Democracy in Occupied Japan

This book offers a detailed assessment of the legacies of the U.S. occupation on Japanese politics and society, discussing the long-term impact of the occupation on contemporary Japan. Focusing on two central themes – democracy and the interplay of U.S.-initiated reforms and Japan's endogenous drive for democratization and social justice – the contributors from both the United States and Japan, address key questions:

- How did the U.S. authorities and the Japanese people define democracy?
- To what extent did Americans impose their notions of democracy on Japan?
- How far did the Japanese pursue impulses toward reform, rooted in their own history and values?
- Which reforms were readily accepted and internalized, and which were ultimately subverted by the Japanese as impositions from outside?

These questions are tackled by exploring the dynamics of the reform process from the three perspectives of innovation, continuity and compromise, specifically determining the effect that this period had on Japanese social, economic, and political understanding. The book critically examines previously unexplored issues that influenced postwar Japan such as the effect of labor and healthcare legislation, textbook revision, and minority policy. Illuminating contemporary Japan, its achievements, its potential and its quandaries, *Democracy in Occupied Japan* will appeal to students and scholars of Japanese–U.S. relations, Japanese history and Japanese politics.

Mark E. Caprio is a member of the Department of Law and Politics, Rikkyo University. **Yoneyuki Sugita** is Associate Professor of American History at Osaka University of Foreign Studies, Japan.

Asia's transformations
Edited by Mark Selden
Binghamton and Cornell Universities, USA

The books in this series explore the political, social, economic and cultural consequences of Asia's transformations in the twentieth and twenty-first centuries. The series emphasizes the tumultuous interplay of local, national, regional and global forces as Asia bids to become the hub of the world economy. While focusing on the contemporary, it also looks back to analyze the antecedents of Asia's contested rise. This series comprises several strands:

Asia's Transformations aims to address the needs of students and teachers, and the titles will be published in hardback and paperback. Titles include:

Asia's Great Cities
Each volume aims to capture the heartbeat of the contemporary city from multiple perspectives emblematic of the authors' own deep familiarity with the distinctive faces of the city, its history, society, culture, politics and economics, and its evolving position in national, regional and global frameworks. While most volumes emphasize urban developments since the Second World War, some pay close attention to the legacy of the longue durée in shaping the contemporary. Thematic and comparative volumes address such themes as urbanization, economic and financial linkages, architecture and space, wealth and power, gendered relationships, planning and anarchy, and ethnographies in national and regional perspective. Titles include:

Asia.com is a series which focuses on the ways in which new information and communication technologies are influencing politics, society and culture in Asia. Titles include:

Critical Asian Scholarship is a series intended to showcase the most important individual contributions to scholarship in Asian Studies. Each of the volumes presents a leading Asian scholar addressing themes that are central to his or her most significant and lasting contribution to Asian studies. The series is committed to the rich variety of research and writing on Asia, and is not restricted to any particular discipline, theoretical approach or geographical expertise.

Democracy in Occupied Japan

The U.S. occupation and
Japanese politics and society

**Edited by Mark E. Caprio
and Yoneyuki Sugita**

Routledge
Taylor & Francis Group

LONDON AND NEW YORK

First published 2007
by Routledge
2 Park Square, Milton Park, Abingdon, Oxon OX14 4RN

Simultaneously published in the USA and Canada
by Routledge
270 Madison Ave, New York, NY 10016

Routledge is an imprint of the Taylor & Francis Group, an informa business

Transferred to Digital Printing 2009

© 2007 Selection and editorial matter, Mark E. Caprio and Yoneyuki Sugita; individual chapters, the contributors

Typeset in Baskerville by Wearset Ltd, Boldon, Tyne and Wear

British Library Cataloguing in Publication Data
A catalogue record for this book is available from the British Library

Library of Congress Cataloging in Publication Data
A catalog record for this book has been requested

ISBN10: 0-415-41589-6 (hbk)
ISBN10: 0-415-56059-4 (pbk)
ISBN10: 0-203-96425-X (ebk)

ISBN13: 978-0-415-41589-7 (hbk)
ISBN13: 978-0-415-56059-7 (pbk)
ISBN13: 978-0-203-96425-5 (ebk)

Contents

x   *Contents*

Contributors

Michael A. Barnhart, Professor, State University of New York, Stony Brook
Email: mbarnhart@notes.cc.sunysb.edu

Mark E. Caprio, Professor, Rikkyo University, Tokyo Japan
Email: caprio@rikkyo.ne.jp

H. Richard Friman, Professor, Marquette University
Email: h.r.friman@marquette.edu

Steven J. Fuchs, Assistant Professor, St. Joseph's College, New York
Email: sfuchs@sjcny.edu

Sayuri Guthrie-Shimizu, Associate Professor, Michigan State University
Email: shimizu@msu.edu

Yoshiko Nozaki, Assistant Professor, State University of New York at
    Buffalo
Email: ynozaki@buffalo.edu

Yoneyuki Sugita, Associate Professor, Osaka University of Foreign Studies,
    Osaka Japan
Email: yone@sugita.us

Maho Toyoda, Lecturer, Kansai University, Osaka Japan
Email: maho@ipcku.kansai-u.ac.jp

Preface

The publication of two monumental volumes on the United States occupation of Japan has greatly enhanced our knowledge of this critical period in Japan–U.S. relations. These two volumes are of course John Dower's *Embracing Defeat* and Takemae Eiji's *Inside GHQ*. Both Dower and Takemae offer detailed survey studies of this seven-year period. Our task in putting together this volume was to examine this period from a variety of different angles: the effects that the pre-war and wartime Japanese governments and the occupation period administrations had on the decisions made in Japan during both this period and the decades that followed its conclusion.

The chapters in this volume consider a variety of actors that range from the classroom teacher to the labor representative; the Korean migrant to the drug peddler. The policies covered here that influenced occupation participants include such domestic areas as healthcare and food provision, as well as diplomatic areas of territorial waters and international trade. In our treatment of these issues we rethink the record left by the United States and Japanese administrations regarding their success in fulfilling the occupation's most fundamental goal: democratizing and demilitarizing Japan. Finally, we consider the influence that these efforts have had upon Japan over the decades that followed.

The compilation of this volume would not have been possible without the assistance of Mark Selden who left his fingerprints on every chapter. We are also indebted to the useful comments provided by one other anonymous reviewer. These comments helped raise the quality of the project. In addition, John Van Sant contributed equally valuable comments to the introduction. Finally, we would like to thank the staff at Routledge and particularly Stephanie Rogers and Helen Baker, for their assistance in bringing the project to completion.

Abbreviations

ACHS	Advisory Council on Healthcare System (Iryo Seido Shingikai)
ACSS	Advisory Council on Social Security (Shakai Hosho Seido Shingikai)
AMA	American Medical Association
ASP	American Selling Price
CCP	Chinese Communist Party
CEDAW	Convention on the Elimination of All Forms of Discrimination against Women
CG	Consultative Group
CIE	Civil Information and Education Section
COCOM	Coordinating Committee on Multilateral Export Controls
CPB	Cabinet Planning Board (Kikakuin)
EEC	European Economic Community
ESS	Economic and Scientific Section
FEC	Far Eastern Commission
FRUS	*Foreign Relations of the United States*
GARIOA	Government and Relief in Occupied Areas
GATT	General Agreement on Tariffs and Trade
HIB	Health Insurance Bureau (Hokenkyoku)
I&RD	Industry and Reparations Division
IMF	International Monetary Fund
JCP	Japanese Communist Party
JMA	Japanese Medical Association (Nihon Ishikai)
JMTC	Japanese Medical Treatment Corporation (Nihon Iryodan)
JTU	Japan Teachers Union
LDP	Liberal Democratic Party
LSL	Labor Standards Law
LTA	long-term arrangement
MHW	Ministry of Health and Welfare (Koseisho)
MITI	Ministry of International Trade and Industry
MMA	MacArthur Memorial Archives
MSC	Medical Security Commission (Iryo Hosho Iinkai)
MSY	maximum sustainable yield

NACP	National Archives at College Park
NATO	North Atlantic Treaty Organization
NRS	Natural Resources Section
OECD	Organization for Economic Cooperation and Development
OEEC	Organization for European Economic Cooperation
OPPSSS	Outline of the Provisional Plan for a Social Security System (Shakai Hosho Seido Kenkyu Shian Yoko)
PC&RD	Price Control and Rationing Division
PH&WS	Public Health and Welfare Section
PHW	Public Health and Welfare (Koshu Eisei Kyoku)
PMIC	Pharmaceutical and Medical Investigation Council (Iyaku Seido Chosakai)
POW	Prisoner of War
PRC	People's Republic of China
ROK	Republic of Korea
SCAP	Supreme Commander for the Allied Powers
SDP	Social Democratic Party
SDR	Special Drawing Right
SIIC	Social Insurance Investigation Committee (Shakai Hoken Seido Chosakai)
SJTPA	Sino-Japanese Trade Promotion Association
SSP	Social Security Plan (Shakai Hoshoan)
SSSG	Social Security Study Group (Shakai Hosho Kenkyukai)
SSSO	Social Security System Outline (Shakai Hosho Seido Yoko)
STR	Special Trade Representative
VAT	Value Added Tax
WTUL	Women's Trade Union League

Introduction

The U.S. occupation of Japan – innovation, continuity, and compromise

Mark E. Caprio and Yoneyuki Sugita[1]

Introduction

Post-World War II occupations experimented with new approaches to dealing with defeated nations to rejuvenate erstwhile foes, rather than overburden them with reparations. The U.S. occupation of Japan (1945–1952) was no exception. Setting aside fierce hatreds and dehumanizing wartime images and prejudices, the occupation administration sought to remold Japan and its people in order to create "democratic and representative organizations" that honored "individual liberties and respect for fundamental human rights . . ."[2]

The political, social, and economic effects of the occupation's efforts continue to spark intellectual debate, producing various interpretations of the occupation's historical significance. Some scholars credit this occupation with producing a pluralistic and democratic Japan that has remained one of the United States' most loyal allies into the post-Cold War period.[3] Others focus on the limitations that the U.S. forces faced, restricting their efforts to realize occupation goals.[4] Still others center their discussions on the effects that international crises, namely world capitalism and Cold War politics, had on this experiment.[5] Finally, a number of studies consider the influence of the occupation's policies on the "miracle" economic growth that Japan enjoyed over much of the postwar period.[6] More recent studies have considered this history from the perspective of the Japanese.[7]

Evident from these studies is the critical influence that security and economic issues have had on U.S.–Japan relations over the long, postwar period. The chapters of this study are not exceptional in this regard. They add to our understanding of Japanese development over this period in two important ways. First, they consider the period by examining critical, but previously unexplored, issues that influenced postwar Japan: the effect of labor and healthcare legislation, textbook revision, and minority policy to name a few. Second, the chapters examine these issues from three perspectives: innovation, continuity, and compromise. Specifically, they examine the contribution the period made to Japanese social, economic, and political understanding; the extent to which this contribution benefited from pre-war and wartime Japanese institutions; and the factors that prevented officials from fully realizing the goals established at the occupation's onset.

The U.S. occupation influenced the tone and direction of Japan's postwar history in remarkable ways. The chapters in this volume recognize this period as a watershed in Japanese history. In answer to Herbert Passin's question "did [the occupation] just make a difference, or did it make a big difference?",[8] all of the chapters lean toward the latter. They also demonstrate that this difference can only be understood in the context of what preceded the U.S. administration's arrival and what followed in its wake. Assessing the occupation's contribution requires looking at it as an integral segment that connected two eras of Japanese history, rather than as a period of timely changes that triggered a new beginning for Japan.

Innovation: What the United States introduced to Japan

> ... inside this fringe of industrial and commercial buildings the residential areas were completely flat with destruction. Our bombings of Tokyo ... certainly hit the Japanese home, right where the average man would feel it the most ... The evidence of [Japan's war defeat] is everywhere, inescapable, and in many ways permanent.[9]

History evaluates the legitimacy new rulers acquire following regime change in part by considering whether the innovations they bring – or more precisely, their articulation of the innovations they bring – are accepted, even embraced, by the population they rule. New rulers compose historical records that invariably overstate the shortcomings of the previous regime and the efficacy of measures introduced to chart a new path. The U.S. occupation administration succeeded in introducing important innovations to postwar Japan. Yet, its success rested ultimately on the ability to link these innovations to pre-war and wartime Japanese institutional practices and values.

American occupation participants might be forgiven for overstating their contribution. When they arrived on the islands in September 1945 the Japan that greeted them lay in ruins. John Dower calculates that the United States succeeded in bombing sixty-six of Japan's major cities, and destroying 40 percent of its urban area. This destruction left one-third of its population homeless. Around 2.7 million Japanese – both military and civilians – had died in the war, and another 4.5 million servicemen were injured. In total, 6.5 million Japanese prepared to repatriate to a homeland that already faced critical shortages in food, housing, and employment.[10] These shortages encouraged the formation of black markets that frustrated occupation efforts to administer SCAP's most immediate task: getting the Japanese on their feet and food into their mouths.

Upon his arrival, General Douglas MacArthur, Supreme Commander for the Allied Powers (SCAP), chose to emphasize Japan's depleted spiritual disposition. In a speech prepared for the official surrender ceremony aboard the USS *Missouri*, the general praised Commodore Matthew C. Perry as a messenger of enlightenment to a closed Japanese archipelago:

> We stand in Tokyo today reminiscent of our countryman, Commodore Perry, ninety-two years ago. His purpose was to bring to Japan an era of enlightenment and progress by uplifting the veil of isolation to the friendship, trade, and commerce of the world.

MacArthur then expressed his disappointment in the Japanese' improper use of Perry's gifts: "But alas [the Japanese forged] the knowledge thereby gained of Western science . . . into an instrument of oppression and human enslavement." He interpreted his mission as finishing the task begun by Perry, by enforcing demilitarization and introducing democracy to the Japanese islands.

> We are committed by the Potsdam Declaration of Principles to see that the Japanese people are liberated from this condition of slavery. It is my purpose to implement this commitment just as rapidly as the armed forces are demobilized and other essential steps are taken to neutralize the war potentials.[11]

MacArthur's articulation of this lofty mission in positive terms – as liberation rather than subjugation, even while noting the security framework within which demilitarization would be situated – represents one of the many important innovations that the U.S. occupation team brought to Japan. The United States set out to avoid the mistakes committed by victors in the past, who saddled conquered nations with crippling reparations that created bitterness and fueled the flames of future wars.[12] In fact, in anticipation of demands expected to come from nations that Japan had occupied or colonized, the very first policy report written by occupation officials stipulated that reparations would be limited to the forfeiture of property that remained in Japan's former colonial territories and to materials anywhere in Japan's possession "not essential for a peaceful Japanese economy."[13]

To accomplish its task, the occupation administration revised a post-World War I innovation, trusteeship, as a vehicle for imposing its direct presence in Japan and other defeated territories such as Germany and Italy. Initiated originally as a benevolent alternative to imperial subjugation to administer territories stripped from Germany (primarily its South Pacific island holdings), trusteeship was applied to lands deemed unprepared for self-rule, in order to provide transition to a point where they could eventually become fully sovereign. The post-World War II occupations applied this formula to the defeated axis states and their former colonies, such as Austria and Korea.

The occupations of Germany and Austria that began soon after Franklin D. Roosevelt's death saw the allies (the United States, Soviet Union, Great Britain, and France) administer these two countries by combined authority from the state capitals of Berlin and Vienna. The occupations organized later in Northeast Asia were nominally placed under a Far Eastern Commission and Allied Council staffed by representatives of the allied nations. Despite the outward form, the Truman administration opposed a coalition framework, and insisted that the Northeast Asian occupations be governed by the United States under the direction of Supreme Commander General Douglas MacArthur.[14] Allies that participated in this administration, such as Great Britain, New Zealand, and Australia, were permitted to contribute to occupation policy when their interests coincided with those of the United States.[15]

The United States stipulated the twin ambitions of demilitarization and democratization as its occupation goals in the 1945 Potsdam Declaration that called for Japan's unconditional surrender and later explicitly articulated them in Japan's postwar constitution.[16] These goals contrasted with those of the military occupations following World War I.[17] But as became apparent as early as 1945, the United States effected a scheme to incorporate West Germany and Japan as regional military and economic hubs to facilitate the inclusion of the West European and Asian theaters within the orbit of American power. Japan's regional importance quickly grew as victorious indigenous communist forces achieved power in China under Mao Zedong's leadership and military conflicts erupted in both Northeast and Southeast Asia.

SCAP often amended its democratic script to accomplish these primary goals. The United States initially envisioned a complete break from core provisions enshrined in the Meiji Constitution that altered the emperor's position, prohibited the Japanese from engaging in war, and eliminated peerage beyond that of the emperor.[18] MacArthur entrusted the task of drafting the postwar constitution to the Shidehara Kijurô cabinet, which formed a committee under the directorship of Matsumoto Jôji.[19] MacArthur's top aide, Brigadier General Courtney Whitney, criticized one draft published in a Japanese newspaper as "extremely conservative," insisting that it left the emperor's position "substantially unchanged."[20] Dissatisfied with the Japanese government's draft, MacArthur ordered an American committee to compose a model constitution. When the committee completed its work one week later, SCAP bullied the Japanese government into adopting it.[21] Even though SCAP permitted a number of significant amendments by the Japanese, controversy lingers as to whether this constitution is truly a Japanese constitution.

Three items that received considerable attention in committee and full assembly debates in the Japanese Diet were the emperor's position, gender equality, and Japan's complete demilitarization. The emperor was defined as a symbol of the state and unity of the people, downgraded from his "sacred and inviolable" status in the Meiji Constitution, to the distress of the Yoshida cabinet. Kyoko Inoue documents that the Japanese succeeded in employing ambiguous language in the Japanese text (that is, the Constitution) that positioned the emperor as the "center of adoration [and] the spiritual unity of the [Japanese] people." From this perspective, she contends, the government could insist that his position remained virtually unchanged.[22] Maintaining the Japanese emperor in his official – albeit weakened – position without offering the Japanese people a voice in this decision, compromised the Occupation's democratic mission and delayed Japanese closure to their wartime history.

The status of the Japanese people, however, changed from "subject" of the emperor to "citizen" of the nation in the new constitution. The Japanese government also redirected the American emphasis on gender equality from the family to the institution of marriage as a means to preserve the authority of the (male) household head. At the national level, the American provisions declaring all family members to be equal in influence upset the metaphor of the emperor as the nation's father figure. At the local level, gender equality in family matters threatened the historic practice of primogeniture employed by farming families, who by law would have to divide land to comply with inheritance laws that would give children, regardless of gender or birth order, equal inheritance rights. By refocusing the emphasis of this article on marriage, the Japanese recognized equality of marriage partner choice, but preserved important elements of Japan's patriarchal familial structure.

Finally, the Japanese Diet rewrote Article 9, which abolished "war as a sovereign right of the [Japanese] nation," to redirect attention to Japan's commitment to "international peace" and away from the promise to renounce war, as emphasized in the American draft. Whether Article 9's wording permits the Japanese to defend their country remains controversial to this day. Ashida Hitoshi, who chaired several committees that reviewed the American draft, argued that this change subsequently enabled the Japanese to form an army to the extent that it did not threaten international peace.[23] In 1946 Nosaka Sanzô of the Japanese Communist Party (JCP) argued, "Japan should retain the right to [fight in] just wars of self-defense." However, Prime Minister Yoshida Shigeru held that Japan had surrendered its "inalienable right of self defense ... even for preserving its own security." This would become the Liberal Democratic Party (LDP) position, implying that Japan's defense rested on U.S. military power. In recent decades, the JCP, in league with the Social Democratic Party (SDP), has consistently opposed any attempt to extend Japan's defensive capabilities, while the LDP has repeatedly stretched the parameters of Article 9 to render it virtually meaningless as a war-renouncing instrument, while further stretching the military bond with the United States, as in the dispatch of Self-Defense Forces to Iraq in 2004.[24]

Japan's new constitution laid the foundation for postwar democracy, encoding important civil liberties initially enacted by various occupation directives. Electoral legislation expanded the range of political participation by allowing previously banned leftist groups to organize politically and granting women the right to vote and to run for elected office. Japan's first postwar election, held in April 1946, attracted three-quarters of Japan's eligible voters to the polls. So complete was the turnover in Diet membership that only six representatives from the wartime period were re-elected. The new Diet included thirty-nine women representatives and nine members of the outcast Burakumin group, the first of either group to serve in Japan's national assembly.[25] Occupation historian Takemae Eiji concludes that the 1946 election "changed the social composition of the Diet, adding farmers, physicians, teachers and a former prostitute" to the rolls of parliament.[26]

A second far-reaching action – land reform – empowered landless and land poor farmers by redistributing to them land they had previously tilled as tenants or hired laborers. MacArthur envisioned land reform as a means to back development of "a new class of small capitalist landowners which itself will stand firm against efforts to destroy the system of capitalistic economy of which it will then form an integral part."[27] SCAP's land reform program limited the amount of land landlords could possess to three hectares (twelve in Hokkaido), virtually outlawed absentee land ownership, and mandated state-mediated land purchase transactions.[28] Steven Fuchs notes in his chapter that SCAP reasoned that land reform provided the foundation for "sound and moderate democracy" and acted as a "bulwark against the pressure of any extreme philosophy." The land reform legislation "relocated ... 80 per cent of all tenanted holdings ... A full 57 per cent of rural farmers became farm owners, and 35 per cent became part-owner, part tenant."[29] Takemae Eiji characterized land reform as the "third pillar" of the U.S. "economic democracy programme" after liberation of labor and economic decentralization.[30]

A similar liberating trend took place in labor reform. Union membership increased rapidly. By 1947 Japan boasted 19,000 unions with over five million members.[31] The 1947 Labor Standards Law abolished many labor practices that had subordinated workers to management, including the dormitory system, which confined them to *takobeyas* (octopus rooms), and the *oyabun* (labor-boss) practice that entitled contractors and brokers to kickbacks deducted from the worker's salary. The legislation also established an eight hour workday and a 48-hour workweek. Finally, it targeted discrimination against women and minors by introducing an equal pay for equal work principle, though, as Miho Toyoda demonstrates, principle often clashed with specific gender requirements and social prejudices when officials debated the legislation's practical implementation. Toyoda's study addresses two questions debated at this time: Would this principle be violated should women be granted a provision – menstruation leave – not available to men? Would protecting maternity by prohibiting female night labor offset the limitations this restriction brought to women's employability?

Japan's postwar constitution failed to realize its vision on other accounts. Chapter 3, Article 8 guaranteed that no "discrimination shall be authorized or tolerated in political, economic or social relations on account of race, creed, social status, caste or natural origin." This guarantee, however, was administered selectively. Mark Caprio demonstrates in his chapter that occupation officials set forth policies that blatantly discriminated against Japan's minority residents (primarily Koreans, Taiwanese and Chinese) to encourage their repatriation.[32] By March 1947 close to 1.4 million Koreans had returned to U.S.-occupied southern Korea, but an estimated 600,000 remained in Japan.[33] Under Japanese colonial rule, Koreans and Taiwanese were Japanese colonial subjects. The Japanese government in 1947 would deprive them of Japanese citizenship, leaving many stateless. Occupation authorities later required them to register to provide Japan with a "defensive weapon of alien and subversive control," a requirement that continues to cause friction between foreign residents and the Japanese government.[34]

Continuity: Prewar and wartime Japanese legacies

> The winter wind has gone
> and the long-awaited spring has arrived
> with double-petalled cherry blossoms[35]

Studies that consider Japan's pre-war, wartime, and early postwar histories tend to emphasize continuity. The occupation period drew heavily on ideas generated during Japan's pre-occupation, past and both successes and limitations were in no small part a product of its doing so.[36] That is, while the United States influenced contemporary Japanese society by introducing a number of innovative ideas and institutions, these required the foundation that pre-occupation Japan provided for their success. The occupation successfully purged a large number of Japanese believed to have held positions that influenced the war's progress. These purges were generally concentrated in a select set of ministries – the Home Ministry was hit hardest – and occupations, such as the police and military. A substantial number of bureaucrats, armed with ideas and plans shelved after the outbreak of war, remained in office. Japan's infrastructure was badly damaged but not destroyed. The trains, for example, remained in operation. First impressions, and inclement weather, might have exaggerated the damage. Sherry Moran, who served in the occupation's Naval Technical Mission, observed that when the weather cleared it became evident that "a great many of the buildings [had been] actually untouched."[37]

The U.S. occupation authorities soon recognized the value of this foundation to their mission. The most obvious example was its controversial decision to retain the Showa Emperor, despite heavy pressure to try him as a war criminal. In September 1945, for example, the U.S. Senate adopted a resolution declaring it to be the "policy of the United States to try Hirohito, Emperor of Japan, as a war criminal,"[38] and important U.S. allies (primarily New Zealand and Australia) called for his indictment.[39] The administration, however, decided early on, probably even before the war's end, to retain both the incumbent emperor and the imperial system. Edwin O. Reischauer noted as early as 1942 that the emperor could be used to effectively maintain social order and implement policy. It then took extraordinary measures to protect him from prosecution.[40] On the other hand, by protecting the wartime emperor and allowing him to retain his throne, the occupation authorities made it far more difficult for the Japanese people to come to terms with the military aggression and atrocities of an earlier epoch, or further democratization, either by choosing his successor or abolishing the imperial institution outright.

The emperor would, however, receive a makeover designed to align him with the democratic, demilitarized, and dependent Japan that the United States now envisioned. The deified emperor would have to "come down from the clouds" to accept a human persona. Hirohito's humanization began with his historic recording announcing to his subjects the decision to accept the U.S. surrender terms. It was the first time that this emperor had directly addressed his subjects. The widely distributed photograph of 1945, showing MacArthur with the emperor, further contributed to this process. A relaxed MacArthur dressed in casual khaki garb, as State Department Japan expert John K. Emerson put it, "towered over a pathetic little figure in a morning coat."[41] This provided the Japanese people with a powerful visual representation explaining the reasons for Japanese wartime defeat. Gone were the emperor's military regalia and white horse, replaced by his gentleman's wardrobe and automobile.

Hirohito's declaration of his humanity in his 1946 New Year address prepared the Japanese people for the diminished role he would assume by the end of the year, as stipulated in the postwar Japanese constitution. His tours throughout Japan – reminiscent of his grandfather's tours throughout the Japanese archipelago in early Meiji Japan – signaled that Japan's postwar emperors would be more public than its pre-war emperors. The second most widely circulated picture of the emperor fittingly depicted him walking among his subjects, tipping his hat.[42]

Maintaining imperial continuity to preserve social order compromised the occupation's democratization pledge. It compromised the new constitution by maintaining a powerful institution headed by a figure who gained office from family background rather than popular election. Compromise also weakened the democratic process. The occupation authorities made assumptions as to (but did not attempt to measure) whether popular opinion favored the retention both of Hirohito and of the imperial institution, but also whether Japanese society would collapse if the emperor were removed. John Dower offers evidence that the occupation authorities may have exaggerated this point. The Japanese people might have permitted his abdication, had the institution survived.[43]

The occupation was predicated on indirect rule, with U.S. authority transmitted through a Japanese government that included key personnel and institutions from the wartime administration. In this respect, we note a telling contrast with the U.S. administration of southern Korea and Okinawa. In Korea the U.S. military government governed directly, although it relied on local personnel, many of them colonial-era government, police, or military officials, to carry out government functions. The U.S. delayed national elections until just before the end of occupation rule.[44] The occupation of Japan, with a Japanese mouthpiece to transmit orders, was far more palatable for the Japanese people.

In Japan, SCAP filled government positions by reinstating important Japanese officials from the pre-war era, many of whom had been purged by Japan's wartime governments. Shidehara Kijurô, prime minister from October 1945 to May 1946, had represented Japan as foreign minister at the 1921 Washington Conference, and was interim prime minister after Hamaguchi Osachi's assassination in 1930. His Minister of Foreign Affairs, Yoshida Shigeru, a former ambassador to England, who subsequently became prime minister, was the most influential Japanese figure of the occupation period. The virtual absence of many of these figures from high public office during the war years cleansed them from direct responsibility and spared them from postwar purges. The occupation later permitted the restoration of wartime officials originally purged just after Japan's surrender, three of whom – namely Hatoyama Ichiro, Ishibashi Tanzan, and Kishi Nobusuke – went on to serve as prime minister. In total, close to 360,000 purged Japanese returned to public life. Of those who successfully secured a seat in the Lower House by the first post-occupation elections (October 1952), more than 40 percent had been purged during the early phase of the occupation.[45]

The vast majority of pre-war and wartime civil servants remained in their posts, including many ranking officers. Sheldon Garon writes that the occupation "never attempted to remove the vast majority of higher civil servants who had dealt with labor matters during the war."[46] Chalmers Johnson notes that the economic ministries survived SCAP's purges relatively unscathed, and "emerged with their powers enhanced." He continues: "the occupation era ... witnessed the highest levels of government control over the economy ever encountered in modern Japan before or since, levels that were decidedly higher than the levels attained during the Pacific War."[47] Civil servants who survived the postwar purges were instrumental in drafting legislation necessary to get Japan back on its feet.

This legislation included ideas that these bureaucrats had unsuccessfully proposed both before and even during the wartime years. Maho Toyoda traces this continuity in the postwar debate over labor legislation. The occupation authorities reinstated certain legislation, such as protective labor legislation, soon after the occupation began. Japanese civil servants, many holdovers from pre-war and wartime Japan, immediately began to update this legislation and completed an initial draft of labor legislation by April 1946. Yoneyuki Sugita highlights a similar trend in the Ministry of Health and Welfare. SCAP permitted officials in this ministry a great deal of authority to draft welfare legislation, much of which was first conceived during Japan's pre-war period.

Their fingerprints are also found in the education field. Yoshiko Nozaki qualifies in her chapter a notion that exaggerates the contribution that SCAP's education reforms made to democratizing Japanese society. While important, she argues that viewing the contribution as a postwar innovation overlooks the continuity of educational structures and practices, as well as personnel, from the pre-war and wartime periods. These holdovers faced serious dilemmas, first in confronting Japan's wartime curriculum following defeat, and then in implementing "democratic education" in occupied Japan: How were they to "teach students to think 'independently' and 'develop their personalities?'" How could the schools practice "equal education" for boys and girls when their expectations of these students were so different?[48]

Personnel continuity helped the occupation resolve critical problems, among the most crucial in terms of health and economic development at war's end being malnutrition. Steven Fuchs argues that food shortages negatively affected Japan in two ways: they slowed economic recovery by causing inflation and trade deficits, and stifled labor productivity by forcing workers to, as Chief of the Military Planning Branch's Civilian Supply Section Palmer Hogenson put it, "[scrounge] for food" rather than work. The black markets that appeared soon after Japan's surrender may have exacerbated these shortages. Fuchs explains that SCAP relied particularly on the Japanese wartime "link system" designed to "maximize quota collection by offering cash payments and consumer items for surplus production" to discourage farmers from selling to the black market. SCAP's food policies did not make Japan self-sufficient in food. Rather, they re-established Japan as an important market for U.S. agricultural commodities and "laid the foundation for the Pacific Alliance."

The breakup of the Japanese empire and Japan's nearly depleted fishing industry constituted the primary international reasons for these shortages.[49] SCAP officials regarded the revival of Japan's pre-war and wartime colonial networks as critical to Japan's economic recovery. From the end of the war, Japanese and Americans argued that Japan's economic ties with Taiwan and Korea should be restored as, in Bruce Cumings' words, an "Asian crescent": Japan forging hegemonic and unequal economic relations with Korea, Manchuria, and North China.[50] After the retreat of the Nationalist Chinese government to Taiwan the United States began stressing Japanese ties with South and Southeast Asian states.[51] Japan settled its differences first with these relatively less challenging cases, soon after it agreed to the terms of peace at the 1951 San Francisco Peace Conference. Other more difficult relations, such as those with South Korea, had to wait until diplomatic relations were established before claims could be settled.[52]

Revitalizing Japan's fishing industry provided one important step toward replenishing Japan's food supply. This initiative, as argued in Sayuri Guthrie-Shimizu's chapter, brought American and allied fears that the return of Japanese fishermen to the high seas would renew pre-war disputes over territorial fishing rights and harvesting regulations. SCAP gradually extended the so-called "MacArthur Line" that initially limited Japan's fishermen to twelve nautical miles from its coasts to the south. This protected American fishing waters but infringed on those of its allies, particularly Australia and New Zealand. These states feared a resurrection of the pre-war disputes over fishing rights. Resolution of these postwar disputes helped expedite Japan's return to the international community. In 1950 Japan passed the Marine Resource Anti-Depletion Law, which demonstrated determination to monitor the yields of its fishermen. In 1952 it joined the United States and Canada in signing the North Pacific Fisheries Convention of 1952, the first agreement it negotiated as a sovereign state in the postwar era.

Certain trade relations were revived despite the absence of formal relations, as in Japan's relations with China over the decades that followed its 1949 communist victory. The Japanese could trade with China through barter, which enabled them to procure essential products without using precious hard currency, as was required with their purchases of similar U.S. goods.

The defeat of the Chinese Nationalists complicated the United States' postwar scenario for East Asia. This setback forced the United States to reconsider its regional strategy, and limited the scope of Japan's relations with Mainland China. Prime Minister Yoshida Shigeru, however, believed Japan and China to be "naturally complementary markets." His attitude, that the color of the country – be it "red or green" – did not matter when determining the state's value as a trading partner, ruffled U.S. feathers. Yet, Japan and China continued to trade, albeit at a curtailed level, even after Chinese troops spilled across the Yalu River to assist North Korea in its fight against U.S.-led United Nations forces.[53]

This history suggests either that the United States was cautiously open to the establishment of economic ties with the People's Republic of China, perhaps with the intention of weaning it from Soviet influence, or that U.S. control over the Japanese was less than absolute. Sayuri Guthrie-Shimizu hints at the latter by arguing that many Japanese government

officials drew on the "sense of affinity widely shared by the Japanese populace toward the Chinese continent and a pan-Asian identity sustained by
the persistent collective nostalgia in encouraging this relationship."

Japan's high economic growth period nevertheless rested on its trade
with the United States and Europe, rather than with China. Michael Barnhart observes that the United States opened its markets to Japan more out
of fear that Japan would pursue trade relations with China and Russia,
than out of a need to develop strong bilateral economic relations. The
United States underestimated Japan's economic potential; its miscalcula-
tion led to the staggering trade deficits that brought friction to the
U.S.–Japan relationship over the decades to come. Japan was also quick to
expand trade relations with China from 1972, after the Richard Nixon
administration repaired relations with the PRC.

Compromised vision: reprioritizing democratization and demilitarization

The occupation administration generally stayed the course of promoting
demilitarization and democratization in Japan through 1947. But from
1947 to the end of the occupation, SCAP reorganized its priorities to
emphasize economic recovery and a degree of remilitarization that would
lash Japan firmly in a position of subordination to U.S. military plans. A
number of factors caused SCAP to compromise its initial intentions. First
was the schism in perspective between officials in Washington and policy
makers on the ground in Tokyo. Political and military developments in
East Asia were a second influence, particularly the success of communist
revolutionary movements in China, Korea, and Southeast Asia. The
changes that accompanied the so-called "reverse course"[54] further
strengthened Japan's pre-war, occupation-period, and postwar continuity,
while complicating the process of postwar reconciliation with neighboring
states that fell victim to Japanese wartime aggression.

Just when this "reverse course" began is open to debate. The chapters
in this volume suggest that in some areas the United States began compro-
mising its plan for demilitarization and democratization from around
1947; in other areas this began much earlier. The general situation – a victorious nation occupying a defeated enemy – hardly presented ideal circumstances for democratization. The process of top–down democracy
building, however, has served as the rhetorical foundation for every occupation organized by the United States over the last half-century, from
Okinawa to Iraq. Elsewhere the results invariably fell far short of the goals.
In southern Korea, for example, the United States undercut this goal by
blocking elections for the entire peninsula, out of fear that Communist
Party candidates would be elected to a nascent Korean government.
Throughout the Cold War, the United States actively supported South
Korea's blatantly undemocratic behavior, while criticizing the North

Korean government for totalitarian excesses. South Korea, in return, demonstrated its loyalty to the United States by contributing large numbers of troops to Vietnam in return for access to U.S. markets and other economic and military support.

We see SCAP's compromise of its democratization vision in limitations that it placed on the basic rights of the Japanese people. It curtailed freedom of expression from the very beginning of the occupation. SCAP imposed a complete censorship of any news regarding Hiroshima and Nagasaki from its arrival. On 10 September 1945 MacArthur ordered the Japanese government to issue legislation making it illegal for the Japanese press to carry news that MacArthur or his aides deemed critical of SCAP. Article 1 of this legislation read as follows: "The Japanese imperial government will issue the necessary orders to prevent dissemination of news, through newspapers, radio broadcasting or other means of publication, which fails to adhere to the truth or which disturbs public tranquility." Articles 2 and 3 cautioned the media against publishing news that SCAP deemed to be "harmful to the effects of Japan to emerge from defeat as a new nation," and "false or destructive criticism of the Allied Powers, and rumors." Article 4 limited "news and information broadcasts" to those originating from Radio Tokyo studio, which occupation officials closely monitored. Five days later, SCAP toughened this legislation further by ordering the Japanese government to subject the Japanese media to "100 percent censorship."[55]

SCAP extended censorship to the schools. Yoshiko Nozaki writes in her chapter that SCAP implemented "democratic education ... in an undemocratic manner" by directing school administrators to blacken out militaristic passages from old textbooks, and censored the content of the new textbooks. She shows that in reversing course, SCAP returned imperialists and (ultra)nationalists to positions of influence, which eventually restricted the potential for textbooks (and by extension the Japanese people) to debate issues such as war responsibility and national identity. Occupation officials assigned to the Education Section of the Military Government also made impromptu school inspections to verify that the schools were complying with "democratic education" regulations that governed classroom materials and lecture content. During these visits, officials searched for illegal wall decorations (such as pictures of the emperor), interviewed teachers, and observed classes to monitor progress toward this goal.[56]

Driving this censorship was a condescending attitude that the Japanese people lacked the maturity needed to function as a responsible self-governing people. SCAP's "tough love" was required if Japan was to advance beyond an adolescent stage of development. MacArthur's chief of censorship, Donald Hoover, drove home this point before a group of Japanese journalists briefed on SCAP's new censorship policy. Hoover instructed them on the Supreme Commander's belief that Japan "has not yet demonstrated a right to a place among civilized nations." The Japanese public received daily reminders of their inferior status. Those riding the trains noticed that U.S. officials rode in special cars that were far less crowded and had more comfortable seating. Their representative to the Allied Council, Asakai Kôichirô (later Japanese Ambassador to Washington), was admitted to these meetings as an observer, but only through the building's back door![57]

Such disparaging attitudes, of course, did not originate during the period of U.S. occupation. The Japanese had long experienced expressions and policies of ridicule and condescension from Europeans and Americans. The Pacific War brought out the worst of racist attitudes on both sides, amply documented by John W. Dower in his *War Without Mercy*. These attitudes also did not dissipate with the advent of a new Japan–U.S. relationship begun with the occupation. Yukiko Koshiro writes that the race issue was "transformed from an instrument of wartime hatred into a negotiable part of a broader Japanese-American arrangement ... Racism did not evaporate, it merely moved from the battlefield to the bargaining table."[58]

The Japanese were not the sole object of U.S. racist attitudes, nor were they immune from harboring such attitudes. Japanese held discriminatory attitudes against Asian peoples, including Asian populations living in Japan, notably the large Korean population. In many ways, as Mark Caprio suggests, the occupation signaled a retreat from progress in assimilating Koreans. The occupation adopted a policy that echoed Japanese sentiments of superiority, but differed in solution: Koreans, many of whom were brought to Japan by force, were pressed to repatriate to Korea, rather than being integrated into Japanese society. Occupation authorities refused, however, to force Korean repatriation, as proposed by Prime Minister Yoshida. Orders issued by occupation officials through the Japanese government to close ethnic Korean schools in Kobe and Osaka did, however, set off riots among Koreans living in those cities. Just before the U.S. ended its tenure in Japan, it advised legislation that required foreigner registration. The Japanese government, which regarded Japan's "foreign" population as both a nuisance and a potential threat, welcomed the new legislation, which survives to this day as one of the more controversial (and humiliating) legacies of the occupation.[59]

Signs of significant reversal in the U.S. initial occupation goals began to appear as early as February 1947, when MacArthur ordered the Japanese government to halt the general strike planned for early March to demand official action to alleviate employment, food, and economic concerns. Most researchers, however, date the "reverse course" from 1948, when SCAP began purging leftist Japanese from positions of influence. The "red purge" dramatically altered the original spirit of the occupation that had released progressives, including communists and labor activists, from Japanese prisons and legitimized their movements after decades of suppression. A number of progressives held positions of influence in government, including the office of prime minister, when the socialist Katayama Tetsu served in this capacity from May 1947 to March 1948. The purges forced thousands of Japanese from positions in politics, education, and even the arts. At the same time the U.S. authorities began de-purging many other Japanese, including a number of Class A war criminals, who had been removed from positions of influence at the occupation's onset.

This reversal in occupation policy was influenced to a large extent by fears of a communist threat to U.S. interests. George Kennan, Director of the Policy Planning Staff and father of U.S. containment policy, played an instrumental role in encouraging these policy changes. His discussions with MacArthur in March 1948 reveal several differences over the two men's visions of the future U.S. role. MacArthur argued that the occupation had successfully transformed Japan into a healthy and democratic country, and recommended that the United States negotiate a formal peace treaty with Japan to end its administration. Kennan countered by questioning whether "Japan's powers of resistance to Communism [could] be taken for granted." Kennan believed that a weak and unstable Japan still required American presence. By May 1950 MacArthur publicly denounced the JCP as subversive and stated that he no longer considered it to be a "constitutionally recognized political movement."[60]

A second disagreement arose over the defense of Japan. MacArthur advised maintaining U.S. bases in Okinawa, rather than on the Japanese mainland. He also defended Japanese disarmament by emphasizing that Japan's economic difficulties, its constitutional restraints, and international factors prevented the country from remilitarizing. Kennan noted inconsistency in MacArthur's two arguments. He learned during his 1948 visit to Japan that the occupation was draining Japanese financial resources. One way of rectifying this would be to allow the Japanese to rearm on a small scale. The other option was to retain U.S. troops in Japan. One way or another, Kennan believed, Japan must house troops, whether American or Japanese.[61]

These discussions, in the words of Takemae Eiji, "set the tone for America's Japan policy for the duration of the Occupation" as they "engineered a shift away from such 'destabilizing reforms' as the purge, reparations, the dismantling of the Home Ministry, police decentralization, *zaibatsu* dissolution and trade unionism."[62] Kennan, in memoirs published fifteen years after the occupation, considered this to be the most "significant constructive contribution" that he made in government. He recalled, "on no other occasion, with that one exception, did I ever make recommendations of such scope and import; and on no other occasion did my recommendations meet with such wide, indeed almost complete, acceptance."[63]

These changes in occupation policy were integral to a larger global strategy. Kennan's arrival in Japan came just after the announcement of the Truman "doctrine," which emphasized his administration's growing concern over global communist expansion.[64] They also coincided with the massive U.S. investment in Europe under the Marshall Plan and the increasing costs of the occupation of Japan. In East Asia, they reflected growing concerns regarding Chinese communist forces, and the possibility of communist influence seeping into Japan should economic recovery remain sluggish. U.S. officials, Michael Barnhart reminds us, had early on pinpointed Japanese economic recovery as a prerequisite for its serving as the U.S.'s primary East Asian ally.

These policy shifts also reflected the concerns of veteran Japan hands in the United States. The Washington-based "Japan lobby," organized around former Japan Ambassador Joseph Grew, was influential in returning purged Japanese to positions of influence.[65] This group, comprised of businessmen, politicians and others with connections to pre-war Japan, felt that SCAP's initial purges were overly harsh and, in the case of the *zaibatsu*, unnecessary. Japan required the expertise possessed by many of these Japanese if it were to accept its new economic and military role. The conservatism that subsequently defined Japan's political, social, and economic institutions is in part a legacy of the de-purging carried out over the latter half of the occupation.

While many of the allied forces held Japan's *zaibatsu* (along with its military) responsible for encouraging their country's reckless road to war, others in Washington regarded these conglomerates as a critical key to Japan's future economic success. The U.S. occupation originally decided to dismantle the conglomerates to encourage "the development of organizations in labor, industry, and agriculture, organized on a democratic basis [to promote the] development of a capitalist democracy."[66] SCAP was slow to carry out this task, suggesting its relatively low priority. The anticipated "economic purge" did not take place until January 1947 and the two biggest *zaibatsu*, Mitsui and Mitsubishi, remained intact until the following July. Legislation to "deconcentrate" 325 large firms was finally passed later that year. In the end, however, only eleven firms remained on the list when the occupation was ready to dismantle the *zaibatsu*.[67] George Kennan's arrival in Japan in March 1948 was instrumental in this change in policy as Washington, now far from the New Deal roots of the occupation and focusing on the unfolding Cold War, felt it best to steer the commanding general away from such "destabilizing reforms."[68] With the exception of one (Sanwa), the *keiretsu* (industrial groupings) that drove Japan's postwar economic success all emerged as reconfigured *zaibatsu* from the pre-war period.[69]

A more startling policy reversal transpired from 1948, when the United States began to pressure the Japanese government to remilitarize. This represented a direct violation not only of Japan's surrender terms, but also its constitution. These pressures intensified with communist successes in Northeast Asia and civil unrest in Japan, climaxing just days prior to the outbreak of the Korean War when John Foster Dulles rushed from a tense situation at the 38th parallel to Tokyo, to press Japanese rearmament. Japanese Prime Minister Yoshida, however, refused these overtures, citing the drag that military expenses would have on the still struggling Japanese economy. He eventually agreed to establish a 70,000 strong National Police Reserve, the present-day Self-Defense Forces, but only after fighting had begun on the Korean peninsula.[70]

Japanese demilitarization and repatriation never reached completion during the seven-year occupation period. Many Japanese remained in Japan's former imperial possessions to train people in their specialties. A team of fifty technicians remained in southern Korea to provide technological instruction. More than 500 Japanese troops remained on the Korean peninsula into December 1946, long after Japan's military had been repatriated.[71] Forty-six Japanese technicians remained in North Korea until 1956 before they were repatriated.[72] In Taiwan, former Japanese soldiers assisted the Nationalist Chinese army in military planning and training. These Japanese did not return home until 1969 (see Guthrie-Shimizu's chapter on Sino-Japanese relations).

Japan's military role during the Korean War was complex, but nonetheless significant. Yoshida dubbed the war Japan's "gift from the gods," reflecting on the economic windfall from providing UN forces with war-related supplies. Roger Dingman estimates that Japan's exports over the first two years of the war increased by 53 percent. During this time the United States paid Japan over $3 billion for goods and services to prosecute the war. This jump-started many companies that would drive the Japanese "miracle" during the postwar period. Employees at Toyota, for example, saw their wages double as the war increased the company's production by 40 percent.[73]

Japan contributed to U.S. wars in other important ways. It dispatched twenty minesweepers to In'chón Harbor to clear the way for MacArthur's dramatic landing. Former colonial officials provided the U.S. military with valuable information on North Korea's terrain. The United States also secretly deployed over 1,000 colonial-era Japanese specialists engaged in shipping and transportation to assist the U.S. military in transporting goods;[74] and shipped 3,936 Japanese technicians to Korea, many of whom remained even after the South Korean government demanded their repatriation.[75] The Korean War helped establish a postwar trend that left a demilitarized Japan dependent on the United States for military protection. The national Self-Defense Forces that Japan reluctantly formed then, from Korea to Iraq, has remained subordinate to U.S. security goals rather than to the wishes of the Japanese people. In short, both democratization and demilitarization reversed course.

Conclusion: occupation legacy

The U.S. occupation of Japan ended officially in 1952, yet the ways in which its impact has since been felt have experienced three overlapping stages, all influenced to some degree by the seven-year U.S. occupation. The 1950s and 1960s were influenced first by the U.S.–Japan security treaties and then by the Vietnam War, as young Japanese and the progressive opposition generally took to the streets to protest the U.S. military arrangement with Japan. The arrangement that left U.S. troops in the archipelago with virtually free reign to use Japan as a rear area to wage war across East Asia served as a direct extension of the occupation: as in the seven years of occupation the Japanese government wielded no influence over the activities that the United States conducted on its now-sovereign territory.

By the early 1970s student demonstrations yielded to high economic growth as erstwhile demonstrators, armed with promises of lifetime employment and a seniority-based salary system, traded their headbands and helmets for the drab salaryman business garb to serve on the front lines of what came to be known to some as Japan, Inc. As demonstrated by Michael Barnhart, U.S.–Japan trade friction that intensified from this time was a conflict nurtured from previous decades, and resulted in part from U.S. slighting of its economic relationship with Japan. By the 1980s, when the intensity of this friction peaked, the Japanese faced stinging accusations that refusal to open their markets suggested ungratefulness for U.S. benevolence: Not only did the United States open its markets to Japanese products, it also offered its military to protect the islands from outside threats, went the litany.

These "trade wars" stimulated the 1990s debates over Japan's global position, in economic but also military terms. Japan built a "rich country" (*fukoku*), but failed to provide the other half of the Meiji-era vision, a strong military (*kyôhei*) needed to protect its national riches. Could it continue to rely on its U.S. ally in this capacity and still claim to have national sovereignty? Japan's military impotence hit home in 1991, when the Japanese government was humiliated by charges from some Americans that it had "merely" contributed $13 billion to support the Gulf War, without providing Japanese troops. Subsequently Japanese participation in UN peace-keeping missions set the stage for Japan's return to the battlefield in 2002 as a participant in the U.S.-led coalition organized to fight the second Iraq War. In addition to the dispatch of several hundred troops in non-combat roles, the Maritime Self-Defense Force plied the Arabian Sea, refueling U.S. and coalition ships.

The debate that transpired across this decade essentially dealt with shedding the occupation legacy that prohibited Japan from becoming what one influential political figure termed a "normal country" (*futsu no kuni*). At the heart of this debate was the claim that a normal country accepted the task of defending its national interests, both those close to home (its borders) as well as those overseas (its oil supply). Critics responded that a "normal country" did not docilely follow another country into an illegal and immoral war. In the event, Article 9 constrained Japan's troop commitments internationally.

Peace groups have been vocal but hardly influential in their efforts to protect Japan's "peace constitution." The government's success in dispatching troops to the Middle East, in the face of significant public opposition, was one important step of many to undermine the spirit of Article 9. Since 1976, directed by Prime Minister Miki Takeo's pledge, the Japanese government has with few exceptions kept its military budget at or under 1 percent of its gross national product. More important is the tremendous buying power that Japan's economic growth has permitted the Ministry of Defense. By the late twentieth century Japan's military budget rose to third highest, after the United States and the Soviet Union.[76] U.S.–Japan Security Treaty revisions have extended Japan's defense responsibilities to cover the sea-lanes that pass by the islands. This record hardly represents the spirit of peace delivered by Article 9.

This trend is indicative of the lethargic attitude that many Japanese have adopted regarding politics in general in the wake of Japan's high economic growth. Japanese ambivalence to politics opened the door to the reintroduction of many pre-war practices. The government reintroduced national patriotism to Japanese schools, and by extension to Japanese society, by establishing the *hi no maru* (rising sun) as Japan's "national flag" and *Kimi ga yo* as Japan's "national anthem." It further mandated that the flag be raised and the anthem sung at school ceremonies. Teachers who displayed improper attitudes and behavior during these ceremonies were to be reprimanded, fined, and eventually sacked, and students disciplined.

Similar changes appear on the horizon in efforts by the present government to revise the 1947 Education Ordinance. Debate over the early part of the postwar period focused on the need to accelerate learning to allow the Japanese to "catch up" with the West. During the period of high economic growth the discussion shifted to the need to develop the population to lead the world into the twenty-first century by nurturing student creativity. Japan had caught up; now it must lead. Japanese interpret the behavior of its youth as a product of having neglected moral education in its wild frenzy to "catch up." Particularly central to this argument is the need to rekindle a sense of Japanese identity, understood to be associated with imperial ideology. The sections of the wartime textbook blackened out by teachers and students once again required attention. Passively forgetting this history has cast shame over the nation; reviving national identity required that Japanese actively engage their history and culture in ways that accentuate the positive of war and empire.

This debate on history was initiated by the conservative *Atarashii rekishi kyôkasho wo tsukurukai* (The committee to create new history textbooks) out of fears that foreign nationals were directing the issues in Japanese history education. Japanese history must be told as "the Japanese see it," rather than in response to the criticisms of its neighbors.[77] The Japanese government's authorization of the *Tsukurukai* textbook was heavily criticized by Korea and China, who understood it as an attempt to justify Japanese expansion and warfare. Yet, more is involved. The textbook's purpose, to instill national pride in students, is part of a larger effort that seeks to revise the 1947 Education Ordinance so as to base Japanese education on patriotism (*aikokushin kyôiku*).

Rising defense budgets, Yasukuni Shrine visits by prime ministers and Diet members, expanding security responsibilities, and nationalist textbooks send ripples of concern to Japan's neighbors and provoke anti-Japanese behavior. The root of these fears stems, of course, from Japan's pre-war history and the failure in the rush to rebuild Japan to resolve outstanding issues of colonialism and war. Efforts by the United States to keep Japan in its Cold War camp developed a U.S.–Japan relationship at the expense of strong Japan-East Asian relations. The post-Cold War era has provided space for these neglected issues to resurface. Japan's economic and political influence has forced the state to confront the issues in the context of its contribution to regional peace and harmony, rather than simply as a loyal ally under the protection of the U.S. political and nuclear umbrella. Strengthened nationalist sentiment in Japan and among its neighbors complicates resolution of these issues in which battles over historical memory are compounded by Japan-China and Japan-Korea territorial disputes.

The chapters of this volume offer us background on many of the political, social, economic, and diplomatic issues that confront Japan and the Asia Pacific today.

Notes

1 This chapter was greatly enhanced by the comments of John E. Van Sant, Mark Selden, and two anonymous readers. We alone assume responsibility for its shortcomings.
2 From the "United States Initial Post Surrender Policy in Japan," dated 29 August 1945. The complete text for this document can be found in Young Hum Kim, *East Asia's turbulent century*, New York: Appleton-Century-Crofts, 1966, pp. 308–15. Roger Buckley describes the statement as the State Department's "crowning success in determining measures for the occupation" in his *Occupation diplomacy: Britain, the United States and Japan, 1945–1952*, Cambridge: Cambridge University Press, 1982, p. 60.
3 Edwin Reischauer, *The United States and Japan*, Cambridge: Harvard University Press, 1965; Herbert Passin, *The legacy of the occupation – Japan*, New York: East Asian Institute, Columbia University, 1968; Theodore Cohen, *Remaking Japan: the American occupation as new deal*, New York: The Free Press, 1987.
4 Owen Lattimore, *The situation in Asia*, Boston: Little Brown, 1949; T.A. Bisson, *Zaibatsu dissolution in Japan*, Berkeley: University of California Press, 1954.

5 William Borden, *The Pacific alliance: United States foreign economic policy and Japanese trade recovery, 1947–1955*, Madison: University of Wisconsin Press, 1984; John W. Dower, *Empire and aftermath: Yoshida Shigeru and the Japanese experience, 1878–1954*, Cambridge: Harvard University Press, 1988; Howard Schonberger, *Aftermath of war: Americans and the remaking of Japan, 1945–1952*, Kent: Kent State University Press, 1989.
6 Ronald L. McGlothlen, *Controlling the waves: Dean Acheson and U.S. foreign policy in Asia*, New York: W.W. Norton & Company, 1993; William Guttman, "Miracles of power: America and the making of East Asian economic growth," D. Phil., University of Oxford, 1989.
7 John W. Dower, *Embracing defeat: Japan in the wake of World War II*, New York: W.W. Norton & Co., 1999.
8 Herbert Passin, "The occupation – some reflections," in Carol Gluck and Stephen R. Graubard, eds, *Showa: the Japan of Hirohito*, New York: W.W. Norton, 1992, p. 119.
9 Theodore De Barry's impressions of Tokyo on 24 September 1945 when he entered the city. As recorded in Otis Cary, ed., *From a ruined empire: letters – Japan, China, Korea 1945–46*, Tokyo: Kodansha International, 1975, p. 48.
10 Dower, *Embracing defeat*, pp. 45–6, 48.
11 Quoted from Nishi Toshio, *Unconditional democracy: education and politics in occupied Japan, 1945–1952*, Stanford: Hoover Press, 1982, pp. 40–1. MacArthur even borrowed one of the flags flown by Perry from the Smithsonian Institute for the surrender ceremonies held on the USS *Missouri*. We thank John E. Van Sant for bringing this fact to our attention.
12 Germany lost its colonies to the victors but was not occupied after World War I. It was forced to pay a $33 billion reparations bill that included charges not only for damages to properties of the allied nations, but also the pensions and other allowances to be paid to their soldiers. See Thomas A. Bailey, *Woodrow Wilson and the lost peace*, Chicago: Quadrangle Books, 1963, p. 240.
13 Kim, *East Asia's turbulent century*, p. 314. The External Assets Division of the Civil Property Custodian Division of SCAP estimated the value of Japanese property in Korea to be in excess of $5 billion. Cited in Sung-Hwa Cheong, *The politics of anti-Japanese sentiment in Korea: Japanese-South Korean relations under American occupation, 1945–1952*, New York: Greenwood Press, 1991, p. 48. The Japanese were also billed for much of the expense incurred during the occupation, including the repatriation of Japanese living in the colonies and colonized people living in Japan. They also paid reparations to former colonial territories in the form of "economic assistance." In the case of South Korea, however, this payment was not made until 1965. North Korea still anticipates receiving compensation for this period once it reaches agreement on normalization with Japan.
14 The United States and the Soviet Union agreed to form a trusteeship to govern the Korean peninsula at the Moscow Conference held in December 1945. However, this never materialized during the three years of foreign occupation and the Korean peninsula was divided into North and South under Soviet and American rule respectively. See Choi Sang-Yong, "Trusteeship Debate and the Korean Cold War," in Bonnie B.C. Oh, ed., *Korea under the American military government*, Westport, CT: Praeger, 2002, pp. 13–39; Bruce Cumings, *The origins of the Korean War*, vol. 1, Princeton: Princeton University Press, 1980. For more information on the formation of the Far Eastern Commission and the Allied Council see Eiji Takemae, *Inside GHQ: the allied occupation of Japan and its legacy*, trans. Robert Ricketts and Sebastian Swann, New York: Continuum, 2002, pp. 96–9.
15 For the history of the British Commonwealth role in the occupation see Peter

Bates, *Japan and the British Commonwealth occupation force, 1946–1952*, London: Brassey's, 1993. Christine De Matos' research has focused on the role that the Australian representatives played in influencing occupation policy. See her "The Allied Occupation of Japan – an Australian View," Available HTTP: <http://www.japanfocus.org/article.asp?id=344> (accessed 11 July 2006).

16 The Potsdam Declaration stated that the occupation forces would not withdraw until Japan's military forces had been "completely disarmed," and until its people had secured basic democratic rights. Text for this document is from Kim, *East Asia's turbulent century*, pp. 297–8.

17 The allied powers also dismantled Germany's military capacity after World War I but allowed it to maintain a force of 100,000 soldiers and a specific number of officers, munitions, and ships, an armed force sufficient for self-defense purposes but insufficient for waging war. The allied powers completely demilitarized Germany following its defeat in World War II, but allowed it to remilitarize within the context of its membership in NATO. This would allow West Germany to contribute to the defense of Europe but as a member of a collective so as not to threaten its neighbors. See Thomas J. McCormick, *America's half-century: United States foreign policy in the Cold War*, Baltimore: Johns Hopkins University Press, 1989, pp. 106–8.

18 As listed in a directive presented by MacArthur to the American committee just before they began to draft the Japanese constitution. See Beate Sirota Gordon, *The only woman in the room*, Tokyo: Kodansha, 2001, p. 104.

19 In contrast, the U.S. military government in southern Korea did not finalize a draft for "South Korea" until late February 1947, just as it prepared to appoint an interim government. See *Miguk jónggi chôngbo charyojim, John R. Hodge munsó* [*United States administration period information materials collection, John R. Hodge papers*] vol. 1, Seoul: Hallym daehak Asia yóngu so, 1995, p. 267.

20 See "Memorandum by Whitney for MacArthur, 2 February 1946," in Takayanagi Kenzô, Otomo Ichirô, and Tanaka Hideo, eds, *Nihonkoku kenpo seitei no katei* [*The making of the constitution of Japan*], vol. 1, Tokyo: Yuhikaku, 1978, pp. 40–3, and Ray A. Moore and Donald L. Robinson, *Partners for democracy: crafting the new Japanese state under MacArthur*, Oxford: Oxford University Press, 2002, p. 77. The draft criticized by Whitney was not a finalized version.

21 During his meeting with Yoshida Shigeru and other Japanese to present the constitution draft, Whitney made a point of mentioning how he was enjoying Japan's "atomic sunshine," at which point a B-29 bomber flew overhead. See Takemae, *Inside GHQ*, p. 280.

22 Kyoko Inoue, *MacArthur's Japanese constitution: a linguistic and cultural study of its making*, Chicago: University of Chicago Press, 1991, p. 191.

23 Takemae, *Inside GHQ*, pp. 289–90.

24 Economic affluence provided the foundation that would make it possible for Japan's gross defense spending to become at one point the third highest in the world, after the United States and Russia. Since then China has overtaken Japan in defense spending. Between the late 1980s and 1990s, writes Gavan McCormack, Japan was the "preeminent military power in the [East Asian] region," and became the world's second largest arms importer. See Gavan McCormack, *The emptiness of Japanese affluence*, New York: M.E. Sharpe, 1996, p. 193. As is the case with many other nations, Japan's defense budget does not include important military-related expenditures, for example those that support the United States military in Japan, much of it paid lavishly by the Japanese government.

25 As Vice President of the Upper House, Burakumin Matsumoto Jiichirô became the first outcaste to enter the Imperial Palace. He gained fame in 1948 by refusing to approach the emperor as his inferior. Hiroshi Wagatsuma, "Postwar

political militance," in George De Vos and Hiroshi Wagatsuma, eds, *Japan's invisible race: caste in culture and personality*, Berkeley: University of California Press, 1972, p. 69.

26 Takemae, *Inside GHQ*, pp. 242, 264–5.

27 Supreme Commander for the Allied Powers, *The political reconstruction of Japan September 1945–September 1948*, Washington, D.C.: Government Printing Office, 1948, p. 780, Appendix F: 42.

28 Okurasho zaiseishishitsu, ed., *Showa zaiseishi* [The economic and financial history of Showa Japan], vol. 3, Tokyo: Keizai shinposha, 1976, pp. 202–6.

29 Takemae, *Inside GHQ*, p. 344.

30 Ibid., p. 339.

31 Ibid., pp. 312–13.

32 Japan's Korean population comprised the largest minority (93.1 percent) followed by Taiwanese and Okinawans, to whom occupation documents also refer as a people to be "repatriated." See Yukiko Koshiro, *Trans-Pacific racisms and the U.S. occupation of Japan*, New York: Columbia University Press, 1999, especially chapter 3, and Caprio's chapter below. One of the more comprehensive histories of the Japan-based Koreans during the occupation is Kim Daegi, *Sengo nihon seiji to zainichi chôsenjin mondai: SCAP no tai zainichi chôsenjin seisaku* [*Postwar Japan policy and the Japan-based Korean problem: SCAP's policy toward Japan-based Koreans*], Tokyo: Keisô shobo, 1997.

33 Pak Kyóngsik, *Kaihôgo zainichi chôsenjin undoshi* [*The history of post-liberation Japan-based Korean movements*], Tokyo: Sanichi shobô, 1989, p. 95.

34 Takemae, *Inside GHQ*, p. 499.

35 Poem composed by Emperor Hirohito to celebrate Japan's survival of a bitter defeat and humiliating occupation to emerge virtually unchanged. Quoted in Dower, *Embracing defeat*, p. 553.

36 Yoshida Yutaka attributes the success of Japan's postwar democratization to "the foundation laid during its prosecution of total war." He argues, "state demands for the prosecution of total war agitated conventional social orders. This created a dramatic leveling of interclass relations (*kaisôkan no heijunka*) that prepared Japanese society for postwar democratization." See his "Hajime ni: mittsu no shikaku" ["Introduction: three perspectives"] in idem, ed. *Sengo kaikaku to gyaku kôsu* [*Postwar reform and the reverse course*], Tokyo: Yoshikawa kôbunkan, 2004, p. 18. See Andrew Gordon, *The evolution of labor relations in Japan: heavy industry, 1853–1955*, Cambridge: Council on East Asian Studies, Harvard University, 1985 for a discussion on the pre-war influence on Japan's postwar employment system.

37 Cary, ed., *From a ruined empire*, p. 61.

38 Congressional Record, vol. 92, 79th Congress, 1st Session (18 September 1945) quoted in Yamagiwa and Nakamura, eds, *Shiryo Nihon senryo 1: tennosei* [*Materials from the occupation of Japan 1: the Emperor*], pp. 416–17. A Gallup Poll revealed that only 3 percent of Americans favored the Allies retaining the Emperor. *Foreign relations United States*, VI, 1945, Washington, D.C.: Government Printing Office, 1969, pp. 587–90.

39 See Buckley, *Occupation diplomacy*, Chapter 4.

40 Herbert Bix writes that Washington directed MacArthur in policy document SWNCC 57/3 to "take no action against the Emperor as a war criminal" without order from Washington. He notes that members of the occupation coached former Prime Minister Tojô Hideki to ensure that his testimony did not implicate the emperor. Tojô was even allowed to "correct" his testimony when it suggested imperial responsibility before being sent to the gallows. Herbert Bix, *Hirohito and the making of modern Japan*, New York: Harper & Collins, 2000, pp. 586–7, 604.

41 Quoted in Nishi, *Unconditional democracy*, p. 90.
42 See for example Dower, *Embracing defeat*, p. 335.
43 Ibid., pp. 300–9. It would have been unlikely that the majority of Japanese people would have voted for abdication had they been given a chance through a referendum.
44 Toriyama Atsushi writes that the U.S. intended to keep Okinawa. To Japan, Okinawa was the "Forgotten Island" and the Japanese people believed Okinawans to be different. MacArthur informed George Kennan that "the Japanese look down upon [the Okinawan people] ... They were simple and good natured people, who would pick up a good deal of money and have reasonably happy existence from an American base development." The official announcement of Okinawa's eventual return to Japanese administrative control was not made until November 1969, although this inevitability was clear from as early as August 1964. By 1967 Japanese aid to the islands had exceeded that provided by the United States. See Toriyama Atsushi, "Okinawa's 'postwar': some observations on the formation of American military bases in the aftermath of terrestrial warfare," trans. David Bust, *Inter-Asia cultural studies* 6 no. 3, 2002, p. 415.
45 Takemae, *Inside GHQ*, pp. 491–3.
46 Sheldon Garon, *The state and labor in modern Japan*, Berkeley: University of California Press, 1987, p. 233.
47 Johnson adds, "only 42 higher officials ... were purged from the Ministry of Commerce and Industry – the wartime Ministry of Munitions – and only 9 from the Ministry of Finance." Of the civilians purged, 70 percent came from the police bureau and officials from the Home Ministry. Chalmers Johnson, *MITI and the Japanese miracle: the growth of industrial policy, 1925–1975*, Stanford: Stanford University Press, 1982, pp. 41–2.
48 Jacob Van Staaveren's accounts of his experiences as school inspector in Yamanashi Prefecture during the occupation are especially revealing in this regard as instructors struggled to instill gender equality and individual thinking in their classrooms. See his *An American in Japan: a civilian view of the occupation*, Seattle: University of Washington Press, 1994, especially Chapter 6.
49 John W. Dower estimates that the colonies had provided Japan with 31 percent of its rice, 58 percent of its soybeans, and 45 percent of its salt. Dower, *Embracing defeat*, p. 91.
50 This argument appeared even before the Japanese had surrendered, and after the authors of the Cairo Communiqué declared that Japan would be stripped of its colonial possessions. For one example see Frank Kent's "A way out for Japan," as reported in I.F. Stone, *The Truman era*, New York: Vintage Books, 1973, p. 15.
51 Bruce Cumings, *The origins of the Korean War: the roaring of the cataract, 1947–1950*, Princeton: Princeton University Press, 1991, p. 50.
52 Much of the economic assistance that Japan offered to these states was tied to the purchase, or acceptance, of Japanese goods. The package agreed upon by Japan and South Vietnam in 1953, when the two states established diplomatic relations, is exemplary. The $55.6 million package included $39 million in reparations that included a $37 million hydroelectric power plant and $2 million for factories, $7.5 million in Japanese government loans, and $9.1 million in private economic cooperation loans. Thomas Havens, *Fire across the sea: the Vietnam War and Japan, 1965–1975*, Princeton: Princeton University Press, 1987, p. 16. The 1965 treaty that normalized Japan's relations with the Republic of Korea was similar in content.
53 For information on postwar Sino-Japanese relations, see Tanaka Akihiko, *Nitchû kankei, 1945–1990* [Japan-China relations, 1945–1990], Tokyo: Tokyo daigaku

shuppankai, 1991, Soeya Yoshihide, *Nippon gaikô to Chûgoku, 1945–1972* [*Japanese diplomacy and China, 1945–1972*], Tokyo: Tokyo daigaku shuppankai, 2000, and Sayuri Guthrie-Shimizu's chapter on Sino-Japanese relations in this volume.

54 Use of the term "reverse course" (*gyaku kosu*) has generated controversy since November 1951, when the *Yomiuri shinbun* ran a series of articles on the occupation. Takemae Eiji disagrees with this terminology: "Occupation policy after 1948 represented a change in emphasis, a course adjustment or shifting of gears not a volte-face." Takemae, *Inside GHQ*, p. 473.

55 See Nishi, *Unconditional democracy*, pp. 86–9.

56 Jacob Van Staavern recollects his experiences as one such inspector in his *An American in Japan*.

57 Takemae, *Inside GHQ*, p. 100.

58 Koshiro, *Trans-Pacific facisms*, p. 2.

59 The 1952 Alien Registration Act introduced by the U.S. occupation borrowed from the 1940 Alien Registration (Smith) Act and the 1950 Internal Security (McCarran) Act, which aimed to suppress communists by according the U.S. government "broad powers of surveillance and control, detention and deportation." Takemae, *Inside GHQ*, pp. 498–9. The Japanese government has recently taken steps to ease this humiliation, primarily by first covering, and then eliminating, the fingerprints that appeared on the alien registration card that all non-Japanese residents are required to carry on their person.

60 Takemae, *Inside GHQ*, pp. 477–8. Yoshida Yutaka identifies two currents that existed within GHQ, one "practical" (*risôshugiteki*) and the other "anti-communist and conservative." See his "Hajime ni: mittsu no shikaku," p. 28.

61 George F. Kennan, *Memoirs, 1925–1950*, Boston: Little Brown and Company, 1967, Chapter 16.

62 Takemae, *Inside GHQ*, pp. 458–9. He cites Bruce Cumings' depiction of this maneuver as the "Kennan Restoration."

63 Kennan, *Memoirs*, p. 393.

64 Hata Ikuhiko argues that the Truman Doctrine was instrumental in the occupation's policy reversal. See Sadao Asada's summary of this article in his "Recent works on the American occupation of Japan: the state of the art," *Japanese journal of American studies* 1, 1981, pp. 180–2.

65 This group, disturbed by occupation policy, carried out an active "anti-SCAP" campaign in the United States. See Takemae, *Inside GHQ*, pp. 459–60 for a summary of this lobby's activities.

66 Kim, *East Asia's turbulent century*, p. 312.

67 Dower, *Embracing defeat*, pp. 532–3. See also Takemae, *Inside GHQ*, p. 335.

68 Takemae, *Inside GHQ*, pp. 458, 461.

69 Dower, *Embracing defeat*, pp. 545–6.

70 See John W. Dower, *Empire and aftermath: Yoshida Shigeru and the Japanese experience*, Cambridge: Harvard Council on East Asian Studies, 1980.

71 These figures are found in statistics provided in HQ, USAFIK [United States Armed Forces In Korea] G-2 Periodic Reports.

72 Takasaki Sôji, "Kikoku mondai no keika to haikei" ["The process and background of the repatriation movement,"] in Takasaki and Pak, eds, *Kikoku undo to hwa nan datta no ka*, Tokyo: Heibonsha, p. 20.

73 Roger Dingman, "The Dagger and the gift: the impact on the Korean War on Japan," *The journal of American-East Asian relations* 1, Spring 1993, p. 42.

74 Takemae, *Inside GHQ*, pp. 489–90.

75 Cheong, *The politics of anti-Japanese sentiment in Korea*, p. 134.

76 Japan has since slipped behind China.

77 Nishio Kanji, *Kokumin no rekishi* [*The people's history*], Tokyo: Sankei shinbunsha, 1999, p. 768.

1   Feeding the Japanese

Food policy, land reform, and Japan's economic recovery

Steven J. Fuchs

Food was at the heart of the economic turmoil the Supreme Commander for the Allied Powers (SCAP) General Douglas MacArthur and his staff inherited in Japan in 1945. Japan's economy deteriorated rapidly during the last two years of World War II; the effects of wartime social and economic dislocation manifested in full during the occupation. Within this landscape Washington expected SCAP to demilitarize and democratize Japan while holding the Japanese responsible for the economy. SCAP, however, quickly realized the inherent contradiction in Washington's instructions; the facilitation of demilitarization and democratization could not be divorced from economic recovery. SCAP believed that the impending food crisis was the largest obstacle to achieving the occupation's political and economic goals. MacArthur, SCAP, and the Japanese therefore fashioned policies designed to maximize food production, collection, and distribution and to supplement domestic production with imports. In the process, MacArthur laid the foundation for the Pacific Alliance.

Historians acknowledge that Japan's cities were bombed out, that the 1945 harvest was one of the worst on record, and that the Japanese government contributed to the economic malaise through the ill-conceived policy of releasing food and natural resources in the last days of the war. They have not, however, examined how SCAP and the Japanese government attempted to tackle the food shortage. Nor have they evaluated the effect of food policy on Japan's economy. SCAP is often portrayed as having ignored Japan's faltering economy and the food crisis.[1] One historian takes a particularly critical view of MacArthur as an apathetic bystander, unfazed by "falling production, rising unemployment, soaring inflation, and widening trade deficits" who believed that only "time and emergency relief . . . would assure recovery."[2]

Occupation policy was certainly designed to "destroy" all vestiges of Japan's military, economic, and political structure that had contributed to the debacle of wartime Japan. Too much attention, however, has been paid to the apparent tendency of the Basic Directive for Post-Surrender Military Government in Japan Proper (JCS 1380/15) to foist responsibility for Japan's economic recovery on the Japanese. Widely cited is the directive's statement, "You [SCAP] will not assume any responsibility for the economic rehabilitation of Japan or the strengthening of the Japanese economy." The Japanese alone were made responsible for avoiding "acute economic distress."[3] The question is: To what extent did MacArthur and SCAP accept the limitations laid down in this directive and others? According to the Chief of the Government Section of SCAP, Brigadier General Courtney Whitney, MacArthur ignored the "no responsibility" clause in order to "minimize the burden upon the American people in the subsidization of food deficiencies."[4] The historian Theodore Cohen, who served as Chief of the Labor Division of SCAP, shares Whitney's assessment. Cohen argued, MacArthur "could never accept the directive's cavalier dismissal of economic recovery as a Japanese responsibility. Without economic recovery, democratization would never last."[5] MacArthur believed that the United States had assumed responsibility for both the political and the *economic* outcome of the occupation.

From 1945 to 1947, SCAP's economic policy was its food policy. MacArthur was the most ardent defender of Japan's right to eat.[6] SCAP viewed food, or the lack thereof, as having precipitated the economic crisis. With Japan's economy shattered and starvation knocking at the door, MacArthur and SCAP attempted to use food policy to resolve the immense economic problems that Japan faced. From SCAP's perspective, farmers' half-hearted participation in the quota and collection system negatively impacted rationing and prices. The resulting food shortage forced workers to migrate to the countryside in search of food, shelter, and employment. Factories struggled to maintain their labor force as food shortages led to the reduction or complete stoppage of supplementary rations for industrial workers, since the staple food ration received priority. Workers, having suffered from diminished rations for six years, displayed "mental lethargy and inability to carry out prolonged physical labor characteristic of chronic malnutrition." "Absenteeism" and "food holidays" prevailed as workers made "foraging expeditions to secure food." Food accounted for approximately 70 percent of a family's budget in 1946, as purchasing food on the black market and inflation devoured wages. Reduced labor efficiency increased the unit cost of manufactured goods. As production costs rose due to inflation, rising wages, and the scarcity of natural resources, exports became less competitive. But the survival of Japan's economy and the maintenance of a reasonable standard of living depended on sufficient exports of manufactured goods to pay for imports of food and raw materials; the more money that was diverted to paying for imports, the less money was available for rebuilding. "The most serious immediate effect of the food shortage," argued the Price Control and Rationing Division of the Economic and Scientific Section, "was in its adverse effect on the already crippled Japanese economy."[7]

The reverse course is frequently defined as the shift in occupation policy from democratization and demilitarization to economic recovery, beginning in 1947. At no time, however, did SCAP's policy undergo a reverse course in its food policy. With food production as its central goal, SCAP pursued reform when necessary and recovery when needed. "SCAP," MacArthur stated shortly after moving into the Dai Ichi building, "is not concerned with how to keep Japan down, but how to get her on her feet again." Only "vigorous and prompt action" could "prevent pestilence, disease, starvation, or other major social catastrophe."[8] Because industrial productivity remained below pre-war levels, SCAP did not give the appearance, at least to Washington, of promoting economic stabilization and recovery prior to 1947. The Nine Point Stabilization Plan, largely conceived by Under-Secretary of the Army William H. Draper, Jr. in 1947 and 1948 and later implemented by President Harry S. Truman's special economic adviser Joseph M. Dodge, altered the approach to economic recovery. While the Nine Point Stabilization Plan emphasized controlling inflation and promoting exports,[9] MacArthur and SCAP focused on food.

The food situation in 1945 proved to be worse than SCAP and the Japanese had anticipated. Food imports dropped from a 1941 wartime peak of 4.36 million metric tons to 1.85 million metric tons. Rice imports, having averaged 1.8 million metric tons from 1936 to 1942, fell to 236,000 metric tons. In August, the Ministry of Agriculture and Forestry had estimated the rice crop at 8.4 million metric tons. Cold weather, a major typhoon in September, and October floods decimated it. When wartime dislocation and fertilizer shortages are factored in, the result was the worst domestic crop in 30 years – 6.45 million metric tons in 1945, compared to a wartime peak of 10.02 million metric tons in 1942. Since millions of repatriated Japanese arriving in 1945 and 1946 would further exacerbate the pressure on the food supply, the Ministry lowered its estimates of the amount of food indigenous production could provide for Japan's anticipated population of 77 million people from 1,782 calories to 1,375 calories per person per day. The Ministry's request for imports stood at a staggering 6.12 million metric tons in rice equivalents.[10]

From the outset, SCAP doubted the accuracy and feasibility of Japanese estimates. By November 1945, however, no audit had been conducted. MacArthur's September announcement that only 200,000 American soldiers were needed in Japan furthered SCAP's dependence on the Japanese government for setting the quota and administering the food collection and distribution programs. The Natural Resources Section (NRS) believed that the Ministry's goals were unattainable "under emergency conditions anticipated in 1946." Since the Japanese themselves had been unable to provide 2,160 calories per person per day during the war, SCAP did not feel obliged to do so. Even a ration of 1,800 calories required importing 3.31 million metric tons in rice equivalents, an unlikely event in 1945 and 1946.[11]

Questionable estimates did not deter SCAP from its primary goal of collecting the 1945 rice crop. Maximizing domestic production to reduce the likelihood of starvation and to justify imports called for a proactive approach to resuscitating Japan's economy. Hoarding, transportation difficulties, population dislocation, fears of food shortages, and a lack of commercial goods worked against SCAP. That the occupation began in September created another problem because the rice crop, which accounted for approximately 60 percent of agricultural production on a caloric basis, would be harvested in October and November. With little time to gain a complete picture of the agricultural situation, SCAP decided in November to utilize the existing government machinery, in spite of concerns about its monopolistic control. The uncertainty of imports and the potential for further aggravating the food situation by disrupting the quota and collection system mitigated against changing it.[12]

The basis of Japan's wartime food policy was the 1942 Foodstuff Control Law, which created a national collection and distribution system for staple foods, including rice, wheat, barley, sweet potatoes, and potatoes. Because of overlapping bureaucratic jurisdictions, the process of setting farmers' collection quotas allowed for a great deal of negotiation and local autonomy. Local officials often underestimated production and the acreage under cultivation. After estimating local production yields, the Prefectural Food Inspection Office passed the information to the prefectural governor, who then gave it to the Ministry of Agriculture and Forestry. After collecting the data, Ministry officials, prefectural governors, and local officials met to finalize food quotas for each prefecture. Prefectural quotas were then broken down by city, town, and village, with local officials setting individual farmers' quotas. Farmers sold their quotas to the Agricultural Cooperative Association, which credited each farmer's account. The Bank of Japan financed the system through food bonds.[13]

The distribution system did not give urbanites and farmers the same quantity and quality of food. The NRS realized that legal measures alone were insufficient to regulate consumption in rural areas. Though doubting the enforceability of such a policy, the NRS limited farmers, who usually consumed 2,200 calories per day, to 2,000 calories in an effort to enhance collection. The tendency of farmers to ignore these limits or sell food on the black market made securing food for the urban population that much harder. Throughout the 1946 rice year (November 1945 to October 1946) the staple ration for an adult was 1,042 calories, with supplementary rations distributed when available. Unable to survive on such meager rations, the Japanese relied on various sources to provide the difference between life and death: home production, family assistance, the black market, charitable organizations, emergency distributions, and imports.[14]

Initial collection rates for the 1946 rice year were well below SCAP's expectations. Typically, the government collected between 85 and 95 percent of the rice quota by the end of February. By the end of February 1946, however, only 60 percent had been collected. Farmers' suspicions of the government, social dislocation, hoarding, and the fear of starvation before the fall harvest, all contributed to the poor results. Matters were further aggravated by black market prices that were astonishingly higher than rationed prices, and the government's past failure to deliver goods earned through the link system, which offered farmers bonuses for meeting or surpassing their quotas. The rationing system was on the verge of collapse. Food, which was central to SCAP's political and economic agenda, was needed immediately to avert starvation and the discontent that would accompany it.[15]

To equalize the food supply throughout Japan, SCAP instituted the deficit transfer program. Deficit transfers involved moving food stocks from surplus to deficit areas in order to equalize "the burden of the food deficit between food producers and consumers and between food surplus prefectures and deficit prefectures." While allowing SCAP to alleviate acute food shortages with Japanese supplies before distributing imports, local officials did not embrace the program. The threat of a food shortage made local officials wary of sending food to other prefectures to assist their more unfortunate brethren without guaranteeing a supply for their own constituents. An appeal by the Emperor and SCAP's warning that imports would not be distributed until the deficit transfer program had been completed resulted in grudging support.[16]

In February 1946, the Japanese government issued the Emergency Imperial Food Ordinance. Government expropriation of undelivered rice quotas was legalized, providing that the farmer receive the official price. The law also strengthened fines and jail sentences for interfering with rice collection, instigating others not to cooperate, and falsifying records. The Emergency Imperial Food Ordinance provided the legal backbone for compelling the agricultural community's cooperation with the collection program. To complement the stricter legal measures, in March SCAP more than doubled the official price of staple foods to inspire farmers to sell more produce to the government. SCAP did not believe that this move would stoke inflation or wage demands, since rationed prices were still well below black market levels. Farmers responded favorably to the higher official prices.[17]

The delay in collecting the rice quota, however, caused turmoil in the distribution system. Urban stock levels plummeted, and the distribution of fifteen days of staple rations at one time became impossible. Furthermore, staple rations had to be delayed in many cities. By May, residents of Tokyo received only 775 calories from the official ration, with total consumption falling to 1,352 calories. For most cities, the crisis became acute in August. Delays were often followed by cancellations. Surveys revealed that diseases stemming from malnutrition peaked during the summer. Colonel Crawford F. Sams, Chief of the Public Health and Welfare Section, feared that urbanites would be "near the danger point of mass starvation" from May to August. Delays, or even the fear of them, sent black market prices and inflation soaring. SCAP estimated that in early 1946 the staple food ration, which provided 75 percent of the total food for a family, cost 35 yen, while the 25 percent acquired on the black market amounted to over 230 yen.[18]

Fear of starvation sparked food demonstrations throughout May. On 1 May 1946, over one million people gathered in cities across Japan to demand food. On 12 May, residents of the Setagaya Ward tried to enter the Imperial Palace to petition Emperor Hirohito for rice. A week later, on "Food May Day," 250,000 Japanese took part in a "give us rice" rally at the Imperial Palace Plaza. By clamping down on the demonstrations, MacArthur missed an opportunity to support the popular democracy he himself had been nourishing. The riots, however, reinforced his conviction that food should remain the number one priority. The significance of the rallies was not lost on Japan's new prime minister, Yoshida Shigeru. Sensing that his career depended on remedying the food crisis, Yoshida warned the nation "a satisfactory solution of the food problem is the basic requirement for Japan's national rehabilitation." Until October, the shortage would be the equivalent of one month's worth of national consumption. Yoshida proposed a national effort to collect the 1946 rice crop by expanding the link system and creating committees to establish consumption and collection plans. In addition, high-class restaurants were to be closed, industrial rations re-evaluated with emphasis on strategic importance and worker productivity, and people asked to move out of the cities. Failure to resolve the food shortage would cause the "collapse" of the modest gains made in industrial production. If all else failed, Yoshida promised to work toward securing the highest level of food imports.[19] In a stroke, Yoshida offered the Japanese hope, while making it clear to SCAP and Washington that the Japanese were willing to sacrifice to help themselves.

These measures resulted in the collection of an additional 700,000 metric tons of rice during March and April. By June, rice deliveries reached 79 percent of the quota. Rice continued to trickle in so that by mid-July the government had collected 86 percent of the quota. Of Japan's forty-six prefectures, six met or surpassed their quota, twelve fulfilled more than 90 percent, ten satisfied over 80 percent, and eighteen failed to meet even 80 percent of the quota.[20] The joint effort made by the Japanese government and SCAP had not fully overcome the legacy of the war or the uncertainty of the future. Inaccurate reporting, dislocation, the threat of starvation, and hoarding pushed the rationing system to the breaking point.

Enhanced collections and regulating supplies could not make up for the 15 to 20 percent of the food supply Japan historically imported. While the Japanese government, SCAP, and Washington hotly debated import levels throughout the occupation, no voice was louder than MacArthur's in insisting that the United States had an obligation to feed the Japanese. In seeking to stabilize Japan's economy, MacArthur couched food imports in politically acceptable terms: to "prevent disease and unrest," to pursue the goals of the occupation, and to supplement exhausted Japanese resources. When these received a lukewarm response, MacArthur relied on plan two: scare the hell out of them. In his requests to the War Department, the Department of the Army, and the Joint Chiefs of Staff, MacArthur outlined the themes SCAP used to justify imports during the first three years of the occupation. He painted a bleak picture of the food situation in 1946, calling it the worst in thirty years. He predicted that extreme food shortages would force the suspension of rations for urbanites by May. To maintain the staple ration of 1,042 calories, Japan would have to import 2.6 million metric tons of rice equivalents between May and September. Failure would bring disastrous consequences, especially for the middle and lower classes. Poverty and hunger would ravage the country, providing a fertile breeding ground for disease and for subversive political ideologies looking to spark "an explosive situation" and "uprisings of a major character." MacArthur gave Washington a stark ultimatum: "Either food or soldiers must be brought to Japan without fail." If food is not sent, MacArthur warned, "I request that it be brought to the personal attention of the President in order that there may be no future question as to the chain of responsibility."[21]

To strengthen its case, SCAP had to address another problem. A study by the Economic and Scientific Section (ESS) revealed that from October 1945 to March 1946, occupation personnel consumed enough alcohol to feed 267,000 people on the standard ration for one year. From April 1946 to March 1947, the food equivalent would rise to rations for 415,000 people. To avert Congressional hostility and justify more imports, SCAP restricted consumption of indigenous food by occupation personnel. In December 1945, SCAP declared all public eating and drinking establishments off limits if the food was prepared with Japanese supplies. Because the food crisis was expected to reach a critical level during the summer of 1946, SCAP suspended the manufacture of liquor from Japan's food supplies during June and July. Alcohol, however, was an essential part of the link system; any prolonged stoppage could interfere with collection. The ban on Japanese liquor for occupation personnel was kept in place after being lifted for the Japanese. SCAP also limited the amount of food diverted to alcohol production, particularly rice. As a result, SCAP estimated total alcohol production at a mere 37 percent of 1935–1939 levels. In setting production, SCAP had to balance the need for food with the demand for alcohol. Too restrictive a policy could have led to the soaring production of bootlegged alcohol, thus obliterating the sought-after benefits.[22]

The Departments of State, War, and Agriculture sent Colonel Raymond Harrison to Japan in the spring to verify MacArthur's dire picture of the food situation. The Harrison Mission concluded that the need for food imports was indeed great, though perhaps not so great as to require the levels requested by SCAP. Former President Herbert Hoover, who led the United Nations Relief and Rehabilitation Agency Mission that arrived in early May, also attested to the precarious nature of Japan's food supply. His conclusions were blunt: without imports, SCAP would end up presiding over conditions much like those at "the Buchenwald and Belsen concentration camps." Maintaining order, never mind promoting economic recovery, would be impossible. These two missions, combined with what one observer has called the "irrefutable fact" that Europe was threatened by famine, helped to pave the way for food imports. The trickle would soon become a stream as Washington realized the potential of agriculturally based foreign aid programs.[23]

Emergency distributions and imports played a critical role in making up for the shortfall. During 1945 and 1946, SCAP authorized the distribution of sizable quantities of U.S. army surplus food stocks, Japanese army surplus stocks, and Japanese government supplies. These measures, while still providing a ration well below minimum dietary requirements, helped to patch the holes in the distribution system. From May to October 1946, SCAP also released imports of cereals and canned goods totaling 594,838 metric tons in rice equivalents. In June, imports equaled 62 percent of Tokyo's rations and 41 percent of Yokohama's. During July and August, imported food jumped to 100 percent of Tokyo's ration. For all of Japan, imports equaled 3.5 percent of the ration in May, 9.8 percent in June, 34.2 percent in July, 33.5 percent in August, and 27.2 percent in September. Imports, SCAP claimed, ensured that "the food shortage did not take the form of mass starvation or widespread disease and civil unrest." According to SCAP, "food imports to defeated and prostrate Japan convinced millions of Japanese of the true democratic aims of the Occupation" and saved as many as 11 million people from starvation.[24]

SCAP efforts went beyond policies designed to overcome the immediate food shortage. From SCAP's perspective, the creation of a democratic and prosperous agricultural community rested on its ability to improve the plight of the 28 percent of farmers who owned no land and the 40 percent who owned insufficient land to support their families. Taking a long-term perspective, Wolf I. Ladejinsky of the NRS argued that an average farm of 2.4 acres kept the population tied to the land. Larger farms were needed to raise the standard of living and to push the excess farm population into other professions – the same prescriptions being offered to American farmers. Agricultural reforms had to coincide with steps to expand Japan's industrial base and non-farm employment opportunities.[25] Thus, Japan's agricultural community needed farm consolidation, ownership, and higher income.

In December 1945, SCAP ordered the Japanese government to "take measures to insure that those who till the soil of Japan shall have a more equal opportunity to enjoy the fruits of their labor." Later that month, MacArthur pushed the Japanese to "remove economic obstacles to the revival and strengthening of democratic tendencies ... and to destroy the economic bondage which has enslaved the Japanese farmers to centuries of feudal oppression." Poverty and hardship, SCAP believed, had led farmers to sympathize with "extremist political movements" and militarism.[26] While Japanese leaders conceded that land reform was needed, a year of negotiation followed before the two sides agreed on how to implement it. In October 1946, the Diet passed the Agricultural Adjustment Law and the Special Measures Law for the Establishment of Owner-Cultivators, which empowered the government to purchase all land owned by absentee landlords, corporate land not tied to industrial operations, owner-operated land and tenant land in excess of retention rates, and all reclaimable land. Not only were the financial terms favorable, the government also granted buyers further protection by waiving mortgage payments during years of poor harvest and limiting mortgage payments and operating expenses to no more than one third of a farmer's gross income. With locally elected agricultural commissions administering the program, tenants and small farmers now had the power to decide the most important question raised by land reform: Who would get what land?[27]

Land reform destroyed the most potent threat to Japan's democratic and capitalist system. MacArthur argued, "there can be no firmer foundation for a sound and moderate democracy and no firmer bulwark against the pressure of any extreme philosophy" than land reform.[28] In addition to removing the vestiges of the economic and political system that had led farmers to support militarism, it also allowed SCAP to pre-empt communist infiltration of the countryside by co-opting their platform. Reflecting on its motivations for undertaking land reform, SCAP announced, "the elimination of this malignancy was recognized as vital to the promotion of maximum production staple foods and requisite social and economic stability." Land reform served another purpose: it allowed farmers to purchase land cheaply, while declining land prices made land an unprofitable investment for non-farmers. Capital would then be available for investment in industry. Farmers' improved purchasing power provided industry with more consumers. As industrial revival advanced, higher wages and new employment opportunities would draw surplus labor back to the cities. Finally, land reform stimulated agricultural production by increasing the amount of cultivated land and by granting farmers access to land.[29]

In addition to strengthening democracy and capitalism, SCAP never wavered in believing that land ownership would increase agricultural production. The redistribution of approximately 4.5 million acres – a third of Japan's cultivatable land – would unleash the productive capability of the Japanese people. The burden of "expanding agricultural production for a starving urban population was of greatest urgency" for SCAP and the Japanese. The basis of all agricultural programs was "centered, first of all, on increased agricultural production," argued Ladejinsky. No reform or technical improvement would alleviate the food shortage unless farmers had the incentive to produce. As a result, SCAP refused to accept any half-hearted proposals for reforming tenancy. By July 1949, the Japanese government had acquired 4.59 million acres, of which 4.46 million acres had been sold. The cost of the program was nearly 8 billion yen.[30]

During the first year of the occupation, SCAP and the Japanese government boosted food production and collection through a combination of short and long-term policies. Though insufficient time to prepare for the harvest limited SCAP's control over food collection, SCAP did not balk in the face of the dire social and economic consequences that failure to feed the Japanese would bring. Though other factors contributed to Japan's economic malaise, SCAP remained convinced that the food shortage was the main cause of inflation, wage and price pressures, the trade deficit and dollar shortage, and lagging industrial production. SCAP and the Japanese increased the food available for distribution by closing restaurants, restricting occupation personnel's access to Japanese food supplies, and stiffening surveillance and legal measures. Deficit transfers, while not equalizing distribution, moderated shortages in the hardest hit areas. By improving the fertility of the land through reclamation, revitalization projects, and the application of fertilizer, SCAP set the stage for larger crop yields. Land reform brought political and economic stability to a segment of the population that had once been active supporters of militarism. SCAP's sponsorship of the fishing industry provided desperately needed protein. Finally, when domestic sources of food proved inadequate, SCAP turned to imports. Led by MacArthur, SCAP was the most outspoken supporter of resuming U.S.–Japanese agricultural trade. As SCAP and the Japanese celebrated their surviving the famine months from May to October, the next rice crop was ready for harvest.

Originally estimated at 8.62 million metric tons, the 1946 bumper rice crop of 9.21 million metric tons surprised everyone. The timing could not have been better. In November 1946, SCAP raised the basic ration for non-producers from 1,042 calories to 1,246 calories to bring the ration closer to the subsistence level. Due to SCAP and the Japanese government's inability to enforce the 2,000-calorie ration for producers, SCAP increased their ration to 2,200 calories. SCAP also planned to provide an average of 568 calories per day in supplemental rations to 7.6 million industrial workers. Finally, the 3.8 million repatriated Japanese had to be fed. Having already notified farmers of their quotas, SCAP and the Japanese government recalculated the quota to 110 percent of the original quota to ensure the collection of as much of the rice crop as possible. By the end of February, however, collection rates reached only 77.5 percent.[31] Something had to be done to avoid a repeat of the 1946 summer food crisis; recalcitrance on the part of farmers was not acceptable.

The quest to feed the Japanese during the 1947 rice year (November 1946 to October 1947) began with imports. In August 1946, MacArthur informed Chief of Staff General Dwight D. Eisenhower that aid should continue for the foreseeable future and that a reversal of policy would "spoil the fruits of our recent victory." In 1946, imports had "prevented disease and unrest"; to build on the economic recovery begun in 1946, the Japanese people needed sufficient nourishment. MacArthur declared, "The first measurable strides toward economic and social rehabilitation will be possible during the coming year." Food remained the "vital incentive" for reaching production goals. While SCAP tried to maximize domestic production to reduce food imports and associated costs, any cut in SCAP's estimates "is false economy" and "will result in dire consequences to the Occupation and to the accomplishment of the Potsdam Declaration directives permitting the reestablishment of a reasonable national economy in Japan."[32] While acknowledging the depth of the global food shortage, SCAP warned, "the serious consequences of the food shortage must not be underestimated and should not be permitted to recur in 1947." Insufficient food had stymied industrial production as poorly fed workers opted to search for food. As a result, production in basic industries, including coal, fertilizer, and textiles, "was seriously hampered," with negative implications for Japan's ability to pay for imports. W.S. Egekvist, Chief of the Price Control and Rationing Division, cautioned that democratization "cannot be secured if they continue indefinitely on a dietary level seriously below that provided under the old feudalistic and militaristic regime."[33]

The arrival of Palmer Hogenson, Chief of the Civilian Supply Section of the Military Planning Branch, brought the relationship between industrial recovery and imports to the forefront. After touring Japan and Korea from 29 August to 3 October 1946 to evaluate the region's economic state, Hogenson concluded that a 1,042-calorie ration meant that people would spend their time "scrounging for food" instead of working, a circumstance that threatened export and production goals. Only "greater industrial activity" could reduce the cost of the occupation. Hogenson, however, did not find SCAP's record to be flawless. SCAP had lowered initial Japanese demands from 6 million metric tons to 3 million metric tons in rice equivalents during the first year. Hogenson raised the question of how "disease and unrest" were averted and no additional troops needed though only one million tons of food had been exported to Japan. By overplaying the "disease and unrest" card, SCAP constantly fell into a trap. Food imports were needed to provide basic sustenance. But, when signs of turmoil failed to arise, the assumption made by Congress and the world was that SCAP's collection program had not set quotas high enough.[34]

The Joint War, Agriculture, and State Department Food Mission headed by Colonel Raymond Harrison further examined the food situation in February 1947. With tensions between the Soviet Union and the United States escalating and the cost of the occupation mounting, Washington sent Harrison to ensure that Japan's resources were being fully exploited. The Mission found no sign of "acute malnutrition," since average consumption was 500 calories to 750 calories above the 1,246 ration, though evidence of "long-continued dietary deficiencies" was clear. Harrison recommended improving the quality of a Japanese diet deficient in fats, oils, protein, and vitamins rather than increasing the ration. In addition, SCAP and the Japanese government should raise the quota instead of relying on imports. As evidence that dramatic improvement could be realized from indigenous production, Harrison pointed out that 10 percent of rice production and 50 percent of the fish catch ended up in the black market. Food imports were not a replacement for unfulfilled quotas.[35]

SCAP took issue with the Harrison Mission's critical assessment. The Mission's argument that relying on local officials to administer the food collection program "will not result in achieving maximum collections" failed to consider the fact that such was the manner in which the Japanese had traditionally collected food. Centralized control was "foreign" to Japan, would "result in loss of efficiency," and was counter to democratization. Moreover, exports were not likely to pay for imports in the near future. Stabilizing imports on that basis would be "inimical" to the goal of reviving production. SCAP was also acutely aware of the rationing system's weaknesses. While the system was not "perfect," admitted the Chief of the Food Branch, B.F. Johnston, there were inherent statistical difficulties when dealing with "a farm population of 32 million persons and 5.5 million farm units averaging less than 2.2 acres each." Johnston argued against those who reasoned that quotas must be too low if food was available on the black market. Instead, he claimed, farmers were selling a percentage of the food they were allowed to retain. To expect otherwise was foolish, given the profits farmers could make on the black market or the scarce items they could obtain by barter.[36]

While SCAP's debate with Washington raged on, the bumper crop and better enforcement dramatically improved collection rates. However, Egekvist anticipated difficulty in satisfying the last 20 percent of the quota. In spite of SCAP and the Japanese government's efforts, farmers were still dissatisfied with forced collection programs as well as the limited goods obtainable through the link program. Farmers also resented strikes by industrial workers, which slowed down the production of fertilizer and other farm necessities. At the same time that workers demanded better pay, the price of rice remained fixed in an inflationary environment. SCAP reforms to nurture democracy at the local level further interfered with food collection. The recent application of the purge to mayors and association chiefs delayed fixing the quota, while the forthcoming local elections were expected to promote sectionalism.[37] The decentralization of power to local governments, combined with local elections, was evidence of the strides Japan was making toward democracy. Gaining the compliance of locally elected officials in charge of rice collection, however, was not made any easier.

SCAP and the Japanese government diligently pursued 110 percent of the quota. Developed by the Japanese government during the war, the link system was designed to maximize quota collection by offering cash payments and consumer items for surplus production. By redeeming points, farmers could purchase scarce consumer goods such as bicycles, fertilizer, salt, sake, and textiles. On 1 March 1947, the Japanese government announced the new incentives. Farmers received cash bonuses or fertilizer for the last 20 percent of their rice quota delivered by March and additional bonuses for deliveries in excess of the quota by the end of April. Other bonuses were given if a farmer's entire hamlet (*buraku*) fulfilled its quota. Yoshida justified this revision by claiming that "supplying the farmers with fertilizers and other necessities commands the first priority, and we must put up with such hardships until the food crisis is over." The goal was to have farmers sell their produce to government agencies instead of the black market while providing industry with customers.[38]

SCAP and the Japanese government expanded the type and amount of goods offered by the link system. The Price Control and Ration Division suggested including canned food in the link system instead of earmarking it for staple distribution, since only limited quantities were available anyway. In the end, "an 'investment' of canned goods in producing areas will realize a much greater return in the form of rice." The Finance Ministry made more sake available for distribution between January and June 1947 as well as 350 million cigarettes. Repair shops were set up so that farmers who satisfied their quota could have their farming implements fixed. Finally, from February to June, over 5 million pieces of textile goods, rubber shoes, bicycle tires, and tubes were made available to farmers.[39]

In early March 1947, the Japanese government reminded local officials that "the satisfaction of 110 percent of the (rice) quota is prerequisite to the food import request by the Imperial Japanese Government to SCAP." Local police were instructed to strictly enforce all food collection laws; infringement carried up to ten years of hard labor or a 50,000 yen fine. SCAP and the Japanese government also undertook a publicity campaign to stimulate delivery and to "emphasize the role of food in the reconstruction of Japan and the fundamental interrelationship of the farm and non-farm elements of the economy." In addition, Ministry of Agriculture and Forestry officials, members of the Food Management Board, and local officials toured the countryside, stressing the importance of full cooperation with the collection program.[40]

SCAP did not sit idly by as food disappeared from the quota system into the black market. On 5 March MacArthur ordered the Commander of the Eighth Army to step up surveillance of food collection and continue the publicity campaign. Moreover, SCAP required the Eighth Army to submit periodic reports on government officials obstructing food collection and ways to enhance collection. The premise was that farmers did not have the right to refuse to fulfill quotas because of shortages of fertilizer and consumer goods. Congressional "reluctance to appropriate money for shipments of food to Japan and Germany," stated a SCAP directive, required greater efficiency in collecting food. On 7 March, the Eighth Army issued a directive that surveillance be set up to track the kind and amount of indigenous and imported food people received and at what price, how much food was distributed at each level of government, and the amount of "leakages." Because of the hierarchical system of rationing, each level of government had to maintain receipts in order to locate breakdowns in the system.[41]

As a result of the initiatives, collection rates in March and April became much higher than those of February. By 31 August, the total reached 107.1 percent of the quota as the Japanese government collected over 6.09 million tons of rice. On a prefecture-by-prefecture basis, the results of the 1947 ration collection program far surpassed 1946. Two prefectures exceeded 110 percent of the quota, twenty-two collected in excess of 100 percent, eleven collected over 95 percent, nine collected over 90 percent, and only two collected under 90 percent. In order to reduce the impact of an altered diet and nutritional deficiencies, SCAP forced the Japanese government to store rice equivalents of 199,000 metric tons to counter imports released from January to March 1947. Total imports climbed every month, culminating with 215,000 metric tons in August, 287,000 metric tons in September, and 297,000 metric tons in October of rice equivalents.[42]

How can we evaluate MacArthur and SCAP's food policies during the first two years of the occupation? From the outset, SCAP undertook a broadly based program to maximize food production, collection, and distribution. Whether it was reducing consumption by occupation personnel, sponsoring land reclamation and land reform, establishing incentive programs, strengthening the collection and distribution systems, or enhancing enforcement measures, SCAP's number one priority was feeding the Japanese. Food policy also became the first step in the process of industrial recovery. The fertilizer, fishing, whaling, and shipbuilding industries figured prominently in SCAP's plans to improve food production. Fertilizer was essential for restoring and maintaining the soil's vitality while fish consumption provided the protein for a balanced diet. In spite of impressive gains, Japan's food production did not meet demand, which historically had always been the case. Therefore, SCAP doggedly pursued imports from the United States, primarily in the form of GARIOA.[43] SCAP believed that the objectives of the occupation were unattainable unless the Japanese were sufficiently fed; the masses were unlikely to place their faith in social and political reforms unless their stomachs were full.

Facilitating food production had dramatic implications for Japan's industrial recovery, especially the fertilizer industry. Agricultural production and crop yield, while always at the mercy of the weather, depended on the liberal application of fertilizer. Fertilizer production, however, had plunged by the end of the war. By arguing in favor of restoring production instead of importing manufactured fertilizer, SCAP revealed its preference for rebuilding Japan's industrial base and integrating it into the regional economy. By allocating scarce electric power, capital, transportation, and natural resources to the most efficient factories, SCAP assisted in the rehabilitation and rationalization of the fertilizer industry. As a result, production reached pre-war levels as early as 1950. In many ways the fertilizer industry epitomized the transformation of Japan's economy from labor intensive to capital intensive and from light to heavy industry that occurred during the 1930s, 1940s, and 1950s.[44]

The fishing industry was also vitally important to SCAP's goal of providing Japan with a balanced diet. Fish was the primary source of animal protein. Therefore, SCAP authorized the conversion and repair of fishing boats in 1945, with construction of new steel vessels commencing the following year. SCAP also increased ship production, thus stimulating the shipbuilding industry. At the same time, SCAP expanded the fishing zone and petitioned Washington for funds to supply equipment. The fishing and shipbuilding industries were given priority status in obtaining capital, fuel, natural resources, and equipment. To increase the catch, SCAP reinstated Antarctic whaling in 1946. Confined primarily to the waters around Japan in 1945, by 1952 Japanese fishermen using vessels built in Japan could be seen traversing their old fishing grounds as a result of SCAP's persistence. By 1956, Japan could boast of having the world's largest shipbuilding infrastructure.[45]

SCAP's food policy also had profound implications for U.S. economic assistance programs. Prior to World War II, Japan was the number one importer of U.S. agricultural commodities. Throughout 1945 and 1946, however, Washington limited shipments to Japan, out of concern for domestic prices, worldwide shortages, and international pressure. With global food production below pre-war levels and U.S. exports soaring, Congress did not view funding the occupation or reviving U.S.–Japanese agricultural trade as a priority. As U.S. agricultural exports came under pressure in 1947 and surpluses mounted, surplus disposal programs doubling as foreign aid became an appealing option. After assuming control of Congress in 1946, the Republican Party supposedly ushered in a more frugal and cost-driven approach to foreign aid. Yet the Republican Congress continued to fund agricultural assistance programs. Why? Washington and the American farming community found in SCAP's demands for food imports a valuable market in Japan. Preferring to avoid a return to production control, Democrats and Republicans opted for foreign assistance programs based on exporting agricultural commodities. Agricultural assistance programs, such as GARIOA, the Occupied Japan Export Import Revolving Fund, and the Natural Fibers Revolving Fund, were designed to rid the United States of surpluses, stabilize prices, develop markets, and provide Japan with foreign exchange. The Agricultural Trade Development and Assistance Act of 1954 (Public Law 480) marked the epitome of this process.[46]

The diagnosis of the illness afflicting Japan's economy began to change in mid-1947. Washington then and historians since have focused on inflation, budget deficits, dysfunctional trading patterns, the dollar gap, and the dissolution of the *zaibatsu*. Stabilizing Japan's economy through austerity measures and production for export was Dodge's remedy, not SCAP's. SCAP, though concerned about the issues later raised by Dodge, emphasized the connection between food and economic recovery during the first two years of the occupation. In doing so, SCAP laid the foundation upon which Dodge's policies would eventually build, "a fact which Dodge never recognized," concluded Cohen.[47] By 1947, Japan's economy faced problems beyond MacArthur's control; he did not have the authority to set an exchange rate, settle reparations, or finance construction projects. For these, Japan had to wait for Washington to act.

SCAP's approach to stabilizing Japan's economy and restoring food production faced harsh criticism from the nations of the Far Eastern Commission (FEC), an international advisory body.[48] The Far Eastern Commission members, many of whom had tasted Japanese militarism in the 1930s and during World War II, resented SCAP's attempts to funnel scarce resources to their former enemy. Hostility began, not in 1947, after what is typically defined as the beginning of the reverse course, but in 1945. Significantly, the FEC's protests were directed at SCAP initiated programs designed to address the food situation and not policies undertaken by Washington. The FEC was not the weak institution historians have portrayed. While it is true that member nations were unable to coordinate policy, their individual dissent against SCAP and Washington often led to lengthy debates and delays, with resolution coming only after the United States either compromised or threatened to act unilaterally by way of a SCAP directive. SCAP consistently took a much harder stance than Washington against caving in to FEC demands. To dismiss the FEC and its impact on U.S. foreign policy and the occupation is a mistake.

SCAP's measures to increase food production did not reverse Japan's dependence on imports. SCAP's policies did, however, play a key role in facilitating Japan's place as largest export market for U.S. agricultural commodities for much of the postwar period. The occupation brought increased demand for imports of wheat, corn, and other types of staple foods to supplement domestic production. Hundreds of millions of dollars in agricultural imports during the occupation and the "economic miracle" established a broad market for U.S. agricultural commodities in Japan. Long gone was the bilateral exchange of silk and cotton that defined the 1930s. U.S. agricultural exports to Japan grew from $485 million in 1960 to a projected $8 billion in 2006. To this day, Japan remains a vital market for U.S. agricultural exports.[49]

Notes

I would like to thank Michael Barnhart, Sayuri Guthrie-Shimizu, Mark Selden, Iona Man-Cheong, Mark Hessler, and Ruth Hein for their assistance.

1 See Michael Schaller, *The American occupation of Japan: the origins of the cold war in Asia*, New York: Oxford University Press, 1985, chapter 2; Richard B. Finn, *Winners in peace: MacArthur, Yoshida, and postwar Japan*, Berkeley: University of California Press, 1992, pp. 47–65; Howard B. Schonberger, *Aftermath of war: Americans and the remaking of Japan, 1945–1952*, Kent: Kent State University Press, 1989, pp. 56–75. Notable exceptions include Takemae Eiji, *Inside GHQ: the allied occupation of Japan and its legacy*, trans. Robert Ricketts and Sebastian Swann, New York: Continuum, 2002; Theodore Cohen, *Remaking Japan: the American occupation as new deal*, New York: The Free Press, 1987. For Japan's food situation at the end of the war, see Thomas R.H. Havens, *The Japanese people and World War II*, New York: W.W. Norton & Co., 1978.

2 Michael Schaller, *Douglas MacArthur: the Far Eastern general*, New York: Oxford University Press, 1989, pp. 132–9.

3 Joint Chiefs of Staff, "JCS 1380/15: Basic directive for post-surrender military government in Japan proper," 3 November 1945, folder: Appendix A basic documents, Box 2083, records of the Supreme Commander for the Allied Powers (SCAP Records), RG 331, National Archives at College Park, College Park, Maryland (NACP).

4 Brigadier General Courtney Whitney quote taken from the forward of "Philosophy of the occupation," Box 2083, SCAP Records, RG 331, NACP.

5 Cohen, *Remaking Japan*, pp. 139–40.

6 Ibid., pp. 137–46. See also Michael A. Barnhart, "From Hershey bars to motor cars: America's economic policy towards Japan, 1945–1975," in *Partnership: the United States and Japan 1951–2001*, ed. Akira Iriye and Robert A. Wampler, Tokyo: Kodansha International, 2001, pp. 201–22.

7 Price Control and Rationing Division (PC&RD), Economic and Scientific Section (ESS), "Food situation during the first year of occupation," n.d., folder: Reports 1946–1949, Box 8395, SCAP Records, RG 331, NACP; Public Health and Welfare Section (PH&WS), Natural Resources Section (NRS), "Food situation during the second year of occupation," n.d., folder: Reports 1946–1949, Box 8395, SCAP Records, RG 331, NACP. For Japan's wartime food situation and SCAP's food policy, see B.F. Johnston, *Japanese food management in World War II*, Stanford: Stanford University Press, 1953, chapter 13.

8 General Douglas MacArthur, *Reminiscences*, New York: McGraw-Hill Book Co., 1964, pp. 284, 294; "SCAPIN 47," 22 September 1945, folder: SCAPINS: SCAP's instructions to the Japanese government, Box 77, Records of General Headquarters, Supreme Commander for the Allied Powers (Records of GHQ SCAP), RG 5, MacArthur Memorial Archives (MMA), Norfolk, Virginia. John Dower convincingly argues, "No Japanese leader, at war's end, offered any real vision for creating a new Japan out of the ruins of the old. It became MacArthur's destiny to do this." Dower wavers on MacArthur and SCAP's role in promoting economic recovery. See John W. Dower, foreword to *Dear General MacArthur: letters from the Japanese during the American occupation*, by Sodei Rinjiro, Lanham, MD: Rowman & Littlefield, 2001; John W. Dower, *Embracing defeat: Japan in the wake of World War II*, New York: W.W. Norton & Co., 1999, pp. 75, 89–90.

9 On the reverse course and the Dodge Line, see William S. Borden, *The Pacific alliance: U.S. foreign economic policy and Japanese trade recovery, 1947–1955*, Madison: University of Wisconsin Press, 1984, pp. 3–5, chapter 2; Cohen,

Remaking Japan, pp. 401–42; Finn, *Winners in peace*, pp. 195–227; Yoneyuki Sugita, *Pitfall or panacea: the irony of US power in occupied Japan*, New York: Routledge, 2003, chapter 3; Schonberger, *Aftermath of war*, pp. 161–235; Takemae, *Inside GHQ*, chapter 10.

10 Rations were based on age, gender, and employment. NRS, "Report no. 2: food position of Japan proper for 1945 and 1946," 13 November 1945, NRS, "Report no. 7: rice crop losses from adverse weather conditions in Japan proper in 1945," 11 December 1945, folder: Japan 1942–1945 General Information–Wool and Other Animal Fibers, Box 301, Narrative Reports of Special Agents, Consular Officers, and Agricultural Attaches, 1942–1945 (Narrative Reports), Records of the Foreign Agricultural Service (Records of the FAS), RG 166, NACP; Central Liaison Office, SCAP, "Situation of food in Japan," 29 September 1945, folder: Japan 1942–1945 economic conditions–wool, Box 301, Narrative Reports 1942–1945, Records of the FAS, RG 166, NACP; PC&RD, "Food situation during the first year of the occupation."

11 NRS, "Report no. 2: food position of Japan proper for 1945 and 1946," 13 November 1945; Food and Agriculture Division, Enemy Branch, Foreign Economic Administration, "Wartime food position of Japan proper with special reference to 1945," 14 November 1945, folder: Japan 1942–1945 economic conditions–wool, Box 301, Narrative Reports 1942–1945, Records of the FAS, RG 166, NACP; MacArthur, "Statement concerning the reduction of occupation Forces," 17 September 1945, folder: Appendix F statements by General MacArthur, Box 2084, SCAP Records, RG 331, NACP. Cohen argues that MacArthur's September announcement created 800,000 tons of U.S. army surpluses that SCAP distributed to the Japanese in the coming months. See Cohen, *Remaking Japan*, pp. 143–4.

12 B.F. Johnston, PC&RD, to Chief, PC, "Memorandum for reorganization of food rationing systems in accordance with JCS directives," 16 December 1946, folder: Memo May 1946–June 1947, Box 8394, SCAP Records, RG 331, NACP; NRS, "Report no. 2: food position of Japan proper for 1945 and 1946," 13 November 1945.

13 PC&RD, ESS, Report discussing food controls and administration, folder: Reports 1946–1949, Box 8395, SCAP Records, RG 331, NACP; NRS, "Preliminary study no 6: Japanese food collection program with emphasis on collection of the 1946 rice crop," 11 March 1947, folder: Japan marketing policies–publications 1949–1946, Box 811, Narrative Reports 1946–1949, Records of the FAS, RG 166, NACP.

14 "SCAPIN 1394," 11 December 1946, folder: SCAPIN 1344–1431, Box 4, Records of the Far Eastern Commission, RG 43, NACP; NRS, "Report no. 2: food position of Japan proper for 1945 and 1946," 13 November 1945; PC&RD, "Food situation during the first year of the occupation." On the Neighborhood Association, see Erich Pauer, "A new order for Japanese society: planned economy, neighborhood associations and food distribution in Japanese cities in the Second World War," in *Japan's war economy*, ed. Erich Pauer, London: Routledge, 1999, pp. 85–105.

15 PC&RD, "Food situation during the first year of the occupation."

16 H.F. Alber, Chief, Price and Distribution Division, to Chief, ESS, "Memorandum on role of prefectural governments in rice collections," 8 June 1948, folder: Memorandum January 1948–30 June, 1948, Box 8394, SCAP Records, RG 331, NACP; PC&RD, "Food situation during the first year of the occupation."

17 "Emergency imperial food ordinance," 17 February 1946, folder: Japan export policy–foodstuff 1946–1949, Box 808, Narrative Reports 1946–1949, Records of the FAS, RG 166, NACP; PC&RD, "Food situation during the first year of the occupation."

18 PC&RD, "Food situation during the first year of the occupation"; Crawford F. Sams, *Medic: the mission of an American military doctor in occupied Japan and wartorn Korea*, New York: M.E. Sharpe, 1998, p. 59; Dower, *Embracing defeat*, pp. 100, 139–48.

19 Dower, *Embracing*, chapter 8; *Oriental economist*, "Rice Rally," 6 June 1946; *Oriental economist*, "Two government programs," 29 June 1946; MacArthur, "Press release," 20 May 1946, Reel 90, Records of GHQ SCAP, RG 5, MMA.

20 PC&RD, "Food situation during the first year of the occupation"; *Oriental economist*, "Review of the week," 13 July 1946.

21 SCAP to WARCOS (JCS), 23 January 1946, SCAP to JCS (General Eisenhower), 21 February 1946, folder: Food import radios, Box 8395, SCAP Records, RG 331, NACP; SCAP to WARCOS, 21 May 1946, folder: War Department February–May 1946, Box 160, Collection of Messages (Radiograms), RG 9, MMA.

22 Victor Boswell, Scientific Consultant, Agriculture Division, "Memorandum on occupation forces use of Japanese foodstuffs in the form of alcoholic beverages," 27 June 1946, folder: 11, Box 8819, SCAP Records, RG 331, NACP; NRS, "Report no. 24: foodstuffs used in the manufacture of alcohol beverages in Japan," 22 March 1946, folder: 5, Box 8819, SCAP Records, RG 331, NACP; Industry and Reparations Division (I&RD), ESS, "Memorandum on consumption of liquor by occupation forces," 10 July 1946, SCAP, "Civilian food supplies," 15 December 1945, Egekvist, Chief, PC&RD, "Food materials used in alcoholic beverages," 26 February 1946, "SCAP circular 11: civilian food supplies," 26 April 1948, folder: Economic policy, Box 8397, SCAP Records, RG 331, NACP. See Yukiko Koshiro, *Trans-Pacific racisms and the U.S. occupation of Japan*, New York: Columbia University Press, 1999 for an examination of SCAP's policies through the lens of race relations.

23 Harrison to Anderson, Secretary of Agriculture, and Clayton, Assistant Secretary of State, 16 March 1946, folder: 1 March–14 March 1946, Box 13, Records of the Office of the Secretary of Agriculture, RG 16, NACP; *Oriental economist*, "Hoover's food mission," 18 May 1946; *Oriental economist*, "Coping with Japan's crisis," 1 June 1946; SCAP to WAR, 23 March 1947, folder: Food mission report and SCAP presentation, Box 8396, SCAP Records, RG 331, NACP; Allen J. Matusow, *Farm policies and politics in the Truman years*, Cambridge: Harvard University Press, 1967, pp. 12–18.

24 PC&RD, "Food situation during the first year of the occupation." In the summer of 1946, the Diet passed a multifaceted resolution expressing its gratitude for SCAP's work in overcoming the food crisis. This resolution was in part designed to feed MacArthur's ego. In emphasizing "sharing privations," the Diet was addressing an international community and a U.S. Congress unwilling to send food unless Japan fully utilized its resources. The resolution also reinforced the fact that food helped to defuse wartime hostility and promote cooperation. See GS, SCAP, "House of representatives will express gratitude of people for SCAP food supplies," 16 July 1946, Reel 90, Records of GHQ SCAP, RG 5, MMA; Yoshida Shigeru, *The Yoshida memoirs: the story of Japan in crisis*, trans. Yoshida Kenichi, Boston: Houghton Mifflin Co., 1962, p. 79. Dower asserts that food imports "enhanced the image of the United States as a generous benefactor." Tadashi Aruga contends that MacArthur realized "the occupation could not succeed if the Supreme Commander failed to help the Japanese people enjoy the most basic freedom, that is, freedom from hunger." See Dower, *Embracing defeat*, p. 93; Tadashi Aruga, "Japan and the United States: a half century of partnership," in *Japan and the United States: fifty years of partnership*, ed. Chihiro Hosoya, Tokyo: Japan Times, 2001, p. 2.

25 Agriculture Division, NRS, "Japanese agriculture programs under the occupation," 26 September 1949, folder: Japan: agriculture–agricultural policy, Box

806, Narrative Reports 1946–1949, Records of the FAS, RG 166, NACP; Wolf Ladejinsky, NRS, "Report no. 79: farm tenancy in Japan," 25 June 1947, folder: Japan: labor–land policy 1946–1949, Box 810, Narrative Reports 1946–1949, Records of the FAS, RG 166, NACP.

26 "SCAPIN 411: rural land reform," 9 December 1945, folder: Appendix B elimination of the old order, Box 2083, SCAP Records, RG 331, NACP; Agriculture Division, "Japanese agriculture programs under the occupation," 26 September 1949; Wolf Ladejinsky, NRS, "Report no. 79: Farm Tenancy in Japan," 25 June 1947. The problem was low production per worker, not low crop yield. Therefore, SCAP promoted economic growth to remove excess farm labor. See Richard H. Moore, *Japanese agriculture: patterns of rural development*, Boulder: Westview Press, 1990, chapter 6.

27 Agriculture Division, "Japanese agriculture programs under the occupation," 26 September 1949. For Japanese proposals on agricultural reform, see Yoshida, *Memoirs*, chapter 19.

28 "General MacArthur commenting on the passage today by the Diet of the land reform bill," October 1946, Reel 90, Records of GHQ SCAP, RG 5, MMA.

29 Wolf Ladejinsky, "Report no. 79: farm tenancy in Japan," 25 June 1947; USPOLAD Huston to Secretary of State, 18 June 1949, Box 810, Narrative Reports 1946–1949, Records of the FAS, RG 166, NACP; "SCAPIN 1855: rural land reform," 4 February 1948, folder: SCAPIN 1855–1898 (1948), Box 6, Records of the Far Eastern Commission, RG 43, NACP; MacArthur, *Reminiscences*, p. 314; MacArthur, "Summary of achievements during the first year of occupation," 28 August 1946, folder: Appendix F statements by General MacArthur, Box 2084, SCAP Records, RG 331, NACP; Public Relations, "General MacArthur approves Japanese government proposals on rural land reform," 14 August 1946, Reel 90, Records of GHQ SCAP, RG 5, MMA; Takemae, *Inside GHQ*, pp. 340–6.

30 Wolf I. Ladejinsky, Agricultural Attaché, "The occupation and Japanese agriculture," 3 June 1952, folder: Japan agriculture, Box 292, Narrative Reports 1950–1954, Records of the FAS, RG 166, NACP; Agriculture Division, "Japanese agriculture programs under the occupation," 26 September 1949; Sugita, *Pitfall or panacea*, pp. 26–7. For land reclamation and improvement projects, see Boxes 8781 and 8782, SCAP Records, RG 331, NACP.

31 PH&WS, "Food situation during the second year of the occupation."

32 Imports were addressed first because of fiscal planning deadlines. CINCAFPAC MacArthur to WARCOS Eisenhower, 17 August 1946, SCAP MacArthur to WARCOS, 1 September 1946, folder: Appropriations A-1.92, Box 152, Radiograms, RG 9, MMA.

33 W.S. Egekvist, "Memo for record," 5 December 1946, SCAP to WARCOS, 14 December 1946, folder: Food import radios, Box 8395, SCAP Records, RG 331, NACP.

34 Palmer T. Hogenson, Chief, Civilian Supply Section, Office of the Quartermaster General, "Japan–Korea: final report and recommendations," 2 December 1946, folder: Japan–Korea: final report and recommendations 2 December 1946 Hogenson, Box 8396, SCAP Records, RG 331, NACP; SCAP to WARCOS, 12 November 1945, folder: Food status 1946, Box 6428, SCAP Records, RG 331, NACP. For how SCAP manipulated import proposals, see Cohen, *Remaking Japan*, pp. 143–6.

35 R.L. Harrison, "Memorandum on the results of survey of food and fertilizer situation in Japan by Joint War, Agriculture, and State Department Mission," 15 February 1947, folder: Food mission report and SCAP presentation, Box 8396, SCAP Records, RG 331, NACP.

36 SCAP to WAR, "SCAP responds to Harrison report," 23 March 1947, folder:

Food mission report and SCAP presentation, Box 8396, SCAP Records, RG 331, NACP; Johnston, PC&RD, "Memorandum on partial staff study on black markets as it pertains to food," 8 May 1947, folder: Memorandum for the record March 1947–July 1947, Box 8394, SCAP Records, RG 331, NACP.

37 Egekvist, Chief, PC&RD, to Chief ESS, "Memorandum on food collection program," 13 January 1947, folder: Memorandum May 1946–June 1947, Box 8394, SCAP Records, RG 331, NACP; W.F. Marquat, Brigadier General U.S. Army, Chief ESS, to Chief of Staff, "Memorandum on periodic report on food situation," 3 February 1947, folder: Memorandum May 1946–June 1947, Box 8394, SCAP Records, RG 331, NACP; "MacArthur hails Diet passage of local government reforms," 20 September 1946, Reel 90, Records of GHQ SCAP, RG 5, MMA. MacArthur cited economic reasons for stopping the general strike; "I will not permit the use of so deadly a social weapon in the present impoverished and emaciated condition of Japan ... A general strike, crippling transportation and communications, would prevent the movement of food to feed the people and of coal to sustain essential utilities, and would stop such industry as is still functioning. The paralysis which inevitably would result might reduce large masses of the Japanese people to the point of actual starvation ..." See MacArthur, "Statement calling off general strike," 31 January 1947, folder: Appendix F statements by General MacArthur, Box 2084, SCAP Records, RG 331, NACP.

38 *Oriental economist*, "Two government programs," 29 June 1946; PH&WS, "Food situation during the second year of the occupation."

39 Concerns about the link system had been addressed prior to this as well. Hubert Schenck, PC&RD, to Chief ESS/PC, "Memorandum on making imported canned foods available for link distribution," 19 December 1946, Schenck, PC&RD, to Chief ESS/PC, "Memorandum on distribution of incentive goods to farmers," 30 December 1946, and Marquat, Chief ESS to Chief of Staff, "Memorandum on periodic report on food situation," 3 February 1947, folder: Memorandum May 1946–June 1947, Box 8394, SCAP Records, RG 331, NACP.

40 PH&WS, "Food situation during the second year of the occupation"; Egekvist, Chief, PC&RD, to Chief ESS, "Memorandum on food collection program," 13 January 1947.

41 SCAP to Commanding General, Eighth Army, 5 March 1947 is attached to NRS, "Preliminary study no. 6: Japanese food collection program with emphasis on collection of the 1946 Rice Crop," 11 March 1947; General Eichelberger, "Operational directive 26: Food distribution," 7 March 1947, folder: 8th Army Operational Directives Regarding Food, Box 8397, SCAP Records, RG 331, NACP.

42 PH&WS, "Food situation during the second year of the occupation."

43 Fumio Egaitsu, "Japanese agricultural policy: present problems and their historical background," in *U.S.-agricultural trade relations*, ed. Emery N. Castle, Kenzo Hemmi, and Sally A. Skillings, Washington D.C.: Resources for the Future, Inc., 1982, pp. 148–81. According to Cohen, "By that time (April 1949) the Japanese could not eat the food as fast as the United States was shipping it in." The fact that Japan's domestic production had increased dramatically did not hurt either. See Cohen, *Remaking Japan*, p. 145.

44 For an overview of SCAP's fertilizer policies, see Boxes 6070, 8991, and 8992, SCAP Records, RG 331, NACP.

45 For an overview of SCAP's fishing policies, see Box 8898, SCAP Records, RG 331, NACP; Box 162, Radiograms, RG 9, MMA.

46 Bruce Gardner, "The economics of U.S. agricultural policy," in *U.S.–agricultural trade relations*, ed. Castle, Hemmi, and Skillings, pp. 182–216; Borden, *Pacific*

alliance, chapter 1; Chester J. Pach Jr., *Arming the free world: the origins of the United States military assistance program, 1945–1950*, Chapel Hill: University of North Carolina Press, 1991, pp. 5, 143.

47 Theodore Cohen in *The occupation of Japan: economic policy and reform*, ed. Lawrence H. Redford, Virginia: MacArthur Memorial, 1980, pp. 78–80.

48 The Far Eastern Commission replaced the short-lived Far Eastern Advisory Commission on 27 December 1945.

49 USDA, "Outlook for U.S. agricultural trade," 24 May 2006, Available HTTP: <http://usda.mannlib.cornell.edu/reports/erssor/trade/aes-bb/2006/aes50. pdf> (accessed 12 June 2006). On U.S.–Japanese trade, see Borden, *Pacific alliance*, pp. 182–6; Yutaka Yoshioka, "The personal view of a Japanese negotiator," in *U.S.–agricultural trade relations*, ed. Castle, Hemmi, and Skillings, pp. 341–67; Aaron Forsberg, *America and the Japanese economic miracle: the cold war context of Japan's postwar economic revival, 1950–1960*, Chapel Hill: University of North Carolina Press, 2000; Sayuri Shimizu, *Creating people of plenty: the United States and Japan's economic alternatives, 1950–1960*, Kent: Kent State University Press, 2001.

2 Occupation policy and the Japanese fisheries management regime, 1945–1952

Sayuri Guthrie-Shimizu

Since pre-modern times Japan has heavily depended on marine fisheries as a source of food protein, and a cluster of technological innovations in the early twentieth century opened the way for development of fisheries as a modern industrial sector for the island nation.[1] In the interwar period, Japanese fishermen began to utilize larger and mechanized vessels, employ various catching devices that permitted efficient harvesting of marine resources, and adopted refrigeration techniques to embark upon distant-water operations. Japanese commercial fishing boats began to expand their sphere of activities beyond the nation's coastal waters across the Pacific Ocean, well into the high seas off Alaska and Canada's British Columbia province. That Japanese fishing fleets began operating in the high seas in the far-off Northeast Pacific meant that it was necessary for them to share the zone of commercial cultivation with North American fishing boats with pre-existing stakes in that part of the ocean. The commingling of fisheries in a shared and increasingly crowded ocean space brought to the fore a dissonance of ideas and practices between Japanese and North Americans and led to frequent international conflicts involving this primary industrial sector.

The most noteworthy of the U.S.–Japan disputes that erupted over the use of ocean resources prior to World War II entailed the catching of salmon in the Northeast Pacific. Just as the relationship between governments in Washington and Tokyo cooled precipitously, from the summer of 1937 through early 1938, over Japan's resumed military aggression in China, a Japanese mother-ship fishing fleet appeared in the high seas off Alaska and began catching salmon in the name of scientific investigation. Fishing interest groups in Alaska (then a U.S. territory) and U.S. Pacific coastal states (Washington, Oregon, California) regarded the sudden appearance of the Japanese fishing and research boats as a threat, arguing that the Japanese would overharvest in the areas in the high seas over which the North Americans had virtually enjoyed exclusive control before the arrival of the Japanese fishing fleet. They demanded an end to Japan's "research" expedition, through well-organized political agitation, thus turning the local fisheries question into a diplomatic issue involving the highest echelons of the U.S. State Department and the Japanese Ministry of Foreign Affairs. As a result of top-level diplomatic negotiations through the winter months of 1937–1938, the Japanese government and fishing industry agreed, albeit grudgingly, to refrain from catching salmon in the high seas in Alaska's Bristol Bay, for the time being. The outbreak of the full-scale war between the two countries in 1941 forced Japan to whittle down, and eventually suspend, its distant-water fishing near American territories, among other places. The inter-governmental conflict over claims to fish stocks, an elusive form of natural resource due to its migratory nature, and the modern industry devoted to their commercial exploitation was fortuitously pushed to the backburner of U.S.–Japanese relations.[2]

This international fisheries conflict was rekindled in the early postwar period. The policy of the Supreme Commander for Allied Powers (SCAP), as it related to Japanese fisheries, reflected the policy priorities of the American government and placed an overwhelming emphasis on restoring Japan's self-sufficiency in domestic food supply. To achieve this overriding policy objective in the immediate wake of Japanese surrender, SCAP embarked upon a program to rehabilitate Japan's near-defunct fishing industry. This SCAP policy elicited angry reactions from two parties invested politically in the question of Japanese fisheries. Australia and New Zealand feared Japan's postwar resurgence as a key player in marine fisheries and whaling. These allies in World War II resented what they perceived as an American attitude exceedingly lenient towards the former enemy, notorious for its perceived disregard for international codes of conduct. They thus consistently opposed the SCAP attempts to promote Japanese pelagic fisheries and whaling, in their capacities as members of the Far Eastern Commission.[3] In addition, SCAP's pro-Japan fisheries policy encountered fierce opposition from America's domestic interest groups, particularly those in the Pacific coastal states and Alaska, which anticipated a resumption of heedless overfishing by Japanese fleets, and destructive competition.[4]

As the State Department was exposed to the vocal opposition to Japanese pelagic fisheries emanating from both international and domestic sources, policy advocates from within the department began to call for the imposition of some type of restraint on post-war Japanese fisheries in the summer of 1948. Echoing the voices of fishermen and boat owners in Pacific coastal states, these internal dissenters urged the department's leadership to acknowledge the need to rein in SCAP's pro-Japan fisheries policy and obtain some kind of commitment from the Japanese government to abide by an international arrangement regarding marine resource conservation. Some of these advocates saw it more as politically expedient with their focus on eventual peace-making with Japan.

In this altered political environment, Washington policy planners began to stress systematic conservation efforts based on the concept of "maximum sustainable yield (MSY)," a rallying cry for U.S. West coast fisheries groups and growing ranks of scientists since the pre-war years, as an important agenda item to be discussed at the prospective peace talks with Japan. For those Washington policy makers who pushed for a peace treaty at an earlier, rather than a later, date, the conflation of local fisheries problems with peace-making meant that the ratification of a prospective peace treaty might be obstructed by domestic special interest groups attaching themselves to anti-treaty forces within the U.S. Senate. They thus sought to prevent such an unwelcome political coalition from forming by negotiating these two issues in separate diplomatic venues. The North Pacific Fisheries Convention, a tripartite treaty signed by the U.S., Canada, and Japan in the spring of 1952, was the result of their compartmentalizing efforts. It was not only a technical agreement supplementing the San Francisco Peace Treaty; it also embodied an intersection of the shifting American occupation policy towards Japan's post-war fisheries, a broader public policy conundrum of ocean resource conservation and management faced collectively by the late twentieth century world, and diplomatic maneuvering by Pacific coastal nations over a natural resource no longer regarded as limitless by a critical mass of scientists and other stakeholders.

The question of international marine resource management and Japan's integration into that multilateral regulatory regime after World War II has been explored extensively by legal scholar Harry Scheiber. The problem of postwar Japanese fisheries, however, has received scant attention from historians of the Allied occupation of Japan. This chapter seeks to fill that gap in the existing literature on occupation-era reforms by reinterpreting Japan's entry into the international marine resource conservation regime as a legacy, albeit a flawed one, of the U.S. occupation policy and the post-World War II peace-making. It also aims to shed light on how the United States and Japan bargained as they designed an institutional framework for regulating this extractive industry multilaterally, and to show how the 1952 tripartite fisheries convention, which catered strongly to American regional interest groups, was delivered to the government in Tokyo as the keystone of its postwar fisheries policy as soon as Japan regained its national sovereignty. This last point would demonstrate that the "reforming" of Japan undertaken through the U.S. postwar occupation was, in some key permutations, powerfully motivated and thus curtailed by narrow American interests, both national and regional.

U.S.–Japan North Pacific fisheries dispute and the territorial waters question

The 1930s saw a rapid expansion of Japan's distant-water fisheries, made possible by major advances in fish-catching and oceanic transport and storage technologies. At the same time, the growing presence of Japanese fishing vessels in the waters far from the nation's coastlines sowed the seeds of a new type of international discord. Due to the very nature of the conflict, fisheries issues were inevitably intertwined with the question of territorial waters and offshore jurisdiction – the geographical area and the resources contained therein to which the sovereign powers of a national government might extend beyond its coastlines under international law, or how far from national coastlines the venerable principle of freedom of the seas should apply. The 1937–1938 conflict between the United States and Japan over the salmon fishing in Bristol Bay was no exception. Not only was it a prime example of how technological advances in fisheries and maritime transport helped to shrink the distances between two sovereign states and generated a new type of inter-state clash of interests. It was also prototypical of mid-twentieth century fisheries disputes in that it pointed to the erosion of the three-mile offshore jurisdiction principle, the legal position taken at the time by the world's majority of nations, including the United States, and the need for finding a supra-national mechanism for addressing a regulatory question pertaining to the ocean commons.

In the fall of 1937, Japan's experimental salmon fishing took place in the high seas outside America's three-mile territorial waters off Alaska. But legal technicalities meant little to those fishermen operating out of Alaska and Seattle who had enjoyed a monopolistic control of salmon stocks there, but had also been bound by federally mandated regulatory requirements. They saw the unregulated Japanese presence as nothing but a disruption to their civilized backyard. Further, an image of Japan as a hostile predator at sea was then widely held by American fishermen because of the nation's refusal to sign international whaling conventions, and other deviations from Western norms in fishing practices. Japan had also achieved notoriety the world over for its heedless exploitation of some fish stocks. Because of the resumption of Japanese military aggression on the Chinese mainland in the summer of 1937, general American public opinion regarding Japan was already reaching a nadir. In this political milieu, the tension generated by the encounter between U.S. and Japanese salmon-fishing vessels off Alaska quickly escalated to a point where American fishermen threatened to fire at the perceived interlopers. It did so partly because the widespread image of Japan as a law-breaker or invader was blown out of rational proportion by some local politicians and news outlets.[5]

Spurred by the rising call from Alaska and the State of Washington for a wholesale exclusion of Japanese fishermen from Alaskan waters, Secretary of State Cordell Hull formally requested the government of Prime Minister Hirota Koki that it order Japanese fishing boats to leave Bristol Bay, and even hinted at the possibility of imposing economic sanctions should Tokyo fail to comply with the request. At the core of the argument the State Department made in demanding the Japanese retreat from Alaskan waters was an important precedent-setting theory, foreshadowing the evolution of American ocean policy in the post-World War II era. Hull argued that America's own policy of three-mile offshore jurisdiction did not apply to the high seas encompassing Bristol Bay. In defense of this position, Hull cited the existence of conservation measures enforced by the federal government to regulate fishing activities by U.S. nationals. He also held that salmon, an anadromous fish species, spawned in rivers in the interior of Alaska and matured in the open sea off Alaska. It followed that even if they were caught in the international waters in Bristol Bay, the salmon came under the national jurisdiction of the United States. What Hull's position demonstrated was that America's traditional ocean policy resting on the three-mile territorial waters rule and adherence to the freedom of the seas principle was showing signs of erosion even before the outbreak of World War II. As will be shown later, this transitional American argument opened the legal door to the abandonment of these long-standing principles in the postwar era by other nations as well as the United States for the purposes of fisheries resource development and conservation.[6]

Bowing to Hull's stern warning, made against Ambassador Joseph Grew's recommendation, the government of Hirota Koki consented in March 1938 not to issue fishing licenses to Japanese nationals and withdrew the salmon research fleet from Bristol Bay. Although it refused to accept Washington's expanding offshore jurisdictional claims, the Foreign Ministry wanted to avoid gratuitous frictions with the U.S., given the uncertainty of the military situation in China. In its official response to Washington the ministry hastened to emphasize that the current Japanese concession on Alaskan waters by no means meant the abandoning of three-mile offshore jurisdiction as the norm in international law and reaffirmed its subscription to the freedom of fishing and navigation in the high seas. Self-restraint on the part of the Japanese government as a voluntary act of the sovereign state had been often employed as a solution to U.S.–Japanese disputes. One of its earliest examples was the "voluntary" banning of Japanese labor immigration to the U.S. in the 1907 Gentlemen's Agreement. Also in the fall 1937, the restriction of Japanese textile exports to the U.S. was hammered out as a private-sector arrangement. This formula allowed the Japanese government to prevent Washington's discriminatory application of a general principle of international law or U.S. domestic legislation to Japan by pre-emptively eliminating the need for such action.[7]

Alaska and Pacific Northwest fishing groups maintained that the easiest and most effective step the federal government could take to keep Japanese distant-water fishing fleets from advancing to the Northeast Pacific was to extend its claim of coastal jurisdiction to the oceans beyond three miles from the U.S. coast. Since this policy deviated from America's traditional adherence to the freedom of the seas principle and the three miles offshore jurisdiction rule, however, such an action would have required careful consideration by legal experts within the federal bureaucracy. In this regard, the so-called Truman Proclamations made in September 1945 regarding the U.S. position on the continental shelf and offshore resources marked a major landmark in U.S. ocean policy and they represented a subtle move towards a modification of the traditional American adherence to the three-mile territorial waters principle. As scholar of the Law of the Seas Ann Hollick has demonstrated, these policy pronouncements, simply inherited from Truman' predecessor, were a product of bureaucratic in-fighting revolving around the Department of the Interior and the State Department that lasted intermittently during the war.[8] In the proclamation regarding offshore living resources, the Truman Administration contended that, under specific circumstances, the U.S. government could enforce federal regulations aimed at conserving fisheries resources in the high seas beyond three miles from the nation's coastlines, even if that might entail exclusion of fishing boats registered with foreign countries. Such specific circumstances would be deemed to exist when only U.S. nationals had engaged in fishing activities in the high seas area in question, and if the entry of fishermen of other nations might exceed the maximum sustainable yield of the fish resources maintained as a result of Americans' conservation regime. If so, the U.S. government could declare the sea area its conservation zone even if it lay beyond three miles from its shores. Since this unilateral declaration referred specifically to salmon fisheries off Alaska, it showed that the U.S.–Japan fisheries dispute before World War II had compelled the U.S. government to re-evaluate its traditional position on the freedom of the seas principle and the three-mile coastal jurisdictional claim.[9]

SCAP's ocean resource policy towards Japan

Japan had been one of the world's leading fishing nations prior to World War II, and its efficient and aggressive harvesting in pelagic fisheries caused concern and fear in oceans around the world. Both image and reality blended into notoriety. As Japan drove militarily into Asia in the 1930s and expanded the areas of its political control, Japanese distant-water fishing fleets, consisting of trawlers and on-site factory ships, advanced to adjacent waters and greatly expanded their areas of operation. The combination of military aggression and expansion of fishing areas tended to create the image that Japan's fishing fleets were also law-breakers and predators, often to an extent not warranted by their actual practices. Similarly, the accumulation of research in oceanography in Europe and the United States at the time entrenched the notion that the ocean's living resources were exhaustible and that, if subjected to untrammeled harvesting beyond maximum sustainable yield, would become depleted.

The concept of maximum sustainable yield had thus been adopted into the ocean resource policies of most nations in the West, albeit in some cases as a token gesture. The United States and Canada entered into a bilateral ocean resource conservation agreement in the 1930s and placed halibut fishing in the high seas in the North Pacific and the Bering Sea under joint regulation. In this regard as well, Japan's distant-water fishing practices and fisheries policies were liable to be branded unlawful, disruptive, and uncivilized. That fisheries groups in Alaska, British Columbia, and the U.S. Pacific Coast states perceived Japan's salmon research fleet as a dangerous interloper reflected Japan's policy and ideological incongruence with the incipient international ocean resource management regime then largely dictated by the United States and Europe.[10]

When the Allied occupation of Japan began, SCAP's Supreme Commander, General Douglas MacArthur, banned the open-sea expedition by limiting what remained of Japan's ocean-going fleet to the high seas beyond twelve miles from Japan's coastlines. The so-called McArthur Line was subsequently redrawn and Japan's fishing zone was expanded incrementally, beginning with SCAP's conditional permission to resume Japan's distant deepwater fishing two months later. The high seas that were opened to occupied Japan's fishing vessels encompassed the bulk of the East China Sea, stretching to the Southwest of the Japanese archipelago. The zone's southern perimeter, however, was set far north of the tropical islands, formerly mandated by the League of Nations and placed under U.S. military occupation after Japanese surrender. The drawing of the MacArthur Line far north of these U.S.-occupied islands was necessitated by security imperatives expressed by the U.S. navy, but this particular demarcation incurred displeasure, and suspicion from Japan's Asian neighbors that SCAP was seeking to deflect Japan's "predatory" fishermen away from the mandated tropical islands towards the high seas of Asia. In June 1946, when the Asians' anger was still smoldering, SCAP incensed them even more by nearly doubling Japan's fishing zone, citing the exigency of the acute food shortage being experienced by the Japanese population. The high seas areas newly opened to Japanese fishing were estimated to contain approximately 80 percent of the nation's pre-war catches, and this second SCAP decision only left banned to the Japanese the salmon stocks in the seas north of Hokkaido, adjacent to the Soviet-controlled island chain, tuna fishing around the U.S.-occupied southern tropical islands, and all forms of fisheries in the Northeast Pacific (including salmon off Alaska).[11]

During 1946, SCAP took another step regarding Japanese marine activities, which further enraged former Allied powers: limited resumption of Japanese whaling. This decision incurred the particularly intense wrath of Australia and Great Britain. MacArthur, however, summarily rejected objections raised by these key members of the Far Eastern Commission as a self-interested policy that pandered to domestic interest groups seeking to eliminate Japanese competition. The general's lack of regard for the allies' grievances was evident from his decision to permit Japanese whaling expeditions to the Arctic in the subsequent years of the occupation. From

MacArthur's perspective, the resumption of Japanese whaling was perfectly consistent with SCAP's policy priority: to promote Japan's economic recovery once the acute food shortage of the immediate postwar years had been brought under control. As the tension between the U.S. and the Soviet Union intensified elsewhere in the world, SCAP began to shift the emphasis of its policy further, and the resumption of Japanese fisheries came to be legitimated in terms of Washington's long-term strategic objective of buttressing the Japanese economy as an anti-communist redoubt in the Far East. Within SCAP, the Natural Resources Section (NRC) was in charge of supervising Japanese fisheries. Its policy towards Japanese fishing activities could be more accurately characterized as "industrial policy" aimed at increasing catches and efficient use of fuels and fishing equipment, rather than ocean resource conservation. In other words, SCAP's fisheries policy rarely manifested concern for prevention of overfishing or multilateral coordinated action for resource conservation.[12]

In the early years of the occupation, SCAP launched its Japan-friendly fisheries policy in all directions. For instance, the United States battled the Soviet delegation on the Far Eastern Commission as the latter maneuvered to block the resumption of Japanese salmon fishing in the Bering Sea. SCAP and Japanese fishing interest groups also directed their gaze eastwards, eyeing the salmon in the Northeastern Pacific, including Bristol Bay. At a time when the consumption of tuna as an inexpensive source of protein was rapidly increasing in the United States, the Japanese fishing industry sought to tap into this new treasure trove of export opportunity. It implored SCAP to lift the ban on tuna catching around the mandated tropical islands and to permit the export of marine products to the United States. Between 1949 and 1950, SCAP began preparing for the resumption of Japanese exports of tuna to the U.S., despite the vehement opposition by fishing groups in the U.S. West Coast. Reminiscent of the solid regional front they had formed at the time of the Bristol Bay dispute in the late 1930s, the West Coast groups banded together to pressure local officials and Congressional members through organizations such as the Pacific Fisheries Conference, formed in 1946 to advance the interests of Pacific Coast fishermen. This inter state interest group would become the standard bearer of campaigns to contain Japan's distant-water tuna fisheries in the 1950s.[13]

While Japan's fishing industry benefited from SCAP's preoccupation with maximizing Japan's food production and capabilities to export marine products, some elements within SCAP began calling for the imposition of some form of conservationist restrictions on Japanese fisheries, based on scientific research. The person who most forcefully advocated this new policy was William Herrington, who became the director of SCAP's Natural Resource Section in late 1948. An oceanographer trained at the University of Washington in Seattle, Herrington was guided by a firm belief in the necessity for marine resource conservation backed by cutting-edge scientific knowledge. He infused a novel idea into SCAP's fisheries policy circles, that Japan, as a member of the postwar multilateral cooperative system, must engage in reasoned harvesting and conservation of marine resources. As a SCAP official, Herrington also believed that the Japanese government must, of its own initiative, adopt conservation measures to make SCAP's pro-Japan ocean policy palatable to Great Britain, Australia and New Zealand. Herrington left discernible marks on SCAP's fisheries policy formulated in the latter part of the U.S. occupation. In 1948, Japan's Fisheries Agency was established under the supervision of SCAP's Natural Resources Section. The new government agency was given a mandate to regulate Japan's trawl fishing in the East China Sea to prevent fish stock depletion. Japanese politicians and interest groups with stakes in fisheries also pledged to take conservation measures seriously, in order to improve their image in the eyes of the world. In May 1950, the Japanese Diet passed the Marine Resource Anti-Depletion Law. In this landmark legislation in the history of Japan's ocean policy, the Ministry of Agriculture and Forestry was vested with the administrative authority to order reduction of Japanese fishing fleets for the purpose of marine resource conservation.[14]

During the occupation period, the Japanese government, SCAP, and the State Department's Northeast Asian Bureau shared the general goal of expanding Japan's fishing zone with deliberate speed and ensuring Japan free and equal access to ocean resources. As Herrington was keenly aware, the chief obstacle to achieving this diplomatic objective was America's former allied powers and liberated areas in the Western Pacific. South Korea, Nationalist China, the Netherlands, Australia, New Zealand and the Philippines continued to object to Japanese whaling after SCAP permitted its resumption in 1946. They also attempted to block the further expansion of Japanese fishing activities elsewhere in the Pacific. For instance, the Philippines government declared a 200 mile zone around its territories and tried to exclude Japanese fishing boats from this area. Facing a phalanx of opponents to its ocean policy for the Western Pacific, SCAP nevertheless decided in the summer of 1948 to permit Japanese fishing activities near the mandated southern tropical islands, incrementally. Again, SCAP justified this policy in the name of stabilizing Japan's economy and promoting exports.[15]

This latest round of SCAP policy predictably invited another wave of fierce opposition from several quarters in Washington's policy-making circle, including the Department of the Interior, the federal agency in charge of fisheries regulation around the mandated islands, and the U.S. navy, concerned with military security. The most vocal objection, however, came from Wilbert McLeod Chapman, a marine biologist who assumed the post of special assistant to the Under Secretary of State for Fisheries and Wildlife, a new office created within the State Department in the summer of 1948. Chapman had strong political connections with the U.S.

West Coast tuna industry, and from the very beginning of his appointment at the State Department did not hesitate to criticize openly the way SCAP was nurturing occupied Japan's distant-water fisheries. Chapman's heady political maneuvering in Washington did not sit well with MacArthur. In an October 1948 memorandum addressed to the Secretary of the Army, he vilified Chapman as a mouthpiece of the West Coast special interest groups scheming to obviate future competition from Japanese fishermen, to the detriment of the United States' foreign policy objectives. As long as the SCAP Supreme Commander justified SCAP's decision to permit Japanese tuna fishing near the mandated islands in terms of the principle of free and equal access to the world's resources, a veritable provision in the Atlantic Charter and reiterated in the Potsdam Declaration, the Army's top brass had no alternative but to support SCAP's proposal to expand Japan's fishing zone ever closer to the U.S.-occupied Southern Pacific islands.[16]

In considering SCAP's shift towards greater concern for resource conservation after 1948, Chapman was another key player in this new policy trend. Like Herrington in the Tokyo post, Chapman belonged to the first generation of American oceanographers trained at the University of Washington. What distinguished Chapman from Herrington was the former's political ambition and drive. While Herrington took care to be politically neutral and invariably articulated moderate positions, Chapman consciously defined his role as an advocate for the West Coast fishing industry and acted so while he served as special assistant to Under Secretary of State. Until he left the post in June 1951, Chapman exercised his strong personality and consistently opposed what he saw as SCAP's pro-Japan fisheries policy. In the fall of 1948, Chapman's first order of business was to eliminate the threats of Japanese fishing fleets from the Eastern Pacific where U.S. West Coast groups had direct stakes. In order to achieve this objective, Chapman lost no time in drafting, at his own initiative, a bilateral fisheries treaty with Japan, and a tripartite treaty including Canada as an alternative plan. His draft treaty sought, first and foremost, to make the Japanese government promise to prohibit Japanese fishing boats from operating in the high seas within 150 miles of the coastlines of the North American continent. Chapman sought to legitimate this scheme by proposing the doctrine of "mutual forbearance." At first brush, this doctrine appeared equal and reciprocal in the sense that American and Canadian fishing boats also pledged to keep the same distance from the Japanese coastlines. In practice, however, they had no interest in fishing near the Japanese islands. Chapman's doctrine thus virtually entailed unilateral abstention by Japan; it was in fact a thinly disguised attempt to exclude Japan from Northeast Pacific fisheries.[17]

In October 1949, Chapman requested to SCAP that it commence fisheries negotiations with the Japanese government on the basis of his draft treaty, in preparation for the nation's eventual independence. MacArthur, seeing through the true intent and practical effects of Chapman's "mutual" forbearance idea, rejected this proposal out of hand. What MacArthur found most objectionable about Chapman's draft was the precedent-setting nature of a bilateral or a trilateral fisheries agreement envisioning Japan's unilateral forbearance in practice. In the likely event that Japan negotiated fisheries agreements with other former belligerents in World War II, Japan would be hard put to fend off demands for similar one-sided abstention from fishing in other parts of the Pacific. The prevailing opinion within the State Department sided with McArthur. The department's Far Eastern specialists and economic policy makers supported SCAP's position, calling for giving Japan unconditional permission to undertake fishing activities near the southern tropical islands, and equal and free access to fish resources in the high seas in the Pacific. For the State Department's mainstream faction, the overriding mission of the time was to build the new world order on the basis of multilateralism and non-discrimination. At a time when the U.S. government was working hard to create various international organizations embodying these visions, Chapman's draft fisheries treaty appeared to be a throwback to the days of discrimination and bilateral arm-twisting.[18]

Towards negotiation of the North Pacific fisheries convention

A fundamental difference of opinion existed among State Department policy makers concerned with Japan's fisheries question, but this divide was all but bridged after the summer of 1950 for several reasons. The key impetus for policy coordination came from an international source, as the military situation in the Far East began to swing in a direction decidedly beneficial to Japan. In the fall of 1949, the Chinese Civil War ended in Communist victory, and this turn of events added a further impetus to the Truman administration's inclination, already evident by then, to grant Japan a relatively lenient peace. Once the Korean War broke out in the following summer and the People's Republic of China intervened in the conflict by sending in "volunteer" troops, it appeared as though there was no reason left to object to Japan's economic rehabilitation and reinstatement as a reliable ally, as far as Washington's strategic priority was concerned. In the summer of 1950, SCAP lifted remaining restrictions on tuna fishing by Japan's mother-ship fleets near the mandated southern tropical islands. Chapman had claimed that this privilege should only be offered as a bargaining chip to force Japan to accept a fisheries treaty incorporating 150-mile mutual forbearance. SCAP's decision to permit unconditionally Japan's access to the highly coveted fishing zone signified a defeat of Chapman's hard-line strategy and a major victory for the Japanese government and fishing industry.[19]

The Canadian government, which had embarked on preliminary

discussions with the State Department over a Japanese fisheries treaty in 1950, also stood in Chapman's way by not consenting to negotiate with the U.S. or Japan on the basis of Chapman's draft treaty. Ottawa opposed a key element of Chapman's draft 15-year, 150-mile mutual forbearance proposal, on the grounds that other former World War II belligerents would probably try to impose comparable one-sided restrictions on Japanese fisheries in the Western Pacific. Canada also feared that even if it should succeed in excluding Japanese salmon and halibut fishermen from the Northeast Pacific, its fellow British Commonwealth countries with stakes in Pacific fisheries, Australia and New Zealand, would not take kindly to such a blatant attempt to protect Canada's narrow national interests by riding on the Americans' coat tails.[20]

Aside from Canada's moderating influence on the overall U.S. negotiating position, other factors embedded in international relations also worked against the 150-mile mutual forbearance scheme pushed by Chapman. Latest oceanographic investigations were indicating at the time that the high seas off the coasts of Central and South America harbored massive and largely undeveloped tuna stocks comparable to those in the high seas near the mandated Southern Pacific islands. But Central and South American countries, most notably Mexico, were attempting to restrict tuna catching by foreign vessels in the adjacent high seas, even at points beyond three miles from their coastal waters. America's hemispheric neighbors justified their restrictive actions by arguing that the U.S. government itself had already jettisoned the three-mile offshore jurisdiction principle in the 1945 Truman Proclamations. If American West Coat tuna fishermen were to contest such enclosure-like endeavors by Latin Americans, they found it expedient that their national government reaffirm its adherence to the traditional three-mile rule. Chapman, seeing himself first and foremost the ally and advocate of Southern California tuna fishing groups, apparently concluded that it was necessary to sacrifice part of the West Coast fishing interests, i.e. salmon fishing in the North Pacific, in order to protect the interests of his own constituents by pressing for three-mile coastal jurisdiction. By mid-1950, Chapman's draft treaty was pushed into the background of U.S.–Japanese dialogue on fisheries policy, and Chapman began to tone down his position on 150-mile mutual forbearance.[21]

What came to the fore instead in late 1950 was a formula whose effectiveness had been amply proven from the pre-war times: to rely on Japan's willingness to restrain its own action to avert a head-on clash with American interests that might trigger unilateral U.S. action.[22] The American official who pushed bilateral fisheries discussions forcefully in that direction was John F. Dulles, appointed special consultant to the State Department to take charge of peace negotiations with Japan. At the time, Dulles was receiving a deluge of requests and proposals from U.S. West Coast fishing groups and their legislative representatives. This political pressure impressed the astute Washington insider with the risk of the fisheries question jeopardizing the entire peace treaty, particularly if West Coast Senators should demand a definitive exclusion of Japanese fishing from "their" waters as a condition for treaty ratification. Since there were a myriad potential complicating factors already existing in the negotiation and ratification of the prospective peace treaty, Dulles wished not to create a situation where a second-tier issue such as fisheries might stymie the whole process.[23]

What Dulles did to achieve this overriding objective was, first, to treat fisheries arrangements and a peace treaty as completely separate negotiations, and second, to garner some kind of assurances from the Japanese government ahead of time in order to mollify West Coast fisheries malcontents.[24] Besides, historical evidence strongly suggests that Dulles was not entirely sympathetic to Japan specialists within the State Department and SCAP who pressed for lenient treatment of Japan's fisheries needs. Rather, he appeared to believe that Japan, the defeated party at the peace table, was duly expected to make concessions to accommodate the victor's needs. Dulles's view along these lines was clear from the fact that when he met with Chapman prior to his visit to Japan in January 1951, he raised the topic of the 1907 U.S.–Japan Gentlemen's Agreement on immigration restriction at his own initiative. At the meeting, Chapman informed the Tokyo-bound chief peace negotiator of Japan's "voluntary" renunciation of North Pacific salmon fishing off Alaska in 1938. This additional information convinced Dulles that Tokyo should adopt this tested formula since it did not require Japan to give up any rights under international law as a sovereign nation. Dulles then ordered Chapman to draft an aide-memoire to be exchanged with the Japanese government. Chapman's draft letter to Prime Minister Yoshida Shigeru requested that the Japanese government announce its intention in writing to refrain from catching fish species that had already been exploited to maximum sustainable yield levels and placed under conservation regimes. In specific terms, it meant salmon, tuna, herring, sardine, and halibut in the Bering Sea and the Eastern Pacific.[25]

The State Department's Northeast Asian specialists and economic officials opposed requiring Japan to deny itself North Pacific fisheries as a price of peace. But since Dulles himself desired Japan's self-restriction, and these officials also feared that West Coast legislators might otherwise try to block the treaty's ratification, they had to accept this negotiating strategy.[26] In January 1951, Dulles visited Japan to discuss a peace treaty and handed Chapman's draft letter to Yoshida. Japan's positions as conveyed by Yoshida were actually not that far removed from Dulles's plan. The Japanese government stated that it would not accept discriminatory restriction on its fishing activities in the high seas after gaining independence, since free access to fish resources in the high seas was an established general principle of international law. At the same time, the Japanese government expressed its readiness to abide by international law and to participate in and cooperate with existing international conservation agreements and scientific investigations regarding whaling, otters, halibut, salmon, and tuna. Since eliminating diplomatic obstacles to a peace treaty was his paramount priority, Yoshida was not averse to packaging politically sensitive fisheries issues in a gentlemen's agreement, as long as the deal constituted a part of a reciprocal fisheries treaty. Chapman's draft aide-memoire received slight adjustment in wording by the Japanese government and grudging concurrence by Japan's industry representatives, and the Dulles-Yoshida exchange of letters was released on 13 February.[27]

The signing of the tripartite North Pacific Fisheries Convention

In the Dulles-Yoshida aide-memoire, the Japanese government agreed to enter into negotiations with the United States on the development and conservation of marine fisheries after Japan had signed a peace treaty and regained its sovereignty. Until such agreement was reached, Yoshida's letter stated, the Japanese government, as a policy of a sovereign state, was prepared to restrict fishing activities by vessels of Japanese registration. This policy of self-restraint would be applied to fish species that had already been placed under conservation measures by countries other than Japan and in the exploitation of which Japan had not been engaged as of the year 1940. This category included salmon, halibut in the Northeast Pacific, and herring, sardine, and tuna in the Eastern Pacific – in other words, all Pacific fish species in which the U.S. had commercial stakes. Yoshida's decision to accept such a comprehensive self-denial upon the resumption of national sovereignty was, predictably, resisted by the fishing industry. Government officials, however, successfully suppressed the criticism by arguing that it was a necessary price to pay for a peace treaty and long-awaited national independence.[28] It must be also noted that Yoshida's February 1951 pledge to Dulles did not cover the Western Pacific, where Japan held greater fisheries stakes. In this regard, it was not an exceedingly self-negating policy either.[29]

Even after the release of the Dulles-Yoshida letters, however, U.S. West Coast fishing groups did not relent in their pressure on Washington to exclude Japanese vessels from Northeast Pacific fisheries. The State Department, alarmed by these ominous political clouds, began to concentrate its energy on separating all aspects of the fisheries question from the general peace negotiations. These efforts culminated in the final structure of the San Francisco Peace Treaty, Article 9 of which provided for Japan to enter into negotiations with former belligerents over fisheries in the high seas after the restoration of national independence. The two-track formula was heartily welcomed by the Japanese government, for it had feared that, of those nations invited to San Francisco, Australia and the

Philippines would try to impose harsh terms on fisheries, among other things, as a condition for signing a peace treaty. Three months before the peace conference was convened, there was also a personnel change at the State Department. This reshuffling was hailed by Japan's fisheries officials and industry leaders with a collective sigh of relief: Chapman completed his appointment as special assistant for Fisheries and Wildlife and moved on to become director of investigation for the American Tuna Boat Association, headquartered in San Diego. To the Japanese' delight, the man appointed as Chapman's successor was Herrington, who had been intimately involved in the rehabilitation of Japanese fisheries as SCAP's chief fisheries official since 1948 and had earned Japanese trust for his scientific expertise and personal integrity. Beginning in the fall of 1951, Herrington presided over the preliminary work towards formal fisheries negotiations between Japan and Canada and played a key role in drafting and revising what ultimately became the 1952 tripartite fisheries convention.[30]

Herrington's administrative leadership had a distinctive characteristic. He emphasized the use of objective scientific data in key aspects of treaty negotiations. Herrington believed that the concept of maximum sustainable yield supported by rigorous oceanographic research should be the only basis for applying the principle of mutual forbearance in the proposed tripartite conservation regime. He was of the opinion that the previous U.S. demand of 150-mile mutual forbearance, pushed forcefully by Chapman in the preceding two years, was unnecessarily harsh towards Japan and incompatible with the freedom of the seas principle traditionally subscribed to by the U.S. government. Reflecting his belief in rational decision-making based on scientific data, Herring was instrumental in establishing a panel of experts, composed of an equal number of scientists chosen by each government, to gather and analyze relevant findings. Under the terms of the tripartite treaty, this expert commission was to meet annually and make recommendations on the selection of fish species to which the principle of forbearance should be applied. Further, Herrington believed that the principle of mutual forbearance should not be applied to a designated area of the high seas, as was the case with Chapman's draft treaty. Instead, he proposed that it should apply only to designated fish species judged by the tripartite expert commission to have been developed at a level close to maximum sustainable yield. Once Herrington began steering the treaty's drafting, the State Department formally abandoned Chapman's goal of keeping a 150-mile belt of the Eastern Pacific off the North American continent off-limits to Japanese fishermen.[31]

Herrington was by no means insensitive to the needs of American fishing interest groups. Rather, he exhibited a keen sense of balance in equalizing the intersecting and sometimes contradictory interests of various segments of the fishing lobby. He presided over U.S. negotiations with Canada with a similarly demonstrated sense of balance and political realism. The Canadian government was concerned that a prospective tripartite fisheries agreement involving Japan might disrupt the bilateral U.S.–Canadian conservation arrangements governing North Pacific halibut and salmon that had been in place since the 1930s. In particular, the Canadians feared that additional restrictions might be imposed on salmon fishing by Canadian nationals in the Bering Sea, and thus sought a guarantee against such a contingency. Herrington skillfully negotiated with the American fishing industry to deliver just such an assurance to Canadians before both delegations headed for formal negotiations in Tokyo in November 1951.[32]

Herrington's rigorous adherence to scientific data was not entirely welcomed by the West Coast tuna industry, which had been accustomed to project its political clout into the policy-making process in Washington through Chapman, for not all scientific data could be expected to serve the industry's interests. For instance, the discovery of tuna stocks that had not reached the MSY level in the Eastern Pacific off Latin America was welcome news, but this oceanographic research in effect showed that the tuna stocks in the Pacific as a whole were still far from facing the threat of overharvesting. What that meant for the treaty negotiation was that the principle of mutual forbearance, even if it was incorporated into the tripartite convention, could not be applied to tuna, thus leaving the massive tuna stocks off the coast of Central and South America wide open to distant-water expeditions by reconstructed Japanese fishing fleets. That is why Chapman, after returning to private industry, and the West Coast tuna lobby, demanded the exclusion of tuna from the list of fish spices to be covered by the treaty, prior to the opening of the formal negotiations in Tokyo. That was why the final tripartite fisheries convention signed in May 1952 made no reference to tuna, the only one of the five fish species mentioned in the draft treaty. For Herrington and diplomats in the State Department, the exclusion of tuna from the final treaty was a necessary concession to an all-too-powerful political interest group that could scuttle the treaty's ratification.[33]

Conclusion

The formal negotiations on the North Pacific Fisheries Convention between the United States, Canada, and Japan were held in Tokyo from November 1951 through March 1952. Japan participated in the discussions as a sovereign state, although the conference began and ended before the San Francisco Peace Treaty came into effect. The choice of Tokyo as the site of negotiation was intended by the American officials involved to visually showcase to the world Japan's new status as an independent sovereign state. The composition of the delegations barely masked the nature of the negotiations as a flashpoint of special interests, as the U.S. and Canadian delegation dispatched to Tokyo, as well as that of the Japanese host, included a number of interest-group leaders.[34] The North Pacific Fisheries Convention, signed in March 1952, was the very first international treaty negotiated and signed by postwar Japan.[35] The historical significance of this treaty lay in the fact that the so-called Doctrine of "Mutual Abstention" was incorporated into the agreement and became part of international law. Under this treaty, the United States, Canada, and Japan mutually confirmed their intent to voluntarily refrain from commercial harvesting of selected fish spices that were scientifically proven to have been developed near the MSY level and in need of conservation. In the sense that this principle was applied to all treaty parties, it was a reciprocal treaty. In practical application, however, it achieved an effect, desired by American and Canadian fishermen, of mandating unilateral abstention of fishing activities by Japanese distant-water fleets with regard to North Pacific fish species (salmon and halibut) in the high seas off the coasts of Alaska and Canada. In other words, the Yoshida government accepted exclusion of Japanese fishermen from a vast portion of the North Pacific fisheries in the postwar period, as one of its very first acts as an independent state. Since members of Yoshida's cabinet favored a successful conclusion of post-World War II peace-making and the re-establishment of its sovereign status by entering into an international agreement as soon as possible, this commitment, decried by Japan's industry leaders as a humiliating capitulation to America's fishing lobby, was deemed a price worth paying for a greater good. At the same time, the Japanese government promised to practice abstention from certain fishing activities in the high seas beyond the three miles of its national coast, thus weakening its claim of the three-mile offshore jurisdiction rule and the freedom of the seas principle as the norms of the world's ocean governance. Postwar Japan also assumed the risk of the abstention doctrine being applied repeatedly in future fisheries negotiations over the Western Pacific with Asia-Pacific countries.[36] To borrow Scheiber's apt expression, at a time when the ocean "enclosure" movement was quickly becoming a worldwide trend, Japan, albeit against its will, contributed to the construction of a key milestone in the road towards the partitioning of the world's oceans as repositories of natural resources.

Notes

1 Arthur F. McEvoy, *The fishermen's problem*, Cambridge and New York: Cambridge University Press, 1986; Joseph E. Taylor III, *Making salmon: an environmental history of the northwest fisheries crisis*, Seattle: University of Washington Press, 1999, pp. 39–67.
2 Harry Scheiber, "Origins of the abstention doctrine in ocean law," *Ecology law quarterly*, 16, no. 1, 1989, pp. 29–35.
3 Harry Scheiber, *Inter-allied conflict and ocean law, 1945–1953: the occupation commands' revival of Japanese whaling and marine fisheries*, Taipei: Institute of European and American Studies, Academia Sinica, 2001, chapter 3.

4 Ibid., chapter 4.

5 "Japanese government makes official statement on Bristol Bay salmon fishing," *Pacific fisherman*, April 1938, p. 25.

6 Hull's memorandum, 28 November 1937, reprinted in *Foreign relations of the United States* (FRUS), 1951, pp. 763–5; *Pacific fisherman*, April 1937, no. 38.

7 "Japanese fishing areas: pre-war and post-war," *Pacific fisherman*, June 1946, pp. 30–3; Address by Edward Allen, "They fish to eat," June 1949, Edward Allen papers, University of Washington Special Collection, Seattle, WA; John Lynch, *Toward an orderly market*, Rutland, VT: C.E. Tuttle, 1968, pp. 94–7.

8 Ann L. Hollick, *U.S. foreign policy and the law of the sea*, Princeton, 1983, pp. 31–61; Chiyuki Mizukami, *Nippon to kaiyoho* [*Japan and the law of the seas*], Tokyo: Yushindo Kobunsha, 1995, pp. 179–80. The Truman Proclamations were a political misstep. This ill-conceived unilateral declaration by the U.S. government opened the legal door to Latin American nations' expanded off-shore jurisdictional claims between 1945 and 1953. On the other hand, the U.S. government failed to take any specific steps towards conservation, as declared in the proclamation concerning the conservation zone after September 1945.

9 Edward Allen, "The fishery proclamation of 1945," *American journal of international law*, 45, 1945, pp. 177–8; Scheiber, "Origins of the abstention doctrine," p. 34.

10 Memorandum from Herrington to Webb, 30 August 1951, State Department decimile file (DF), 611.946/8-3051, Record Group (RG) 69, National Archives, College Park.

11 Mizukami, *Nippon to kaiyoho*, pp. 180–1; *Japanese fishing under the occupation*, National Fisheries Institute Yearbook, California, 1949, pp. 102–3; "Mission and accomplishments of the occupation in the natural resources field," 26 September 1959, SCAP Records, RG 331, National Archives; Wilbert Chapman, "Tuna in the mandated islands," *Far Eastern survey*, 15, 1946, pp. 317–9.

12 SCAP Natural Resources Section, "Mission and accomplishments."

13 Harry Scheiber, "Pacific Ocean resources, science, and law of the sea," *Ecology law quarterly*, 13, no. 13, 1986, pp. 437–47.

14 Chapman, "Tuna in the mandated islands," p. 31; "SCAP opens foreign trade office in New York," *Commercial fisheries review*, December 1947, pp. 29–30; Memorandum from Herrington to Allen, 27 March 1950, Edward Allen Papers, UW; Memoranda by Herrington, 8 July 1948, 26 January and 5 July 1949, SCAP Records.

15 Letter from Wilds to U.S. members of the Far East Commission, 10 December 1948, DF 894.50/12-1048.

16 Telegram from Flory to Chapman, 7 October 1948, DF 740/00119/10-748.

17 Letter from Chapman to Allen, 12 September 1948, Allen Papers; letter from Chapman to Phister, 23 October 1949, Wilbert Chapman Papers (WCP), University of Washington Special Collection.

18 Letter from Moseley to Allison, 3 February 1950, DF 611.945/2-350; letter from Chapman to Hendrick, 8 November 1949, DF 611.946/8-1050; letter from Martin to Chapman, 3 August 1949; letter from Chapman to Herrington, 11 April 1950, WCP.

19 Memorandum for the Japanese Government, "Mothership-type tuna fishing operations," 11 May 1950, AG 800.217, SCAP Records; letter from Chapman to Phister, 31 May 1950, WCP.

20 Memorandum of conversation between Collings and Johnson, 23 March 1950, DF 611.946/3-2450; memorandum of conversation, Byrd and Southworth, 19 April 1950, DF 611.946/3-2450.

21 Letter from Chapman to Arnold, 3 January 1949, WCP; memorandum from Chapman to Brown, 8 March 1950, Edward Allen Papers.

22 Letter from Rusk to Jessup, 6 July 1950, DF 611.946/7-650; letter from Chapman to Dulles, 5 January 1951, DF 611.946/11-1050; letter from Chapman to Phister, 30 October 1950, WCP.
23 Letter from Knowland to McFall, 7 November 1950, DF 611.946/11-750; letter from Chapman to the Acting Political Advisor for Japan, 7 June 1950, DF 611.946/6-750.
24 Letter from Chapman to Phister, 6 January 1951; letter from Chapman to Phister, 6 January and 5 March 1951, WCP.
25 Letter from Chapman to Phister, 6 January 1951; letter from Chapman to Phister, 18 January 1951, WCP.
26 Open letter from Miller to Acheson, 9 November 1951, DF 611.946/11-950; *Pacific fisherman*, January 1951, pp. 19–20; memorandum from Freeman to Acheson, November 1950, Miller Freeman Papers, University of Washington Special Collection.
27 Scheiber, "Abstention doctrine," pp. 64–5.
28 Department of State bulletin, vol. 24, 1951, p. 351; letter from Chapman to Phister, 10 February 1951, WCP.
29 "Kosho keii kaigi kaisai made" ["Backgrounds of negotiations: towards the opening of the conference"], 7 February 1951, Kitataiheiyo no kokai gyogyoni kansuru kokusai joyaku ikken [Opinion on the international treaty regarding fisheries in the North Pacific], "Nichibeika sangoku gyogyou kyotei koshoni kansuru hoshin," ["Regarding the plan to negotiate a tripartite fisheries agreement between Japan, the U.S. and Canada"], 2 November 1951, Foreign Ministry Records, B'6.4.0.18 (hereafter KKJ), Japanese Foreign Ministry Archive, Tokyo; letter from Chapman to Phister, 10 February 1951; memorandum from Leddy to Chapman, 12 April 1951, WCP.
30 Hollick, *U.S. foreign policy and the law of the sea*, pp. 426–7; Office memorandum from Zurhellen to Johnson, DF 611.946/7-1751; memorandum from Herrington to Phister, 24 July 1951, WCP; "Kitataiheiyo no kokai gyogyoni kansuru kokusai joyaku ikken," "eibun-an" ["An item on the international agreement on fisheries in the North Pacific"], 11 July 1953, KKJ.
31 "Nichibeika sangokukan gyogyo joyakuan no keii" ["The backgrounds of the Japan–U.S.–Canada tripartite fisheries draft treaty"], 10 October 1951, KKJ; letter from Herrington to Freeman, 3 October 1951, WCP.
32 "Yoyaku no igi," *Zaigai gaimu sanko shiryo daiichigo* ["The significance of the treaty: file #1 of the Foreign Affairs reference materials"], 25 December 1951, KKJ; memorandum for the files, 4 September 1951, DF 611.426/9-451; letter from Herrington to Brooding, 1 October 1951, Allen Papers.
33 Letter from Chapman to Freeman, 17 September, 3 October 1951; letter from Chapman to Herrington, 12 October 1951; letter from Herrington to Freeman, 16 October 1951, WCP; office memorandum from Norwood to Corse, 15 August 1951, DF 611/426/8-1555; memorandum from Johnson to Rusk, DF 611.946/7-1051.
34 For a complete list of delegates at the tripartite conference, see "Daihyodan no kosei" ["The composition of the negotiating team"], JKK; memorandum from Chapman to Freeman, 17 September 1951, WCP; letter from Allen to Shiel, 25 August 1955, Allen Papers; report from Bond to DOS, 4 January 1952, DF 611.006NP/1-452.
35 "Joyaku no iIgi," 25 December 1951, KKJ; Selak, "The proposed international convention for the high seas fisheries of the North Pacific Ocean," *American journal of international law*, 46, 1951, p. 323.
36 Scheiber, "Abstention doctrine," p. 27.

3 Protective labor legislation and gender equality

The impact of the occupation on Japanese working women

Maho Toyoda

Introduction

1 April 1999 was an epochal date in Japanese gender politics. It marked the day that a ban on women working late-night shifts and other regulations were repealed by an amendment to the Labor Standards Law (LSL). As a result, visible numbers of women made inroads into workplaces such as public transportation, particularly in railroad companies. Before its amendment, women were prohibited from working between 10 p.m. and 5 a.m.; so railroad companies, which require working at/over night, employed few women. This represents a typical case of protective labor laws narrowing job options for women.

The legislation that restricted female working hours resulted from an active debate over gender equality and protection that began soon after the onset of the United States occupation of Japan. The original LSL, enacted in 1947, was written by the Japanese government under the close supervision of the Supreme Commander for the Allied Powers (SCAP), and thus reflected their biases of this administration. SCAP emphasized gender equality as part of its larger mission to democratize Japan. This ambition is reflected in the original LSL legislation that promoted the principle of equal work for equal pay. Yet, ironically, by this same legislation many women workers lost their jobs through provisions that sought to protect them.

Research to date has credited gender reforms introduced by SCAP with promoting gender equality in Japan. These studies focus on the "alliance" created by SCAP female staff members and their Japanese counterparts to enable "radical" reforms to take shape in postwar Japan.[1] Recent research by Mire Koikari, however, emphasizes that this "alliance" did not always exist. She argues that Japanese representation in this alliance was comprised primarily of women from the privileged classes.[2] What appears to be lost in this debate is the fact that while "radical" reforms may have been articulated in legislation, they were not always carried out in the workplace.

In fact, occupation gender policy was riddled with contradictions. Gail

Nomura found the LSL to be restrictive rather than protective.[3] Nomura, however, fails to consider SCAP's intentions. She also does not fully acknowledge the Japanese government's role in this legislation's creation. Japanese officials wrote the legislation; they cooperated with SCAP officials in legislating it. The legislation's strong commitment to protecting women laborers outlived the occupation and survived until the recent amendment took effect.

This chapter assesses the impact of the U.S. occupation on labor gender issues, particularly the protection of women workers. The debate that accompanied the formation of Japan's LSL focused on two issues: menstruation leave and night labor. Menstruation leave was one of the major demands put forth by labor unions at the time. On the one hand, SCAP urged Japanese female union members not to overemphasize menstruation leave, in order to preserve the ideal of equal pay for equal work. SCAP officials, however, offered a different line for night labor. Here, they argued the necessity of protecting women by prohibiting them from night labor.[4] This chapter analyzes the historical development of the discussion to evaluate the influence that SCAP's gender policies had on Japan's contemporary female labor force.

Drafting the Labor Standards Law

Protective legislation in pre-war Japan

The Japanese government first prohibited women from night labor in the 1919 Factory Act, although it postponed enforcement of this legislation until 1929. External pressure no doubt encouraged the inclusion of this provision in the Act: the International Labor Organization had adopted a similar prohibition of female night labor that same year. In addition, female workers, with support from the Japanese Federation of Labor (*sôdômei*), appealed for the prohibition. "The wartime situation forced the Japanese government to nullify the Factory Act in the late 1930s. By 1937 it established a wartime exemption that suspended all protective labor legislation. This forced women to work without any protection."[5]

SCAP was fully aware of this legislation. It recognized the pre-war Mining Act and the Factory Act as "the first legislative attempts" to protect workers but criticized this protective legislation as "limited." Moreover, during the "wars of conquest," enforcement of this "scant protection" was neglected; the Japanese government also passed ordinances to nullify its effectiveness. By the end of the war, SCAP realized, protective regulations had "in general been suspended." SCAP understood that in the immediate postwar period workers were "largely unprotected by law." This recognition led SCAP to "suggest" that the Japanese government take immediate measures to enact labor protection legislation.[6]

The restoration of labor protection was included in the "Basic Initial

Post-Surrender Directive to Supreme Commander for the Allied Powers for the Occupation and control of Japan," issued on 3 November 1945 by the U.S. Joint Chiefs of Staff. This directive ordered Supreme Commander Douglas MacArthur to "require the Japanese to remove, as rapidly as practicable, wartime controls over labor and reinstate protective labor legislation." SCAP had already ordered the removal of wartime exemptions in its "Removal of Restrictions on Political Civil and Religious Liberties" of 4 October. The Japanese government responded to this memorandum on 24 October by repealing ordinances that nullified pre-war protective legislation. It also reinstated protective legislation to pre-war Factory Act levels. It continued to suspend the enforcement of pre-war provisions that regulated female labor in mines, to avoid an adverse effect on coal production while replacements were being recruited. To compensate women miners during this period, mine operators agreed to grant them paid maternity and menstrual leaves.[7]

The Japanese government soon realized the flaws in its protective labor legislation, and the need to create new legislation rather than mend old legislation. It began drafting the Labor Standards Bill on 1 March 1946, just after it had established the Labor Protection Division (*rôdô hogoka*) of the Labor Standards Section (*rôdô kijunkyoku*) in the Welfare Ministry (*kôseishô*).

The Labor Protection Division and the Labor Standards Bill

SCAP entrusted the Japanese with the task of drafting the LSL, although it closely supervised their work. As early as 11 April 1946 the Labor Protection Division completed its "Points to Draft a Labor Protective Bill." The following day, Teramoto Kôsaku, Chief of the Labor Protection Division, completed a draft of the legislation.[8] Teramoto's proposal received input from members of the drafting committee, each of whom was assigned responsibility for compiling different sections of the legislation. For example, Tanino Setsu, the only female labor inspector in pre-war Japan, was assigned the section on women and children.

The eventual legislation began to take form when the third draft was completed on 13 May 1946. This draft contained most of the provisions found in the final version of the LSL. Before the legislation was finalized members of the drafting committee held lengthy discussions on its contents and conducted field studies to determine actual working conditions. Tanino, accompanied by Teramoto and Helen Mears, the only female member of the SCAP Labor Advisory Committee, inspected several factories and offered a number of detailed reports.[9]

Menstruation leave received considerable attention during this process. The provision was not included in the first draft, but, influenced by discussion within the Labor Protection Division, was inserted in the second draft.[10] This change may reflect Tanino's efforts. Originally not in favor of the provision, Tanino apparently changed her mind after meeting with Akamatsu Tsuneko, a women organizer for the Japanese Federation of Labor, and other women workers. In the end Tamino proposed that the provision be included in the new legislation if "it would ease the hardship of women workers." She also offered data that demonstrated the need for this provision. At first, Teramoto was against its inclusion claiming that it was too "filthy" to occupy a place in the LSL. Tanino's data revealed the problems that menstruating women faced in the workplace. She submitted studies demonstrating the errors and accidents that women experienced during their periods, in order to strengthen the provision for menstruation leave. History was also on her side. Tanino argued that immediately after the war women coal miners had been afforded this benefit. In the end, she succeeded in persuading a reluctant Teramoto to include menstruation leave in the LSL.[11]

Teramoto expressed his reservations at a meeting with SCAP staff officials on 28 May 1946. Here he revealed that members of the drafting committee "were much troubled by [the menstruation leave] problem" for the following three reasons: First, no other country had included such a provision in its labor legislation; second, when "weak girls" who failed to menstruate were given a month's break to return home, their periods normalized. Therefore, it would be either "unreasonable" to require an employer to grant leaves to those women not menstruating, or to those whose menstruation was normal. And third, girls would rather receive sanitary materials than menstruation leave. He further noted that, according to medical practitioners, not all types of work were "injurious" to menstruation. Therefore, he recommended, "only those employers who employ women in work injurious to menstruation" should be required to grant them leave.[12]

Here we must note that while Teramoto's comments unintentionally revealed factors that at first glance appeared to support menstruation leave, they did not necessarily lead to a logical conclusion to grant the leave. For example, if labor conditions ameliorated, young women would be healthy enough to menstruate regularly; and if the situation of scarce goods improved and the shortage of necessary sanitary supplies was remedied, most women would not need to worry about requesting time off. Both factors were directly related to the immediate postwar situation: the poor working conditions and shortage of basic supplies alone were reason enough for women to require time off during their periods. But the leave was included in the draft because the Labor Protection Division deemed that extra consideration should be given for two reasons: this leave time was a routine item in the demands made by labor, and second that in the immediate postwar period women faced a shortage of sanitary cottons and "facilities," namely restrooms.

At this conference, Teramoto also reported that the Labor Protection Division had solved the problem of the prohibition of night labor by exempting it in the case of the two-shift work system. He explained that, because "girls do not prefer midnight labor as they lose weight and become tired," he had decided that a "proper solution" would be to give forty-five minutes' rest and thirty minutes' exemption for night labor.

Teramoto also addressed the issue of night labor at this meeting, by announcing the Labor Protective Division's decision to admit a small number of exemptions in the case of women working in a two-shift working environment. He explained that because the draft provided that the actual work day be limited to eight hours, it would be necessary to permit exemption until 11 p.m., if one hour was allowed for rest time in the two-shift working environment. He argued that it was possible not to allow exceptions if the rest time was thirty minutes, but only if this thirty-minute rest period was used for eating and not as a break. As a "proper solution," he proposed allowing women working day shifts a forty-five minute break (an additional fifteen minutes to the thirty-minute meal time break) and only thirty minutes' exception for those working the night shift.[13]

The drafting committee met with Theodore Cohen, Chief of SCAP's Labor Division, Economic and Scientific Section (ESS), for the first time in the summer of 1946. Upon reading the draft Cohen remarked that he was "surprised and impressed" to see "a bewildering array of protection minutiae" in its contents. He thought the draft represented "more than a law; it was a labor code for all industry." He advised Teramoto and his committee to continue to work on the legislation because labor protection was not a part of SCAP's "mission," and added, "there was no reason for SCAP to object [to] a code like this."[14]

The Japanese government officially submitted the draft to SCAP at a meeting with the Labor Division, ESS on 24 August. At this meeting the Japanese gained the impression that the Labor Division supported the draft, complimenting it as good and sufficiently progressive. The Labor Division "offered no objection to submitting it to public hearing in the present form to serve as a basis for further discussion." SCAP approved the prohibition of night labor (along with other restrictions on women and underage laborers) as "essential." It further stated that the provision "should not be changed during the course of public hearings."[15] Through these discussions both SCAP and the Japanese drafting committee defined adult female laborers as a class sharing characteristics with underage laborers, but separate from adult male laborers.

The Japanese government held public hearings between 5 and 17 September. Specialists on women's issues, including Ichikawa Fusae and Yoshioka Yayoi, attended the morning sessions on 14 September to offer their views. During the afternoon sessions women working in fields such as textiles, transportation, and telecommunications were given the chance to voice their ideas.[16]

Laborers used the public hearings to voice opposition to the night labor exemptions. They requested that the exemptions be rescinded out of fear that they would eventually "become principle" over the course of the legislation's application. Female workers noted the difficulty of night labor, particularly during their menstrual periods. Ichikawa, a leading feminist in pre-war Japan, voiced concern that this prohibition, combined with the principle of equal pay, might encourage employers to eschew employing women. On the other hand, employers in a number of industries requested that their industries be exempted from the prohibition. After the completion of the public hearings, the Labor Protection Division expanded the number of exemptions to night labor prohibitions, primarily as a result of requests from employers.[17]

The public hearings also addressed – critically – the issue of menstruation leave. Yoshioka, a prominent female doctor, vehemently expressed her opposition to the provision, asserting that menstruation leave was not necessary and that women who suffered during menstruation were sick. She supported this argument with data demonstrating that less than 5 percent of all women required special breaks during their periods. Employers also expressed their reluctance to offer women this benefit, suggesting that it be granted to women only after they had been medically diagnosed as in need of this time off, to avoid abuse. Moreover, they suggested it be offered as paid sick leave to avoid the ill-balanced situation of having to offer women a benefit not available to their male counterparts.[18]

In contrast to this opposition, a coalition of workers, employers, and medical practitioners voiced strong support for menstruation leave, insisting that every working woman who suffered during her period be granted leave irrespective of the industry for which she worked. Workers demanded that leave time be given with pay and without medical approval. Many women asserted that their work was "injurious to menstruation." A "bus girl" from the transportation union impressed the audience by describing the painful experiences that she endured while working during her period. These arguments gained the support of the Japan Medical Society, which contended that menstruation problems differed from person to person.[19]

Appeals by women workers, as well as the favorable opinions expressed by workers, employers, and the Japan Medical Society, may have been instrumental in keeping the menstruation leave provision in the bill, despite the fierce criticism from its opposition. Arguments put forth by workers trumped the employers' demand for medical diagnosis. The bill refrained from characterizing this time off as "sick leave," nor did it stipulate whether this would be paid leave or how long a leave would be allowed. The members of this coalition, coming from workers, employers, and the Japan Medical Society, influenced the bill's widening of women eligible for menstruation leave to include all those who experienced difficulty while working during their period, rather than targeting only those employed at jobs deemed "injurious . . . to menstruation."

In November 1946, Japanese members of the bill's drafting committee met with Golda Stander, a labor economist who had just been appointed as Chief of the Wages and Labor Conditions Branch, the Labor Division, ESS. The arrival of Stander, a specialist in labor standards, expedited the negotiations of the bill. Despite difficult exchanges, she ultimately agreed with SCAP policy that protective legislation such as LSL should be determined by the Japanese themselves. For example, Stander initially considered the menstruation leave provision to be "unnecessary and frivolous." However, she ultimately followed Cohen's advice to "stand aside": this "was a Japanese bill, and if [they wanted menstruation leave included] there was no justification for SCAP's intervening."[20] While it is basically true that during the drafting process SCAP refrained from openly expressing opposition to the Japanese inclusion of menstruation leave in the bill, Stander, however, "cruelly" voiced her view to Tanino that menstruation leave was "overprotective" and that it would have a "bad influence" "upon women's employment opportunities" should it be included. Nonetheless, she deferred to Japanese wishes by not objecting to its inclusion in the bill's final draft.[21]

The Labor Legislation Committee (*rômuhôsei shingikai*) of the Welfare Ministry approved the LSL on 24 December 1946, and the Japanese Cabinet held meetings to review the legislation between 6 and 22 February of the following year. After gaining Cabinet approval the bill was submitted to the 95th Imperial Parliament, its final session under the Meiji Constitution. The House of Representatives gave its approval to the bill without change on 18 March after twelve days of deliberation.[22] The bill was sent to the House of Peers the next day, where it was approved on 25 March. This legislative body raised a number of penetrating questions regarding female protection and equality. It pointed out the incompatibility between the principle of equal pay and female protection. Including a provision for menstruation leave, it noted, might negatively influence female employment opportunities.[23] This animated discussion in the Japanese parliament – perhaps influenced by SCAP's tacit approval – produced no major changes to the proposed legislation. On 27 March the bill was passed unanimously, and it went into effect on 1 April 1947, to be enforced from 1 September of that year.

Enforcing the LSL: SCAP's female labor policy

Menstruation leave and SCAP views on gender equality

SCAP continued to maintain a noninterventionist stance toward menstruation leave. Stander repeated her stance at the August 1947 Magazine Conference, just at the time the LSL was to be enforced, that the issue was one that Japanese women must address themselves. She noted that the problem stemmed from "a lack of sanitary conditions, hygiene, etc." during the postwar social disorder and added "these conditions may make it necessary for women to take leave periodically."[24] Mead Smith, newly appointed to the Wages and Labor Conditions Branch of SCAP's Labor Division, also indicated that leave was necessary "in view of the lack of rest rooms, sanitary facilities, and modern personal hygiene in Japan today."[25] Stander and Smith both taking the position that the special postwar circumstances required women taking time off during their periods diminished the chances that the occupation administration would attempt to change the provision.

However, opposition to the provision appeared periodically. Stander herself insisted that "it should be the right of the woman worker to decide for herself" whether she could work or not during her period.[26] This suggests Stander's tacit opposition to the demand by labor movements that every woman take menstruation leave every month.

Opposition also focused on the potential abuse of this benefit: women might take this monthly leave even if were unnecessary. On 28 June, Smith met with Tanino Setsu, then Chief of the Women's and Children Section (*fujin-shōnenka*) of the Labor Standards Bureau. The two agreed as a basic principle that menstruation leave would be provided only "for the benefit of those who actually need it." Smith noted that "at the present time Japanese women do not appear to recognize this principle." They took menstruation leave "each month automatically," whether they needed it or not. This "abuse" of the provision, Smith warned, would be "completely out of keeping with women's efforts to obtain equal treatment with men." Tanino concurred with her on this point and vowed to include the problem on her list of areas to be emphasized in the educational activities organized by her section.[27]

Stander spoke out against menstruation leave on 16 October 1947, claiming that the provision would obstruct the principle of equal pay and would thus serve as an obstacle to true gender equality in employment opportunities. She noted that menstruation leave had never been an issue in the United States. All workers there were "free, of course, to decide when and where they will work." She stressed that most female workers in the United States continued at their jobs during their time of menstruation; if they were too ill to work, they simply took the day off. "However," she continued, "most government agencies as well as a number of private employers" had a sick leave policy that permitted their employees to take time off if they felt ill. Finally, she carefully added that this sick leave policy applied "equally to men and women."[28]

Despite Stander's obvious objections to what she interpreted as a gender-biased provision, she continued to insist that issues such as "whether women should demand from their employers menstruation leave as a right," "whether or not they actually [were] too ill to work," and "whether they should require payment for such leave as a right" were ones that the Japanese women must address. She advised women to look at menstruation leave in a broader context. The question of balance –

ending wage discrimination – was the more pressing issue. She reminded her audience that the LSL also included a provision for equal pay: Women "must weigh in the balance what they want more – equal pay for equal work or special leave provisions which negate the principle of equal pay for equal work." She continued:

> [Japanese women] must decide for themselves whether they do not stand to lose more be demanding payment for such time not worked when payment is not granted to men for sick leave in terms of possible loss of employment opportunities as well as in terms of achieving true equality with men.[29]

In this speech Stander clearly outlined her core arguments in opposing menstruation leave, and left little room to doubt her support for its inclusion under a sick leave provision equally applicable to both men and women. A provision for menstruation leave, a benefit only available for female workers, was inherently discriminative. She chastised the labor unions for insisting that women receive paid menstruation leave, and their demands that every female worker take this leave whether she needed it or not.

SCAP attempted to restrict the use of menstruation leave as it strove to enforce the LSL. Over the seven-year occupation period SCAP revised every statement issued by the Japanese government, including the leaflet "Is Menstruation Leave Necessary for Working Women?" Before it was issued to the public, the leaflet was translated into English and, after instructions and revisions were issued by SCAP staff members, it was retranslated back into Japanese. During this process, Mead Smith attempted to influence women unionists toward negotiating sick leave instead of menstruation leave, on the grounds that the latter would be discriminatory as it applied only to women. She added the following to an item in the leaflet that discussed menstruation leave in other countries: "In the United States, in those establishments where sick leave is provided for both men and women, a female worker who finds difficulty in working on [her] menstruation day is allowed to take sick leave."[30] She suggested additional clarifications after a statement that acknowledged the trade unions' right to request pay during the leave: "It is necessary that women members of the union should be very careful so that opportunities to receive the same amount of pay as men will not be hindered due to the above fact."[31]

We also see her influence in the section on "Menstruation Leave and the Labor Union," which Smith completely rewrote. The final version read as follows:

> Since both men and women are working toward obtaining equal pay for equal work, many trade unionists are thinking over carefully

whether it is desirable to negotiate for the payment of this time taken off from work by women alone. In addition it is possible for unions to negotiate for sick leave for both men and women.[32]

The leaflet concluded by warning that "menstruation leave has the danger of bringing about disadvantages to women," and that in the future, when working conditions improved, menstruation leave would "naturally become unnecessary for the great majority of women."[33]

Prohibition of female night labor: A contradiction in SCAP policy

By opposing menstruation leave, SCAP appeared to demonstrate its support for a policy of gender equality in labor protection. Its stance on the issue of night labor prohibition, which limited the working hours of female labor, contradicted its stance on this principle. In its labor legislation it supported a provision that "protected" women by prohibiting them from night work and gaining employment in areas that required their presence on the job after a certain hour.

SCAP may have been influenced by American society's long tradition of passing gender-biased protection and restrictive legislation. After the 1905 Lochner vs. New York case, where the U.S. Supreme Court ruled against the state's claim that its labor regulations were applicable to all workers, proponents of protective labor legislation changed their tactics to argue the special needs of women for state welfare. Strategically, they emphasized that the "natural weakness" of women required that they receive special protection and that it was the state's responsibility to safeguard the "mothers of the race" as well as the morality of future homemakers. This idea – that women were too weak to fend for themselves in employment negotiations, and that they were the mothers and domestic nurturers – prevailed throughout the "progressive era" and into the 1940s.[34] American staff employed by SCAP carried this bias with them to Japan.

Golda Stander revealed her stance on this idea in an 18 July 1947 statement where she explained that society owed women special protection because they were "the mothers of the race," and because harmful working conditions would adversely affect "the welfare of the race."[35] Mead Smith, on 15 July 1947, stated in a press conference that "the traditionally inferior status" of women and their "exceedingly weak" bargaining position rendered the necessity of "special protection" self evident. She further questioned rhetorically whether giving female workers special protection reduced their chances of employment. Her answer, based on "the experience of workers in the United States," was negative.[36]

Post-World War II American society thinking regarding the issue of female labor protection, however, changed dramatically. The transition is seen in the reaction by Blanch Freedman, Executive Secretary of the New

York Women's Trade Union League (WTUL), to a question posed by a SCAP official regarding female night labor. The WTUL traditionally had advocated labor protection for women. However, on this occasion Freedman felt the question better left "unanswered for the time being." She stated: "With the change in labor standards and conditions [the WTUL] is reconsidering the entire question" of night labor as considerable doubt had been raised over the necessity of continuing this prohibition.[37]

Freedman was perhaps drawing on past precedent. The post-World War I period had witnessed New York City layoffs of female railroad workers, presumably under protective legislation, but more accurately to rehire males returning from the war. The legislation had gone into effect despite claims by women that they were able to mind their own health and moral matters. At this time 800 out of the 1500 female employees had lost their jobs.[38] A similar sequence now occurred in occupation-era Japan as female railroad workers, who had replaced male workers called to war, were laid off after the government enforced a provision in the newly enacted LSL that prohibited female night labor.

Postwar Japan encountered a huge unemployment crisis after 1.3 million demobilized soldiers returned to the work force. Dismissing women workers was seen as one solution to this problem. In July 1947 the Transportation Ministry issued a statement to this effect, claiming that women were "inadequate workers in terms of physical strength and ability."[39] Marusawa Michiyo, Chief of the Women's Section of the Osaka Railroad Workers Union, recognized the desire of women to work at night and petitioned that the LSL be amended accordingly.[40]

Marusawa and other female railroad union representatives petitioned SCAP on 25 August 1947, the eve of the law's enforcement. Their petition stated that "not all women currently on night work can be absorbed in daytime employment." As serving twenty-four-hour shifts was a condition for railroad employment, this sector would find it "difficult to employ women if they cannot work on into the night." This limitation would also cause "future discrimination against employing women on railroads." This concerned not only their promotion, but also their employment in general, for the railroads could very well adopt a "no more employment of women" policy. This group also noted exemptions given to women in other sectors, such as telephone operators and nurses, as "discriminatory": if the LSL could exclude women in these professions, "it seems logical and possible to exclude railroad women."[41]

Stander and Smith rejected the appeal, and SCAP ordered the prohibition strictly enforced. Stander reasoned: "Any law going into effect for the first time creates some hardships for some groups ... such groups should recognize the long-run importance of the provisions of the Law." Both Stander and Smith remarked that it would be "desirable" to extend this same protection to telephone workers and nurses. But since these jobs were "essential to the public," and since these professions relied "almost entirely [on] women," it would be "impossible to prohibit night work without causing extreme disruption and considerable harm to the public." The two labor officials further explained that, as railroad employees were "not predominantly female," there was little reason for women "to be excluded from the Law's protection." In addition, they noted, "the fact that two groups are not able to have protection is no reason to extend exemption to the third." Stander and Smith urged women workers to "consider the seriousness of attempting to change a Law." Once the law was changed, they argued, it would take considerable "time and effort to change it back." Also, "any exemption granted under the Law would tend to weaken the effectiveness of the Law [and] lead to other requests for exemptions."[42]

Female railroad employees were not the only group seeking exemption; however the results were the same throughout. SCAP appeared uninterested in allowing for more exemptions. At a 2–3 March 1948 conference Tanino Setsu passed on to Mead Smith a list of occupations that sought exemption to the LSL provision against female night labor. The law, however, targeted the type of employer, rather than specific occupations – telephone operators employed by railroad companies and police departments were included in the prohibition, while those employed by the telephone company were not. Tanino, who regarded telephone work as being well suited for women, feared that the occupation could become a male profession should women be prohibited from night employment. Her ambition was to broaden the legislation to include exemption for as many telephone operators as possible. She reported that the Labor Standards Section had already issued an ordinance on 17 February that admitted broadening the interpretation of the "telephone" enterprise.[43]

Tanino also strove to gain railroad-crossing watchwomen permission to work at night. She argued that women employed in this profession were generally elderly and uneducated, and thus difficult to place in other employment. They also secured their housing through their employer. She suggested that officials "secretly" accept the status quo: they could gain an understanding with labor officials to refrain from enforcing the law until these workers found adequate housing. Tanino felt that this was the only way to exempt women in other occupations, such as women jailers, policewomen, and women correspondents – if the law could not be amended, it would be ignored.[44]

Smith criticized this proposed solution. She informed Tanino that any such steps would have to be "publicized." In addition, Smith instructed, "responsible Government agencies should not, as in the pre-war time, have secret dealings of any sort." Smith emphasized that "such an agreement just to ignore the Law would open the way for the same lack of enforcement in the future that has characterized Japanese Labor Laws in the past."[45]

SCAP issued a clear warning on exemptions at a subsequent meeting held on 26 April. Here, Smith informed Tanino that night labor by women employed as railroad crossing guards, prison matrons, police-women, dormitory matrons, and women correspondents would "adminis-tratively be permitted." She further warned that such administrative agreements were "dangerous." The above exemptions were merely a tem-porary measure and "not the kind of secret behind-the-door maneuvering which before the war enabled Government officials to avoid responsibility and nullify laws." Smith stressed again that care must be taken to "avoid any further such actions."[46]

At this meeting, Smith also emphasized to Tanino that SCAP greatly deplored any interpretation that the Labor Standards Section had issued. However, SCAP accepted it "with extreme reluctance." SCAP did not sub-scribe to Tanino's "fears that men would take over the industry" if women were prohibited from working night shifts as telephone operators in any noncommunications enterprises.[47]

This assertion, however, did not match reality. Prohibiting women workers from performing night labor did cause many to lose their jobs. SCAP strictly implemented the provision. Clearly, further exemptions would have weakened the legislation's effectiveness. It is also evident that, ironically, this prohibition, aimed at protecting women, pushed them from occupations in which to date they had comprised the great majority of workers. The prohibition also "protected" women from entering traditionally male-dominated professions, areas where women had only recently begun to make inroads.[48] SCAP used gender equality to argue its case against granting women menstruation leave. Its position on female night labor reversed this policy by excluding women from employment opportunities and restricting them to female-dominated, low-wage occu-pations. SCAP's justification for this position – the premise that women were "weak" and "mothers" – was also discriminatory.

Post-occupation discussion on menstruation leave and prohibition of female night labor

Marusawa Michiyo and other Railroad Union officials, by requesting exclusion from the prohibition of female night labor, had already anticip-ated that, should their request be denied, the day would come when there was "no more [female] employment on railroads." Having direct experience of night labor on the railroads, they were in a position to assert that their work was "not so heavy ... as day work."[49] Their anticipa-tion proved to be prophetic. Due to the railroads' policy of twenty-four hour shifts, hundreds of women were dismissed over their inability to work a complete shift. It has only been recently, since the prohibition was rescinded when the LSL was amended in 1999, that women have returned to the railroad industry. This is just one example of women having to wait a full half-century to regain their employment opportunities as a result of this prohibition.

The menstruation leave provision, on the other hand, remained unchanged in this legislation. As SCAP staff members anticipated, menstruation leave became a major target for criticism in terms of women's protection and gender equality in the workplace during the post-occupation period. This issue captured the attention of the Japanese Diet, and predominantly representatives of the socialist and communist parties who enjoyed close ties with labor unions. This opposition has carried the torch of maintenance of female protection.

Discussions on both issues – menstruation leave and night labor – remained virtually unchanged over the fifty years from the first session in 1947 until the most recent in 1997. The Japanese Diet faced consistent resistance to amending the prohibition on night labor. Likewise, Diet members consistently demonstrated support for menstruation leave as a valuable right and means of protecting maternity. Armed with data that demonstrated only a small percentage of women taking advantage of this benefit, legislators pushed for more lenient measures to make it easier for women to take menstruation leave.

During the late 1940s and into the 1950s, when the labor movement was still powerful, women unionists strongly encouraged women to take the leave every month. Their ambition was to counter employer attempts to have the LSL amended to limit its female protection provisions. Particularly during the Korean War, which triggered economic growth and consequently expanded demands, employers viewed these protection measures as obstacles to productivity. The Japan Federation of Employers' Associations (*Nihon keieisha dantairenmei*) and the Japan Board of Trade (*Nihon shôko kaigisho*) presented their views as early as 1951, requesting that the prohibition on female night labor and the provision for menstruation leave be relaxed. Diet members retorted that menstruation leave was necessary to safeguard maternity protection. The Japanese government emphasized that it was a provision available only to those who badly needed it, and not available to women automatically.[50]

In the early 1960s Japan's vigorous economic growth witnessed increased "rationalization" in the business world. The labor influence, in turn, suffered from this development. To improve productivity many employers strove to restrict women from taking menstruation leave. Examples of the ruthless efforts made by employers appeared consistently in the Diet's proceedings over the 1960s. Diet members who addressed this issue were not so much interested in discussing the disadvantages that women who requested leave time faced; rather, they saw it as a right acquired and thus one to be protected. Efforts to prevent women from fully exercising this benefit stimulated workers' efforts to protect their right to this leave. Women having to work under poor working conditions, and denied rest time when they needed it, were not always in a position to question the implementation of menstruation leave. The Japanese government, however, did not budge from its position that menstruation leave was to be made available only to those women in need of rest time during their periods. In 1960, when asked to comment on the fact that a decreasing number of women had been taking menstruation leave, Tanino Setsu, then Chief of the Women's and Minors' Bureau (*fujin shônen kyoku*), parroted the government line: It would be good if women better understood the intention of this leave time. Women should not take menstruation leave unless they absolutely required it.[51]

The government shifted its policy on menstruation leave in the late 1960s and early 1970s, after employers began to argue that women were "overprotected." From this time it viewed the leave as an important maternity protection measure.[52] A 1970 report presented by the Tokyo Board of Trade supported the employers' strong demand that women forfeit this protection if they desired gender equality in the workplace. This view provoked vigorous opposition in Diet sessions, with legislators insisting the provision's necessity to protect maternity. For this reason, the government vowed to make every effort to administratively facilitate women's right to take this leave, as it categorized the leave as "maternity protection."[53] A similar argument is found in a 1970 session. On this occasion, a female Diet member who had long supported the women's right to menstruation leave admitted that the leave would no longer be necessary should their working conditions improve. She immediately added, however, that Japan's substandard working conditions still made leave time necessary.[54]

The International Women's Year of 1975 and the United Nations Decade for Women that followed marked a significant turning point for Japanese government policy toward working women. In 1975 the government established a project team to promote women's issues (*fujin mondai kikaku suishin honbu*). This led to the creation of several other policy-making bodies. In 1978 the LSL study group (*rôdôkijunhô kenkyūkai*), a private advisory group, submitted their report, which declared the necessity to rethink protection to achieve gender equality in the workplace. Again, labor and members of the Diet criticized the Japanese government for supporting the employers' position. Legislators claimed that, to the contrary, sufficient protection was needed to achieve gender equality, without questioning the two different types of protection at issue: maternal protection and occupational health and safety protection. Some legislators insisted that the prohibition of night labor protected maternity. They presented data demonstrating the correlation between birth complications and night labor. Others cited data from the results of a study that showed the positive effect that taking this leave had on pregnancy, to demonstrate that menstruation leave protected maternity.[55]

In 1979, the United Nations adopted the Convention on the Elimination of All Forms of Discrimination against Women (CEDAW). The Japanese government immediately made the legislative adjustments required for its ratification. The Labor Ministry soon organized an experts' board for gender equality [*danjo byôdo mondai senmonka kaigi*], comprised of representatives from labor, management, and the public. After several studies the board agreed that first, Japan's prohibition on night labor should be repealed except in cases involving physically taxing labor, and second, that menstruation leave should in principle be abolished. It also admitted the need for further consideration on this second point. The Japanese government proposed its draft to amend the LSL based on these suggestions. It submitted this proposal, along with a bill for equal employment opportunities, to the Diet in 1984. The discussion on this legislation continued into 1985.

During these discussion sessions legislators reiterated arguments that had appeared in similar sessions over the last few decades: both provisions were required for maternity protection. At public hearings in 1985, a representative of women unionist members insisted that night labor had adverse effects on maternity and that menstruation leave offered women a significant therapeutic impact. One Diet member pointed out that it would be a greater setback for the government to establish standards in accordance with those of men, who worked much longer hours than women. Rather than abolishing it, the protection should be extended to men as well, to allow them a shorter working day and extra days off to compensate for their inability to take menstruation leave. A similar point offered that working hours for men be reduced, to realize gender equality. Actualizing these suggestions, however, was impractical at the time. Diet members, focusing on maternity protection, paid little attention to gender roles. The government admitted that equal labor standards needed to be introduced to achieve equality. However, it also believed that women required special consideration because of their particular "social role" in the home.[56]

In 1985 the Diet passed an amendment to the LSL and enacted the Equal Employment Opportunities Law for Men and Women [*danjo koyôkikai kintôhô*]. This influenced a rise in the number of women workers over the decade that followed, from 15.5 million to 20.5 million. Wage discrepancies, however, remained unchanged: women continued to be paid salaries 60 percent the level of those offered to men.[57] It soon became apparent that the legislation lacked the teeth necessary to reduce sex discrimination. In 1993 the Labor Ministry requested that the Council on Women's and Minors' Problems [*fujin shônen mondai singikai*] reconsider female protection, along with the Equal Employment Opportunities Law and other gender issues regarding childbearing and nursing. In its final report, submitted in 1996, this council concluded that LSL legislation that protected women alone should be abolished and that the exception from night labor should be offered to workers who were pregnant or nursing newborn infants. This bill reached the Diet floor in 1997.

Once again the discussion focused on the repeal of protective legislation for women. One session of the Labor Committee in the House of Representatives was attended by 700 women, who crowded into the gallery and demonstrated their opposition to repealing this protection. Legislators recycled arguments that had dominated previous sessions: night labor affected menstrual functions and complicated pregnancy. They further proposed that men also be afforded provisions of female protection. Once again, Diet members favoring the retention of protections insisted that night labor prohibition be considered as maternity protection. They refused to allow the legislation to limit its focus solely to women's biological maternal function. Rather, they seemed determined not to relinquish the labor protections that they had gained through their predecessors' struggles.

The government, on the other hand, insisted that the new legislation differentiated between the two types of protection and that it should not restrict the women's opportunity to work at night. Night labor, it argued, affected pregnancy only after conception, and thus the prohibition should only be applied to pregnant women. The government's position also stated that menstrual malfunctions, in which night labor was but one of a variety of factors, would not directly affect maternity. Based on its interpretation of standards established by the International Labor Organization, the government concluded that female prohibition on night labor was no longer required as a measure for maternity protection. The government, however, refused to rescind the provision on menstruation leave, as it believed that Japanese working conditions remained substandard. It has only been recently that the government has directed attention toward improving these conditions, as a benefit to both men and women, rather than simply focusing attention on protections available exclusively to women.[58] Despite strong opposition, the new labor law passed in 1998, and went into force from 1 April 1999.

Conclusion

SCAP intended to democratize Japan, and in this endeavor it attempted to spread an ideal of gender equality. This effort encouraged its opposition to menstruation leave, because such a provision contradicted its equal pay principle. By contrast, SCAP demanded the full enforcement of other protective, but discriminative, provisions for women workers, such as the ban on night labor. In this we note a major contradiction.

We might link its attempt to improve working conditions and advocate the prohibition of night labor to U.S. national interests. Helen Mears, a member of the SCAP Labor Advisory Committee, in 1942 pointed out the enormous importance of female labor, which comprised the vast majority of workers in all export industries. She explained:

> For not only did they hold down the general wage level; not only did they hold down the labor movement; but they [also] released the men

workers for heavy industry, for armaments, for the Army. Unconscious, unaware ..., these little girls were creating the "Modern Nation" Japan.[59]

During the occupation, Stander claimed that the exploitation of women had "too long been associated with Japan's industrial system." This exploitation, which had given rise to Japan's vigorous economic competitiveness throughout the world, arose from the militarism and autocracy that SCAP aimed to destroy. Stander emphasized that if Japan wanted to "take its place with the democratic nations of the world," it was "essential" to "revise its economic way of life and establish standards of employment which will no longer make Japan synonymous with 'sweat-shop' labor."[60]

Combined with this policy, SCAP supported the prohibition of night labor. This position may have seemed logical to SCAP, since American society at that time also advocated protective labor legislation applicable only to women. It should be noted, however, that American society was in transition at this time, as demonstrated by the case of WTUL, a key organization advocating women's labor protection. This organization expressed doubts regarding the necessity of continuing the prohibition. In addition, one other group of women also lobbied for a constitutional amendment guaranteeing gender equality, including a provision that made protective legislation applicable to all workers, both men and women. In their opposition to menstruation leave, SCAP staff members also claimed that equal protection should be given to both men and women. They nonetheless advocated the prohibition of night work. SCAP's policy was rooted in the idea, inherited from the so-called progressive era, that women needed protection because they were "weak" and "mothers."

For more than fifty years, the legacy of occupational reforms, embedded with SCAP's ideas, prevented the Japanese government from abolishing the prohibition of night labor as applied only to women. Diet members supported the protection so passionately that it took more than half a century to even start discussing its repeal. It took international pressure from the UN and the ILO to push the government to shift its policy and begin to reconsider the protective measures. The seeds of strong support for protection in postwar Japan were sown during the occupation. At the time when the prohibition of night labor was enforced, women railroad workers appealed unsuccessfully to SCAP for permission to work at night and to be exempted from the prohibition. Voices from women workers who questioned the protections were rarely heard afterwards, and the discourse for reconsidering the protection waned.

Compared to the prohibition of night labor, menstruation leave has yet to be seriously discussed. Debates in Diet sessions clearly show that menstruation leave is considered unnecessary if working conditions are improved. The government should have been aware that it needed to increase its efforts in this area rather than keeping menstruation leave, because SCAP had already warned of this situation during the occupation. A leaflet published by the Women's and Minors' Bureau also indicated that the leave would be unnecessary in the future. Although it is logical enough for the government to support a law once it is enacted, it should be remembered that the government explained menstruation leave's inclusion in the LSL in 1947 as necessary to compensate for Japan's poor working conditions in the immediate aftermath of the war. Although with reservations, SCAP accepted the leave on this basis. In light of the discussion in postwar Japanese Diet sessions, it is valuable to look back at SCAP's attitude toward menstruation leave. SCAP's suggestion that protection be given to both sexes and that menstruation leave eventually be abandoned remains worthy of note.

Notes

1 Two important examples are Susan J. Pharr, "A radical U.S. experiment: women's rights laws and the occupation of Japan," in L.H. Redford, ed., *The occupation of Japan: the impact of legal reform*, Norfolk: MacArthur Memorial, 1977; and Uemura Chikako, "Shūsen chokugo ni okeru fujin kaihō," ["Emancipation of women immediately after the end of war"] *Fujin kyoiku jyoho* 14, 1986, pp. 22–6.
2 Mire Koikari, "Gender, power, and politics in the US occupation of Japan, 1945–1952," Ph.D. dissertation, University of Wisconsin-Madison, 1997, pp. 40–1.
3 Gail Mieko Nomura, "The allied occupation of Japan: reform of Japanese government labor policy on women," Ph.D. dissertation, University of Hawaii, 1978, pp. 144–5.
4 Maho Toyoda, "Amerika senryoka no Nihon niokeru josei rōdō kaikaku," ["Protection or equality?: labor reform for/against women in the U.S. occupation of Japan"] *Amerikashi-kenkyu* [*Studies of American history*] 23, 2000, pp. 43–59.
5 Mutsuko Asakura, *Danjo koyō byōdō hōron* [*Studies on equal employment for both sexes*], Tokyo: Domesu Shuppan, 1991, p. 161; Ayako Oba, *Danjo koyo kikai kintō hō zenshi* [*Pre-history of law for equal employment opportunity of men and women*], Tokyo: Miraisha, 1988, pp. 125–57.
6 GHQ/SCAP, "History of the nonmilitary activities of the occupation of Japan, 1945–1951," pp. 73–7, GHQ/SCAP Records, the National Diet Library. The National Diet Library in Tokyo holds GHQ/SCAP Records on microform. This is a duplicate of RG331 in the National Archives.
7 ESS/LA, "Labor division monthly report," March 1946, GHQ/SCAP Records, Box no. 2015(4), Sheet no. LS-40814–15.
8 Matsumoto Iwakichi, *Rōdō kijunhō ga yoniderumade* [The process of making the Labor Standards Law], Tokyo: Romugyoseikenkyujo, 1981, pp. 34–42; Teramoto Kosaku, *Aru kanryō no shōgai* [Life of a governmental officer], private printing, 1976, p. 92; Watanabe Akira, ed., *Rōdō kijunhō* (1) [The Labor Standards Law], vol. 52, *Nihon rippō siryō zenshū* [The collection of Japanese lawmaking documents], Tokyo: Shinzansha, 1998, pp. 26, 175–8.
9 Helen Mears, "Factory inspection trip; Shikishima Boseki" [Spinning and weaving], Kusatsu, Shiga Ken, 10 May 1946, GHQ/SCAP Records, Box no. 8480(1), Sheet no. ESS(B)-16666–16671; Tanino Setsu, "Rōdō kijunhō no seiritsu nitsuite" ["On the birth of the Labor Standards Law"] (testimony), Kiyoko Nishi, ed., *Senryoka no nihon fujin seisaku* [The policies for Japanese women

under the occupation], Tokyo: Domesu Shuppan, 1985, pp. 137–9; Watanabe, ed., *Rōdō kijunhō* (1), pp. 72–4; Matsumoto, *Rōdō kijunhō ga yoniderumade*, pp. 57–61.

10 Watanabe, ed., *Rōdō kijunhō* (1), pp. 179–87; Watanabe, ed., *Rōdō kijunhō* (2), p. 192.

11 Matsumoto, *Rōdō kijunhō ga yoniderumade*, pp. 238–43; Tanino, "Rōdō kijunhō no seiritsu nitsuite," pp. 141–2.

12 "Conference with Mr. Teramoto," GHQ/SCAP Records, Box no. 8486(4), Sheet no. ESS(I)-01202–01210.

13 Ibid.

14 Theodore Cohen, *Remaking Japan: the American occupation as new deal*, New York: Free Press, 1987, p. 231.

15 Watanabe, ed., *Rōdō kijunhō* (2), pp. 37–65, 364–5; Leon Becker to Cohen, Chief, Labor Division, Collet, Costantino, Davis, and Stanchfield, "Draft of the Labor Standard Bill," 29 August 1946, GHQ/SCAP Records, Sheet no. ESS(I)-01205.

16 Watanabe, ed., *Rōdō kijunhō* (3), pp. 38, 381; Watanabe, ed., *Rōdō kijunhō* (2), p. 117; Matsumoto, *Rōdō kijunhō ga yoniderumade*, pp. 195–202.

17 "Summary of comments at public hearing of the Labor Standards Bill," n.d., GHQ/SCAP Records, ESS(I)-01204; Watanabe, ed., *Rōdō kijunhō* (2), pp. 549–601.

18 "Summary of comments"; Matsumoto, *Rōdō kijunhō ga yoniderumade*, p. 240; Watanabe, ed., *Rōdō kijunhō* (2), p. 591.

19 "Summary of comments"; Watanabe, ed., *Rōdō kijunhō* (3), p. 399; Watanabe, ed., *Rōdō kijunhō* (2), pp. 549–601; Matsumoto, *Rōdō kijunhō ga yoniderumade*, p. 240.

20 Cohen, *Remaking Japan*, p. 233.

21 Tanino, "Rōdō kijunhō no seiritsu nitsuite," p. 142; Matsumoto, *Rōdō kijunhō ga yoniderumade*, p. 242.

22 Watanabe, ed., *Rōdō kijunhō* (3), pp. 657–8.

23 Ibid., pp. 838–40; 852–3.

24 "Magazine Conference" – 12 August 1947, GHQ/SCAP Records, Box no. 5248, Sheet no. CIE(B)-01762–01766.

25 Mead Smith, "Labor standards for women and children in industry" 15 July 1947, GHQ/SCAP Records, Box no. 6321(25), Sheet no. ESS(B)-02378–02380, folder title: "Speeches, articles and press releases – general."

26 Golda G. Stander, "Problems of women in industry and child labor in Japan," 17 February 1947. Box no. 6321(25), Sheet no. ESS (B)-02378–02380; Kinue Sakurai, *Bosei hogo undōshi* [*History of the movement for maternity protections*], Tokyo: Domesu Shuppan, 1987, p. 94.

27 "Conference re preparation of ordinance implementing Article 67 of Labor Standards Law," GHQ/SCAP Records, Box no. 8495(8), Sheet no. ESS(H)-02486–02490.

28 Stander, "Special problems of concern to Women Teacher Trade Unionists," October 16, 1947, GHQ/SCAP Records, Box no. 6321(25), Sheet no. ESS(B)-02378–02380.

29 Ibid.

30 Draft of the leaflet, "Is menstruation leave necessary for working women?" June 1948, GHQ/SCAP Records, Box no. 8492, Sheet no. ESS(H)-02451–02460.

31 Ibid.

32 Ibid.

33 Ibid.

34 Alice Kessler-Harris, *Out to work: a history of wage-earning women in the United*

States, New York: Oxford University Press, 1982, pp. 183–9; Theda Skocpol, *Protecting soldiers and mothers: the political origins of social policy in the United States*, Cambridge: The Belknap Press of Harvard University Press, 1995, pp. 373–7; Susan Hartman, *The home front and beyond: American women in the 1940s*, Boston: G.K. Hall & Co., 1982, pp. 128–30; Susan Ware, *Holding their own: American women in the 1930s*, Boston: Morgan Press, 1982, p. 27.

35 "Informal talk by Miss Golda Stander," 18 July 1947, GHQ/SCAP Records, Box no. 8488, Sheet no. ESS(I)-01276.

36 Smith, "Labor standards for women and children in industry," 15 July 1947, GHQ/SCAP Records, Box no. 6321(25), Sheet no. ESS(B)-02378–02380.

37 Blanch Freedman, executive secretary, New York Women's Trade Union League to Ann Gannon, Labor Education Branch, Labor Division, Economic and Scientific Section, 5 December 1946, GHQ/SCAP Records, Box no. 8495(8), Sheet no. ESS(H)-02486–02490.

38 Kessler-Harris, *Out to work*, p. 194.

39 Sakurai, *Bosei hogo undōshi*, p. 72; Ayako Oba, *Fujin rodo* [Women's work], Tokyo: Akishobo, 1969, pp. 24–8.

40 Michiyo Marusawa, "Rodo kumiai fujinbu no tanjo to kaishoron" ["Birth of the women's section in a trade union and its dissolution"] (testimony), Nishi, ed., *Senryoka no nihon fujin seisaku*, pp. 161–3.

41 "Conference with representatives of women's section of railroad union," 25 August, 1947, GHQ/SCAP Records, Box no. 8495(8), Sheet no. ESS(H)-02486–02490.

42 Ibid.

43 Smith to Stander, "Conference 2 and 3 March 1948 re exceptions to night work prohibition," 8 March 1948; attachment, "The list of enterprises requiring the determination of interpretations or the exclusion of application of the enforcement of provisions which prohibit the employment of women," GHQ/SCAP Records, Box no. 8495(8), Sheet no. ESS(H)-02486–02490.

44 Ibid.

45 Ibid.

46 "Night work exceptions," 30 April 1948, GHQ/SCAP Records, Box no. 8495(8), Sheet no. ESS(H)-02486–02490.

47 Ibid.

48 Nomura, "The allied occupation of Japan," p. 129.

49 "Conference with representatives of women's section."

50 Rodosho, ed., *Shiryō rōdō undōshi, Shōwa 26 nenban* [Data on labor movement, 1951], 1952, pp. 366–72. For example, Labor Committee, Session no. 4, 6th House of Representatives, 1 December 1949; Labor Committee, Session no. 2, 12th House of Councilors, 2 November 1951; Plenary Session no. 46, 13th House of Representatives, 27 May 1952; Budget Committee, Session no. 26, 16th House of Councilors, 29 July 1953.

51 Social and Labor Committee, Session no. 6, 34th House of Representatives, 18 February 1960.

52 For example, Social and Labor Committee, Session no. 14, 51st House of Representatives, 29 March 1966; Social and Labor Committee, Session no. 6, 63rd House of Councilors, 9 November 1970.

53 Social and Labor Committee, Session no. 6, 64th House of Representatives, 17 December 1970.

54 Social and Labor Committee, Session no. 6, 63rd House of Councilors, 11 November 1970.

55 Budget Committee, Session no. 3, 85th House of Councilors, 9 October 1978; Budget Committee, Session 16, 87th House of Representatives, 21 February 1979; Budget Sub-committee 3, Session no. 3, 87th House of Representatives,

1 March 1979; Budget Sub-committee 5, Session no. 4, 87th House of Representatives, 2 March 1979.
56 Cabinet Committee, Session no. 10, 101st House of Representatives, 24 April 1984; Plenary Session no. 32, 101st House of Representatives, 24 June 1984; Social and Labor Committee, Session no. 32, 101st House of Representatives, 10 July 1984; Plenary Session no. 26, 101st House of Councilors, 1 August 1984; Plenary Session, 102nd House of Councilors, 10 May 1985; Social and Labor Committee Public Hearings, 102nd House of Councilors, 17 April 1985.
57 Ayano Yokoyama, *Sengo Nihon no josei seisaku* [Women's policy in postwar Japan], Tokyo: Keiso shobo, 2002, pp. 297–302.
58 For example, Labor Committee, Session no. 2, 140th House of Councilors, 25 February 1997; Plenary Session no. 31, 140th House of Representatives, 6 May 1997; Labor Committee, Session no. 14, 140th House of Councilors, 29 May 1997.
59 Mears, "Factory inspection trip," p. 289.
60 Stander, "Problems of women in industry."

4 The impact of the occupation on crime in Japan

H. Richard Friman

Prominent explanations of crime and crime control in Japan note the transition of the police away from the authoritarian structures of the 1930s and stress the impact of U.S. occupation policies as facilitating the transition towards democracy. Other explanations place greater emphasis on the recentralization of the police and the embedded aspects of social control that followed the occupation and were institutionalized in the 1954 revisions to the 1947 Police Law and the establishment of the National Police Agency.[1] In contrast, relatively little attention has been focused on the unintended legacy of occupation policies on crime and crime control in Japan.[2]

The widespread dislocation in post-war Japan has been well documented by scholars of the occupation. John Dower and Eiji Takemae observe that by late 1945 an estimated 2.7 million Japanese soldiers and civilians had died, 4.5 million servicemen were "wounded or ill," and 6.5 million soldiers and civilians were displaced abroad and returning to the main islands.[3] Japan's major cities were largely destroyed, with the inhabitants facing widespread conditions of homelessness, overcrowding, disease, and shortages of food, medicine and clothing. The occupation's initial focus on purges and reforms of Japan's primary political institutions relegated the issues of economic recovery and health and social welfare to low priority areas of indirect control. Supreme Commander for the Allied Powers (SCAP) directives authorized Japanese ministries to centralize industry and military supplies from wartime stockpiles, and to distribute non-military supplies to the local population.[4] However, diversion from wartime stockpiles and the centralization and distribution processes into the black market was rampant. Though enforcement efforts by occupation and Japanese authorities and gradual economic recovery would make progress against black markets by the early 1950s, occupation policies had already contributed to the emergence of several patterns in crime and crime control. In this chapter, I focus on patterns in drug control.

The illicit drug trade and Japan have a long history. During the first half of the twentieth century, Japan was a major drug source and trans-shipment country with a tightly controlled domestic market. More recently, Japan has been part of the global mass market for illicit drugs despite extensive domestic controls.[5] Though Japan's market for illicit drugs remains relatively limited by international standards, drug trafficking and abuse have posed major challenges to crime control. Since the late 1940s, methamphetamine has been the primary drug of choice in Japan and the centerpiece of yakuza-controlled domestic distribution networks, followed to a much lesser extent by other drugs such as heroin, cocaine, cannabis, and synthetics such as LSD and ecstasy. I argue that the origins of this postwar pattern were influenced by the U.S. occupation.

The occupation had the unintended effects of not only facilitating Japan's illicit drug trade but also institutionalizing selective state responses to organized and migrant crime. On the surface, this argument is paradoxical. Responding to widespread Japanese participation in the illicit drug trade into China during the 1920s and 1930s, occupation policies explicitly focused on drug control.[6] SCAP measures included the introduction of U.S. drug control laws, the creation of drug control agencies and training of drug control agents, direct drug enforcement efforts, and broader control measures aimed at pervasive black markets. By the late 1940s, SCAP authorities also were targeting organized criminal gangs of Japanese and foreigners. However, these efforts were incomplete at best and often inconsistent in policy as well as practice. Occupation drug control efforts focused on narcotics rather than the booming trade in stimulant drugs, and fragmented drug control between the police and narcotics officers under the Welfare Ministry. Police reform measures undercut campaigns against black markets while SCAP prioritization of control efforts focused more on food and other staples rather than drug control. The occupation's selective tolerance and cooperation with organized crime groups also facilitated ties between the police and Japanese crime groups, while reinforcing tensions between the police and foreign minorities.

This chapter explores the impact of the U.S. occupation on drug markets and drug control in Japan. The first section provides a brief overview of the transition from strict domestic control prior to World War II to the rise of the stimulant epidemic in occupation Japan. The second and third sections explore the origins and selective impact of occupation drug polices and enforcement practices. The fourth section addresses how occupation policies facilitated patterns of collaboration and exclusion between the police, organized crime groups (the *yakuza* or *bōryokudan*), and minority foreign population. The final sections briefly explore the legacy of the occupation on Japan and the impact of U.S. polices on drug markets and drug control in Germany.

From control to epidemic

Drug trafficking and abuse in Japan's home islands had been relatively limited prior to the occupation. That said, Japan was no stranger to the illicit drug trade. Prior to and during World War II, elements of the Japanese government and private industry had played significant roles in the illicit transshipment of manufactured narcotics from Europe and the United States into China, as well as in facilitating illicit exports of Japanese-produced manufactured narcotics and promoting and organizing large portions of the Chinese opium trade.[7] Japanese controls on transshipment and exports were lax at best. In contrast, the drug trade into the Japanese home islands, both in manufactured drugs and raw opium and coca, received greater attention from customs officials and prefectural police.[8] Japanese concerns with domestic drug abuse had long reflected fears of China's experience during the nineteenth-century opium trade.[9] Strict domestic drug control regulations on opium and manufactured narcotics initially contributed to holding domestic drug problems largely in check.[10] Domestic production and distribution of opium and manufactured narcotics were regulated through government licensing of farmers and the pharmaceutical industry.[11] The industry had expanded as part of an import substitution industrialization strategy intended to replace products that had been obtained from Germany prior to World War I.[12]

By the 1920s, concerns with rising domestic drug problems began to emerge in Japan. Early reports of drug abuse problems focused on Korean laborers, despite the fact that estimated opium addiction rates in this population were less than 1 percent.[13] In 1929, the head of Japan's League of Nations Association wrote to top government officials pointing to the risk of broader drug problems in Japan as stemming from increased domestic production by the Japanese pharmaceutical industry and the erosion of cultural constraints on drug use among Japanese youth.[14] In 1933, the Association for Relief of Narcotics Addicts, a private association backed by government funding, responded to these concerns by establishing a "narcotics treatment center" in Tokyo. Headed by H. Nagao, a "former Diet member and leading prohibitionist," the center emphasized voluntary treatment "through occupational therapy" and education and prevention.[15] Despite the treatment center, the number of Japanese addicts continued to increase, especially as individuals who had picked up the drug habit in China returned to the home islands.[16] By the late 1930s, constraints on available supply began to slow the rise. The Ministry of Welfare's Public Health Bureau became the primary institutional authority over domestic drug issues and domestic production was channeled into military stockpiles.[17] Tighter domestic and trade controls during the 1940s, as well as civilian shortages of pharmaceuticals, further limited access to supply and, in turn, the growth in the addict population.

As occupation authorities entered Japan in late 1945, they were concerned less with problems of Japanese addiction and more with preventing any resurgence of Japan's role in the illicit international drug trade. U.S. drug control authorities such as Harry Anslinger, director of the Federal Bureau of Narcotics, had long argued that Japan was engaged in the *narcotization* of China and responsible for drug trafficking into the United States during the 1930s and 1940s. Though based in the United States, Anslinger would play an important role in providing information to the International Military Tribunal for the Far East on these charges, and in shaping drug control in postwar Japan. William Walker notes that Anslinger "years later, termed this endeavor one of the major accomplishments of his tenure in office."[18] Anslinger worked with SCAP officials, including Wayland L. Speer in SCAP's Public Health and Welfare Section, to draft directives that would be incorporated into Japanese drug control legislation.[19] Reflecting U.S. concerns, these efforts focused on narcotics. Stimulant drugs received limited attention.

Directive SCAPIN 2 (September 1945) called on Japanese authorities to provide information concerning all stockpiles of drugs and medical supplies. By October 1945, however, occupation authorities focused explicitly on narcotics. Directives SCAPIN 98 (6 October 1945), SCAPIN 130 (October 12, 1945), and SCAPIN 229 (2 November 1945) required the "full itemization" of all stockpiles of narcotics and introduced prohibitions on the import, export, growth (opium) and manufacture of narcotic drugs.[20] Itemization would prove to be no easy task. Theodore Cohen observes that in mid-August 1945, the Japanese cabinet, fearing the pending U.S. confiscation of military supplies, issued a secret directive to "civilianize" military stockpiles. Directive 363 authorized the distribution of stockpiled goods, excluding arms and armaments, to "prefectural governments . . . public bodies . . . [and] private corporations." Manufactured goods already in the pipeline for delivery to the government were returned to factories and records of the transactions were destroyed. After two weeks, once Japanese authorities realized that the occupation would be working with the Home and Welfare Ministries to distribute military stockpiles to the Japanese people, the directive was rescinded and new orders were issued for the return of the supplies. Cohen estimates that 70 percent of military stockpiles were distributed during this two week period under Directive 363. Of these goods, an estimated 30 to 60 percent were returned for official distribution. The remainder would directly enter the black market.[21]

Cohen does not explicitly address the fate of pharmaceutical stockpiles under Directive 363. SCAP reports note the discovery in 1945 and 1946 of narcotic stockpiles "scattered throughout Japan" in military bases, hospitals, medical depots, private firms, and caves.[22] The *New York Times* (31 October 1945) reported one such discovery of opium and other narcotics in one warehouse "near Nagano" worth an estimated $6.0 million "at legal prices" and $50.0 million on the black market. The SCAP reports note an estimated 70 percent of narcotic drug and raw material stockpiles were "in the possession of military authorities," with the remainder in the hands of private firms. Given Directive 363, however, these figures likely overestimate the total quantity of narcotics that ended up under occupation control. As Takemae observes, "after the war, Japan's civilian and former military drug lords managed to conceal large stores of narcotics and later made fortunes from their covert sale."[23] SCAP authorities did seek to establish a "system of centralized control" for the materials they had discovered.[24] Authorities collected raw materials and semi-manufactured narcotics and placed them in storage depots in Yokohama and Kobe. There they would remain until new SCAP provisions in 1947 allowed for limited medical production.[25] Under the October 1945 provisions of SCAPIN 130, SCAP authorities also collected supplies of finished narcotics. These drugs were turned over to the Ministry of Welfare for storage, and eventual distribution to private firms for rationed public allocation.[26]

As argued by Takemae, the introduction of SCAPIN 98 in October 1945 also signaled the beginning of efforts by members of SCAP's Public Health and Welfare Section and the Ministry of Welfare to draft new drug control legislation for Japan.[27] SCAPIN directives shaped by Anslinger were incorporated into a new Narcotics Control Law introduced in July 1948. The law, comprised of six chapters and seventy-five articles, was patterned after the U.S. Harrison Narcotic Act passed in 1914, and focused on the manufacture, distribution and trade in narcotics.[28] In 1947, SCAP directives also ordered the introduction of cannabis control measures. Although Indian hemp had been regulated under Japanese narcotics laws prior to the occupation, domestic production of hemp fiber had been encouraged during the war by Japanese authorities.[29] In July 1948, the SCAP directives were incorporated into a new Marijuana Control Law. Patterned after the U.S. Marijuana Tax Act of 1939, the law introduced extensive licensing provisions for producers and researchers and banned the trade, sale, dispensing and possession of cannabis drugs.[30] Cannabis regulation and federal level criminalization had been a lower priority issue for Anslinger in the United States, compared to the issue of narcotics.[31] Control measures appeared to be introduced in Japan less to curtail potential Japanese participation in the international trade and more to address cultivation, consumption, and trade by U.S. forces stationed in Japan.[32]

In contrast to the SCAP focus on narcotics, the growing Japanese problem with trafficking and abuse of methamphetamine received little attention. The history of the discovery of methamphetamine and its precursors reveals several Japanese connections. Working with samples of the plant *ma hung*, a type of *Ephedra*, in 1885, Nagai Nagoyoshi, an influential chemist at the University of Tokyo, was the first to isolate and synthesize the alkaloid ephedrine. Nagai had spent thirteen years in Germany working with leading chemists and publishing in Berlin before returning to Japan in 1883. Nagai's conclusions that ephedrine was a possible alternative to adrenaline in treating asthma attracted the attention of the German pharmaceutical company E. Merck: natural derivatives had been a source of growth for the company. Two decades earlier, Merck had begun the first commercial production of the coca derivative cocaine hydrochloride. Although Merck scientists replicated Nagai's experiments, the company concluded that there was little market potential for the drug at the time.[33] Ephedrine as derived from *ma huang* was rediscovered during the early 1920s, this time by two Americans, K.K. Chen and Frederick Schmidt, working at the Peking Union Medical College. Published findings by Chen and Schmidt on the sources and effective uses of ephedrine as an asthma treatment led to increased interest and production of the drug by companies including Merck.[34]

Fearing shortages of ephedrine in the face of growing demand, researchers during the 1920s also had turned to efforts at developing synthetic forms of the drug. These efforts led to the discovery of two other compounds with stimulant qualities – amphetamine and methamphetamine. Amphetamine ("phenylisopropylamine, later called dextroamphetamine") was discovered by a U.S. researcher, Gordon Allis, in 1929. Methamphetamine (d-phenyl-isoproplymethylamine hydrochloride) was discovered in 1919 by a Japanese chemist noted in the literature as A. Ogata.[35] During the 1930s, Ogata licensed his production process to the British-based Burroughs Wellcome and Company.[36] Capable of being produced from natural or synthetic ephedrine, as well as other ephedra alkaloids such as pseudo ephedrine, methamphetamine was initially used as a drug for psychiatric treatment in Europe. Medical usage of methamphetamine began in Germany in 1938 and in the United Kingdom in 1940. By 1940, interest in medical use of methamphetamine for the treatment of "mental disorder, narcolepsy and weight reduction" also had spread to Japan.[37]

Japanese government interest in ephedrine and methamphetamine was more extensive than that of the medical community and focused more on the drugs' stimulant effects. During the late 1930s, the Japanese military "produced" and "sanctioned" the use of ephedrine among military forces engaged in the Sino-Japanese War.[38] By the mid-1940s, all branches of the Japanese military as well as factory and construction industries had turned to ephedrine and the more powerful methamphetamine to enhance the performance of military personnel and industrial workers.[39] Though the government contracted production of the drug from the Japanese pharmaceutical industry, the relative production and consumption patterns for the two drugs during the 1940s are difficult to determine. Scholars have noted the terms *Philopon* (interpreted by one scholar as meaning "love of work") and "*Senryoku Zōkyō Kai* (drug to inspire the fighting spirit)" to inconsistently describe one or both drugs in their oral or injected forms.[40]

It is important to note that the use of stimulant drugs during the war was not limited to Japan. American armed forces used amphetamines, though sources differ on the extent to which the drugs were "formal military issue."[41] However, production and usage in Japan during the war was more widespread, leading to large military stockpiles of ephedrine and methamphetamine, and consumption habits introduced to a large portion of the population. As military stockpiles of narcotics were dispersed under Directive 363 and later under broad SCAP-sanctioned rationing systems, so too were stimulant drugs. Industry stockpiles of methamphetamine that had been contracted by the imperial government also directly entered the market. Companies "advertised aggressively," marketing the drugs as ways to "shake off sleepiness and become energetic" and used trade names including Hiropon, and Hylopon, evoking the wartime brand identification.[42]

Combined with postwar dislocation, these dynamics helped to create Japan's first domestic drug-abuse epidemic. Stimulant consumption spread from urban into rural areas, and from workers and students to farmers, rapidly outstripping the wartime stockpile.[43] Masayuki Tamura observes that the first recorded case of hospitalization for stimulant addiction in Japan occurred in September 1946. By 1954, the epidemic had peaked at approximately 200,000 stimulant addicts, over 550,000 "chronic users" and an estimated 2 million former users, roughly 3.8 percent of the country's population.[44] In contrast, the total number of reported narcotics addicts from the entire period of 1946 to 1954 was 8,003 persons.[45] More important from the standpoint of this chapter, SCAP paid little attention to the problem.

Law and omission

As part of a series of SCAP directives aimed at demilitarizing and reorganizing the Japanese healthcare system, Japanese authorities introduced legislative steps in 1948 establishing standards for medical practices. As noted, SCAP's Public Health and Welfare Section had played an instrumental role in the introduction of the Narcotics Control Law in June 1948. However, the growing problem of stimulant abuse did not appear to be a SCAP priority. In July, Japanese authorities introduced a series of laws under SCAP auspices focused more on establishing standards and procedural norms for institutions including medical schools, hospitals, clinics, and pharmacies.[46] The Pharmaceutical Affairs Law (Drug, Cosmetics and Medical Instrument Law) passed on 29 July did include limited control measures for stimulants, but as part of broader requirements that pharmacies require signatures from purchasers of "dangerous" drugs. Faced with rising incidents of stimulant psychosis, the Ministry of Welfare introduced additional measures. In August 1949, the ministry introduced an ordinance banning "production of stimulants in tablet or powder form," but the ordinance did not address the production of stimulants in liquid form. The omission was glaring, given that military production and stockpiles of ephedrine and methamphetamine, as well as postwar commercial production and consumption of methamphetamine, consisted primarily of vials of liquid solution taken orally, or by injection for greater effect.[47] Two months later, the ministry "gave a warning to the principal pharmaceutical companies to suspend" all forms of stimulant production, and followed this warning with a formal ordinance to this effect in 1950.[48]

Unlike the case of narcotics, however, the distribution, possession, import and use of stimulant drugs were not criminalized until the waning days of the occupation. The official warnings and selective prohibitions in the face of growing demand for methamphetamine increased illegal production by pharmaceutical companies and "clandestine" laboratories. The 1951 Stimulant Control Law finally criminalized the stimulant trade, but with penalties less extensive than those for violation of the 1948 Narcotics Control Law. Maximum penalties for stimulant offenses were three years' imprisonment, while maximum penalties for narcotics offenses were five years' imprisonment and a ¥50,000 ($175) fine.[49] As discussed below, law enforcement resources also were targeted more at narcotics control. The combination of increased criminalization, selective enforcement, and booming demand accelerated illegal production of methamphetamine and facilitated the rise of organized crime groups. In the immediate aftermath of the occupation, Japanese authorities shifted the focus of control efforts from narcotics to stimulants. In addition to enhanced enforcement efforts, the Stimulant Control Law was amended in 1954 and 1955 with the inclusion of stiffer penalties, compulsory hospitalization in mental hospitals for stimulant addicts, and controls on the importation of ephedrine and other precursors.[50]

SCAP historical monographs on the occupation's non-military activities in Japan offer extensive detail on the issue of narcotics control but make no mention of the problem of stimulant drugs.[51] Henry Brill and Tetsuya Hirose observe that by the late 1940s there had been little research on methamphetamine, or amphetamine, addiction and psychoses and thus "it was not surprising that the Japanese did not consider methamphetamine a hazard in 1945 when the stores were released."[52] This argument is not only flawed but fails to explain why the Japanese authorities did not take more extensive steps as problems with stimulant abuse became readily apparent. The answer lies in the impact of the occupation on Japanese drug control, and the resistance of Anslinger and, in turn, SCAP authorities to extending drug control efforts beyond narcotics and marijuana.

Stimulant abuse was a growing but low-priority area of concern in the United States by the late 1940s. Amphetamine-based nasal inhalers (e.g. initially sold under the trade name Benzedrine) had emerged as an area of concern in the mid-1930s. Research on the physiological effects of amphetamine use and national media stories warning of the risks had already begun to emerge in the United States, albeit with little impact on consumption. Amphetamine inhalers were not covered by the 1906 Pure Food and Drug Act as amended in 1938, and continued to be available without prescription, despite warnings by the American Medical Association, until 1959.[53] Other forms of amphetamine were only partially covered by prescription regulations, and the regulations were not well enforced. Regulations on methamphetamine prescriptions, sold primarily in tablet form (Methedrine), were not tightened until the mid-1960s. As abuse problems increased, and in the face of a political maneuvering over a broader international drug control movement, the United States criminalized the non-prescription trade in amphetamine and methamphetamine in 1970 under the U.S. Drug Abuse and Control Act.[54]

As director of the Federal Bureau of Narcotics, Anslinger had a major impact on retarding the initial movement toward stimulant controls in the United States and, in turn, the position of occupation authorities on stimulant control in Japan. Scholars of drug control observe that Anslinger vehemently opposed efforts at home and internationally to expand the drug control regime beyond narcotics. David Musto writes that "Anslinger 'put sandbags up against the door' whenever anyone suggested that the Federal Bureau of Narcotics police barbiturates and amphetamines." Anslinger viewed the extension of the drug war as "bureaucratic suicide for an enforcement agency with a small budget and staff." Anslinger also sought to facilitate narcotics control by working with federal and local judges, and viewed an extension of the drug war to the large numbers of "ordinary citizen" users of barbiturates and amphetamines as likely to lead to judicial backlash.[55] Philip Jenkins points out that Anslinger also sought to facilitate narcotics control by maintaining good relations with leading U.S. pharmaceutical companies. These companies happened to have a large stake in the manufacture of stimulant drugs.[56] By the early 1950s, the U.S. manufacturer Merck and Company, a former affiliate of the German parent company, was the sole U.S. producer of ephedrine hydrochloride, exporting 80 kilograms in 1952 to East Asia alone. By the late 1950s, U.S. manufacturers also were producing 3.5 billion amphetamine tablets per year.[57]

During the early 1950s, Anslinger increasingly acknowledged that the consumption and abuse of amphetamines, and especially barbiturates, were emerging as problems in the United States, but he continued to stress that the Federal Bureau of Narcotics needed to focus instead on "really dangerous drugs."[58] Individual states could take action but the federal government should not. Testifying before Congress in 1951, Anslinger argued that the problems surrounding federal steps to control the barbiturate trade would be "worse than [alcohol] prohibition." Control efforts would be hampered by the lack of necessary resources, the absence of public support, and widespread domestic production.[59] In 1955, Anslinger reiterated these arguments in congressional hearings on federal controls on barbiturates and amphetamines. Anslinger supported his opposition to controls by noting that the United Nations Commission on Narcotics Drugs, on which he served, had "never considered this on an international level ... because of the fact that there is no international problem or no international trafficking."[60]

The statement was flawed on several counts. As early as 1949, the World

Health Organization Expert Committee on Habit-Forming Drugs had noted the rising problem of stimulant abuse. The United Nations Commission on Narcotic Drugs also first discussed the issue of stimulant abuse in 1955.[61] More important, none of Anslinger's testimony, or that by any other expert, in the 1951 and 1955 hearings mentioned that Japan was in the midst of a stimulant abuse and trafficking epidemic. Though Anslinger was well aware of drug conditions in Japan, the stimulant epidemic "had not been widely publicized in the United States."[62] Anslinger's only discussion of Japan before Congress in 1955 was to testify that narcotics trafficking from the People's Republic of China was leading to a postwar rise in Japanese heroin addiction.[63] As Kato observes, the total number of narcotics addicts in Japan did increase during the early 1950s, from 659 addicts in 1953 to 999 addicts in 1954.[64] However, these figures paled in comparison to the country's stimulant addiction problems.

Enforcement and omission

Scholarship on the police in occupied Japan reveals that the country's law-enforcement resources were no match for the general proliferation of black markets and organized crime groups during the late 1940s. Purges and reorganization of the police had left the country with a decentralized, inexperienced, and minimally armed force. SCAP pressures for crackdowns against black markets in the late 1940s focused resources on curtailing illicit trade in food and raw materials. The police arrested millions of "ordinary Japanese" for black market violations, 1.5 million in 1948 alone.[65] In this context, law enforcement resources dedicated to the rising stimulant problem were limited at best.

Democratization was a primary initial goal of the occupation, and as David Bayley notes, the remaking of the police was one of the occupation's "demonstration projects."[66] Occupation authorities faced the difficult task of reforming the centralized "police state" while relying on the police as the primary institution to maintain "internal order."[67] As an initial step, SCAPIN Directives, including Numbers 93 (October 1945) and 550 (January 1946), disbanded the Military Police (*Kenpei*) and the civilian Special Higher Police (*Tokkō*) and turned to broader purges of "militarists and ultranationalists" from the police ranks.[68] The *Tokkō* legacy of suppressing political and social opposition was seen as a primary impediment to democratization, especially by SCAP's Government Section under Brigadier General Courtney Whitney. SCAP purges focused on *Tokkō* members and supporters, removing 96 percent of the country's prefectural police chiefs, 11 to 15 percent of all police inspectors, assistant inspectors, and sergeants, and 3.2 percent of patrolmen. Christopher Aldous observes that though "less than six percent of the total police force" the focus on senior leadership levels meant that "the effects of the purge were disproportionate to its size."[69]

The ability of the police to facilitate order was a primary concern of other SCAP offices, including the General Staff Section G-2 (Intelligence) under Major General Charles A. Willaughby, and the Public Safety Division under Colonel Howard E. Pulliam, as well as the concern of the Japanese government. In late 1945, SCAP had authorized the creation of a new civilian police force of almost 94,000 personnel, rejecting Japanese government requests for a larger and better-equipped force. Voluntary departures, illness, and purges resulted in a force by 1946 optimistically estimated at 88,000, and pessimistically by Pulliam at closer to 66,000. The new force lacked experience and equipment. Aldous writes that by August 1946, "75 percent of the force had less than one year's experience."[70] The police also lacked firepower, especially relative to emerging crime threats.

SCAP directives in 1945 had called for the government to "collect, record and dispose of all military stores and armaments, including ammunition and small arms." The police participated in this process even though the Instrument of Surrender, signed in September 1945, had explicitly exempted the "general police forces" from disarming. There were exceptions. By late 1945 occupation authorities were still discovering unreported stockpiles of rifles, machine guns, and ammunition in police stations. By early 1946, SCAP officials had clarified the requirements and explicitly authorized the police to carry small arms. Two years later, SCAP had yet to provide the requisite supplies of pistols and ammunition. By late 1948, SCAP had allocated only 18,000 pistols, resulting in a police force armed primarily with wooden batons.[71]

Under the Police Law of 1947, the force was expanded on paper to over 125,000 authorized personnel but, in a move opposed by Willaughby and Pulliam, decentralized into a system of independent metropolitan and rural police. Metropolitan areas with populations greater than 5000 were required to establish Local Municipal Police forces. Locally financed and administered by independent prefectural public safety commissions, these forces in total were limited to 95,000 personnel. In contrast, towns and rural areas with populations less than 5000 became the responsibility of the new 30,000-member National Rural Police force, administered at the prefectural level but under a National Public Safety Commission.[72] Problems with coordination, financing, and staffing and equipment shortages plagued the new structure from its introduction in 1948, leading to initial steps towards recentralization in 1951 and more extensive reforms in the new Police Law of 1954.[73]

Occupation authorities largely bypassed the police as the central agency for coordinating the enforcement of drug control laws and ordinances.[74] In January 1946, under SCAPIN 644, authorities turned to a reorganized Ministry of Welfare to coordinate distribution of wartime stockpiles of medical supplies, including narcotics.[75] The ministry's role was expanded further in April 1947. SCAP reorganized the ministry by elevating its Narcotics Division to the Section level and expanding the new section's administrative and support personnel. The new section was empowered to serve as the "central agency" for implementing measures to control the licit distribution of medicinal narcotics and to suppress the illicit trafficking in narcotics and other dangerous drugs.[76] The Narcotics Section was initially authorized to deploy no more than 200 Narcotics Control Officers (*mayaku tōseishuji*), assigning between two and twenty officers per prefecture to "supervise and investigate narcotics control."[77] Of these control officers, a portion were to be designated as Narcotic Agents (*mayaku torishimariin*). In September 1947, five months after the reorganization, Diet Law Number 112 granted narcotic agents "judicial powers of arrest for narcotic violations."[78]

SCAP's Public Health and Welfare Narcotic Section played an instrumental role in the Ministry of Welfare Narcotic Section's focus on narcotics enforcement. Beginning in March 1948, SCAP established a series of narcotics control schools in Tokyo, to train the personnel of the Narcotics Section as well as those agencies that would be under the section's supervision. Instruction focused on "methods of investigation of criminal cases concerned with narcotics."[79] In addition, SCAP authorities were able to provide "personal instruction" to the agencies "under the [Section's] direction" including the police.[80] The focus of this instruction was on narcotics. The July 1948 Narcotics Control Law and Marijuana Control Law, and the December 1948 Partial Amendment of the Narcotics Control Law, reinforced the central role of the Ministry of Welfare and its narcotics agents. The Partial Amendment increased the total number of narcotics officers to 250.[81] The Narcotics Law superceded Law Number 112 and authorized narcotics agents to engage in control measures against narcotics, marijuana, and, under Japan's Criminal Code, Chapter 14, prepared opium.[82] More important, for the first time the law also granted narcotic agents the authority to carry firearms.[83]

In practice, by December 1948, the Ministry of Welfare Narcotics Section's staff of thirteen officials and ten clerks had oversight responsibility for 151 narcotics agents, 377 administrative officials, and 137 clerks. These resources were limited, especially given the task of monitoring 88,300 registered narcotics dealers, ranging from manufacturers to retailers, let alone curtailing the illicit trade.[84] The ability of narcotics agents to obtain the firearms they were authorized to carry, in light of the shortages faced by the police, also is uncertain. Through the 1940s, narcotics agents, by statute and by training, were focusing on narcotics, marijuana, and opium rather than stimulants. This SCAP emphasis on narcotics carried over into training of police at the local municipal and rural levels. In 1947, Japanese authorities arrested and prosecuted 692 persons for narcotics offenses, primarily involving "internal traffic" in medicinal opium, heroin, morphine, cocaine, and codeine. In 1948, the number arrested increased to 1070 persons and in 1949 to 2152 persons.[85]

As concern at stimulant abuse began to increase during the late 1940s, however, Japanese authorities began to shift resources away from narcotics and towards the regulation of the stimulant trade. In the context of strong demand for stimulant drugs, the stimulant regulations of 1947–1949, although limited, had prompted an increase in illicit production and trade by pharmaceutical companies as well as clandestine pharmaceutical producers and distributors. In 1950, 2917 persons were arrested for violations of the pharmaceutical law's signature provisions and ministerial ordinances regulating stimulant production.[86] The 1951 Stimulant Control Law, and its wider criminalization provisions, prompted a new wave of enforcement efforts and a staggering increase in arrests. In 1951, 17,528 persons were arrested for stimulant control violations compared to 2232 persons arrested for violations of narcotics, opium, and cannabis control laws combined. Stimulant seizures in 1951 alone consisted of "4.6 million vials of injectable liquids, 8000 tablets and 77 kilograms of stimulant powder."[87] As enforcement efforts increased, arrests for stimulant law violations surged to over 38,000 in 1953 and peaked at 55,664 in 1954. By comparison, annual arrests through the 1950s for narcotics, opium, and marijuana violations combined fluctuated between only 1400 and 2162 persons.[88]

Collaboration and exclusion

The combination of strong demand for stimulants, the gradual criminalization of stimulant production and trade, and the limited resources for enforcement of this criminalization created incentives for organized crime groups to enter the trade. Occupation policies did little to alter these incentives. In addition to the impact of police reforms discussed above, occupation policies dealing with organized crime were limited in general and inconsistent in practice. Cutting across these issues, Japan's minority population of Korean and Chinese emerged as a focal point of collaboration and exclusion between occupation authorities, the police, organized crime, and the newly liberated minorities themselves.

SCAP officially discovered organized crime in Japan in May 1947, with the Public Safety Division's report on the challenges posed by the *oyabun-kobun* system of "bosses and henchmen." The report broadly classified crime groups by their primary activities, noting the threats posed by gambling syndicates (*kashimoto* or *bakuto*), street stall associations (*tekiya*), and more modern and violent gangster groups (*gurentai*).[89] SCAP committees and crackdowns on organized crime groups beginning in September 1947 focused on disrupting large-scale black market operations with little sense of the accommodations that had emerged between these groups and the police during the war and the early years of the occupation. As a result, the impact of the crackdowns was undercut by the reluctance of police, public safety commissions, and prosecutors to take action against organized crime groups. SCAP control efforts were undermined further by collaborative linkages between organized crime and members of SCAP's GS-2 section aimed at curtailing the rise of the Japanese left, as well as broader linkages between occupation reconstruction efforts and gang-affiliated labor contractors.[90]

In this context, organized crime syndicates, integrating groups with *bakuto*, *tekiya*, and *gurentai* operations, began to consolidate during the occupation. In the mid-1940s, for example, the Yamaguchi-gumi was one of many small crime groups operating in the Kobe waterfront district. By the early 1950s, the gang had moved into gambling, protection, and drug markets in Kobe and neighboring Osaka, relying on a combination of strict hierarchical control, gang wars, and incorporation of defeated opponents. By the 1960s, the Yamaguchi-gumi was well on its way to becoming the most powerful crime syndicate in Japan, with over 340 affiliated gangs, 10,000 members, and an operational reach throughout the country. In the Tokyo/Yokohama area during the 1940s and 1950s a similar pattern of consolidation was taking place leading to what would become the major rival syndicates to the Yamaguchi-gumi, the Sumiyoshi-kai and Inagawa-kai. The stimulant trade offered crime syndicates an increasingly lucrative source of income, especially as economic recovery began to erode the role of black markets in meeting demand for food and consumer goods.[91]

Japanese crime groups by 1950 faced competition in illicit stimulant production and distribution from groups of displaced Koreans and Chinese, mainland and especially Formosan. Derogatively referred to as *sangokujin* (third country people), these groups became a central piece in the integration dynamics of organized crime syndicates. Japanese labor recruiting during the early 1900s and conscription and forced migration during the 1930s and 1940s had resulted in over two million Koreans and over 40,000 Chinese in Japan by 1945. Repatriation programs under the occupation eventually reduced these numbers to an estimated 530,000 to 620,000 Koreans, 10,000 to 17,000 Formosans, and 18,000 to 22,000 mainland Chinese.[92] The legal status of the remaining foreign population, in terms of nationality and legal protections and jurisdictions, was confusing at best. SCAP authorities introduced and then removed protections as U.S. concerns increased over what were seen as challenges posed to the occupation by an increasingly vocal and organized Korean minority.[93] Initially designated as "liberated peoples" in November 1945, Koreans by 1946 had become the target of SCAP directives authorizing increased surveillance, police crackdowns, and Japanese rather than occupation criminal jurisdiction. In contrast, Formosans and mainland Chinese retained their status as UN nationals and thus "were removed from Japanese criminal jurisdiction" through the 1940s. By the early 1950s, under amended Alien Registration Laws, strict Japanese nationality laws, and the Peace Treaty with the United States, Chinese as well as Koreans lost extraterritorial protections and became permanent foreign resident aliens.[94]

Facing large-scale unemployment due to economic dislocation and discrimination, groups of Koreans and Chinese turned to the black market, where they soon clashed with Japanese rivals. In 1946, roughly 30 percent of the "open air merchants" selling black market goods in Osaka were non-Japanese.[95] During the late 1940s, these merchants and their distribution networks were incorporated into syndicates of Japanese criminal groups consolidating in the Kobe–Osaka area. The Yamaguchi-gumi, having established its dominance in Kobe, extended its reach into Osaka, defeating and incorporating the operations of rival gangs including the Meiyu-kai, a leading Korean gang. But it was in the Tokyo–Yokohama area where the greatest clashes between foreign and Japanese groups took place. In Yokohama, a turning point in the rise of the Inagawa-kai crime syndicate lies in the late 1940s turf wars that displaced rival Korean and Chinese gangs from the area. Inagawa Kakuji's initially small gang, the Kokusai-kai, waged a more "ruthless" war against its foreign rivals for control of black markets rather than following the incorporation strategies of the Yamaguchi-gumi. By the 1960s, the Kokusai-kai had moved beyond Yokohama to become one of the major gangs vying for control over Tokyo.[96]

Opportunities in the Tokyo market gave rise to numerous challengers. In the proliferating open-air markets, gangs vied for control over lucrative *tekiya* networks. Chinese and Korean gangs fought with Japanese rivals in violent clashes over control of the black markets in the Shibuya, Shinjuku, Shimbashi, and Ginza areas. These clashes would facilitate the consolidation of black market networks in the early years of the occupation, coordinated by crime bosses including Ozu Kinosuke and Matsuda-gumi founder Matsuda Giichi.[97] By the late 1940s, black markets and entertainment operations in the lucrative Ginza district increasingly came under the control of Machii Hisayuki (Cheong Geong Yong), and his "largely [South] Korean" Tôsei-kai. By the early 1950s, the Tôsei-kai was dominating the Tokyo methamphetamine trade and by the 1960s had established a working relationship and "blood brother" ties with the leadership of the Yamaguchi-gumi.[98]

Much as in the case of Japanese crime groups, foreign participation in the methamphetamine trade was facilitated initially by access to supplies diverted from military and industrial stockpiles. Prior to 1946, diverted supplies of ephedrine and methamphetamine were obtained from American servicemen as well as Korean and Chinese middlemen contracted by SCAP to disburse pharmaceutical supplies.[99] As noted above, illicit production of stimulants began in earnest soon after this practice was banned in 1950. Ephedrine hydrochloride in powder form provided the base for production of injectable methamphetamine solutions as well as methamphetamine powder. According to Richard Deverall, one kilogram of ephedrine power could be used to produce 200,000 ampoules of injectable methamphetamine solution.[100] Unregulated by SCAP, stockpiles of ephedrine hydrochloride had been turned over to the Ministry of Welfare and allocated to pharmaceutical producers and distributors. Beginning in 1946, SCAP also allowed the Ministry of Welfare to selectively import raw materials and medicines to fill production gaps.[101] By the early 1950s, the United States was a primary licit source of imported ephedrine hydrochloride, with Merck and Company exporting 49.5 kilograms to Japan in 1952 alone. The importation of ephedrine would not be prohibited until the 1955 amendment to the Stimulant Control Act was passed. Illicit trade in ephedrine took place as well, routed into Japan primarily through the British colonies of Hong Kong and Macau, though allegations by the mid-1950s posited the role of direct shipments from the People's Republic of China.[102]

In this context, clashes between crime groups for control of the docks of the Kobe/Osaka and Tokyo/Yokohama areas shaped access to the licit and illicit import of ephedrine. Control over open-air markets also shaped access to domestic supplies of raw materials and distribution networks for finished products. The actual control of the stimulant trade by Japanese relative to *sangokujin* is difficult to determine accurately. Given the SCAP focus on narcotics, available statistics on stimulant offenses are limited at best.[103] The crackdown following the 1954 amendment to the Stimulant Control Law offers the most detail, but the potential for bias in enforcement patterns requires that arrest patterns be viewed with caution. In October 1954, the police made 5974 arrests for stimulant offenses: 27.9 percent for sale or purchase and 46.4 percent for possession. A total of 223 persons were arrested for stimulant production. Of these, Deverall, citing Metropolitan Police Board figures reported in the Japanese press, notes that 101 persons were Japanese while 122 were Korean.[104] Koreans and Chinese also were stimulant users, and thus a portion of the lucrative market, but here again accurate figures are difficult to obtain.[105]

From the standpoint of the inexperienced and poorly equipped Japanese police, both foreigners and foreign crime groups were a threat to social order. The relationship between the police and Japan's foreign minority populations had always been tenuous at best. Well prior to the occupation, the police were instrumental in perpetuating a broad pattern of anti-foreign distrust and stereotyping. Koreans were portrayed as the crime-prone "enemy within" and police helped to incite anti-Korean riots in the aftermath of the Great Kanto Earthquake.[106] Chinese laborers in Japan were viewed with suspicion as well.[107] In the waning months of the war, strikes and violent revolts by conscripted Korean and Chinese laborers in Japan's coal mines resulted in brutal police and militia crackdowns. The incidents increased the sense of the threat posed by foreigners.[108] SCAP liberalization of Koreans and Chinese, and the initial exclusion of these groups from the authority of Japanese police and courts, increased this sense even further.

The police were ill equipped to respond to tensions partially of their own making. Individual acts of retribution against Japanese, public protests by large groups of *sangokujin*, and their expansion into black markets led the police to look to organized crime groups for support. In the Shibuya Incident of 1946, for example, a fight between "hundreds of Formosan venders and over a thousand Matsuda-gumi toughs" ended up in a gun battle in front of the Shibuya police station.[109] In Kobe, the mayor even directly appealed to the Yamaguchi-gumi for assistance to remove 300 *sangokujin* occupying a police station, a request that established "a long term debt of duty."[110]

The accommodations between the police and the *yakuza* that emerged during the occupation selectively tolerated organized criminal activity as a means to achieve broader social order.[111] Accommodations had taken place during the early 1900s, as the *yakuza* joined forces with the police against left-wing labor and political movements. By the late 1930s and war in China, accommodation had eroded, resulting in prison for those gang members who did not enter the military or, in the case of *tekiya*, groups that did not work with the police to regulate distribution of increasingly scarce supplies.[112] Police reliance on associations such as the Street Stall Tradesmen's Union (*Roten Dōgyō Kumiai*) in Tokyo, beginning in 1943, would carry over into the occupation, but with the relative power of the police and gangs reversed. Led by *tekiya*-boss Ozu Kinosuke, the union expanded its control of Tokyo's open air markets in 1945 and 1946, vying with foreign as well as Japanese competitors to organize an estimated 45,000 stalls by 1947. Ozu's organization served as an "administrative authority" as well as a social safety net for "demobilized soldiers and repatriates" and a source of additional income for the beleaguered police.[113] As Ozu became the target of the SCAP crackdown against the *oyabun-kobun* threat in 1947, his organization's influence beyond the Shinjuku-Shimbashi area waned and other crime groups such as the Tosei-kai and Sumiyoshi-kai emerged to fill the gap.[114]

Minoru Shikata and Shinichi Tsuchiya point to the dramatic decline in arrests of gang members for penal code offenses – from over 30,000 in 1946 and 1947, to 12,110 in 1948 and fewer than 2500 by 1951 – as evidence of the success of police crackdowns against Japanese organized crime during the occupation.[115] However, this interpretation is misleading. The police did intensify crackdowns against black market operations under occupation pressure in 1947 by increasing raids and sweeps of train stations and open air markets.[116] That said, the efforts were far from successful. The police tended to focus on small rather than large-scale operations. They engaged in "active and passive" interference with investigations, at times facing interference from local Public Safety Commissions.[117] Alfred Oppler, Chief of the Courts and Law Division of SCAP's Government Services Section, observes that personnel and resource problems with Japan's criminal justice system often led to those arrested being released on bail, their trials delayed, and only occasional prosecution for minor offenses.[118] Robert Whiting points out that even with these constraints "fully half of the known 50,000 underworld figures in the country were arrested" in the SCAP crackdowns in late 1947. But, as Whiting observes further, "only two percent wound up doing any time." He cites the case of Ozu as an example: though arrested and convicted, the *tekiya* leader was released for health reasons and behavior that, in the eyes of police, prosecutors, and judges alike, had demonstrated "high moral character."[119] David Kaplan and Alec Dubro also observe that although Tôsai-kai leader Machii was arrested "ten times" between 1946 and 1958, he only "received three sentences [and] . . . served very little time."[120]

Accommodations between the police and Japanese organized crime during the occupation partially reflected the increasing ability of the *yakuza* to keep unorganized crime and foreign crime in check.[121] SCAP's role in this pattern of accommodation partially reflected an initial lack of understanding of the existence and role of organized crime groups. In 1946, for example, occupation authorities approved the Tokyo Metropolitan Police Board's request for renewing the *Roten Dōgyō Kumiai* monopoly over administering the city's street stalls, mistaking the association for "a cooperative association."[122] As noted, by mid-1947 SCAP's Public Safety Division was cracking down on Ozu's operation as part of a broader campaign against *oyabun-kobun* relationships. However, lack of understanding is not a sufficient explanation of SCAP's role. Some SCAP divisions were more tolerant of linkages between organized crime groups and elements of the Japanese government and actively promoted them. Kaplan and Dubro argue that members of SCAP's G-2 section had extensive ties with Japan's conservative politicians and the *yakuza*, relying on the latter – directly and through right-wing political cutouts such as Kodama Yoshio – for strike-breaking operations, attacks on organized labor leaders, and attacks on communist political leaders and supporters.[123]

SCAP backing also reflected increasing concerns with the destabilizing presence of the Korean and Chinese minority, and by the late 1940s, the minority's political activism. By 1947, U.S. army intelligence was arguing that the League of Korean Residents in Japan (*Choryón*) was "heavily involved in illegal entry [of migrants], smuggling and black marketeering and was funneling the proceeds from these illicit activities to the [Japanese] Communist Party." Right-leaning groups such as the Korean Residents Union (*Mindan*) and their *yakuza* supporters received less attention.[124] The bottom line is that SCAP did little to counter the anti-*sangoku-jin* dimension in the growing linkages between the police and organized crime, and instead directly and indirectly encouraged it. By 1946 SCAP-sponsored immigration policies included measures allowing authorities, in practice, to curtail illegal entry to suppress smugglers and exclude "subversive elements" and added deportation provisions to remove the same.[125] In turn, the police were able to leverage the threat of deportation to selectively crack down on the Korean minority. An indirect form of SCAP sanction appeared in the treatment of reporting practices by the Japanese media. Though required to suppress "anti-foreign propaganda," SCAP censors did little to stop anti-Korean diatribes in the Japanese press. Newspaper articles emphasized the social disorder caused by the *sangoku-jin*, including their dominant role in the drug trade and other illegal activities, while downplaying the activities of Japanese.[126]

Legacy

The end of the occupation left Japan with a relatively decentralized and democratized police force, an extensive narcotics control framework, structurally embedded organized crime groups, poorly integrated foreign minorities, and a stimulant drug epidemic. By the mid-1950s, Japanese authorities had begun to significantly recentralize the police force, and de-emphasize narcotics control relative to the stimulant trade. The *yakuza*'s role in the booming stimulant trade had overstepped the boundary of tolerance for a newly recentralized police, and the police cracked down.[127] Enforcement steps against the *yakuza* and Korean and Chinese methamphetamine production and distribution networks curtailed drug supplies. Stepped-up arrests, increased penalties under amended drug control laws, compulsory hospitalization, and widespread education campaigns curtailed demand. By the late 1950s, the epidemic had ended.[128]

Unfortunately, this did not signify the end of Japan's drug problems. Crackdowns against organized crime groups during the 1950s resulted in imprisonment of Japanese gang members and deportations of foreign producers and traders. However, the major *yakuza* syndicates remained intact. The accommodations that had emerged between the police and organized crime during the 1940s continued, with the intensity of police crackdowns against organized crime varying in relation to the extent to which *yakuza* activities overtly crossed the line of disrupting rather than facilitating social order.[129] The recentralization of the police at the national level, with the formation of the National Police Agency, and expansion of police powers and inroads into daily life did not change a basic pattern of police reliance on the *yakuza* to self-regulate entertainment districts and help limit foreign crime threats.[130] The syndicates briefly explored the heroin trade during the late 1950s and early 1960s, but limited societal demand and police crackdowns over the narcotics trade, as well as gang violence stemming from broader turf wars, curtailed *yakuza* interest. By the early 1970s, the stimulant trade had remerged in Japan as a primary source of *yakuza* income. The trade remains firmly entrenched to this day. In contrast to the 1950s, the *yakuza* turned to foreign supplies of methamphetamine, initially relying on affiliated producers in South Korea, and later in Taiwan and China. These relationships have drawn on ties with Korea and China established during the occupation as well as ties established as the *yakuza* moved abroad into drug, gambling, sex trafficking and other operations in East and South-east Asia.[131]

The occupation patterns of accommodation and exclusion entered a new stage from the 1990s. Faced with intrusive anti-gang legislation and the severe economic downturn, *yakuza* entered a new phase of violent confrontation within and between the major syndicates that, in turn, sparked a new wave of police crackdowns. Seeking sources of income and a lower public profile, major and minor *yakuza* groups diversified into brokering migrant labor and subcontracting retail drug distribution to Iranian and other foreigners. Other *yakuza* groups have moved into the distribution of newer drugs such as ecstasy, older drugs including heroin and cannabis, and moved upstream seeking new sources of methamphetamine, including North Korea. At the same time, however, lax immigration policies during the economic bubble years of the 1980s, and illegal migration patterns since the 1990s, facilitated by the *yakuza*, have increased the presence of foreign groups vying with the *yakuza* for control of Japan's entertainment districts. The police, having long relied on the *yakuza* to deal with foreigners, have taken steps to address this issue. Much like the 1940s, however, they remain relatively unprepared to deal with an increasingly diverse population, let alone respond to the challenges posed by foreign crime groups.[132]

Epilogue: why no stimulant epidemic in Germany?

If, as I have argued, U.S. occupation policies shaped patterns of drug problems and drug control in Japan, why did the U.S. occupation of Germany not lead to a similar stimulant epidemic and collusion between a fragmented police and organized crime? The U.S. occupation brought the same focus on narcotics control to Germany as it had to Japan. Authorities focused on the democratization and decentralization of the police, and liberated a large foreign minority population. Elements of this population as well as Germans participated in an extensive black market. However, differences in context and policy choices between the two cases help to explain variation in outcomes.

U.S. concerns with Germany as a country engaged in the illicit production and trafficking of manufactured narcotics largely disappeared by the 1930s. With the 1929 Opium Act, German policy makers incorporated provisions of international drug control conventions, including those that had been pushed by the United States. Occupation authorities who entered Germany in 1945 focused on re-establishing drug controls that had eroded in the latter years of the war rather than seeking to remake German drug control policy or, more importantly, preventing Germany from playing an international role in the illicit narcotics trade. In all four occupation zones, authorities reintroduced the provisions of the Opium

Act. By 1947, officials were focusing on how to coordinate the different institutional frameworks that the British, French, and Soviets had adopted to implement the Opium Act.[133]

In contrast to Japan, German drug control policy prior to the occupation had included controls on stimulant drugs. As in Japan, German policy makers relied on the extensive use of stimulant drugs among the military during the war but the countries diverged in this practice in the early 1940s. German policy makers became concerned with the adverse physical effects of stimulants, both amphetamine and methamphetamine, and in June 1941 moved from promoting military usage to restricting stimulant distribution and use under the country's primary drug control law, the 1929 Opium Act.[134] The Opium Act's provisions on narcotics as well as stimulant control help to explain how authorities were able to avoid the postwar problems of Japan despite the occupation's primary emphasis on narcotics. By 1947, in the four states (*Länder*) that comprised the U.S. occupation zone there were 2600 reports of possible drug addiction and 408 cases of confirmed addiction in the zone's population of approximately sixteen million. In the confirmed cases, the majority involved narcotics while only six involved the dominant methamphetamine brand Pervatin as the primary drug of addiction.[135]

Black markets were rampant in Germany, dominated by trafficking in cigarettes, currency, food, and consumer goods.[136] That said, there was no German equivalent to Japan's Directive 363. Full-scale invasion of Germany had resulted in the allied forces discovering abandoned military and industrial stockpiles, including stockpiles of pharmaceuticals. The stockpiles initially were distributed haphazardly until a more coordinated distribution system was established. By 1946, occupation authorities estimated that 90 percent of narcotics stockpiles had been "recovered and restored to legitimate channels." Thefts from these channels and illicit trafficking drawing on undiscovered stockpiles continued through 1947.[137] Diversions from the production facilities of pharmaceutical companies also were a source of illicit trafficking. In the case of stimulants, however, control over such diversion was facilitated by the zonal division of Germany under the occupation. The primary producer of Pervatin, Temmler-Werke of the Vereinigte Chemische Fabriken, was located in the Soviet zone, and the Soviets expropriated the facility and its remaining contents.[138]

Actual control over illicit drug markets in the dislocation of postwar Germany required enforcement capacity. In contrast to Japan, the occupation of Germany was more direct. The U.S. army initially had considered a Japanese-style occupation, with occupation forces supervising a German police force that, while "backed by U.S. tactical units," would have primary responsibility for the provision of "security and order."[139] Concerns over how such a step would be received in the United States and Europe, however, eventually led to the creation of an American "constabulary" in the U.S. occupation zone. Occupation troops would gradually be phased out and, by mid-1946, replaced with troops organized for a policing role. The force was authorized at 38,000 troops, roughly "one constable . . . for 450 Germans" in the U.S. zone.[140] In addition to the constabulary, occupation forces turned to the German police.

Occupation reforms of the police took place in the context of a broader process of de-Nazification, demilitarization, democratization, and decentralization. Occupation forces dismantled and purged the Nazi "police machinery," including the order and security police forces and their specialized agencies such as the *Gestapo*.[141] Although decentralization took place in each of the occupation zones, Allied authorities differed in the extent to which responsibilities were shifted to the state (*Land*) or municipal level. In general, decentralization of the police across the zones was facilitated by a tradition of police organization at the *Land* level. The tradition of municipal level organization varied across the *Länder* and would lead to recentralization efforts by German policy makers in the late 1940s. In the U.S. zone, authorities emphasized municipal-level organization, with individual forces in all cities with populations of more than 5000 persons and a state-level police for rural areas. Though the structure was similar to that introduced in Japan, the size of the police force in Germany was greater. In 1945, U.S. authorities established a force of 22,000 police in their occupation zone. By 1949, there were 40,000 German police in the four *Länder* that comprised the U.S. occupation zone or roughly "2.3 police officers for every thousand inhabitants" compared with roughly 1.6 police per thousand in Japan.[142]

Issues of experience and equipment faced the German police, much like their Japanese counterparts. German police were armed initially with wooden nightsticks, before being authorized to carry small arms in late September 1945.[143] However, the patterns of accommodation and exclusion found in Japan, and the role of the occupation in shaping these patterns, differed in Germany. Part of the reason lies in the relatively larger police force and the more direct role of occupation policing. Germany also lacked organized native groups comparable to the *bakuto* and *tekiya* that played an important role in the rise of the modern *yakuza*. The police in occupied Germany did face a rough equivalent to the *sangokujin* in the form of 5.2 million former conscripted laborers and prisoners of war. The largest populations of these displaced persons were from Eastern European countries, such as Poland, and the Soviet Union. Roughly 2.5 million displaced persons were in the U.S. occupation zone, housed primarily in camps, pending repatriation. By late 1945, repatriation had dramatically decreased this figure to approximately 600,000 and the numbers would decline further during the occupation.[144] From the standpoint of the German authorities, and increasingly the occupation forces, the remaining displaced persons posed a threat to security and order. As liberated peoples, the displaced persons had access to supplies from the occupation forces, "privileged status under the occupation, and virtual immunity from the German police," leading to the displaced person camps becoming centers of black market activity. Armed gangs of displaced persons would also stage raids on Germans in the areas surrounding the camps. Occupation authorities worked to set up police forces within the camps and, where these efforts failed, coordinated raids on the camps with the German police.[145] Although organized groups of displaced persons played an active role in the black market, occupation authorities made no reference to such groups playing prominent roles in the black market drug trade.[146]

Unlike Japan, occupation polices in Germany did not have the unintended effects of facilitating the rise of the stimulant trade or structurally embedded relations between the police and organized crime. However, the U.S. occupation would influence drug crime and crime control in Germany in other ways. The territorial legacy of a divided Germany on the front lines of the Cold War included the unique status of Berlin and a substantial deployment of American troops on German soil. By the 1970s, Berlin had emerged as a major gateway for the drug trade into Europe. Drug abuse problems among the more than 200,000 American troops based in Germany facilitated the trade, while jurisdictional disputes over military bases and growing American interest in the potential for drug trade through Europe into the United States would influence the institutional relationships between the *Länder* and the Federal government on drug control. Jurisdictional disputes and U.S. pressures for Japan to cooperate in a new war on drugs also emerged from the 1980s, once again shaping patterns of crime and crime control in Japan.[147]

Notes

I thank Craig Frizzel and Kilic Kanat for their research assistance.

For authors writing in Japanese, names are presented below in the order family-name given-name.

1 For an example of the former, see D. Bayley, *Forces of order: police behavior in Japan and the United States*, Berkeley: University of California Press, 1976; of the latter, see P. Katzenstein, *Cultural norms and national security: police and military in postwar Japan*, Ithaca and London: Cornell University Press, 1976.
2 Notable exceptions include C. Aldous, *The police in occupation Japan: control, corruption and resistance to reform*, London and New York: Routledge, 1997; and D. Kaplan and A. Dubro, *Yakuza: Japan's criminal underworld*, Berkeley: University of California Press, 2003.
3 J. Dower, *Embracing defeat: Japan in the wake of World War II*, New York: W.W. Norton, 1999, pp. 45–6, 54, 93, 103; and E. Takemae, *Inside GHQ: the allied occupation of Japan and its legacy* [translated and adapted from the Japanese by R. Rickerts and S. Swann], London and New York: Continuum, 2002, p. 406.
4 Takemae, *Inside GHQ*, p. 406.
5 H. Friman, *Narco diplomacy: exporting the U.S. war on drugs*, Ithaca and London: Cornell University Press, 1996.

6 Ibid.
7 The literature here is extensive. For example, see F. Merrill, *Japan and the opium menace*, New York: Arno Press, 1981 (reprint of publication by Foreign Policy Association 1942); and K. Meyer and T. Parssinen, *Webs of smoke: smugglers, warlords, spies, and the history of international drug trade*, Boulder: Rowman and Littlefield, 1998.
8 For example see State Department diplomatic records, RG59, narcotics, internal affairs of Japan: 894.114/198 (18 September 1935: Secretary of State to U.S. Embassy Tokyo), 202 (9 October 1935: Kobe to Department of State).
9 Japan's Opium Law incorporated strict domestic controls that initially appeared in trade agreements with the United States and Great Britain in the late 1850s. See, Ministry of Foreign Affairs, *Japan and narcotic drugs*, February 1950; and M. Vaughn, F. Huang and C. Ramirez, "Drug abuse and anti-drug policy in Japan: past history and future directions," *The British journal of criminology*, 1995, vol. 35, no. 4, pp. 493–4.
10 The primary domestic regulations consisted of the Opium Law of 1898 as amended, Home Office and Imperial Ordinances, and provisions of the Japanese penal code (State Department diplomatic records, RG59, narcotics, internal affairs of Japan: 894.114/N16/2-2745 (League of Nations to Department of State, 27 February 1945).
11 See Friman, *Narco diplomacy*, pp. 40–1; and Meyer and Parssinen, *Webs of smoke*, p. 97.
12 K. Yamasaki and G. Ogawa, *The effect of the World War upon the commerce and industry of Japan*, New Haven: Yale University Press, 1929; and Bureau of Foreign Trade, Department of Commerce and Industry, Japan, *The industry of Japan*, Tokyo: Maruzen, 1930.
13 M. Kato, "An epidemiological analysis of the fluctuation of drug dependence in Japan," *The international journal of the addictions*, 1969, vol. 4, no. 4, p. 598.
14 State Department diplomatic records, RG59, 1925 Geneva Conference: 511.4A6/6 (18 July 1929: League of Nations Association to Premier Y. Hamaguchi, Foreign Minister Baron Shidehara, Minister of the Interior K. Adachi, and Minister of Justice Viscount C. Watanabe).
15 State Department diplomatic records, RG59, narcotics, internal affairs of Japan: 894.114/167 (4 April 1935: Department of State to Geneva); and Ministry of Health and Welfare, *A brief account of drug abuse and countermeasures in Japan*, 1972, p. 2.
16 Kato, "An epidemiological analysis," p. 598. See also *Japan chronicle* articles (December 1934) in State Department diplomatic records, RG59, narcotics, internal affairs of Japan: 894.114/153 (1–2 December 1934) and 157 (8 December 1934).
17 Established in 1937, the ministry took over responsibility for opium and narcotic drug related matters from the Home Ministry's Hygiene/Sanitary Bureau. See, M. Barnhart, *Japan prepares for total war: the search for economic security, 1919–1941*, Ithaca and London: Cornell University Press, 1987, pp. 71–2.
18 W. Walker, *Opium and foreign policy: the Anglo-American search for order in Asia, 1912–1954*, Chapel Hill and London: University of North Carolina Press, 1991, pp. 102, 135, 165 [quote], 167–8.
19 In 1947, Speer, a narcotics agent, would become head of the "Narcotics control branch of SCAP's Public Health and Welfare Section" (Walker, *Opium and foreign policy*, p. 168).
20 Monograph 19: Public Health September 1945–December 1950, in Supreme Commander for the Allied Powers, Historical Monographs 1945–1951, *History of the nonmilitary activities of the occupation of Japan*, Volumes 1–55, World War

Two Records Division, NARS [Available on microfilm, Center for Research Libraries], pp. 220–1; and *New York Times*, 19 October 1945.

21 T. Cohen, *Remaking Japan: the American occupation as new deal*, New York: The Free Press, 1987, pp. 340–2. See also Dower, *Embracing defeat*, p. 114.

22 Monograph 19, p. 220.

23 Takemae, *Inside GHQ*, p. 643.

24 Walker, *Opium and foreign policy*, pp. 167–8.

25 Under a June 1947 memorandum, these goods were "turned over to the Japanese government ... for manufacture of narcotic drugs for medical and scientific purposes" by companies in Tokyo and Osaka. See, Ministry of Foreign Affairs, *Japan and narcotic drugs*, p. 16.

26 Monograph 19, pp. 221–3. Storage facilities were located in Sendai, Tokyo (two locations), Niigata, Osaka (four locations), Okayama, Takamatsu, and Fukuoka. See, Ministry of Foreign Affairs, *Japan and Narcotic Drugs*, p. 16.

27 Takemae, *Inside GHQ*, p. 416.

28 Monograph 19, p. 223; and Ministry of Foreign Affairs, *Japan and narcotic drugs*, pp. 13–15.

29 Ministry of Health and Welfare, *A brief account*, p. 5.

30 Monograph 19, p. 225.

31 For example, see D. Musto, *The American disease: origins of narcotic control*, New York and Oxford: Oxford University Press, 1973, pp. 221–9. For the argument that Anslinger was the driving force in marijuana control, see E. Brecher, *Licit and illicit drugs: the consumers union report*, Boston: Little, Brown, 1972, pp. 415–20.

32 Ministry of Health and Welfare, *A brief account*, p. 5.

33 B. Holmstedt, "Historical perspective and future of ethnopharmacology," *Journal of ethnopharmacology*, 1991, vol. 32, pp. 14–15; and S. Karch, *The pathology of drug abuse*, New York: CRC Press, 1996, p. 195.

34 Karch, *The pathology*, p. 195.

35 Ibid., p. 199; and J. Cadet, "Free radicals and drug-induced neurodegeneration," Paper presented at the 6th Internet World Congress for Biomedical Sciences, 2000 (available at http://www.uclm.es/inabis2000).

36 The company "sold methamphetamine in the United States under the brand name of Methedrine" until the late 1960s. See, Karch, *The pathology*, p. 199. The company was established in London in 1880 by two American pharmacists (see company history at http://www.bwfund.org).

37 H. Brill and T. Hirose, "The rise and fall of a methamphetamine epidemic: Japan 1945–55," *Seminars in psychiatry*, 1969, vol. 1, no. 2, 185; Kato, "An epidemiological analysis," p. 592 [quote]; and Karch, *The pathology*, p. 199.

38 Vaughn, Huang and Ramirez, "Drug abuse and anti-drug policy in Japan," p. 497.

39 For example, see Japan International Cooperation Agency, *Anti drug activities in Japan*, Tokyo: National Police Agency, 1989, p. 26; and Vaughn, Huang and Ramirez, "Drug abuse and anti-drug policy in Japan," p. 497. The latter note (p. 497) that the Japanese government first used stimulants (Philopon) during the 1930s in the Sino-Japanese war.

40 For example, Karch (*The pathology*, pp. 195, 202) uses the term Philopon to describe ephedrine, and Hiropon to describe the name of postwar methamphetamine. Kato ("An epidemiological analysis") uses only the term *senryoku* to describe wartime methamphetamine and makes no mention of ephedrine. Vaughn, Huang and Ramirez ("Drug abuse and anti-drug policy in Japan," p. 497) note the stimulant Philopon and the broad designation of *senryoku* for war stimulants. Japan International Cooperation Agency (*Anti drug activities*, p. 26) and Masayuki Tamura ("Japan: stimulant epidemics past and present,"

Bulletin on narcotics, 1989, vol. 1, pp. 83–93) notes the general term of Philo-pon for wartime stimulant drugs. Hiroshi Suwaki, Susumu Fukuiu and Kyohei Konuma ("Methamphetamine abuse in Japan: its 45 year history and the current situation," in H. Klee ed., *Amphetamine misuse: international perspectives on current trends*, United Kingdom: Harwood Academic Publishers, 1997, p. 201) note that Philopon and Sedrin were commercial names for over-the-counter methamphetamine sold in Japan beginning in 1941.

41 For example, see "Energy in pills," *Business week*, 15 January 1944, pp. 40–4; L. Grinspoon and P. Hedblom, *The speed culture: amphetamine use and abuse in America*, Cambridge: Harvard University Press, 1975, pp. 18–19; and Karch, *The pathology*, p. 201.

42 Kato, "An epidemiological analysis," p. 592; Ministry of Health and Welfare, *A brief account*, p. 2; and Vaughn, Huang and Ramirez, "Drug abuse and anti-drug policy in Japan," p. 498.

43 T. Shimomura, "Japan," *Drug enforcement*, 1975–1976, 39; and C. Spencer and V. Navaratnam, *Drug abuse in East Asia*, Kala Lampur: Oxford University Press, 1981, p. 52.

44 Tamura, "Japan," pp. 83–93. See also Brill and Hirose, "The rise and fall of a methamphetamine epidemic," p. 186.

45 Kato, "An epidemiological analysis," pp. 594–5.

46 Takemae, *Inside GHQ*, p. 415.

47 Monograph 19, pp. 197–201; Brill and Hirose, "The rise and fall of a Methamphetamine Epidemic," p. 181; and Tamura, "Japan," pp. 83–93.

48 Kato, "An epidemiological analysis," p. 592; and Tamura, "Japan," pp. 83–93.

49 *Annual reports of governments [under the 1931 drug convention as amended, 1946]: Japan, communicated by the government of the United States of America, annual report for 1948*, p. 6 [located in 894.111 Narcotics/8-1549; hereinafter cited as Annual report Japan 1948]; and Tamura, "Japan," pp. 83–93.

50 Health and Welfare, *A brief account*, p. 7; and Tamura, "Japan," pp. 83–93.

51 Monograph 19, p. 50.

52 Brill and Hirose, "The rise and fall of a methamphetamine epidemic," p. 185.

53 "Two new drug hazards," *Science news letter*, 13 December 1947; J. Kramer and R. Pinco, "Amphetamine use and misuse: A medico-legal view," in D. Smith and D. Wesson eds, *Uppers and downers*, Englewood Cliffs, NJ: Prentice Hall, 1973, pp. 9–22; and Grinspoon and Hedblum, *The speed culture*, pp. 11–13. Karch (*The pathology*, p. 201) notes, "Inside each inhaler were eight folded paper sections impregnated with 250 mg of amphetamine. Abusers opened the inhaler and chewed the papers."

54 Kramer and Pinco, "Amphetamine use"; and Grinspoon and Hedblum, *The speed culture*, pp. 12–13, 20–2.

55 Musto, *The American disease*, p. 213.

56 P. Jenkins, *Synthetic panics: the symbolic politics of designer drugs*, New York and London: New York University Press, 1999, pp. 36–7.

57 R. Deverall, *Red China's dirty drug war: the story of the opium, heroin, morphine and philopon traffic*, New York and Tokyo: American Federation of Labor, 1954, p. 188; and Grinspoon and Hedblum, *The speed culture* 1975, p. 20.

58 U.S. Congress, House, *Traffic in, and control of, narcotics, barbiturates, and amphetamines*, Hearings before a Subcommittee of the Committee on Ways and Means, 84th Congress, October–December 1955, January 1956, p. 192.

59 U.S. Congress, House, *Control of narcotics, marijuana and barbiturates*, Hearings before a Subcommittee of the Committee on Ways and Means, 82nd Congress, 1st Session on HR 3490 and HR 348, April 1951, pp. 204–8.

60 U.S. Congress, *Traffic in, and control of, narcotics*, p. 192.

61 K. Bruun, L. Pan and I. Rexed, *The gentlemen's club: international control of drugs*

and alcohol, Chicago and London: The University of Chicago Press, 1975, p. 17. On the steps leading to the eventual inclusion of stimulant control in the 1971 Vienna Convention, see ibid, pp. 243–68); and W. McAllister, *Drug diplomacy in the twentieth century*, London and New York: Routledge, 2000.

62 Kramer and Pinco, "Amphetamine Use and Misuse," p. 14. Another example of Anslinger's awareness is that the back cover of Deverall's book (*Red China's dirty drug war*), which includes several chapters on drug problems in Japan includes this statement of support from Anslinger: "Your booklet ... is going to be of great use to us in our efforts to suppress this traffic."

63 U.S. Congress 1956, *Traffic in, and control of, narcotics*, pp. 199–203.

64 Kato, "An epidemiological analysis," p. 597.

65 Aldous, *The police in occupation Japan*, p. 70; and Dower, *Embracing defeat*, p. 45 [quote].

66 Bayley, *Forces of order*, p. 185.

67 Aldous, *The police in occupation Japan*, pp. 49–50; and Takemae, *Inside GHQ*, pp. 296–7.

68 "Monograph 55: Police and public safety, in Supreme Commander for the Allied Powers, historical monographs 1945–1951," *History of the nonmilitary activities of the occupation of Japan*, volumes 1–55, World War Two Records Division, NARS, p. 11 [Available on microfilm, Center for Research Libraries]; and Takemae, *Inside GHQ*, p. 296.

69 Monograph 55, p. 11; and Aldous, *The police in occupation Japan*, p. 51.

70 Aldous, *The police in occupation Japan*, pp. 57–8.

71 Ibid., pp. 61–2 [quotes], 184; and Takemae, *Inside GHQ*, pp. 57, 108, 296.

72 Aldous, *The police in occupation Japan*, pp. 175–9; and Takemae, *Inside GHQ*, pp. 298–9.

73 For example, see A. Oppler, *Legal reform in occupied Japan: a participant looks back*, Princeton: Princeton University Press, 1976, p. 248; J. Perry, *Beneath the eagle's wings: Americans in occupied Japan*, New York: Dodd, Mead and Company, 1980, pp. 147–8; Aldous, *The police in occupation Japan* 1997, pp. 180–207; and Takemae, *Inside GHQ*, p. 537.

74 The SCAP historical monograph "Police and public safety" details the reorganization and roles of the police, but makes no mention of narcotic or other drug enforcement. The closest link would be as part of SCAP pressure on the police to crack down on the *oyabun-kobun* relationship (see Monograph 55).

75 Monograph 19, pp. 9–10; and Takemae, *Inside GHQ*, pp. 413–14.

76 *Annual reports of governments [under the 1931 drug convention as amended, 1946]: Japan, communicated by the government of the United States of America, annual report for 1947*, p. 1 [US National Archives: located in 894.111 Narcotics/5-2748; hereinafter cited as Annual report Japan 1947].

77 Laws and regulations [communicated in compliance with the terms of the 1931 drug convention as amended, 1946]: Japan, p. 5 [located in 894.111 Narcotics/8-2049].

78 Annual report Japan 1947, p. 5; and Monograph 19, pp. 225–9.

79 Annual report Japan 1948, p. 7.

80 Annual report Japan 1947, p. 5.

81 These numbers would be increased further under the 1953 Narcotics Control Law, which required local governments to establish narcotics officers to "investigate crimes concerning narcotics and other dangerous drugs" Vaughn, Huang and Ramirez, "Drug abuse and anti-drug policy in Japan," p. 499.

82 Opium offenses were prescribed in Chapter 14 of the Penal Code, Law No. 45 of 1907 (Annual report Japan 1948, p. 7).

116   H.R. Friman

83 Annual report Japan 1948, p. 5. It is unclear whether the narcotics agents actually were more likely to obtain small arms compared to the police.
84 Annual report Japan 1948, p. 7; and Monograph 19, p. 224.
85 Annual report Japan 1947, p. 7; Annual report Japan 1948, p. 9; and *Annual reports of governments [under the 1931 drug convention as amended, 1946]: Japan, communicated by the government of the United States of America, annual report for 1949*, pp. 7–19 [located in 894.53/10-1550].
86 Japan International Cooperation Agency, *Anti Drug Activities*, p. 24.
87 Tamura, "Japan," pp. 83–93.
88 Health and Welfare, *A brief account*, p. 30; and Tamura, "Japan," pp. 83–93.
89 Monograph 55, p. 87; Aldous, *The police in occupation Japan*, pp. 108–9; and Kaplan and Dubro, *The yakuza*, pp. 39–40.
90 A. Oppler, *Legal reform in occupied Japan*, p. 248; Aldous, *The police in occupation Japan*, pp. 110–15; and Kaplan and Dubro, *The yakuza*, pp. 40, 60–3.
91 H. Iwai, "Organized crime in Japan," in R. Kelly, ed., *Organized crime: a global perspective*, Totowa, N.J.: Rowman and Littlefield, 1986, pp. 214–33; and Kaplan and Dubro, *The yakuza*, pp. 26–7, 61, 74–5.
92 General Headquarters, Supreme Commander for the Allied Powers, *History of the nonmilitary activities of the occupation of Japan, 1945–1950*, volume VI – legal reform, public safety, and freedom of expression – part 4: "Treatment of foreign nationals," p. 102 [Volume 16 in the Japanese series, on file at the National Diet Library; hereinafter cited as SCAP, "Treatment of foreign nationals"]; R. Mitchell, *The Korean minority in Japan*, Berkeley and Los Angeles: University of California Press, 1967; M. Weiner, *Race and migration in imperial Japan*. New York and London: Routledge, 1994; and A. Vasishth, "A model minority: the Chinese community in Japan," in M. Weiner, ed., *Japan's minorities: the illusion of homogeneity*, London and New York: Routledge, 1997, pp. 108–39.
93 Mitchell, *The Korean minority*; C. Sung-hwa, "A Study of the origin of the legal status of Korean residents in Japan: 1945–1951," *Korean journal*, 1992, vol. 32, no. 1, 43–60; and Takemae *Inside GHQ*, pp. 448–52.
94 SCAP, "Treatment of foreign nationals," p. 73; and Takemae, *Inside GHQ*, pp. 451, 498–9.
95 Aldous, *The police in occupation Japan*, 113; and Takemae, *Inside GHQ*, p. 451 [quote]. Dower (*Embracing defeat*, p. 580), citing SCAP data, notes that an estimated "16,000 third-country people, mostly Korans and Formosans were actively involved in illegal black market activity" by early 1946.
96 Kaplan and Dubro, *The yakuza*, pp. 74–5.
97 Aldous, *The police in occupation Japan*, pp. 108–110; Dower, *Embracing defeat*, pp. 140–4; and Kaplan and Dubro, *The yakuza*, pp. 35–6.
98 R. Whiting, *Tokyo underworld: the fast times and hard life of an American gangster in Japan*, New York: Pantheon Books, 1999, pp. 26, 80, 85, 317; and Kaplan and Dubro, *The yakuza*, pp. 228–9.
99 Friman, *Narco diplomacy*, p. 66. On the broader role of American servicemen in the diversion of supplies, see Whiting, *Tokyo underworld*, pp. 14–22.
100 Deverall, *Red China's dirty drug war*, p. 187.
101 Monograph 19, pp. 193–4.
102 Deverall, *Red China's dirty drug war*, pp. 187–8; and Tamura, "Japan," pp. 83–93. Deverall (p. 188) notes that in contrast to 1952, Merck and Company exports of ephedrine hydrochloride to the "Far East" dropped to 6.6 kilograms in 1953 with none of the materials being sent to Japan.
103 In contrast, the SCAP annual reports on narcotic drugs as submitted to the United Nations offer extensive detail on seizures of heroin, morphine, opium and other narcotics by nationality of the offender.

104 Deverall, *Red China's dirty drug war*, pp. 189–90; and Tamura, "Japan," pp. 83–93. Deverall (p. 190) posits further that by 1954 an estimated 2000 to 3000 Koreans were involved in the illicit stimulant trade.

105 For a breakdown on narcotics addicts, see Kato, "An epidemiological analysis," p. 597. Suwaki, Fukuiu and Konuma ("Methamphetamine abuse in Japan," p. 201) note the first cases of stimulant addiction appearing in the Kobe–Osaka area in 1946. David Courtwright (*Forces of habit: drugs and the making of the modern world*, Cambridge: Harvard University Press, 2001, p. 82) notes that most addicts were "young men from slum districts, often of Korean or Chinese ancestry."

106 For example, see Mitchell, *The Korean minority*, pp. 39–40, 91–2; and Weiner, *Race and migration*, pp. 60–83.

107 Vasishth, "A model minority," pp. 108–39.

108 Takemae, *Inside GHQ*, p. 312.

109 Oppler, *Legal reform in occupied Japan*, p. 249; Dower, *Embracing defeat*, p. 143[quote]; Takemae, *Inside GHQ*, pp. 451–52; and Kaplan and Dubro, *The yakuza*, pp. 35–6.

110 Kaplan and Dubro, *The yakuza*, p. 35.

111 The third player in these accommodations was Japan's conservative politicians. For discussion, see Aldous, *The police in occupation Japan*; and Kaplan and Dubro, *The yakuza*.

112 Aldous, *The police in occupation Japan*, pp. 110–11; Whiting, *Tokyo underworld 1999*, pp. 11–12; and Kaplan and Dubro, *The yakuza*, pp. 20–6, 75.

113 Aldous, *The police in occupation Japan*, pp. 110–11, 117 [quote]; and Kaplan and Dubro, *The yakuza 2003*, p. 38.

114 Whiting (*Tokyo underworld*, pp. 27, 80) argues that the Sumiyoshi-kai was vying for control with Tosei-kai in the Ginza area with both gangs referred to as the "Ginza Police." Dower (*Embracing defeat*, p. 141) notes the Ueda gang as being in control of the Ginza black markets during the early years of the occupation.

115 M. Shikata and S. Tsuchiya, eds, *Crime and criminal policy in Japan from 1926 to 1988*, Tokyo: Japan Criminal Policy Society, 1988.

116 Cohen, *Remaking Japan*, pp. 313–14.

117 Oppler, *Legal reform in occupied Japan*, p. 248; Aldous, *The police in occupation Japan*, pp. 70–9, 98–9 [quote]; and Dower, *Embracing defeat*, pp. 143–4.

118 Oppler, *Legal reform in occupied Japan*, pp. 246–7.

119 Whiting, *Tokyo underworld*, p. 17.

120 Kaplan and Dubro, *The yakuza*, pp. 228–9.

121 In addition, the *yakuza*, especially in the Kobe–Osaka area, began to emerge as an institution that would offer socioeconomic advancement for members of the Japan's minority populations, including Koreans. For example, see G. DeVos and K. Mizushima, "Organization and social function of Japanese gangs: historical development and modern parallels," in R.P. Gore, ed., *Aspects of social change in modern Japan*, Princeton: Princeton University Press, 1967, pp. 289–325; and Kaplan and Dubro, *The yakuza*.

122 Aldous, *The police in occupation Japan*, p. 110.

123 Kaplan and Dubro, *The yakuza*, pp. 44–55, 62–4.

124 Takemae *Inside GHQ*, pp. 451–2, 454 [quote]; and Kaplan and Dubro, *The yakuza*, pp. 225, 229. In contrast, Sung-hwa ("A study of the origin of the legal status," p. 48) posits that SCAP focused on both organizations. SCAP posited Choryón "as a major crime organization," but also "ordered the Japanese government to dissolve violent Korean organizations including terroristic right wing ones."

125 Takemae, *Inside GHQ*, p. 449.

126 Ibid., p. 452. Dower (*Embracing defeat*, pp. 406–7, 435) notes that formal censorship was "terminated in October 1949" but "continued in altered forms" until 1952. By 1953, the pattern of anti-foreign press reporting was well entrenched. Positing the drug trade in Asia as a communist-directed enterprise, Deverall (*Red China's dirty drug war*, pp. 191–5) reviews Japanese press reports during 1953–1954, excerpting stories to buttress his claim of the "deep complicity of the North Korean minority" backed by the Japanese Communist Party (JCP), and Chinese smugglers in the stimulant trade. In contrast, stories concerning Japanese offenders, without ties to the JCP and with ties to organized crime groups, receive little mention.

127 Tamura, "Japan," pp. 83–93. For broader arguments on the issue of accommodation and crackdown, see Aldous, *The police in occupation Japan*, p. 231; and Kaplan and Dubro, *The yakuza*.

128 Tamura, "Japan," pp. 83–93; and Vaughn, Huang and Ramirez, "Drug abuse and anti-drug policy in Japan," pp. 491–524.

129 Friman, *Narco diplomacy*; and Kaplan and Dubro, *The yakuza*.

130 Katzenstein, *Cultural norms and national security*.

131 M. Tamura, "The yakuza and amphetamine abuse in Japan," in H. Traver and M. Gaylord, eds, *Drugs law and the state*, Hong Kong: Hong Kong University Press, 1992, pp. 99–118; H. Friman, "Obstructing markets: organized crime networks and drug control in Japan," in H. Friman and P. Andreas, eds, *The illicit global economy and state power*, Lanham: Rowman and Littlefield, 1999, pp. 173–99; and Kaplan and Dubro *The yakuza*, pp. 223–50.

132 Friman, "Obstructing markets," pp. 173–99; H. Friman, "Snakeheads in the garden of Eden: immigrants, smuggling and threats to social order in Japan," in D. Kyle and R. Koslowski, eds, *Global human smuggling in a comparative perspective*, Baltimore: Johns Hopkins University Press, 2001, pp. 294–317; and Kaplan and Dubro, *The yakuza*, pp. 273–6.

133 Friman, *Narco diplomacy*, pp. 20–5, 88–9.

134 Ibid., p. 90.

135 *Annual reports of governments [under the 1931 drug convention as amended, 1946]: Germany*, communicated by the Office of Military Government for Germany (US), Annual Report for 1947, pp. 6–7 [located in 862.114 Narcotics/11-3048; hereinafter cited as Annual Report Germany 1947].

136 H. Zink, *The United States in Germany, 1944–1955*, Princeton: D. Van Nostrand, 1957, pp. 139–40; F. Davis, *Come as a conqueror: the United States army's occupation of Germany 1945–1949*, New York: Macmillan Company, 1967, p. 148; and E. Ziemke, *The U.S. army in the occupation of Germany, 1944–1946*, Washington, D.C.: U.S. Army, Center of Military History, 1975, pp. 353–4.

137 *Annual reports of governments [under the 1931 drug convention as amended, 1946]: Germany*, communicated by the allied control authority, Annual report for 1946, p. 5 [quote] [located in 862.114 Narcotics/12-147]; and Annual report Germany 1947, pp. 9, 12.

138 Friman, *Narco diplomacy*, pp. 88–90.

139 Ziemke, *The U.S. army in the occupation*, pp. 339–41.

140 Davis, *Come as a conqueror*, pp. 163–72 [quote]; and Ziemke, *The U.S. army in the occupation*, pp. 341, 443.

141 R. Kempner, "Police administration," in E. Litchfield *et al.*, *Governing postwar Germany*, Ithaca: Cornell University Press, 1953, pp. 406–7.

142 W. Friedmann, *The allied military government of Germany*, London: Stevens and Sons, 1947, pp. 106–7, 170–1; Kempner, "Police administration," pp. 407–13 [quote]; Zink, *The United States in Germany*, pp. 304–5. Comparison figures for Japan are estimated based on an authorized force of 125,000 police for a Japanese population, by the late 1940s, of approximately 80 million.

143 Friedmann, *The allied military government*, p. 106; and Ziemke, *The U.S. army in the occupation*, pp. 270, 357.

144 Ziemke, *The U.S. army in the occupation*, pp. 284–90, 355.

145 Davis, *Come as a conqueror*, pp. 172–4; and Ziemke, *The U.S. army in the occupation*, pp. 355–8 [quote].

146 For example, see Annual report Germany 1947, p. 11.

147 Friman, *Narco diplomacy*, pp. 73–84, 90–1.

5 Educational reform and history textbooks in occupied Japan

Yoshiko Nozaki

A series of educational reforms launched and implemented in Japan during the years of occupation involved intricate politics and practices, ideologically or otherwise, both at national and local levels. Education as effected by a modern nation-state is crucial to the consciousness and identity of a nation, and the occupation forces pursued a series of educational reforms designed to remake Japanese cultural and political identities. The issues then at stake concerned war, nation building, and educational policy and practice, and they resonate today in the context of a resurgent Japanese nationalism manifested in recent textbook controversies, prime ministerial visits to Yasukuni Shrine, and conflicts between Japan and its neighbors such as China and Korea.

Previous research on the occupation accepted a view that the educational reforms were among the most successful achievements in the democratization of Japanese society. A popular view also seems to prevail that the United States and its allies rebuilt Japan from total ruins, and that a pacifist, democratic nation and education emerged through that rebuilding. Although not entirely false, these views are misleading on at least two major grounds. First, they tend to overlook the continuity of educational structures and practices from presurrender to the postwar period. Second, they conflate the official (legal) pronouncements of democratic education with the actual (cultural and political) processes and practices. Japan was defeated in the war, but its internal power structure, school systems and operations, and workforce (teachers and administrators) were intact at the beginning of the postwar education program.

This chapter examines not only the events that took place at the level of the Japanese state and occupation authorities but also the reactions of schools and teachers. How did the people involved in the education system, from officials in the Ministry of Education to textbook authors and schoolteachers and administrators at local sites, respond to the news of Japan's defeat and the events and reforms that followed? What were the conflicts and contradictions? The chapter also analyzes the history textbooks written and published during the period to assess the extent to which the events of war, defeat, and reforms transformed the consciousness of Japanese people as it was embodied in those texts. The chapter demonstrates that educational reforms during the occupation period underwent socially, culturally, and politically complex processes that contained a multitude of tensions.

Japan's surrender and the "blacking out" of textbooks

The surrender

On 15 August 1945, the day Emperor Hirohito announced Japan's acceptance of the Potsdam Declaration to his subjects, the Suzuki cabinet resigned en masse. Ôta Kozo, the outgoing Education Minister, presented his final instruction to the schools on that day.[1] His message was that Japan's defeat had been brought about by the people's insufficient dedication to the emperor, along with their failure to bring into full play the spirit nurtured by their imperial education. Hereafter, he concluded, students and teachers must devote themselves wholly to their duties as imperial subjects, and to the maintenance of the *kokutai*.[2] In referring to *kokutai*, Ôta had in mind the emperor, as the presurrender doctrine regarded his inherited authority as the essence of the nation and nationhood. Like many other officials who had promoted ultranationalistic and emperor-centered education in the service of war, Ôta persisted in his determination to secure the imperial state even in defeat.

Ôta (along with other wartime government leaders) was not alone in unwavering loyalty to the emperor and the imperial nation – many teachers and school administrators made the same plea. For example, at one rural school in Hokkaido, teachers gathered in front of the *hôanden*, a hall built in the schoolyard where the photos of the emperor and empress were enshrined, where they groveled and cried. The feeling was that the war was lost "because of our lack of effort," and so "[we] apologize for it."[3]

An official record entry for 15 August at another local school read, "At noon today, His Majesty's broadcast was heard." It continued:

> We can only shed tears ... Unaware as we are that the situation of the time has worsened to this degree, we can only regret the lukewarmness [of our efforts]. From now on, whatever situations we may encounter, we will only resolutely proceed to maintain *kokutai*, without forgetting the history of three thousand years.[4]

Students' expressions also reflected the official emperor-centered ideology to a significant degree. A third-grade boy at another school wrote: "I'm disappointed at losing the war. It is like a bad dream ... I now surely want to make Japan a great nation when I grow up. I want to grow up quickly and next time win the war."[5] A fourth-grade girl wrote that at noon her family "sat up straight in front of the radio" and "heard the music of the song 'Kimigayo' [Emperor's reign],[6] playing reverentially." For "the first time," she was about to hear "the direct voice of His Majesty Emperor [Hirohito]." Unfortunately, she could not understand what was said, and so her mother had to explain his message to her. As she put it:

> I could not understand what was going on at all. My mother said to me "Kyôko, we lost the war. . .," woefully while wiping her tears. We all cried together loudly . . . I thought, "Oh, we were bad, we should have tried harder. . . .[7]

To be sure, some teachers (and parents) welcomed the news with relief. Isoda Takeshi, an English teacher, who listened to Hirohito's radio announcement with acquaintances at the home of his wife's parents, noted that the people crying in the room were not "simply grieving Japan's defeat." Rather, he thought, they cried only because of "the stereotypical forms of expressions and ideas that had become habitual over the years," and the truth was that "they cannot suppress the joy that springs in their hearts." Isoda might have been mistaken about the emotions and feelings of others, but he himself felt "a relief that he had never experienced before," since he had for some time passively resisted the ultranationalist education at his school.[8] Isoda, clearly sensing a kind of liberation, was perhaps in the minority among teachers, as the feelings expressed by teachers at the news of defeat were commonly of emptiness, mortification, and apprehension.[9] However, this did not mean that many people, including teachers and students, would oppose the idea of building a different, democratic future for the nation. Indeed, in the subsequent developments of postwar social and educational reforms, teachers would become a strong force that promoted the idea of democratic education, even though the transformation of their consciousness was often painful and gradual.

Reopening schools

During the last years of the war, the Japanese government increasingly used its schools as sites of wartime labor service. Some school buildings were converted into munitions plants and storehouses. Students in secondary and higher education (and older primary school students from late 1944) were mobilized to work at these facilities year round. Even primary school students, whom the state had in principle exempted from labor services, were engaged in various year-round labor services, including cultivating the schools' gardens (converted from playgrounds) and gathering acorns, locusts, and other edible things from the fields. Schools and teachers assisted and supervised these labor activities.[10] The summer of 1945 was no different. Even though academic classes were not in session, many teachers and students came to school anyway. In fact, some teachers and students heard Hirohito's radio announcement at their school. The nation lost the war, but the schools did not lose their grip on the students.

Schools reopened for the second term from the end of August to the middle of September, even though they received no direct instructions from the Ministry of Education (*Monbushô*) about what they should teach and how they should instruct their students. While coping with the new situation was important, resuming normal school business took priority. Many teachers, however, found it difficult to tell their students about Japan's defeat, because they had previously taught that it would never happen to Japan.[11] In these circumstances some teachers began to reflect on their responsibility for the wartime ultranationalist education.

Nagai Kenji, an elementary school substitute teacher, attended his school's staff meeting on 19 August (his school would reopen the following day), where the teachers debated the issue. At this time the principal suggested the use of the term "discontinuation" instead of "defeat," to avoid student criticism. After the staff meeting, Nagai cleaned up his classroom, took down several pro-war posters, and wondered about his responsibility for having taught concepts such as "the divine nation of Japan" and "Imperial Japan's [ultimate] victory," and for representing "Americans and the British as demons and animals."[12]

The following day most of his students were back, which was perhaps a relief to Nagai. They asked him whether Japan had really been defeated or had simply discontinued the war. Nagai could not say the term "defeat" to his pupils, even though he would have liked to. His decision was not based on the principal's suggestion, but because he thought that if he were to admit Japan's defeat, he would have to apologize to his students for having taught "lies." He was not sure whether he should do this, and, if so, how to do it. Many teachers shared his dilemma. However, one colleague, Mr. Kanamura, who thought that teachers bore no responsibility for what they had taught during the war, admitted to his students that Japan had been defeated. Kanamura explained to Nagai and others: "I was taught that [the divine nation Japan would not be defeated], and the government said that. A mere teacher bears no responsibility." Nagai was not convinced. Several days later he admitted Japan's defeat to his students and apologized. He eventually left teaching in the spring of 1947.[13]

Ichijô Fumi, an elementary school teacher who on 15 August was with her students working in the school's wheat and buckwheat patches, also confronted this issue of teachers' responsibility for wartime education. Following instructions from her school's principal, she remained at her boarding house for several days after Hirohito's radio announcement. During this time, she and her colleague and housemate, Miss Tabe, contemplated resigning. Tabe argued that they should resign because they were responsible for having implemented the militarist education program, and that she could not in good conscience teach the things that would "uproot" and "upset" the lessons she had taught during the war.

Ichijô did not disagree with Tabe but felt that she could not desert her students, who were from poor families in a mountain village and who were dearly attached to her (Ichijô had been a very enthusiastic teacher). Ichijô and Tabe wondered whether those teachers capable of successfully making "an internal self-conversion" would be the only ones to continue teaching. In December 1945, it was Ichijô who left teaching when she realized her inability to "turn 180 degrees."[14]

Blacking out textbooks

The Japanese government's postwar education policy – which was primarily concerned with textbooks and curriculum – began "blacking out" (*suminuri*) textbooks. At the end of August 1945, while considering how to maintain the *kokutai*, the Ministry of Education instructed schools to exercise "discretion" in using the existing textbooks when the schools reopened in September. On 20 September, the ministry notified all schools that they were to instruct teachers to delete the militarist content from textbooks and other educational materials.[15] In all likelihood, however, the ministry's true intention was more to conceal, than to negate, militarism. Some officials later recalled its purpose as trying to make a favorable impression by hiding militarist content from the eyes of the occupation forces.[16]

Nor did the blacking out of textbooks aim to eliminate the emperor-centered educational content that had fervently been stressed during the war. While the Ministry listed several general criteria for content removal, in only one case – that of second-semester elementary school Japanese language textbooks – did it specify the exact items to be removed. Moreover, the items it specified were mainly war and military related, and not items illustrating adoration of the successive emperors (e.g. *Kimigayo*, which was contained in textbooks).[17] Finally, the Ministry recommended an introduction on the *kokutai* and moral establishment in case the blacking out process produced a shortage of educational materials. This provision implicitly prescribed the use of the Imperial Rescript on Education, a document that had been read by principals and teachers at school ceremonies during the years leading up to war and defeat. It was, in essence, a narrative of Japan's nationhood in terms of imperial sovereignty.[18]

As notification of the Ministry's instructions reached the local schools, teachers began to ask their students to black out – in some cases, cut out with scissors or paste over with glue – the lines and pages in the textbooks that they perceived as military related. The Ministry's instructions lacked specifics, and so prefectoral and local officials, schools, and teachers developed their own lists to identify items for removal. In some instances, it was the prefecture that developed the list; in others, school officials and teachers developed it. These locally developed lists often included far more items for removal than the instructions given by the Ministry. In any case, no two textbooks emerged from this process exactly alike, indicating that each classroom teacher took some liberty in determining which items were to be removed.

By the middle of November 1945, the Ministry of Education completed a list of items to be removed from all school textbooks in use, and in February 1946, it sent a second notice to the local schools. However, the notice contained only items for elementary Japanese language and math textbooks. It thus failed to provide schools with a complete set of instructions for carrying out this task.[19] The Ministry allowed the schools to use the blacked-out textbooks until 31 July 1946. In April 1946 (the beginning of the 1946 school year), it published and distributed "stopgap" textbooks in the subject areas permitted by the occupation forces. These textbooks were printed on large, coarse paper and folded in the shape of a newspaper. They were also in short supply, which provoked criticism from both teachers and parents.[20]

What were the reactions of local schools and teachers toward this blacking out process? It seems that many local schools and teachers believed that the occupation forces, or simply the *American* force, had ordered it. The schools and teachers tried to remove as much militaristic and ultranationalistic content as possible, since "it was most important to perform this task in a way that would prevent any problem from arising."[21] One teacher felt that "new orders came one after another from the American side," and that he had to follow them "without due (re)composition of his thoughts and feelings."[22]

The task, however, presented a considerable psychological conflict in those teachers who had been committed to wartime militarist, emperor-centered education practices and who were conscientious enough to be self-reflective. Popular novelist Miura Ayako, who was one such teacher, later wrote:

> While watching my students black-out [their textbooks], I wondered if there had ever been anyone who made their students do this kind of work. The textbooks I had [used] ... until yesterday contained things that should not have been taught ... Were the things I had taught really wrong? ... If they were, what should I say to apologize [to my students]? ... Thinking this way, it became painful for me to continue standing in front of my students as their teacher.[23]

Miura realized that "having [the students] black-out their textbooks made her distrust not only the government and politics but also all human beings." She finally left teaching in March 1946.

Blacking out textbooks gave Itakura Mie, an elementary school teacher, an eye-opening experience as well. Itakura was so firmly committed to the emperor-centered ideology that she went to the Imperial Palace on 16 August and pledged to continue to teach the emperor-centered view of history. However, after learning that the order to black-out textbooks came from the Japanese Ministry of Education, rather than the occupation forces, she began to reflect critically on her wartime teaching. As she put it: "I was told that [the textbook blacking-out] was the order of the Ministry of Education. I thought [they] must have mistaken [the Ministry] for GHQ [General Headquarters of the occupation forces]. But it was the Ministry.... I felt this beyond bearing."[24] Itakura also realized that she faced physically weak children, who were pale and afflicted by malnutrition and rashes. Recognizing her responsibility in promoting the war compelled her to leave teaching. (She continued to study, however, and became interested in teaching social studies. This encouraged her to return to teaching in the early 1950s.)[25]

In these early months of the occupation and its rapidly changing atmosphere, a good number of teachers left teaching – though the majority stayed in the job. Regardless of their decision, having to admit Japan's defeat to students and having them black-out their textbooks forced many teachers to realize that they had made serious mistakes by teaching a militarist, ultranationalist curriculum and promoting the war. In subsequent years, their repentance would manifest in their efforts to build Japan's postwar democratic education. As the above examples suggest, however, at this point they had a very limited perspective on the question of their personal (and collective) responsibility for the war. They felt responsible for the lessons they had taught their students, not for the atrocities that their nation and its military had committed toward other peoples and countries.

The last state-authored history textbooks

Initiatives for postwar history education and textbooks

The Supreme Commander for the Allied Powers (SCAP) began to issue its directives concerning education in general, and the curriculum and textbooks in particular, in October 1945. On 22 October SCAP prohibited the promotion of militaristic and ultranationalistic ideologies in and through education and suggested the establishment of an education system that would teach ideas and concepts of basic human rights. It also ordered the purge of militarist and ultranationalist teachers, and the reinstatement of those who had been removed because of their resistance to wartime education. On 30 October SCAP gave more specific instructions for the purge: those teachers who had implemented extremely militaristic education would be fired; all present and prospective teachers should be evaluated in terms of their wartime deeds (and current beliefs) to be qualified as adequate for postwar education.[26]

On 15 December SCAP ordered the abolition of any government propagation of Shinto, including a ban on the use of state-authored teaching materials, such as *Kokutai no Hongi* [The True Meaning of the National

Polity] and *Shinmin no Michi* [The Path of the Imperial Subject]. SCAP's informal pronouncements made it clear that Japanese history textbooks would have to be rewritten. Finally, on 31 December, SCAP ordered that teaching of morals (*shûshin*), Japanese history, and geography be suspended and that textbooks and teachers' guides prepared for these subject areas be withdrawn.

SCAP's 31 December order encouraged Japanese historians such as Ienaga Saburô to articulate ideas for postwar history education and textbooks. In the presurrender period, historical research conducted at the higher education level had been separated from the history instruction offered in primary and secondary schools. This allowed wartime history instruction in schools to become extremely ultranationalistic, and to center its curriculum on Japanese myths and other fallacies. Soon after the 31 December directive, Ienaga and others began to address the issues of Japan's postwar history education. They began by criticizing the separation of history teaching from historical research. Ienaga called for a history curriculum based on historical scholarship, an education that would teach verified – *kagakuteki* [scientific] to use his word – facts. As he stated:

> How do we search for the correct knowledge of Japanese history that should be the content of the correct teaching of the national history? I believe there is no other way but to seek it through the right kind of research on national history [*kokushigaku*]. It has often been said that history as a specialized discipline and the teaching of history are different. Some critics have even argued the two to be completely separate, but I have always disagreed with this view. In my view, the correct teaching of history has to be based on historical scholarship to the utmost.[27]

In early 1946, Ienaga published *Shin Nihonshi* [New Japanese History], a text that reflected his view that education should convey democratic values and the desire for peace (this project preceded his involvement in writing a state-authored textbook, *Kuni no Ayumi* [The Course of the Nation], discussed below). He wrote *Shin Nihonshi* as a vision of a history textbook (and education) for a postwar democratic nation. Although at this point Ienaga published the text through Fuzanbo, a commercial press, for the general audience, he was eventually able to publish it as a school textbook after the state introduced its textbook screening system and began to certify history textbooks for primary and secondary schools.[28]

Meanwhile, in the fall of 1945, the Ministry of Education began its project of writing new history textbooks.[29] First, in December, the Ministry formed an official committee to examine the contents of existing elementary and secondary school history textbooks. It then commissioned

Toyoda Takeshi, a compiler from the Ministry's Textbook Bureau, to write a history textbook. From the beginning, there was conflict between SCAP and the Ministry. While SCAP saw it necessary to write entirely new history textbooks, the Ministry insisted that it was sufficient to simply eliminate the militaristic content from already existing textbooks. Toyoda's textbook began with accounts of Japanese history in terms of some archaeological findings, which pleased SCAP's Civil Information and Education Section (CIE). But the text also included the mythology on Japan's divine origin – an element that the CIE could not overlook.[30] The project was canceled in May 1946, just after the account of the ancient period had been completed. SCAP suggested that the Ministry form a new history textbook writing committee with historians who had not previously served on the Textbook Bureau.[31]

The ministry launched a new project to develop three textbooks (for elementary schools, secondary schools, and teacher training colleges), each dividing Japanese history into four periods: ancient, medieval, early modern, and modern/contemporary. The site of this project was the refectory of the Historiographical Institute at Tokyo Imperial University. It commissioned eleven historians for the project, with each member selecting and organizing the textbook content for their assigned sections. All eleven, however, followed three common principles: (1) no propaganda of any kind; (2) no militarism, ultranationalism, or propagation of Shintoism; and (3) the inclusion of the accomplishments of ordinary people in the areas of economy, invention, scholarship, and art, with mention of the successive emperors' achievements whenever appropriate. SCAP had its Japanese employees examine the manuscripts daily, and although it never actively asked the authors to include specific descriptions (except for some phrases referring to the building of a democratic Japan that were inserted at the end of the textbooks), it did screen some passages.[32]

Ienaga was asked to write about the ancient period for the elementary school textbook, later entitled *Kuni no ayumi*.[33] He used Toyoda's draft as a basis because he faced severe time restrictions – the manuscript had to be finished in one month's time. But Ienaga extended Toyoda's revision in some significant ways. For example, he deleted much of the mythology that Toyoda had included. He also began the text with a description of Stone-Age civilization, and proceeded objectively to describe the formation of Japan as a state.[34] *Kuni no ayumi*, published in September 1946, was the first postwar state-authored history textbook. It was also the first school textbook to list the names of the actual authors. The Ministry published two other textbooks: *Nihon no rekishi* [History of Japan, published in 1946] for secondary schools, and *Nihon rekishi* [Japanese History, published in 1947] for teacher training colleges. These first three books were also to become the last state-authored history textbooks in the course of postwar educational reforms.

The Tokyo war tribunal and limited perspectives and sources for history textbooks

The authors of the first (and last) postwar state-authored textbooks attempted to overcome the militaristic influence of wartime educational policies and textbooks, and SCAP did not dictate what they should write. The authors were, however, still constrained by the political, social, and cultural conditions of the period. With respect to the material on World War II, they changed the name of the war from *Daitôa Sensô* [The Great East Asian War], the term created by the Japanese government and used in wartime textbooks, to *Taiheiyô sensô* [The Pacific War]. This change reflected SCAP's prohibition of the official use of the former term and its promotion of the latter. Beginning in December 1945, SCAP ordered all major newspapers, as well as the Nippon Hôsô Kyôkai (NHK), a public broadcasting company, to run a series of articles and radio programs concerning the war. These were written and produced by the CIE as part of a re-education effort for the Japanese. The articles and programs used the term *Taiheiyô sensô*, which quickly spread among the Japanese.[35]

To change the name of the war in the textbooks was much easier than addressing the far more complicated question of war responsibility. This latter task was not only more immediately political, but also required profoundly critical perspectives and self-reflective insights. Time did not allow the authors of the last state-authored textbooks to think this question through; even if they had been given the necessary time, however, it seems somewhat doubtful that they could have adequately addressed the question. (Subsequent history shows that it took years for Japanese intellectuals and historians, including Ienaga, to develop the critical perspectives and knowledge necessary to address this question.) At the time, the information on the war (and Japanese war crimes) was limited; the evidence produced in the Tokyo war tribunal sessions was sometimes the only source available to the authors.

In addition, the Tokyo war tribunal, which was the main instrument for uncovering Japanese war crimes and dealing with the question of war responsibility, did not fully accomplish its mission. At the tribunal court, which began on 3 May 1946, SCAP and Japan's ruling forces found themselves, coincidentally or not, in agreement over the question of Emperor Hirohito's war responsibility. SCAP was inclined to use the authority of the emperor to implement occupation policies and reforms. The Japanese ruling classes – especially those close to the Imperial Court – actively helped indict Japan's top wartime military leaders (mostly from the Japanese army, such as Tôjô Hideki, a general and the prime minister from October 1941 to July 1944). This was to shift the war responsibility onto them and to avoid the prosecution of the emperor. (This framework also allowed ordinary Japanese citizens to avoid questions concerning their personal and collective war responsibility – though there were, of course, a few individuals who were deeply concerned with the issue.)

The process of the Tokyo tribunal increasingly reflected U.S. interests, particularly as signs of the impending Cold War surfaced. For example, the United States granted immunity from prosecution to military officers and personnel involved in the experiments of Unit 731, Japan's bio-warfare unit, in exchange for the information they had accumulated from their experiments. Also, the verdict of the Tokyo war tribunal (handed down in November 1948) for the most part disregarded Japan's respons-ibility for the war in Asia. The tribunal's findings regarding Japanese war crimes were (extremely) limited and involved only a small number of the indicted leaders. Besides, the tribunal faced difficult legal issues concern-ing the punishments of individual high-ranking officials for the war crimes committed by the state.[36] The decision, for example, acknowledged the deaths of more than 200,000 civilians and POWs in Nanjing and its out-skirts within six weeks after the Japanese army occupied the city in 1937 (an event known as the Nanjing Massacre) and sentenced the command-ing officer of the operation, General Matsui Iwane, to death. The tribunal, however, did not necessarily deal with all the questions concerning the atrocity.

In October 1948, before the tribunal submitted its November verdicts, the United States officially decided to place the importance of Japan's economic recovery above its democratization in order to counter the com-munist threat of the Eastern bloc, and for this reason, it decided not to hold further tribunal sessions. In fact, though the execution of seven war criminals sentenced to death in November, including wartime prime minister Tôjô Hideki, took place on 24 December, several A-class war crime suspects still detained and awaiting trial were set free the next day. Those released included Kishi Nobusuke, who later became prime minis-ter, and the second and third rounds of prosecution previously intended were canceled.[37]

Another problem was that the tribunal did not regard some of the Japanese war atrocities as war crimes. The existence of comfort facilities and comfort women, for example, had been known. In fact, at the end of war, the Allied forces (mainly U.S. forces) took many comfort women – mostly Korean women – into custody as POWs (they belonged to the Japanese military). While aware through interviews that many of the women had been forced to work in the comfort facilities, the Allied forces did not consider the matter a war crime that required prosecution of the Japanese involved. Except two cases – one involving Dutch women in Indonesia, and the other involving Guam female residents – they did not feel obligated to conduct further investigations. Nor did the tribunal court.[38]

War-related materials in the last three state-authored history textbooks

The extent to which the process of the tribunal directly influenced the authors of the last state-authored history textbooks is largely a matter of conjecture. The textbooks indicate only that the authors recognized Japan's wrongdoings in the war – at least to the extent to which those crimes could be known at that time (mainly through the tribunal's fact-finding processes). They also attempted to address the question of responsibility, but they were not able to go beyond the tribunal findings.

All three textbooks, for example, described the 1937 Nanjing Massacre from a critical perspective (albeit modestly and briefly). These descriptions offered a stark contrast to that given in the wartime state-authored elementary school history textbook (published in 1943), which described the event as one of the heroic moments of Japanese military operations in China. In its words: "[H]ighly loyal, strong, and brave imperial officers and soldiers ... captured the capital Nanjing on 13 December and flew the flag of the Rising Sun from the top of the fortress."[39] Contrary to this wartime description, *Kuni no ayumi*, in its section of modern and contemporary history written by Ienaga's co-author Okubo Toshikane, wrote, "[Our military] ravaged Nanjing, the capital of the Republic of China."[40] The statement was brief, but it clearly indicated that the event was now seen as one of Japan's wartime atrocities.

Nihon no rekishi, the textbook for secondary schools, included the line, "Our army committed atrocities while occupying Nanjing."[41] Further, *Nihon rekishi*, a textbook for the teacher training colleges, stated: "The war situation became more and more complicated, and the resistance on the Chinese side grew more intense, triggered by the Japanese army's atrocities in Nanjing."[42] These descriptions were not extensive, and they dealt with the matter in a somewhat passing manner; nonetheless, they represented the textbook authors' view that the event involved atrocities committed by the Japanese army during wartime. It was clear that the authors felt that the event deserved attention in the textbooks.[43]

Discussion on various questions concerning the responsibility for the war (e.g. what kinds of responsibilities existed and who bore ultimate responsibility for Japan's war of aggression) was another matter, however. All three textbooks basically blamed the military. For example, in describing the beginning of Japan's aggression against China, *Kuni no ayumi* stated:

> There was peace for a while after the end of World War I in Europe, but from that time, the atmosphere of our nation gradually changed. In particular, the influence of the military spread throughout the spheres of politics and the economy, and society became turbulent, leading to such bloody events as the 15 May and 26 February incidents. Finally, because of the affairs in Manchuria, a troublesome

entanglement developed with the Republic of China, and peace in the East fell into disarray.[44]

It described Japan's defeat as follows: "Our nation was defeated. The people suffered greatly because of the long war. The military's suppression of the people and its waging a reckless war caused this unhappiness."[45] The text did not in any way consider Emperor Hirohito's responsibility for the war. In fact, the textbook cited Hirohito's January 1946 statement as a new direction for Japan as a democratic nation. In this statement, Hirohito stressed the importance of rebuilding Japan as a peaceful nation by referring to the Imperial Covenant of Five Articles (the famous oath taken by the Meiji Emperor in 1868 at the beginning of his reign).

The three textbooks were not without their shortcomings. *Kuni no ayumi*, perhaps because it was the first of the three to appear, was criticized by the Japanese left wing[46] and by several foreign countries for failing to completely eradicate the "emperor-centered view of history" (*kôkoku shikan*).[47] Ienaga himself also admitted its shortcomings. However, to be fair one must note that, in rewriting history, especially the history of the war, these authors had only limited access to sources since, strictly speaking, research on the subject had yet to be conducted. In any case, the publication of the last three state-authored history textbooks clearly marked the beginning of Japan's postwar historical studies, the teaching of its history, and the controversy over its textbooks.

The 1947 constitution and the struggle over new curricula

The 1947 constitution and the Fundamental Law of Education

The "democratization" of Japan under the occupation moved along swiftly, at least on the surface. The new constitution, promulgated in November 1946 and put into effect in May 1947, offered a picture of nationhood that differed remarkably from the militarist, (ultra)nationalist, and emperor-centered nation of the presurrender period. The postwar constitution stated that sovereignty resided with the people, gave the emperor (and his successors) a status as "symbol" of the nation (Article 1), guaranteed basic human rights (Article 11), and renounced war (Article 9). (Because of its renunciation of war, it has often been called the Peace Constitution.) At the same time, the constitution guaranteed academic freedom (Article 23) and the people's right to an education (Article 26), thus giving shape to the "new education."

On 31 March 1947, the Japanese government proclaimed both the Fundamental Law of Education (*Kyôiku Kihonhō*) and the School Education Law (*Gakko Kyōikuhō*).[48] The Fundamental Law of Education articulated the key principles of postwar education, including the goal to provide "full development of personality" (Article 1), as well as provisions for "equal opportunity in education" (Article 3), and "coeducation" (Article 5). The law also instituted "nine years of free compulsory education" (Article 4), by which schools would be reorganized into a 6–3–3 system (six-year elementary, three-year junior high, and three-year high schools).[49] Most important, it stated that "Education shall not be subject to improper control, but it shall be directly responsible to the whole people" (Article 10), the concern here being a fear of the state's oppressive control over education.[50] The law served, in a sense, as an educational constitution. As the Ministry of Education put it, the legislation was "a declaration of new educational ideals" in the nature of "an absolutely indispensable law with regard to educational matters." Since the law was designed to shape the subsequent course of educational law and policy, it served to replace the Imperial Rescript on Education.[51]

In contrast, the School Education Law, which dealt with the practical operation of schools (including textbook policy), allowed the state to continue to hold its control over schools. For example, although both the first U.S. education mission to Japan and the Japanese Education Committee (formed to welcome the mission, and chaired by Nambara Shigeru) suggested that textbooks be freely published and freely selected,[52] the School Education Law stipulated that elementary school textbooks were to be screened, approved, or authored by "competent authorities" (*Kantoku-chô*, Article 21). The law also stipulated similar procedures for secondary school textbooks. At first, it was understood that "competent authorities" would consist of the Ministry of Education as well as the prefectural education boards to be created. However, through the School Education Law Enforcement Regulations issued in May 1947 (which was not an actual piece of legislation), the ministry defined itself as the sole "competent authority." This interpretation was, in the Ministry's words, to be in force "for the time being," but subsequently it became permanent.

Interestingly, the first postwar curriculum policy reflected more of the democratization ideal of Japanese education than the textbook policy as stipulated by the School Education Law. The Ministry of Education's *Gakushûshidô Yoryô: Ippanhen (Shian)* [Instructional Guidelines: General Guide (A Tentative Plan), hereafter the *1947 General Guide*], which was prepared in late fall 1946 and published on 20 March 1947, just before the promulgation of the two laws, criticized Japan's presurrender education and its policies over their having brought uniformity to schools. It argued, instead, that, within certain goals and frameworks, each school and teacher should creatively devise educational content and teaching methods appropriate to the needs of their students, school resources, and community environments. As such, the guidelines were "tentative," rather than "prescriptive." Indeed, the *1947 General Guide* defined itself as not the teachers' manual of the past, but a "guide" (*tebiki*): "[This volume] is written as a guide for teachers to inquire into ways to make use of [ideas for] a course of study (*kyōiku katei*) that has newly arisen to meet the demands of students and society."[53]

In fact, the volume presented the results of curriculum research rather than statements on curriculum standards, so as to give teachers ideas and examples. This approach was new to most teachers, and it was particularly encouraging for enthusiastic teachers with progressive and innovative inclinations. For example, Ogino Sue, an elementary school teacher, at first found "the title *Instructional Guidelines* strange" and "its horizontal writing hard to read." The phrase "tentative plan," however, captured his attention. As he put it:

> My honest feeling was that it [the meaning of "tentative plan"] *hardly made sense*. It was explained as follows: "It is hoped that those who read this text, keeping in mind that this was created as a mere trial, give [the Ministry] plenty of suggestions and cooperate in producing a perfect one hereafter." For the first time [in my life], I felt close to the Ministry of Education, which was a government office, one that I had [previously] perceived as existing [far] above the clouds.[54]

Ogino attended the meetings where officials from the prefectural education department explained the guidelines. As he recalls, he saw many teachers repeatedly asking the same question: "Is it all right" for teachers to decide actual lesson plans and daily curriculum? The curriculum approach was quite different from that used during the presurrender period. Ogino, like other teachers, asked about the meaning of "tentative plan," and one official responded with a smile, "This is the Ministry of Education's book. [We] would like to have teachers make the actual one." Ogino felt his pulse racing with "a sensation full of life and energy."[55]

In subsequent years, local schools and teachers, encouraged by the idea of empowering teachers in the domain of curriculum deliberations – the most radical idea conveyed by the 1947 guidelines – made numerous efforts to develop their own curricula to suit their districts and schools.[56] In the 1950s, however, as conservatives regained control of the government, the Ministry of Education began to reverse this policy. It removed the phrase "tentative plan" and announced that its guidelines were a "legally binding force." This obligated schools and teachers to base their instructions on the educational content that the guidelines prescribed.

The replacement of history education with "social studies"

While the institutional reorganization of Japanese education – in particular the transition to the 6–3–3 system – was underway, the idea for replacing history education with a new, integrated subject called "social studies" (*shakaika*) was also being introduced. In September 1946, after the publication of *Kuni no ayumi*, SCAP allowed schools to resume the teaching of history, though the extent to which they actually did differed. About one month later, however, the Ministry of Education (with the support of some SCAP officials) announced the introduction of social studies for the 1947 school year.

The new subject would integrate four previously separate subjects – morals, civics, geography, and history – into one course in which students would explore several major problems in relation to their own experiences. This curriculum design, which basically precluded teaching history in its chronological narrative form (*keitô gakushû*), sparked controversy within and outside the ministry. Most historians, for example, opposed the idea of social studies because they thought that the chronological teaching of history was necessary to explain origins and developments of historical events. Some CIE officials involved in the state-authored history textbook project also opposed the idea, since it would render the three history textbooks – two of which had just been published and the other being prepared for publication – useless from April 1947.[57] This dissent was not, however, powerful enough to reverse the policy.

Just when most people thought they had seen the last of chronological history teaching, however, a certain faction of the Ministry of Education succeeded in having a subject called "national history" (*kokushi*) included in the required subject list for grades eight and nine (the last two years of compulsory education) of the *1947 General Guide*. An already confusing situation became more so with this insertion, because the volume containing the subject guidelines for "national history," one that was required to immediately follow the *1947 General Guide*, had yet to be developed. That is, the content of "national history" remained undefined and textbooks unavailable. It was also not clear whether "national history" should mean "chronological history." Rather, it seemed that the door was ever so slightly reopened to allow proponents of history education to resist "social studies" and to revive some kind of history teaching. In any case, the Ministry of Education was thus compelled to notify schools that the implementation of social studies would be postponed, and that *Nihon no rekishi*, the state-authored history textbook for secondary schools, might be used to teach "national history."[58]

Schools began teaching social studies in September 1947, but high school education under the 6–3–3 system was to start in April 1948. In the fall of 1947, the pro-history faction within the Ministry again succeeded in adding "national history" (later renamed "Japanese history") to the required high school subjects. The ministry then created the Committee for Compiling Secondary School National History Textbooks (*Chûtô Kokushi Kyôkashô Hensan Iinkai*). It invited notable historians of different traditions, not including imperialists and ultranationalists, to join this committee. The ministry's intent was to gather support from these historians for the idea of teaching history within a social studies framework, and to develop national history textbooks compatible with the idea of social studies. This effort failed as the views of most of the committee members differed from the ministry's. Consequently, the committee was unable to develop the textbooks.

Under these circumstances, in the fall of 1948, the ministry notified high schools of an amendment to the high school subject guidelines, with social studies consisting of one required subject (general social studies) and four electives (national history, world history, human geography, and current events). Although the Ministry announced that these subjects would be implemented during the 1949 school year, it failed to issue the appropriate instructions on time. The Ministry did not complete the subject guidelines for high school Japanese history until 1951 (publishing them in 1952). Because of this, even though it introduced the textbook screening system in 1948, it was years before the Ministry could accept manuscripts for high school Japanese history textbooks. In any case, a new situation emerged from the struggle for a social studies curriculum: while history in elementary schools was replaced with social studies, the idea of teaching history within a framework of social studies did not really materialize at the secondary school level.[59]

How the schools and teachers dealt with curriculum changes during these years varied with each specific instance, especially within the elementary schools, where social studies gained some acceptance. According to a memoir written by Kanazawa Kaichi, an elementary school teacher (and later a principal) in Tokyo, Japanese history was not taught at his school during the early years of the occupation. Then one year, to his surprise, he found that his students wanted to study Japanese history. As he put it:

> On 8 January, 1950, after the opening assembly for the [third] term, I asked my sixth-grade homeroom students, "Well now, you have only three months to go as sixth-graders. Let's study hard to be sure that you have nothing to regret later. So tell me what, if anything, you want to be taught before your graduation." One of the students said, "Please teach Japanese history." ... I was shocked because I had not taught anything like history [during the occupation years]. Because other students also said that they wanted to be taught [the subject], for three months until their graduation, I forgot myself and taught [them] Japanese history. This was during the Occupation, when teaching history was not welcome ... [I used] *Kuni no ayumi* as a textbook.[60]

Kanazawa was somewhat critical of the way social studies was implemented during the occupation. The approach was more top-down, at least in its initial stage. Sakurada Elementary School – the school next to his – specialized in social studies curriculum research and occupation officials sometimes visited that school. In Kanazawa's view, Sakurada implemented social studies education "for the United States." One example he gave concerned the story of a street urchin:[61] when the child found a job in the area of Sakurada and wanted to attend the school, it refused to admit him on the grounds that "*Our* school is a school for social studies research, ... [and so it] cannot admit street urchins." The school's refusal to admit the student left Kanazawa with a poor opinion of the school. As he put it in his memoirs:

> If social studies is a subject that is based on the surrounding area, and on dealing with the problems that arise there, the problem of street urchins was the most pressing, real problem [social studies had to address] in [our] area of Shinbashi, Tokyo, at the time. Furthermore, it was a problem that involved children, [one that the students can reflect upon] as their own. I thought that if [Sakurada] had been [truly] a school of social studies research, it should have been that much more willing to admit the child.[62]

This street urchin ended up in Kanazawa's class. Kanazawa himself stated he "was not able to adapt to the social studies [practiced] during the occupation." The subject, in his view, was U.S.-centered rather than one that addressed the problems facing the Japanese people.[63] The Ministry's top-down implementation of the subject seemed to have met with resistance from teachers like Kanazawa who were in the process of developing critical perspectives and consciousness in these early postwar years.

To be sure, Kanazawa did not oppose the core idea of social studies. The above quote suggests that he had a good grasp of what the subject should be – to teach students about societal problems by examining their experiences in the surrounding communities. Indeed, in the 1950s, a greater number of progressive teachers became involved in developing social studies lesson plans at local levels, and these plans were more or less along the lines of the idea expressed by Kanazawa. Ironically, around the same period, as the conservatives regained power, the Japanese government came to see that social studies education was too progressive in its original model with an orientation toward curriculum integration and problem solving, and began to change its form and content. In response, progressive teachers and intellectuals began to counter such state efforts by promoting and defending social studies.

Postwar textbook screening and history textbooks

The introduction of postwar textbook screening

In September 1947, the Ministry of Education announced that it would introduce a textbook screening system in 1948 (for the 1949 school year textbooks), without clarifying that it would halt the publication of state-authored textbooks. The Ministry formed several committees to develop ideas and policies for the system, and the Japan Teachers Union (JTU) also sent its representatives. Furthermore, around this time, the Ministry suggested that schools, in consultation with their teachers, select textbooks appropriate to their own educational needs, though it failed to legally define who would have the authority to adopt these textbooks.[64] Many concerned with education, including teachers, scholars, and the editorial staffs of publishing houses, welcomed the Ministry's position, and immediately initiated a number of new textbook projects. Even the JTU launched its own textbook projects, and eventually submitted nearly sixty manuscripts for screening.

Textbook screening under the occupation was a complicated and convoluted, twofold process. Publishers were required to submit both Japanese and English versions of their manuscripts, with the Ministry of Education responsible for screening the Japanese manuscripts. In the Ministry's screening process, five commissioned examiners evaluated the manuscripts, and sixteen appointed committee members made decisions regarding approval. The CIE screened English-language versions of approved manuscripts. Then, if the CIE requested a revision, the publishers or authors had to revise and resubmit the manuscript to the Ministry's committee. The 1948 textbook screening was a rushed process, and only a small number of textbooks gained approval. As of 11 August, 418 of the 584 texts submitted had passed the Ministry's screening, but only ninety of those gained CIE clearance.

From 25 August the textbooks that passed the screening process were displayed in local school districts. Only sixty-two textbooks were in time for this stage, including two written by the JTU. Many teachers visited the display halls to examine the texts; the atmosphere was one of excitement and enthusiasm, an attitude that continued in subsequent years. Tokutake Toshio, then an editorial staff member of the Chūkyō Shuppan publishing house, recalled: "I visited the display hall everyday. It was around the time of 1950–55. There were always groups of teachers examining, comparing, and discussing the textbooks."[65]

In general, because teachers felt obligated to promote the "non-governmental" textbooks, the state-authored textbooks lost a significant share of the market. In 1950, the Ministry of Education announced that it would cease writing textbooks, though it made one last futile attempt to reintroduce its own "standard textbooks" in 1952. After this failed, the Ministry finally decided to stop publishing state-authored textbooks (which was indeed a gradual process, beginning in 1953 and taking several years to complete). This did not mean, however, that the Ministry would abandon its control over textbooks, but that it began to influence textbook content by way of textbook screening and other means.

The content of non-government history textbooks

Many textbooks that were not state authored represented Japan's war with China and its occupation of other countries as Japanese "aggression" (*shinryaku*). For example, a survey of fifteen junior high school textbooks on Japanese history published in the early 1950s (ones examined by the author for this chapter) revealed that twelve used the term "aggression" in one way or another to describe Japanese military activities in, and conflicts with, China from the early 1930s. This was especially true of descriptions of the Manchurian Incident of 1931 – when Japan conquered Manchuria, established a puppet government in Manchukuo and appointed Henry Pu-yi, the heir to the Manchu dynasty, as "provisional president."[66]

Several textbooks also included descriptions of the Nanjing Massacre of 1937. *Gendai Nihon no naritachi* [The origin of contemporary Japan], a high school textbook published in 1952, contained the line, "The Japanese Army's ways of pillaging and assault, including 'the violent incident of Nanjing,' brought it worldwide notoriety."[67] *Gendai Sekai no naritachi* [The Origins of the Contemporary World], another high school textbook published in 1952, read: "The occupation of Nanjing resounded throughout the world because of the notoriety of 'the violent incident of Nanjing,' so-called because of the Japanese Army's destruction of the city, its pillaging, and its assaults."[68] Another textbook *Chûgaku shakai* [Junior high school social studies], published in 1954, provided even more details of the massacre:

> [The Japanese] army occupied northern China within the year and captured Nanjing. At that time, the army, entering the fortress Nanjing in triumph, inflicted severe acts of violence on the civilians. Because of this, the people of the world increasingly denounced Japan and sympathized with China.[69]

Moreover, some textbooks also recognized Japan's aggression in other Asian regions. *Chûgaku shakai* made the following reference to Japan's war crimes and the anti-Japanese resistance in Southeast Asia:

> Because the Japanese military committed violent acts in the various territories it occupied, it incurred [native] inhabitants' enmity. In places such as the Philippines, Malaya, Indochina, and Indonesia, the inhabitants sustained covert resistance movements for independence from Japanese occupation.[70]

Such descriptions suggest that early postwar history textbook authors recognized Japan's atrocities as war crimes, and understood the importance of representing them as such in school textbooks. In other words, one can see signs suggesting that the authors' intention was to increase coverage of Japanese aggression in future editions.[71]

These non-government textbooks published in the early 1950s, however, did not pursue the question of war responsibility to the extent that a contemporary critic might wish. Many framed their discussion around the results of the Tokyo war tribunal. In this regard, their perspectives were limited, as were those of the three state-authored history textbooks discussed earlier. Most textbooks blamed the military for aggression in Asia and tyranny in Japan, but none questioned, or referred to, Emperor Hirohito's war responsibility. Several textbooks represented Hirohito as a figure whose authority and power were exploited by the (fascist) military leaders and as a monarch who, in the end, suppressed the pro-war military and ordered the war's end.

Nor did the textbooks explore the issue of the responsibility of the Japanese citizens for the war. Instead, they generally represented the Japanese people as having been deceived by propaganda filtered through the military's control of the media, education, and other information outlets. For example, the 1955 edition of *Atarashii shakai* [New social studies] referred to civilians twice in its section on the Asia-Pacific War. One reference appeared in the textbook's discussion on the rise of the Japanese military dictatorship during the early 1930s. It explained the relationship between ordinary Japanese and the military dictatorship as follows:

> Around this time, the political parties lost the trust of the people because they connected with the *zaibatsu* [financial conglomerates] to pursue only their own interests and ignored the people's sufferings. The military cleverly took advantage of this and attempted to end the party system and impose a military dictatorship ... After the February 26 incident, members of the armed forces secured all important political positions ... Even liberals and believers in democracy, not to mention socialists, were denounced as traitors to the nation. In this way, the people were gradually driven into war.[72]

A second reference appeared in the textbook's discussion of wartime Japan, specifically its description of the people's lives during the war's final phase:

> The people's lives were unusually difficult. They faced starvation, their houses were burned down, and they lived on a day-to-day basis with fear of air raids. They came to hope that the war would end. However, the military did not listen to the people's wishes and only clamored for the decisive battle on the homeland.[73]

People here were not portrayed as active participants in history but, instead, as people who were manipulated, had no voice, and were forced to obey. This image, while not entirely false, was a selective representation of a rather heterogeneous population, many of whom were, in fact, strong-minded ultranationalists at grassroots levels.

Conclusion

The postwar reforms that took place in Japan at the very beginning of the occupation spoke of a new social framework centered on ideas such as "democracy" and "freedom." Without question, the occupation brought significant changes to the legal and institutional frames and arrangements of Japanese education, including coeducation and the extension of free compulsory education to nine years, to name a few. However, it is also the case that at least some of these reforms caused confusion and conflict. They also did not necessarily eradicate all the administrative, pedagogical, and cultural practices of Japanese education developed under the wartime emperor-centered and ultranationalist regime. Rather, the occupation forces introduced reforms through the existing presurrender system, and continued the top-down approach that was in place before their arrival. This allowed them to quickly introduce reforms that reached the local schools in a short period of time. But it also created a fundamental contradiction – educational reforms intended to initiate democracy being implemented in a rather undemocratic manner.

It should be noted, however, that occupation-era educational reforms also opened up space that allowed seminal struggles for alternative and oppositional national narratives and identities, along with a new perspective on history as research and education, to emerge at different locations in the educational system. The authors of the last state-authored history textbooks attempted to develop new national narratives; teachers and administrators in local schools began to reflect critically on their wartime education. Yet their perspectives were limited and ambiguous on some important questions concerning the responsibility for the war in general, and ones concerning the emperor's role and the people's responsibility in particular. Such limitations and ambiguities in the three state-authored textbooks, as well as in daily school/classroom practices, are perhaps to be expected. After all, a nation's perception of who "we" are cannot be changed overnight, and so, in a circumstance like the occupation, schools and teachers may serve both as agents of social change and criticism as well as the conservers/repository of dominant culture and tradition.

Textbook publication through the state screening system, which allowed private publishing houses to write and publish textbooks, produced substantive developments both in the variety and the quality of textbooks. These textbooks indicated that the question of war responsibility, a significant part of Japan's national narrative and identity, would be further explored, and that insights on these issues would deepen in the future. However, in the later stages of the occupation, the United States shifted its policy emphasis from the demilitarization and democratization of Japan to the establishment of an anti-communist bloc, thereby allowing Japan to remilitarize. This shift enabled Japan's imperialists and (ultra)nationalists to recover from their set-back of the nation's defeat in the war. The Japanese conservative power bloc gained control of the state in the 1950s. Although it fell just short of changing the 1947 constitution in the late 1950s and 1960s, it did succeed in reversing many postwar educational reforms, either by legislation or by regulation.

Notes

1 Japanese names in this chapter follow the Japanese name order, except author names for their English publications.
2 Monbushô, "Shûsen ni kansuru ken" [The matter concerning the end of war, Monbushô Kunrei Dai-5-go, 15 August 1945], cited in Nagahama Isao, *Nihon fashizumu kyôshi-ron: Kyôshi-tachi no hachi-gatsu jûgo-nichi* [On Japan's fascist teachers: The teachers on August 15th], Tokyo: Akashi shoten, 1984, p. 95. The term *kokutai* is often translated as "national polity," but I would suggest "emperor-centered nationhood" as its proximate meaning (the exact translation of the term is difficult). For further discussion, see Richard Minear, *Japanese tradition and Western law: emperor, state, and law in the thought of Hozumi Yatsuka*, Cambridge: Harvard University Press, 1970, pp. 56–83.
3 Miura Ayako, *Ishikoro no uta* [A song of stones], Tokyo: Kadokawa shoten, 1979, p. 289. Miura, one of the most popular female writers in postwar Japan, was a schoolteacher at the time of Japan's surrender. The book is one of Miura's autobiographical works.
4 A school record entry, Maruko Chûô Elementary School, cited in Nagahama, *Nihon fashizumu*, p. 93.
5 Nagai Kenji, *Kyôshi wa haisen wo dô mukaetanoka: Kunô to mosaku no hibi ninenkan no kyôiku nisshi* [How the teachers met defeat: The educational record of two years of agony and groping], Tokyo: Kyôikushiryô shuppankai, 1999, pp. 95–6.
6 "Kimigayo," a song wishing for the long reign of an emperor on the throne, was played at national, state, and school ceremonies before and after the war, but it was only 1991 when it legally became Japan's national anthem. Since then, the legal designation of "Kimigayo" as the national anthem has been controversial. For further discussion, see, for example, Tanaka Nobumasa, *Hinomaru kimigayo no sengoshi* [The postwar history of the flag hinomaru and the song kimigayo], Tokyo: Iwanami shoten, 2000; and Yamagishi Shigeru, *"Kimigayo" wo utaimasuka?: Anatani totte kokka towa* [Would you like to sing Kimigayo? What "national anthem" means to you], Tokyo: Waseda shuppan, 2000.
7 An entry from *Ina-shôgakko hyakunenshi* [The hundred year history of Ina Elementary School], cited in Nagahama, *Nihon fashizumu*, pp. 124–5.
8 Isoda Takeshi, *Aru kyôshi no kuju no kaiso: Komesôdô kara kinpyô made* [A teacher's bitter memoirs: From the rice riots to the Kinpyo struggle], Osaka: Shikishobô, 1977, pp. 148–9.
9 Nagahama, *Nihon fashizumu*, p. 93.
10 See also Yasukawa Junosuke, *Jûgonen sensô to kyôiku* [The fifteen-year war and education], Tokyo: Shinnihon shuppansha, 1986, pp. 178–84.
11 Teachers had taught students that a *kamikaze* (divine wind) would blow and beat the enemies (as it had blown off the Mongolians invading Japan in the thirteenth century).
12 Nagai, *Kyôshi wa haisen*, pp. 1–11.

13 Ibid., pp. 88–91.
14 Ichijo Fumi, *Awaki wataame no tameni: Senjika Shimokitakata nôminso no kiroku* [*For pale cotton candy: A record of Shimokitakata peasantry during the war*], Tokyo: Domesu shuppan, 1976.
15 For more details, see John Caiger, "Ienaga Saburô and the first postwar Japanese history textbook," *Modern Asian studies*, 3.1, 1969, pp. 1–17.
16 See, for example, Nakamura Kikuji, *Kyôkasho no shakaishi: Meiji ishin kara haisen made* [*A social history of textbooks: from the Meiji restoration to defeat in the war*], Tokyo: Iwanami shoten, 1992, pp. 220–1; and Yoko H. Thakur, "History textbook reform in allied occupied Japan, 1945–52," *History of education quarterly*, 35.3, 1995, pp. 261–78.
17 See Yamazumi Masami, *Nihon kyôiku shôshi* [*A concise history of Japanese education*], Tokyo: Iwanami Shuppan, 1987. For the song "Kimigayo," see note 6 above.
18 For additional discussions, see, for example, Byron K. Marshall, *Learning to be modern: Japanese political discourse on education*, Boulder: Westview Press, 1994, pp. 58–62; and Teruhisa Horio, *Educational thought and ideology in modern Japan*, Tokyo: University of Tokyo Press, 1988, pp. 65–72.
19 See Nakamura, *Kyôkasho no shakaishi*, pp. 220–38.
20 The stopgap textbooks were distributed in the 1947 school year also. For further discussion of the stopgap textbooks, see Tokutake Toshio, *Kyôkasho no sengoshi* [*The postwar history of textbooks*], Tokyo: Shin Nihon shuppansha, 1995, pp. 44–5; and Kyôiku no Sengoshi Henshû Iinkai, ed., *Sengo kyôiku kaikaku to sono hôkai heno michi* [*Postwar educational reform and the course of its collapse*], Tokyo: San'ichi shobô, 1986, pp. 131–2.
21 Nagahama, *Nihon fashizumu*, p. 311.
22 Kanazawa Kaichi, *Aru shôgakkôchô no kaisô* [*Memoir of a school principal*], Tokyo: Iwanami shoten, 1967, pp. 45–6.
23 Miura, *Ishikoro no uta*, pp. 292–3.
24 Kawana Kimi, *Onna mo sensô wo ninatta* [*Women also took part in the war*], Tokyo: Tôjusha, 1982, pp. 64–5.
25 Kawana, *Onna mo sensô*, p. 67.
26 This process of teacher evaluation turned out to be very problematic, because all the teachers had collaborated with the wartime Japanese government and the difference was only a matter of degree. For further discussion, see Nagahama Isao, *Kyôiku no sensô sekinin: Kyôikugakusha no shisô to kôdô, zôho* [*Education's war responsibility: Educational researchers' thoughts and deeds, enlarged edition*], Tokyo: Akashi shoten, 1992, pp. 268–309.
27 Ienaga Saburô, "Kongo no kokushi kyôiku" ["The future of national history education"], *Shôchô*, October 1946, p. 14. Ienaga also stressed the importance of empirical studies of history, and criticized not only studies conducted by imperialist historians of the presurrender period, but also the arguments made by Marxist historians who revived the tradition immediately after Japan's defeat.
28 See Ienaga Saburô, "Sengo no rekishi kyôiku" [Postwar history education], in *Iwanami kôza Nihon rekishi*, vol. 22, *bekkan*, supplement, no. 1, Tokyo: Iwanami shoten, 1968, p. 319.
29 Ienaga, "Sengo no rekishi," p. 316.
30 See Ienaga, "Sengo no rekishi," pp. 314–17; and Thakur "History textbook reform," pp. 267–8.
31 Another project, this one for teacher training schools, was also in progress under the leadership of Maruyama Kunio, who remained as an author for the new project.
32 See Yamazumi Masami, *Shakaika kyôiku no shuppatsu* [*The start of social studies*

education], Tokyo: Nihon tosho senta, 1981, pp. 16–8; and Ienaga, "Sengo no rekishi," pp. 318–19.

33 Ienaga's specialty was in the area of ancient Japanese history. His Ph.D. dissertation was on eighth- to twelfth-century Japanese cultural history. According to Ienaga, most of the members were "empiricist" (*jisshōshugi*) historians who were generally apolitical around that time and who had had little experience teaching history in grade schools. See Ienaga, "Sengo no rekishi," p. 319.

34 See Caiger, "Ienaga Saburô," pp. 12–13, for the actual citation of the opening paragraphs of the textbook.

35 The term is still popular. See Yoshida Yutaka, *Nihonjin no sensôkan: sengoshi no nakano henyô* [*Japanese views on the war: changes in postwar history*], Tokyo: Iwanami shoten, 1995, pp. 26–34.

36 For further discussion, see Richard H. Minear, *Victors' justice: the Tokyo war crimes trial*, Princeton: Princeton University Press, 1971.

37 The early release did not apply to B- and C-class suspected war criminals.

38 Tanaka Toshiyuki, "Naze beigun wa jûgun ianfu mondai uo mushi shitanoka: Jo" [Why did the U.S. forces ignore the issue of war comfort women?: Part 1], *Sekai*, 627, 1996, pp. 174–83; and Tanaka Toshiyuki, "Naze beigun wa jûgun ianfu mondai o mushi shitanoka: Ge" [Why did the U.S. forces ignore the issue of war comfort women?: Part 2], *Sekai*, 628, 1996, pp. 270–9. See also, Yuki Tanaka, *Japan's comfort women: sexual slavery and prostitution during World War II and the US occupation*, New York: Routledge, 2002.

39 Monbushô, *Shotôka kokushi ge* [*Primary school national history*, vol. 2], Tokyo: Tokyo shoseki, 1943, p. 174.

40 Monbushô, *Kuni no ayumi ge* [*The course of the nation*, vol. 2], Tokyo: Nihon shoseki, 1946, p. 49.

41 Monbushô, *Nihon no rekishi ge* [*History of Japan*, vol. 2], Tokyo: Chûtôgakko kyôkasho kabushikigaisha, 1946, p. 104.

42 Monbushô, *Nihon rekishi ge* [*Japanese history*, vol. 2], Tokyo: Shihangakko kyôkasho kabushikigaisha, 1947, p. 204.

43 See also Tawara Yoshifumi, "Nankin daigyakusatsu jiken to rekishi kyôkasho mondai" [The Nanjing massacre and the history textbook controversy], in Fujiwara Akira, ed., *Nankin jiken wo dô miruka: nichi, chû, bei kenkyûsha niyoru kenshô* [*How to understand the Nanjing massacre: verifications by Japanese, Chinese, and US scholars*], Tokyo: Aoki shoten, 1998, p. 118.

44 Monbushô, *Kuni no ayumi ge*, p. 48.

45 Ibid., p. 51.

46 The critics consisted mainly of Marxist historians, but included some "ethno-historians" such as Wakamori Tarô, who advocated research on and the teaching of the history of ordinary people.

47 For these criticisms, see Thakur, "History textbook reform," pp. 270–1; Yamazumi, *Shakaika kyôiku*, pp. 18–19; and Kimijima Kazuhiko, *Kyôkasho no shisô* [*Thoughts on textbooks*], Tokyo: Suzusawa shoten, 1996, pp. 274–8.

48 After the first postwar election, Katayama Tetsu, chair of the Japan Socialist Party (*Shakaitô*), formed a coalition cabinet in June 1947, and supported the educational reforms, but was not able to finance basic matters, such as schoolhouse reconstruction. See Kyôiku no Sengoshi Henshû Iinkai, *Sengo kyôiku kaikaku to sono hôkai heno michi*, pp. 115–29.

49 Compulsory education during the war was six years.

50 Horio, *Educational thought*, p. 121.

51 See Horio, *Educational thought*, pp. 108–29. In fact, the edict lost its effect because of the Diet resolution in 1948.

52 For more information about the 1946 U.S. Education Mission, see Gary H.

Tsuchimochi, *Education reform in postwar Japan: the 1946 U.S. education mission,* Tokyo: University of Tokyo Press, 1993.

53 Monbushô, *Gakushûshidô yôryô: Ippanhen (shian) [Instructional guidelines: General guide (a tentative plan)],* Tokyo: Monbushô, 1947, p. 2. The quote is the author's translation. SCAP requested the Ministry of Education to translate the guidelines into English, and the translation of *1947 General guide,* entitled *A tentative suggested course of study: general,* lingers today, which is reprinted in Kokuritsu Kyôiku Kenkyûjo-nai Sengo Kyôiku Kaikaku Shiryô Kenkyûkai, ed., *Monbushô gakushûshidô yôryô,* vol. 1, Tokyo: Nihon tosho senta, 1980. There are slight differences between the Japanese and English versions.

54 Ogino Sue, *Aru kyôshi no shôwashi [The history of Showa experienced by a teacher],* Tokyo: Hitotsubashi shobô, 1970, p. 134.

55 Ogino, *Aru kyôshi,* p. 135.

56 For further discussion of a series of the *Instructional guidelines* in the late 1940s, see Nagao Akio, *Shin karikyuramuron [New curriculum theory],* Tokyo: Yûhikaku, 1989, pp. 14–17; and Yokoyama Yoshinori, "Kyôkasho saiban to gakushûshidô yôryô" [The textbook lawsuits and the instructional guidelines], in Kyôkasho Kentei Soshô o Shiensuru Zenkokurenrakukai, ed., *Rekishi no hôtei [The court of history],* Tokyo: Ôtsuki shoten, 1998, pp. 109–10.

57 See Kimijima, *Kyôkasho no shisô,* p. 280; and Usui Kaichi *et al., Atarashi chûtô shakaika heno izanai [An invitation to new secondary social studies],* Tokyo: Chirekisha, 1992, pp. 155–62.

58 In practice, schools ended up using *Kuni no ayumi,* since *Nihon no rekishi* turned out to be rather difficult for junior-high students. See Kimijima, *Kyôkasho no shisô,* p. 281.

59 See Kimijima, *Kyôkasho no shisô.*

60 Kanazawa, *Aru shôgakkôchô,* p. 61.

61 There were many street urchins in Tokyo during those years because of the war.

62 Kanazawa, *Aru shôgakkôchô,* p. 60.

63 Readers may detect a certain kind of nationalism in Kanazawa's words. The later occupation years saw signs of postwar grassroots nationalism among the Japanese. Such nationalism was not expressed overtly during the occupation, but after Japan's independence there was a surge of grassroots nationalism. See Yoshida, *Nihonjin no sensôkan,* pp. 38–41 and pp. 72–5.

64 The ministry even suggested that each classroom could adopt different textbooks. See Tokutake, *Kyôkasho no sengoshi,* p. 57, and Nakauchi Toshio *et al., Nihon kyôiku no sengoshi [The postwar history of Japanese education],* Tokyo: Sanseido, 1987, p. 105.

65 See Tokutake, *Kyôkasho no sengoshi,* p. 59.

66 A list later compiled by Hirotake *et al.* contains nineteen entries of junior high school Japanese history textbooks published for use during the years 1952–1954, fifteen of which were examined for the present study. In a similar vein, forty-one entries of junior high school social studies history textbooks are found in the list as published for use during the years 1952–1955. Among them, twelve were examined for the present study, of which six texts use the term "aggression" in describing the Manchurian Incident and Japanese military activities leading up to it. See Hirotake Nagayoshi, Nakamura Kikuji, and Kato Saneharu, *Kyôkasho kentei sôran: Chûgakkôhen [A general list of screened textbooks: junior high],* Tokyo: Komiyayama shoten, 1969, pp. 104–9.

67 Wakamori Tarô, *Gendai Nihon no naritachi ge [The history of contemporary Japan,* vol. 2], Tokyo: Jitsugyô no nihonsha, 1952, p. 105.

68 Nakaya Kenichi and Onabe Teruhiko, *Gendai sekai no naritachi ge [The history of contemporary world,* vol. 2], Tokyo: Jitsugyô no nihonsha, 1952, p. 94.

146   *Y. Nozaki*

69 Mutai Risaku, *Chûgaku shakai ge* [*Junior high school social studies*, vol. 2], Tokyo: Kairyûdô, 1954, p. 105.
70 Mutai, *Chûgaku shakai ge*, p. 108.
71 See also Tawara, "Nankin daigyakusatsu jiken," pp. 118–19.
72 Atarashii Shakai Henshû Iinkai, ed., *Atarashii shakai 3* [*New social studies*, vol. 3], Tokyo: Tokyo shoseki, 1955, p. 170.
73 Atarashii Shakai Henshû Iinkai, *Atarashii shakai 3*, p. 173.

6 Universal health insurance

The unfinished reform of Japan's healthcare system

Yoneyuki Sugita

Introduction

The Asia-Pacific War and the U.S. occupation of Japan led to the rapid development of health insurance protection for broad segments of the Japanese population. Both during the war and after, the Japanese government dramatically expanded and increased its control over health insurance programs. Circumstances in the immediate postwar period also induced the introduction of more egalitarian healthcare features, which became the basis for the eventual introduction of health insurance coverage for the entire population in Japan.

From the late 1930s to 1961, the period of time healthcare coverage in Japan is reviewed in this chapter, the most far-reaching attempt to introduce a fully socialized national healthcare program came in the early years of the U.S. occupation of Japan. In those years, reform-minded Japanese scholars and civil servants in Japan's Ministry of Health and Welfare (MHW) put forward a series of ambitious, government-funded, progressive healthcare programs. In proposing these programs, these scholars and officials tried to take advantage of the nationwide zeal for democracy that was evident almost immediately after Japan's defeat, to carry out a comprehensive reorganization of Japan's healthcare services. Despite differences in both outlook and understanding of how the machinery of the Japanese government and U.S. occupation worked, the general goal was to achieve universal health insurance coverage. Some initial proposals went so far as to advocate full nationalization of healthcare services. But, faced with resistance by fiscally conservative Japanese, and U.S. officials who worried about Japan's shaky postwar national finances, more modest proposals that could be accepted by higher authorities in the Japanese government and U.S. occupation were offered. These were based on a hybrid structure of public sector agencies supplemented by private sector hospitals and physicians in private practice. The Dodge Line of 1949, however, shattered hopes of implementing even these more modest proposals. The Dodge Line ended up barring government funding of the proposed public–private health insurance programs, which forced the

Japanese government to turn to the private sector to provide healthcare services in place of any cohesive government-run system.

Nevertheless, by 1961 Japan had managed to put in place the basic outline of an egalitarian healthcare system. This system, while not nationalized, was prescribed by the government, which had assumed firm control of the rules, regulations and modes of payment covering Japan's hospitals, clinics and private-practice physicians. The motivation for making this possible came largely from the desperate postwar need to alleviate the miserable living conditions of Japan's war-ravaged population. The healthcare system that was functioning by 1961 provided universal healthcare coverage, unrestricted access to healthcare facilities and low co-payments. That the Japanese people living in the twenty-first century enjoy the longest lifespans in the world is partly attributable to the healthcare system that emerged forty-five years ago. This system, however, was the product of ad hoc and quantitative expansions of existing pre-war and wartime programs, rather than the result of efficient and coherent comprehensive postwar reorganization. As has become clear in recent years, the creation of universal coverage has in many ways postponed problems inherent in Japan's healthcare system forty-five years ago, which the nation as a whole must now deal with.

"Private ownership and national management" in Japan's healthcare system

In 1922, the Japanese government established its first health insurance system. This provided limited coverage to factory workers and mineworkers employed by companies with over 300 full-time employees. But it was not until the late 1930s that the government initiated large-scale programs to protect the health of the Japanese people at large. In October 1937, the Cabinet Planning Board (CPB), a government agency established under the control of the prime minister, began comprehensive national planning, mainly in regard to all-out wartime mobilization strategies, including healthcare. In the 1930s and the 1940s, civil servants on the CPB, who were greatly influenced by the command-economy ideas of socialism and Nazism, insisted on reforms which became, in effect, measures to create a planned and controlled national economy. Two of the most prominent officials behind the reforms were Kishi Nobusuke, Vice-Minister of Commerce and Industry, and Hoshino Naoki, President of the CPB, both of whom had experience implementing a state-controlled economy and maintaining social order in Manchuria. Middle-ranking officials who supported the reforms were Okumura Kiwao, Minobe Yoji, Mouri Hideoto, and Sakamizu Hisatsune. Their cooperation with the military helped form a powerful faction of civil servants in the early 1940s.

During the Asia-Pacific War, this mix of high and middle-ranking so-called "reform-minded civil servants" intervened extensively in broad areas of the economy. Rejecting nationalized or rigidly planned economies, they embraced private ownership. But they also advocated government assumption of responsibility for management of private assets, believing that private corporations should increase productivity in accordance with national guidance.[1] They dismissed market-oriented, open, and unrestrained competition. Instead, they emphasized cooperative work and equal distribution of the product of one's labor as a way to preserve social harmony in Japan and discourage non-participation in work for the betterment of society. The philosophy of this group, assisted by the imperatives of war, contributed greatly to the reform of Japan's healthcare system during the late 1930s and early to mid 1940s.[2]

From the late 1930s until almost the end of World War II, militarism and healthcare services developed hand in hand in Japan. The Japanese government expanded its power over healthcare policies during this time to meet military demands for healthier men in the army and to provide benefits to the families of those who died in action. As a result, the Asia-Pacific War precipitated the rise of progressive healthcare policy making in Japan.[3] This result can at least be partly explained by the need, as understood by Japan's wartime leaders, to ease the burdens imposed by modern warfare on Japanese society. Aside from the obvious need for healthy conscripts, Japan's government concluded that it was necessary to provide those families deprived of potential breadwinners with widespread benefits in order to rally public support for the war. Japan's war-fighting needs did not put social improvements on hold; on the contrary, some rather unexpected social policy proposals rose to the surface and were implemented.[4] For example, in 1938 the government took the unprecedented step of expressing its concern for the health of the entire nation by establishing the Health and Welfare Ministry, which was charged mainly with improving the physical capacity of the Japanese people and instituting wide-reaching health improvement programs. In the same year, the government enacted the National Health Insurance Law, which mandated health insurance protection for about 60 percent of the population, especially those living in rural areas.[5] The government expected that the main beneficiaries of the new health insurance law would be young men who would someday become conscripts in the Japanese army. This law was vital, because the military recognized that those living in rural areas had become so physically weak that many were unable to pass the basic health checkup required of conscripts.[6]

But the government was also enthusiastic about expanding its health insurance programs to the rest of the country.[7] In 1939, the passing of the Clerical Health Insurance Law and the Seamen's Insurance Law expanded the coverage of health insurance to urban workers primarily in the service industry and to sailors, respectively. In September 1940, Ishihara Takeji, Head of the National Health Insurance Division of the MHW, said: "Providing all Japanese people with medical treatment was the essence of a new healthcare system.... [For this purpose] both physicians and the government must make efforts to decrease medical fees."[8] In January 1941, the cabinet endorsed the Outline of the Establishment of Population Policy. This policy included a provision that stated "the government should expand and strengthen health insurance systems to cover all Japanese people. In addition to medical care benefits, the government should also prepare various kinds of benefits necessary for preventive care."[9] Koizumi Chikahiko, who served as Minister of the MHW from July 1941 to July 1944, became in 1942 the first official in his position to use the term "universal health insurance." In his view, universal health insurance coverage constituted the core of any government-administered medicine program.[10] By 1943, 95 percent of municipal governments had established national health insurance societies, and more than 70 percent of Japanese were enrolled in the National Health Insurance program.[11] Although these figures appear somewhat impressive, many of the societies were inactive and provided very little, if any, basic preventive medical care.

In June 1938, another important action taken by the government was its initial effort to reorganize the Japanese Medical Association (JMA), which consisted primarily of private practitioners. Since the Meiji era, private practitioners rather than physicians working in hospitals had played the dominant role in providing healthcare to anyone who could afford it. Unless the government established control over the JMA, it would be difficult to operate a healthcare program that could effectively serve the nation. Moreover, the government established the Pharmaceutical and Medical Investigation Council (PMIC), chaired by the Health and Welfare Minister, to devise appropriate measures to improve the nation's healthcare system. In October 1940, the PMIC stated that there was a need to reorganize the JMA to make it more subordinate to the MHW. But at the same time it recommended the mandatory establishment of local medical associations subordinate in turn to the JMA. In addition, the PMIC advised the government to require all physicians to participate in these medical associations and to strengthen its supervisory power over the JMA by making the association's chairmanship a cabinet appointment.[12] In November 1941, the Council for New Medical World System, sponsored by the *Taiseiyokusankai*, a central organization for national mobilization headed by the prime minister, strongly insisted on nationalization of healthcare services and effective national management of healthcare, which, in effect, would abolish private practice in healthcare services. The Director of the Health and Medical Bureau of MHW later stated that, "[as] the New Medical World System insisted, it was necessary for the government to control the medical service."[13] In short, taking advantage of the wartime emergency, the Japanese government sought to make extensive changes in the supply-side of healthcare services, which, up to that point, had mainly been managed and controlled by the JMA.

In February 1942, the Japanese government enacted the National Medical Law. About two-thirds of this law concerned the Japanese Medical Treatment Corporation (JMTC), an organization that the Japanese government planned to use to oversee the Japanese healthcare programs in place of the JMA. In April 1942, it promulgated the Japanese Medical Treatment Corporation Law. According to these two laws, the JMTC was founded with a capitalization of 100 million yen, paid in full by the government. The JMTC had three official tasks: to prevent and eradicate tuberculosis, to send physicians to medically-underserved areas and to improve and disseminate medical services.[14] In public, the government stated that the JMTC would never be used to nationalize healthcare services. Its role was to emphasize cooperation with the JMA without lessening the control private physicians had over their own individual medical practices.[15] In fact, however, the government tried to manage each individual physician and control the whole healthcare services by expanding the scope of JMTC's activities.[16] Above all, the National Medical Law of 1942 compelled reorganization of the JMA. Henceforth, the JMA's main purpose was to cooperate with government efforts to improve the physical strength of the Japanese by improving and developing medicine and healthcare instruction. All physicians were required to join their local medical associations. Furthermore, the JMA and prefectural medical associations were now required to reorganize in a hierarchical way so that the MHW could implement Japan's healthcare policies through its effective control over the JMA. The details were stipulated in the Law of Japan Medical Association and Japan Dentist Association that was proclaimed in August 1942. This law stipulated most recommendations made by the PMIC. The Health and Welfare Minister had the authority to order the JMA to implement necessary measures to improve healthcare services. In effect, the government had put the JMA under its control, forcing it to become a national institution placed in the service of a state-directed campaign to nurture healthy and robust people. In January 1943, a thoroughly reorganized JMA began to operate, with the approval of Health and Welfare Minister, Koizumi Chikahiko, who appointed Inada Tatsukichi, Governor of JMTC, as the JMA's new president. Consequently, the government was now using both the reorganized JMA and the newly established JMTC as a two-pronged approach to achieve its national medical policy objectives.[17]

The Japanese government instituted another major wartime healthcare reform measure in February 1942, when it revised both the National Health Insurance Law and the Health Insurance Law. These reforms dramatically increased governmental control over health insurance policies. Prior to the revisions, these two laws were important because they served as the basic framework for regulating Japan's healthcare services; however, because of the wartime revisions, healthcare in all of Japan was transformed into a more centralized and extensive system.

Specifically, the revised National Health Insurance Law accomplished the following:

1   The establishment of national health insurance societies had formerly been a voluntary undertaking for local authorities, but henceforth the chief administrator of the local authority could order the establishment of such societies. Once a society was established, all local residents had to join. In one stroke, the National Health Insurance went from being voluntary to mandatory in many parts of the country.

2   The revision stipulated that whenever one-half (previously, this had been two-thirds) of the residents of a particular community became members of a voluntary national health insurance society, the chief administrator had the authority to make membership in the community compulsory for all its residents.

3   The revised law also ordered the replacement of JMA-administered group health insurance contracts based on fixed-fee payments by subscribers with a new government program in which physicians would receive direct health insurance payments based on a fee-for-service schedule.[18]

This altered payment system became the basis for promoting health insurance among physicians in the postwar era, because the treatment of a higher volume of patients covered by insurance resulted in an increase in their income.[19] Moreover, the administration of the new payment arrangement became independent of the JMA. The government gradually established a system of reviewing the content of medical treatment and deciding the level of reimbursement payments to physicians by giving the Health and Welfare Minister, in consultation with the JMA, the authority to decide medical service fees.[20] This constituted a major change in the history of Japan's healthcare. The power to decide important issues concerning health insurance, such as the appointment of insurance physicians, the supervision of physicians, and medical service fees, had been taken out of the hands of the JMA and given to the government. This wartime action, alone, fundamentally altered the balance of public versus private control of Japan's healthcare system.[21]

The government also revised the Health Insurance Law in the following ways:

1   The Health Insurance program and the Clerical Health Insurance program would merge. This step was necessary to curb the proliferation of health insurance programs that hindered management of an effective and coherent healthcare service.

2   Prior to the revision, the Health Insurance Law was only applicable to corporations with five or more employees in specific sectors, such as mining and railroads. But with the revision, the Health Insurance Law

was applied to corporations with five or more employees in a wide variety of sectors. This particular revision was important for setting in motion an expansion of Health Insurance and was in line with the government's goal of achieving universal coverage.

3   The Health Insurance program had provided family allowance as an ex gratia benefit, but the revision stipulated that the family allowance, with the newly added childbirth expenses of the spouse, should be a legal benefit. This revision was important, to make the program more attractive.

4   As with the revised National Health Insurance Law, the revised Health Insurance Law ordered the replacement of JMA-administered group health insurance contracts based on fixed-fee payments by subscribers with a new government program in which physicians would receive direct health insurance system payments based on a fee-for-service schedule. The government also acquired the power to enforce designation of physicians as legal insurance physicians.

These epoch-making changes allowed the MHW to exert direct control over individual physicians. Thus, between 1938 and 1944 the Japanese government created the basic framework for a nationwide system of health insurance and established strong control over health insurance programs. In particular, the number of people covered by social health insurance dramatically increased during the period of full-scale war. In 1937, before national health insurance was established, Japan's social health insurance covered about 3.8 million people; by 1944, the number of insured individuals reached more than 50 million.[22] However, the government failed to provide financial support for the rapid expansion of health insurance coverage. Moreover, despite the government's investment of time and energy in extending healthcare coverage programs to much of the nation, most Japanese considered the provision of insured medical services to be a temporary, wartime-related emergency action.[23]

Social welfare and the question of equality

In 1940, Ernest Bevin, British Minister of Labour, asked William Beveridge to critically assess the existing social security system in Great Britain and propose reforms. In December 1942 Beveridge published his results in a report on social insurance and allied services (the Beveridge Report), where he recommended that the British government act to eliminate five major social problems: want, disease, ignorance, squalor and idleness. What became known as the Beveridge Plan served as a model for the creation of the modern welfare state in countries around the world after World War II.[24]

Japan's MHW obtained a copy of the Beveridge Report during the war. The ministry's review of the plan greatly affected the concept of social security among civil servants working in the Health Insurance Bureau (HIB) of the MHW. Unlike previous social insurance programs in Japan, one of the key features of the Beveridge Report was enrolling the entire nation in such programs. As the HIB viewed it, the major purpose of a Japanese-style Beveridge Report would be to eliminate poverty by providing the Japanese people with a minimum income based on a redistribution of national wealth. Social insurance played a central role in the plan. Individuals might use private insurance if they wished to be covered above the basic needs. The Beveridge Report was premised on equal benefits and payment of equal premiums.[25] The fact that Japan's government decided to provide all Japanese people with a national minimum income, as advocated in the Beveridge Report, acquired crucial social significance for the development of Japan's postwar social security system.[26] The postwar Japanese government sought a broad and egalitarian health insurance coverage that emphasized equality among the Japanese people as its guiding principle.

With the end of the war, Japan was quickly engulfed in a whole series of problems, the most serious of which were hyperinflation, acute food shortages, widespread disease and internal population dislocation. Seven million Japanese abroad, including demobilized servicemen, were waiting to return to Japan. By the end of 1946, after about five million Japanese had returned home,[27] a general sense of despondency prevailed throughout the country. Alcoholism, drug addiction and crime had become rampant. All this pointed to imminent social collapse. Drastic reforms and a massive program of public assistance were necessary if Japan was to maintain social unity.

Occupied Japan was temporarily isolated from the international community in the immediate aftermath of the war – a situation that was advantageous for Japan because it allowed the Japanese authorities to implement drastic domestic reforms without having to worry about such international constraints as trade deficits and defense expenditures. The Allied powers controlled Japan's trade and U.S. assistance covered Japan's trade deficit. This assistance amounted to 92 percent of Japan's imports in 1947 and 75 percent in 1948. Therefore, Japan did not suffer from topsy-turvy global economic conditions that were causing havoc with other national economies at that time. Moreover, since the United States provided military protection, Japan was able to get by with minimum defense expenditure. Being placed under Allied economic and military protection allowed Japanese officials and the mostly American personnel working for the Supreme Commander for the Allied Powers (SCAP) to focus much of their time and budgetary resources on formulating progressive social reforms.[28]

Occupation policy of placing Japan under indirect rule allowed Japan to preserve the fundamental structure of its pre-war and wartime civil service in the postwar era. Most of the civil servants working for MHW during this period were carryovers from the pre-war era.[29] SCAP left the task of redeveloping Japan's health insurance programs largely in the hands of Japanese government officials.[30] The experience and familiarity that these officials brought with them from the wartime expansion of Japan's healthcare policies equipped them with the authority, knowledge and confidence to orchestrate and administer the welfare programs conceived during the occupation and influenced by the principles of the Beveridge Report. As a result, the MHW continued to expand its influence over the lives of Japanese people in the postwar period.

One immediate postwar problem that the Japanese government could not ignore was the spread of epidemics. Between 1 September 1945 and 31 August 1946, more than 30,000 Japanese were found to be suffering from infectious typhus. The presence of this and other epidemics provided the state with the opportunity to institute strong preventive medical care. With SCAP's support, the Japanese government enacted the Preventive Vaccination Law in 1948. This enabled the government to implement mandatory immunization programs to treat a wide range of diseases, including typhus, as well as cholera and dysentery. Japan's national immunization program was groundbreaking and on a scale scarcely witnessed in other countries.[31] SCAP immunized approximately thirty-one million people with BCG by May 1949.[32] Providing broad-based equitable healthcare treatment and controlling the spread of infectious diseases inherently increased the power of the government over the health and life of the nation.

On a more general level, the reality of wartime destruction and the resulting postwar misery forced the Japanese government to take as one of its first post-surrender actions the provision of emergency relief to the population at large. The confused social situation in the immediate postwar period, along with hyperinflation, combined to reduce millions to a marginal economic existence.[33] For the Japanese government, postwar Japan began with public welfare assistance programs that became the foundation for the postwar Japanese social security system.

In December 1945, worried that ubiquitous poverty and economic misery in postwar Japan might precipitate serious social disorder, SCAP suggested that the Japanese government devise a program for relief and welfare. At the end of December, the Japanese government responded to SCAP with a basic plan for providing emergency support to needy persons. Not satisfied with the plan's content, SCAP issued a directive (SCAPIN775) to the Japanese government in February 1946 outlining four major principles for public assistance: national responsibility, indiscriminate equality, the separation of public and private affairs, and unlimited necessary expenses.[34] After it accepted these principles, in April 1946, the Japanese government enacted the Poor-Assistance Law, which took effect in October.[35] The enactment of this law marks the point at which Japan's postwar system of social security began in rudimentary form, based on the provision of public assistance to those suffering from extreme poverty. Naturally, livelihood protection became a central component of Japan's social security. Consequently, from the very beginning Japan's postwar social security system emphasized a minimum standard of living for all.[36] In addition, the wartime policy of powerful government action to control prices and wages in the interests of promoting an equitable and stable standard of living carried over into the postwar era. In short, Japan retained its pre-war and wartime emphasis on egalitarianism in the postwar period.[37] This emphasis on egalitarianism became a founding principle and ever-present feature of Japan's postwar social security system.

Using social security to promote egalitarianism became a prominent feature of Japan's postwar life, partly because the Allied Powers regarded the "welfare state" as a vehicle for securing a minimum standard of living through democratic rather than totalitarian, autocratic or military dictatorship means, and partly because a welfare state was seen not merely as an economic policy or another kind of social system but as a positive ideal that could be applied to prevent the re-emergence of militarism or fascism.[38]

Ambitious plans

The remaking of Japan through the powerful SCAP-directed democratization process provided opportunities in the postwar period to promote additional progressive social security measures. Progressive scholars, politicians, and government officials influenced by the Beveridge Report introduced a series of policy proposals, such as a comprehensive healthcare system that combined the Health Insurance and the National Health Insurance programs, a welfare medical assistance system and a dependent family allowance system.[39]

In February 1946, a group of progressive scholars, Kondo Bunji, Ohkochi Kazuo, Suetaka Makoto, Sono Kenji, and Hirata Tomitaro, formed the Social Security Study Group (SSSG), an informal study group, to formulate a model health insurance program that would cover all Japanese people. They were among the few Japanese scholars at that time who were familiar with the newly emerging concept of social security and the details of the Beveridge Report. The group issued Japan's first postwar proposal for a comprehensive "Social Security Plan" (SSP) in July 1946, which included a call for a universal healthcare system. The SSP contained measures that would prove to be more progressive than those in the Beveridge Report. For example, they introduced a premium system that would be determined by income rather than fixed, as proposed under the Beveridge Report. The SSP also stated as an ultimate objective the nationalization of Japan's healthcare system. Until nationalization could be put into effect, the SSP called on the government to establish medical care facilities directly managed by social insurance programs throughout the country.[40] However, Crawford F. Sams, Director of SCAP's Public Health and Welfare (PHW) section, was opposed to nationalized healthcare: "SCAP is not establishing nor advocating socialized or state medicine in Japan."[41] He later argued that nationalized healthcare was normally adopted by communist or totalitarian regimes.[42] As the SSSG was an informal group, the SSP that it published had no official status; however, because most SSSG members later went on to join governmental consultative bodies, they used the knowledge they had acquired on social security policies to present influential recommendations to these bodies.

In March 1946, the Japanese government established the Social Insurance Investigation Committee (SIIC), an official consultative body to the MHW consisting of more than fifty members, chaired by Kanamori Toku-jiro, a member of the House of Peers and former Director-General of the Cabinet Legislation Bureau. Most of the scholars affiliated with the SSSG also participated in the SIIC. In April 1946, the Health and Welfare Minister asked the SIIC about the future course of the social insurance system. In December 1946, the SIIC submitted an official report with a list of recommendations. Many of these were based on those contained in the SSP that the SSSG scholars had formulated. One recommendation called for the merger of the Government-Administered Employment-Based Health Insurance and the National Health Insurance programs, which would be administered by regional associations. Unlike the pre-war National Health Insurance program, the establishment of and participation in regional associations was to be compulsory for all residents not covered by other insurance programs such as the Corporate-Sponsored Health Insurance or the Government-Led Mutual Aid Insurance programs. The SIIC report left the Corporate-Sponsored Health Insurance programs and the National Public Service Mutual Aid Health Insurance programs virtually untouched. It did, however, advocate the abolition of family allowances. Finally, unlike the SSP issued in July 1946, the SIIC report did not mention nationalization of healthcare services; instead, it insisted that the government should expand and improve the network of national and public medical facilities.[43] The SIIC's report was still progressive and comprehensive in nature; however, it was more politically and financially feasible than the SSP. Receiving the SIIC report, the MHW looked into the situation of the National Health Insurance program, and whether it would be possible to integrate this program with Government-Administered Employment-Based Health Insurance and other measures recommended, but the MHW also had to deal with day-to-day pressing needs that required its immediate attention.

During the war, the Japanese government established national health insurance associations throughout Japan, but it found these associations financially difficult to maintain after defeat. In May 1946, the All-Japan Federation of National Health Insurance Associations, a central organization to represent interests of the national health insurance associations, advocated an increase in government subsidies as the best way to overcome this financial difficulty. According to the National Health Insurance Law, the government was able to provide subsidies "within the limits of the budget" and gave small subsidy amounts to the national health insurance associations, depending on the number of persons they insured.[44] Immediately responding to this need, the MHW decided to increase its subsidies as an ad hoc measure to alleviate the financial burdens of the National Health Insurance associations. In September 1946, the government added 150 million yen in subsidies to the National Health Insurance budget, which represented more than double the amount offered in the budget of fiscal year 1946.[45] On 14 June 1947, the PHW section under SCAP made public its position with respect to Japan's National Health Insurance for the first time since Japan's defeat. In a public statement, PHW insisted that the revival and strengthening of the National Health Insurance system would be indispensable for the stability of economic life in Japan. For this purpose, PHW encouraged the Japanese government to significantly increase government subsidies for the inadequate National Health Insurance program. It also requested that Japan's multiple health insurance programs – which included Corporate-Sponsored Health Insurance, the National Public Service Mutual Aid Health Insurance, the Government-Administered Employment-Based Health Insurance, the National Health Insurance – be integrated into a single health insurance system.[46] Both Japanese progressive scholars and government officials on the one hand, and PHW officials on the other, shared the idea that Japan's multiple health insurance programs should be integrated for the sake of efficiency. They also shared the belief that the national government should play a far more extensive role in managing healthcare and provide much larger subsidies for health insurance programs.

But despite the radical reconception of Japan's healthcare system, as proposed by the SIIC, SSSG or other consultative bodies, the Japanese government decided that the nation could not afford any major wholesale changes at that time. Instead, the government's priority in 1947 and 1948 was to get the existing multiple health insurance programs, now in a state of paralysis, to start functioning again. The Insurance Bureau at the MHW took the lead in insisting that revitalizing existing insurance programs should be the top priority and that making small-scale improvements and enrolling more of the Japanese population would be sufficient, at least for the time being.[47] The Finance Ministry warned that the government did not have adequate financial resources or manpower to make fundamental healthcare revisions. Given the cautious approach recommended by powerful bureaucratic interests, the only immediate step taken by the government was to make minor revisions to the National Health Insurance Law in June 1948, transferring the responsibility for managing the National Health Insurance from national health insurance associations to municipal governments. An overall reorganization of Japan's healthcare system and the creation of a much larger healthcare budget had been forestalled.[48] Thus, despite the fact that progressive and comprehensive schemes for reorganizing Japan's health insurance programs had been discussed and proposed, the Japanese government had to deal with pressing financial problems.

The SIIC, on the other hand, was convinced that the time to implement a democratic and comprehensive reorganization of Japanese health insurance programs had arrived. In October 1947 it submitted a Social Security System Outline (SSSO) to the MHW.[49] Japanese and SCAP officials considered it to be a Japanese version of the Beveridge Report. Through the SSSO, the SIIC advocated for Japan a universal social security system to replace the existing social insurance and welfare public assistance systems that remained from the wartime years. They deemed these systems to be inadequate for the task of securing "the minimum standards of wholesome and cultured living" stipulated in Article 25 of the new postwar Japanese constitution.[50] This social security system they envisioned was not to be a mere patchwork of existing social insurance programs. Instead, it would provide the Japanese people with a progressive and comprehensive set of social insurance protections, including public assistance programs. According to the SSSO, everyone who was insured would be responsible for paying insurance premiums, with amounts proportionate to income levels. The government would be partly responsible for medical treatment costs but wholly responsible for all processing expenses.

The SSSO was in some ways more socialist and progressive than the Beveridge Report. For example, while the Beveridge Report called for fixed premium payments regardless of income, the SSSO proposed income-graduated premiums. However, in comparison with the SSP, the SIIC wanted its SSSO proposal to be more realistic in the context of Japan's current circumstances. Thus, the SSSO recommended that employers pay premiums for low-income employees. It also abandoned the idea of nationalizing healthcare services. Nevertheless, a strong strain of progressive thinking existed in the SIIC. One important member, Kondo Bunji, felt that eventually Japan's healthcare system should be nationalized. To accomplish this, Kondo believed that the government should build more national and public hospitals and incrementally nationalize the medical practices of private practitioners.[51] Moreover, Ohkochi Kazuo, another important progressive member, regarded the SSSO as a mere first step toward the destruction of capitalistic "liberal society" and a decisive shift toward socialism.[52]

However idealistic the SSSO may have been, the PHW was against it because of financial difficulties: "Preliminary estimates that at maturity of the plan the cost of social insurance alone will amount to 35% of all payrolls indicate that it is extremely doubtful whether the Japanese Government is capable of financing the program."[53] The SSSO was criticized from various sources immediately upon release for making unrealistic financial assumptions. Moreover, SCAP regarded the plan as too socialist. Even some SIIC members considered the plan too idealistic and impossible to realize.[54] The Japanese government simply ignored the report that was criticized for its impractical financial figures and its inability to receive the blessing of SCAP.

By request from the Japanese government, SCAP in August 1947 invited a five-person U.S. team of social security experts led by William Wandel to Japan, to study possibilities for revamping social insurance programs. In December 1947, Wandel submitted a report that contained his recommendations to SCAP. After making its review, SCAP considered the report too left-leaning, but nevertheless released it to the Japanese government in July 1948. The Wandel Report, which was dismissive of the SSSO, presented a plan for realizing a moderately progressive but less far-reaching social insurance program. Whereas the SSSO advocated introducing a completely new social security system, the Wandel Report settled for strengthening and rationalizing the current system. The recommendations in this report appeared more attainable than those found in the SSSO. One of the most important recommendations was the integration of employees' health insurance except for the Corporate-Sponsored Health Insurance and recognition of two main health insurance programs, the Health Insurance and the National Health Insurance. While the Wandel report strongly emphasized Japanese government financing of National Health Insurance, the other health insurance programs would have to depend on paid-in employer and employee premiums.[55] The report gave considerable attention to welfare public assistance, which it agreed would stall the development and implementation of idealistic social security plans centered on social insurance that progressive scholars and officials had proposed during the early stages of the occupation.[56] Partly because of the Wandel Report, previous arguments for integrating the Corporate-Sponsored Insurance and the National Health Insurance gradually died out.[57] Based on the recommendation put forth in this report, the Japanese government established the Advisory Council on Social Security (ACSS) in December 1948, which served as an important official advisory body to the prime minister.

The Wandel Report also recommended that the government fund the expansion of national and public hospitals rather than subsidize social insurance payments, the sole exception being the National Health Insurance program.[58] In addition, SCAP aimed at the reorganization of the system of healthcare providers along the axis of national and public hospitals. In May 1948, the Advisory Council on Healthcare System (ACHS) of MHW also proposed establishing a well-organized system of medical facilities centered on national and public hospitals, supplemented by doctors in private practice.[59] Some SIIC members still supported direct public management of healthcare services.[60] In the early period of the occupation, the MHW considered adopting a system based on the British Health

Service. This might have put Japan on the road to nationalizing its health-care.[61] Nevertheless, because of the unavoidable postwar reality limiting public financing, the government had to rely on the private sector to build new hospitals and increase the number of hospital beds.

On SCAP's invitation, in August 1948, the American Medical Association (AMA) jumped in with its own health insurance proposals. Strongly critical of the PHW plan to establish a seemingly socialist social security system as called for in the Wandel Report, and upset that various proposals in circulation would result in greater governmental control of Japanese healthcare policies, the AMA sponsored its own study of Japan's healthcare system. Unsurprisingly, this report opposed the recommendations made in the Wandel Report, claiming that they were too idealistic, indeed more so than anything Americans enjoyed. The AMA report submitted in December 1948 pointed out that Wandel accepted a system of social security that was both controlled and subsidized by the government and that introduced a coercive healthcare program – provisions that were essentially no different from those that had been employed in nations with totalitarian governments, including those of the defeated Axis Powers. The AMA Mission "maintains that the worthy objective will not be attained using means that will inevitably push the Japanese farther along the road of centralization of power back to the totalitarianism."[62] The AMA strongly advocated a fundamental democratic reorganization of the Japanese healthcare system based on market-oriented principles. The Wandel Report assumed that the Japanese healthcare and social security systems were on the right track and required only minor adjustments at certain points. The basic AMA assumption, however, was that the system contained totalitarian features that needed fundamental democratic, rather than socialist, reform. The AMA regarded the Wandel plan as too socialist, and prone to undermine individualism and the vitality of the private sector. It was convinced that in any healthcare system, labor and capital (i.e. private sector actors) should be responsible for its financial administration. Government intervention should be avoided at all costs.[63] In comparison with the Japanese progressive ideas and schemes on health insurance programs, the AMA provided the most laissez-faire plan. Faced with a series of socialist-oriented proposals for Japan's future health insurance programs, devised by MHW committees, PHW seemed to defer to the AMA position;[64] however, in the end, the AMA proposal did not have much concrete influence on the Japanese government.

As the above indicates, a hodgepodge of ideas concerning the postwar direction of Japan's healthcare system was in circulation in the late 1940s. These ranged from the ultimate nationalization of healthcare services to a laissez-faire plan that sought to avoid all government intervention. These ideas came from Japanese progressive scholars and civil servants, SCAP, and the AMA, and any one or a combination of them appeared to have a chance of being adopted. Some ideas, such as the SSSO, suffered an early death, while others, such as those coming from the AMA, created a brief sensation in policy-making circles. To some, the swirl of ideas, proposals, plans, and advisory committees represented chaos. The arrival of the Dodge Line and its austere budget plan, however, effectively terminated the debate. Implemented in 1949, this plan served as a turning point in the development of Japan's postwar health insurance system.[65]

The Dodge Line: The turning point for Japan's health insurance system

Hyperinflation widened the gap between high-end private medical fee payments and low-end medical fee payments covered by health insurance. Japanese doctors in private practice were reluctant to accept insured patients. In fact, they viewed insured treatment as a form of charity. Their reluctance placed the future of current health insurance programs in jeopardy. It also forced the MHW to conclude that some kind of action was needed.

In August 1948, the MHW decided to raise the price of fee payments for medical services and established the Social Insurance Medical Fee Payment Fund to speed up insurance payments, a ploy designed to maintain physician support for the current health insurance system. As a result, the number of cases treated under the health insurance system increased.[66] Also, the payment method for the Corporate-Sponsored Health Insurance programs changed from a bulk contract to a fee-for-service system, thereby making these insurance programs more attractive to physicians.[67]

Another problem was that the health insurance programs faced a financial crisis after the war. A large deficit of around 180 million yen in 1946 threatened the National Health Insurance program with collapse.[68] The cause of the deficit was the large sums being paid by the Japanese government following the increase in payment prices for medical services and the use of government subsidies to pay off the debts of the health insurance programs.

These circumstances threatened Japan's social stability, including, of course, the healthcare system. The Dodge Line, implemented in early 1949, was designed to lower hyperinflation. Named after Joseph M. Dodge, the president of the Detroit Bank and the person entrusted by President Harry S. Truman to take firm charge of Japan's government finances, the Dodge Line was an economic austerity program that played a significant role in destroying idealistic and progressive health insurance ideas that would have invited large governmental subsidies. The Dodge Line became one of the most important deflationary fiscal and monetary policies in modern Japanese history. In February 1949, Dodge recommended a tight monetary/anti-inflation policy, which he described as absolutely vital for balancing Japan's budget. Specifically, Dodge recommended the following measures: (1) balancing Japan's consolidated budget; (2) more efficient tax collection; (3) tighter credit; (4) lower wages and higher product prices; (5) controlled trade; (6) allocation of resources to exporters; (7) increased industrial and mining production; (8) establishment of a fixed exchange rate; and (9) a decrease in the amount of currency in circulation.[69] Implementation of the Dodge Line brought an immediate result: The inflation rate dropped from an annual rate of 80 percent by 1948 to 24 percent in 1949.[70]

When the Dodge Line took effect, it spurred an extraordinary increase in health insurance payments. With a disinflation policy now in effect, even the relatively high-income class of people began to use health insurance. This result was encouraged by a gradual change of view by the Japanese people regarding health insurance in general, now seen as a civil right rather than as charity.[71] By 1950, insurance users outnumbered private patients.[72] Japanese physicians, too, gradually lost most of their private patients and became heavily dependent on the health insurance system as health insurance became more prevalent in Japan from 1948 onward.[73]

Because the Dodge Line led the Japanese people increasingly to utilize health insurance programs, they became more and more dependent on these programs. Consequently, it became much more difficult for the government to abolish the current program outright and precipitate new designs from scratch. Moreover, the fact that the Dodge Line secured a balanced budget made it next to impossible to carry out any large-scale reorganization of the Japanese health insurance program within the then-existing limits of the national budget. Under this circumstance, in June 1950 the ACSS announced a tentative scheme, the "Outline of the Provisional Plan for a Social Security System (OPPSSS)," which was aimed at achieving universal healthcare coverage. It proposed insuring all employed workers, with Japan's prefectural-level instead of municipal-level governments serving as their insurers. One exception was large companies, which would be allowed to establish their own health insurance societies for their employees. OPPSSS recommended having the government establish well-organized and systematic medical and health networks throughout Japan. Funding would be based on the Japanese government assuming 20 percent of expenditures for preventative health measures and treatment and all administrative expenditures.[74]

PHW indicated its displeasure with the OPPSSS: "As a general conclusion, however, it is believed that the recommended program is too ambitious in relation to Japan's present resources." The PHW also considered it impossible for the Japanese government to achieve universal health insurance because of financial difficulties. "Compulsory national health insurance is not acceptable under SCAP policy, and should be eliminated from the recommendation."[75] PHW did not design any elaborate, comprehensive social schemes for occupied Japan; however, given Japan's

unstable financial condition, PHW did criticize those Japanese governmental councils which advocated far-reaching progressive social security
plans that were long on idealism.[76]

In October 1950, the ACSS followed up OPPSSS with a "Recommendation with Respect to a Social Security System" submitted to the office of
Prime Minister Yoshida Shigeru. All the idealistic plans for reform
hatched in the early postwar years finally led to this recommendation. At
its most fundamental level, the "Recommendation" was a comprehensive
social security plan that the ACSS believed should be implemented swiftly
through the government and various public institutions. The assumption
underlying the "Recommendation" was that because the Japanese people
had a basic right of survival, and the government had a duty to assure a
minimum standard of living for all, the government had to take greater
responsibility for the welfare of its constituents, as directed by the new
postwar constitution. It was the increase in government expenditures,
rather than an increase of premiums paid by insured people, that should
support the expansion of Japan's social security provisions. The "Recommendation" emphasized the importance of universal healthcare coverage
and a substantial increase in government subsidies for health insurance
programs. Drawing on the Wandel Report, the ACSS "Recommendation"
also contained guidelines for developing a Japanese healthcare system
centered on national and public hospitals.[77]

The ACSS "Recommendation" of October 1950 marked the height of
postwar idealistic fervor among Japanese civil servants and SCAP officials
who were trying to advance social security reforms. However, they were
forced to deal with the reality of immediate relief for the population and
social reconstruction under the Allied occupation, particularly after the
Dodge Line was implemented. Neither the national nor local governments
had enough funding for its implementation.[78] Because the implementation of the Dodge Line was now in full swing, there was no room for
grandiose and financially risky health insurance schemes. In October
1950, Japan's leading business newspaper, the *Nihon Keizai Shimbun* [The
Japanese economics newspaper], stated that the most critical health insurance issue facing Japan was the need to examine the relationship between
the ACSS 1950 "Recommendation" and Japan's fiscal condition. The
newspaper described the "Recommendation" as an armchair plan that
had to be reconsidered from the practical point of view of what Japan
could afford.[79] Inaba Shuzo, Deputy Director-General of the Secretariat of
the Economic Stabilization Board, argued that it would be quite difficult
for Japan to stabilize the economy and maintain a balanced budget at the
same time. Consequently, prompt implementation of the "Recommendation" would be next to impossible.[80] After Prime Minister Yoshida received
the "Recommendation," he established a Cabinet Official Roundtable
Conference on the Social Security System in November 1950 to nominally
consider the future social security system, but did nothing more with the

"Recommendation" itself. Largely ignored by the government,[81] the ideals and objectives contained in the "Recommendation" were not implemented. Japan was left to continue relying on ad hoc measures concerning health insurance programs. As a result, the postwar Japanese health insurance system became more broadly based, while lacking an overarching central government policy perspective to guide it.[82]

U.S.–Japan alliance and Japan's healthcare policy

Demilitarization, one of SCAP's most important objectives in Japan, also influenced the development of Japan's postwar health insurance programs. This demilitarization, led by the United States, and anti-military campaigns by Japan's civilian leaders, which culminated in the war-renouncing clause (Article 9) in Japan's new postwar constitution, greatly contributed to the promotion and acceptance of pacifism by the Japanese. But without a substantial military to defend itself, Japan's government came under strong pressure from Washington to accept the continuation of U.S. military bases within Japan as well as the gradual promotion of rearmament. The hallmark of the Japanese postwar state was the combination of pacifism, military subordination and reliance on U.S. military power, including the U.S. nuclear umbrella.

This situation precipitated a three-way heated debate on Japanese national security after the termination of the occupation. First, vocal left-wing political groups, such as the Socialist and Communist parties, disparaged the U.S.–Japan Security Treaty as unconstitutional and imperialistic, accusing the United States of seeking to use Japan as a forward base to oppose the Soviet Union. These leftwing groups advocated the dissolution of the U.S.–Japan alliance. Second, and more importantly, the right wing and pro-rearmament forces such as former Colonel Hattori Takushiro, former Lieutenant General Tatsumi Eiichi who was Prime Minister Yoshida's private adviser in military affairs, the Democratic Party led by Foreign Minister Ashida Hitoshi, and Hatoyama Ichiro of the Liberal Party, criticized the Japanese government for an excessive reliance on U.S. military protection. These right wing forces argued that Japan should have an independent military force strong enough to command respect in the world community. The pro-rearmament forces were clearly nationalists, who favored unfettered rearmament as a means of eliminating U.S. influence in Japan. Third, a group of centrists, led by Prime Minister Yoshida, searched for a more practical approach. The centrists regarded the stationing of U.S. military forces in Japan as the only available way open to Japan to insure its self-defense. Up to a point the centrists agreed with Japan's rearmament, on condition that the United States provide substantial economic assistance and economic opportunities to cover the costs of rearmament and to promote economic growth.[83]

In order to both preserve the U.S.–Japan alliance and prevent the alliance from exploding into a debilitating public debate that could threaten to seriously undermine Japanese social stability, a practical approach favored by Yoshida was continued by successive post-occupation Japanese cabinets. Japanese prime ministers and the government expended much energy on creating policies that allowed the Japanese population to enjoy the benefits of close ties with the United States that provided not only economic and military assistance but also considerable access for Japanese goods to the U.S. market. Moreover, U.S. military assistance to neighboring Asian countries became a reason to purchase goods made in Japan, which became an important catalyst of Japan's high-speed economic growth in the 1950s. As all this enabled Japan's economic pie to become larger, Japan's government was able to widen the scope of social security and provide it with greater financial support.[84] Thus, the 1950s was a time of winning political acceptance from the Japanese people for a coherent and interrelated set of policies: the U.S.–Japan alliance, economic growth, and the expansion of the social security system.

Economic recovery and expanding social security were two among a small number of national goals that struck a popular chord with the overwhelming majority of Japanese. Moreover, as long as the government was able to maintain this popular backing, it could restrain the rise of both the right and the left wings in Japanese politics. With the policies of the Dodge Line still very much alive, the primary agenda of Japan's Ministry of Finance became securing a balanced budget. Nevertheless, as the 1950s became a decade of sustained economic growth for Japan, the government took advantage of the larger economic pie to painlessly advocate a more extensive program of social security benefits. Worried by the severe ideological confrontations over security alliance-related issues, the conservative and pro-business Liberal Democratic Party (LDP) actively supported policies in the few areas where a consensus among the Japanese people was possible, particularly an expanded welfare state. One of the main ways the LDP could attract popular support was to ostentatiously back improvements in Japan's postwar healthcare services.[85] Although the competing Socialist Party was the first political party in Japan to articulate the need for extensive social welfare protections, the LDP and other conservative parties quickly adopted the same position.

The Democratic Party, also conservative and led by Prime Minister Hatoyama Ichiro, announced "peaceful coexistence [with the Communists] and social security" as the party slogan in the 1955 election.[86] Japan did not face the dilemma of choosing between economic growth and the expansion of social welfare. Instead, Japan was able to choose both, and the governing conservative parties took advantage of this to keep the ideological clash over national security issues, including the military alliance with the United States, in check in Japan in the immediate aftermath of the U.S. occupation. In short, the 1950s was a period of fiscal conservatism and absolute growth in the size of the economic pie. Consequently, the

Japanese government avoided any major reorganization of health insurance programs that would be time-consuming and require using a substantial amount of budget as well as political capital; instead, as Japan's economy grew, the government resorted to merely incremental increases in the size of existing health insurance programs, such as an expansion of governmental subsidies, raising insurance medical service fees, and enrolling formerly excluded people in insurance programs.

Health insurance for the whole nation: light and shadow

Despite a series of idealistic health insurance proposals during the occupation, it was quite evident that Japan's government was having trouble financially supporting national healthcare services. To address this problem, the government made a decision to consolidate government-run national and public hospitals so as to reduce administrative expenses. It also introduced a special accounting system that required, in principle, operating publicly run hospitals on a self-paying basis in 1949 and in 1952 respectively.[87] By the 1950s, the Japanese government had abandoned plans to reorganize the healthcare system on the basis of a network of national and public hospitals, deciding instead to promote the rapid development of private medical institutions.

Various laws were passed to support the development of private medical institutions. The revised Medical Service Law of 1950 introduced the incorporation of medical institutions. The revised Special Taxation Measures Law of 1954 realized a 72 percent deduction from physicians' income generated by social insurance treatments. The number of private clinics and medical corporations had increased rapidly since the government established the Medical Care Facilities Financing Corporation in 1960 to assist private medical institutions by making available long-term, low-interest loans. The Medical Service Law was revised again in 1962 to allow the government to begin restricting the number of beds in public hospitals and accelerate the growth of new, private hospitals and clinics as well as the number of beds in existing private medical institutions.[88] National and public hospitals on the one hand and private hospitals on the other found themselves pitted against each other in free for all competition, without any coherent central government coordination.[89] The hallmark of the postwar Japanese healthcare services on the supply side was dependence on the private sector and uncoordinated development between national and public hospitals on one hand and private hospitals and clinics on the other.

Turning to the demand side of the healthcare services in the 1950s, Japan's policy makers and elected officials began to pay closer attention to the realization of the long-advocated proposal for a universal health insurance system. In short, the government sought socialization of demand for healthcare. On 14 November 1951, the Upper House of the Diet adopted a resolution to promote a social security system. Part of the resolution insisted that the government implement the 1950 ACSS "Recommendation" without delay. Because health-related costs were a major cause of poverty in Japan, providing adequate healthcare at a modest cost was the most pressing issue for the government. In the postwar era, both the Health Insurance and the National Health Insurance often faced financial difficulties. Consequently, more and more voices were raised for increasing government subsidies to support both health insurance programs.[90]

In 1949 the government subsidized 50 percent and then, in 1950, 70 percent, of necessary processing expenses for the National Health Insurance. But with the outbreak of war on the Korean peninsula in June 1950, Japan was able to launch a full-scale economic recovery. U.S. spending on all kinds of wartime necessities helped to fill the Japanese government's coffers with tax revenue. More money was now available to spend on health insurance programs. From 1951, the government began paying the cost of all processing expenses.[91] In July 1953, when the National Health Insurance again found itself facing a severe financial crisis, the government decided to provide subsidies that amounted to 20 percent of medical treatment expenses in addition to the cost of all processing expenses. This provision officially became law in August 1955. Assisted by this legally mandated subsidy, a larger number of municipal governments adopted the National Health Insurance programs. Nevertheless, an inequality gradually crept in as people covered by the National Health Insurance could consult a doctor, but those without it in their community could not access medical care. To eliminate this inequality, more tax money was used to expand the National Health Insurance system, to make it available to the whole nation.[92]

Financial crises in the Government-Administered Employment-Based Health Insurance program rose to the surface in 1954. This delayed payment of the medical service fee, as a reserve fund of 1.8 billion yen had been depleted. Worst of all, the program recorded a 3.9 billion yen deficit. Also in 1954, the Corporate-Sponsored Health Insurance programs experienced an unfavorable balance for the first time in the postwar period. In May 1955, the MHW established a seven-member committee (the Seven-Member Committee) for the purpose of listening to opinions from a wide range of civilian people of experience or academic standing, to investigate these financial problems. In October 1955, the Seven-Member Committee advised in a report that the government should not give any government subsidy to insurance payment for the medical fees in the Health Insurance program. This was the counterattack against the trend of rising public demand for greater government subsidy, even for insurance payments to cover these costs. Instead, the Seven-Member Committee insisted that in fairness the government should make it a priority to assist uninsured citizens – roughly thirty million people at the time. The uninsured were primarily those working for small, urban-based companies having less than five employees. As a concrete measure, the committee advocated the establishment of a special Health Insurance program to cover small corporations with less than five employees.[93]

The Seven-Member Committee's report reaffirmed the importance of achieving universal health insurance coverage. As of 1956, the LDP committed itself to this objective. In January of that year, Prime Minister Hatoyama made an official commitment to universal health insurance coverage, stating: "We will proceed with a plan to achieve comprehensive medical security to cover the whole nation." The declaration was accompanied by a budget prepared by the cabinet.[94] Also in 1956, the MHW issued a white paper that declared that the expansion of health insurance to uninsured people (approximately 32 percent of the total population) was the MHW's most important task.[95] For political reasons, the LDP was motivated to implement universal coverage to undercut the popularity of the Socialist Party. In November 1956, the ACSS submitted to Prime Minister Hatoyama the "Recommendation On a Medical Security System," which recommended that a second-tier health insurance program be established to cover those workers employed in small companies with fewer than five employees.[96]

In July 1956, the MHW established a five-member advisory committee, the Medical Security Commission (MSC), to investigate appropriate methods for establishing medical security to cover the whole nation by around 1960. In January 1957, the MSC submitted a report to Minister of Health and Welfare Kanda Hiroshi, that insisted, in contrast to the May 1955 Seven-Member Committee report and the November 1956 ACSS recommendation, on covering employees in small companies with less than five employees by expanding the National Health Insurance. It argued that creating a new and separate second-tier health insurance system would be ineffective and would face a number of difficult problems, namely:

1   The extremely large number of small firms scattered all across Japan would make it too cumbersome to administer a large population of insured individuals and to collect premiums;
2   Low wage levels among the insured would make it extremely difficult to operate an insurance program without substantial subsidies from government; and
3   Because small companies were using various kinds of labor and wage structures, extreme changes in business performance and a high rate of employee turnover would make it technically too difficult to establish company-based insurance.[97]

The MSC argued that it would be much easier to expand the existing National Health Insurance program than to establish a new one from scratch. In any case, achieving universal health insurance coverage was an essential top priority for the government. Whether this would be achieved by establishing a new, second-tier health insurance system or by extending the existing National Health Insurance, it was merely a quantitative expansion of existing health insurance programs, leaving the need for reorganization and integration of a variety of health insurance programs far behind. As for the health insurance programs, quantitative expansion, rather than qualitative improvement, prevailed.

On 8 January 1957, the Cabinet of Prime Minister Ishibashi Tanzan decided to phase in a universal health insurance program by 1960. The following day, the MSC agreed with Ishibashi, strongly insisting that the government should take "all necessary measures to achieve a nationwide diffusion of National Health Insurance by 1960."[98] The MSC also recommended that the state assume final responsibility for the National Health Insurance, which would lead to the expansion of state power and authority.[99] Finally, the LDP decided to expand National Health Insurance to cover the uninsured rather than institute a systematic improvement or expansion of second-tier health insurance.

In February 1957, the LDP created a four-year plan to implement a universal health insurance program. In March, Japan's leading daily newspaper, the *Yomiuri Shimbun*, reported that first the Ishibashi cabinet and then the cabinet of Prime Minister Kishi Nobusuke both emphasized social security, especially medical security, policies. The core of the two cabinet's medical security policies was the realization of health insurance for the whole nation. When a member of the Socialist Party criticized the government's four-year plan for realizing universal health insurance coverage, likening it to "wax fruit," Prime Minister Kishi replied that because bringing health insurance to the whole nation was a critically important policy, he would take it upon himself to achieve that goal.[100]

In November 1956, the ACSS submitted its recommendation, claiming that it would be necessary to establish a framework for universal health coverage, even without solid substance, to provide the Japanese people with satisfactory medical services.[101] In June 1957, the *Mainichi Shimbun*, another leading Japanese daily newspaper, reported that over 20 million people were excluded from health insurance benefits, 10 million low-income people were dependent on welfare medical assistance programs in the event of illness, and 60 percent of the time illness was responsible for a family moving onto the welfare rolls. The *Mainichi* considered it essential that the medical security network be expanded without delay to those who were uninsured.[102] The rise in popular demand for social security protection forced all political parties to support an expansion of social security benefits. During the period of high-speed economic growth in the 1950s, the LDP carried out incremental improvements to social security because government officials assumed that such improvements would not strain the national budget.[103]

In October 1957, the MHW announced its intention to seek a fully-fledged revision of the National Health Insurance Law, which would require all municipal governments to implement a National Health Insurance program by 1960. In the national elections of May 1958, both the LDP and the Socialist Party pledged to improve social security.[104] Finally, on 1 April 1961, National Health Insurance programs took effect across the nation. Japan had finally achieved universal health insurance. Because egalitarianism was a basic principle of Japanese social security in the postwar era, the Japanese government established a framework of universal health insurance coverage in order to win popular support, without paying much attention to qualitative improvement of the health insurance programs, by integrating them into a comprehensive program or at least making appropriate adjustments to a variety of existing programs. Reorganization of the existing various health insurance programs would have been time-consuming and would have required the use of a substantial amount of financial resources, much political capital and muscle; instead, Japan's politicians took the easier route of implementing ad hoc measures to extend the reach of the patchwork of the existing health insurance programs.

Conclusion

Just sixteen years after its defeat in the Asia-Pacific War, Japan established the basic form of a democratic and egalitarian healthcare system that provided universal coverage, free access to healthcare facilities, and low co-payments. This system went on to make it possible for today's Japanese to enjoy high standards of health and the longest lifespans in the world. Japan, however, achieved this system in the absence of a comprehensive reorganization of the pre-war health insurance system. It is this system that survives largely intact today.

After the war, many ideas and schemes emerged with respect to the future development of health insurance programs. However, most of them took it for granted that the government would have to assume substantial financial responsibility for a new integrated health insurance program. Social insurance, especially the National Health Insurance, in a sense, would constitute a kind of public assistance. The more broadly the health insurance programs were dispersed, the higher the governmental subsidies would become. On the other hand, the AMA's basic principle that, in social insurance, the private-sector actors should assume financial administration, was sound and healthy.

In 1949, however, SCAP strictly imposed the Dodge Line, which stalled fiscally irresponsible health insurance programs. Japan could have employed more insurance principles, dictating that insurers were primarily responsible in terms of financial administration, a program similar to that which the AMA advocated. Instead, the Japanese government resorted to providing subsidies in an incremental way to cover not only necessary processing expenses but also medical treatment expenses. The

U.S.–Japan alliance and the stationing of U.S. military forces in Japan after the termination of the occupation could be a major source of severe internal confrontation in Japan. To contain this controversial problem, the Japanese government emphasized the incremental expansion of health insurance programs, one of the very few things on which the Japanese could reach consensus. Instead of implementing overall reorganization of health insurance programs that would require a large sum of money and political capital, the Japanese government carried out quantitative incremental expansion of the existing health insurance programs. As more people used insurance more often, and medical technology advanced, government expenditure increased steadily, and ultimately, Japanese tax payers had to shoulder the financial burden. Moreover, the Japanese people came to depend heavily on the government, neglecting their self-help responsibilities as citizens.

Japan finally achieved universal healthcare in 1961; however, there was no efficient coordination among national, public, and private medical institutions, no clear division of labor between hospitals and clinics, and no socialization of health service in the supply side, although the demand side was socialized. Moreover, a variety of health insurance programs coexisted without effective coordination and there was a great difference in terms of premiums, benefits, and fringe benefits among the programs. In short, a patchwork of the existing health insurance programs led to universal healthcare, leaving a mountain of problems behind.

Currently, Japan faces many serious problems in the healthcare field, the most pressing of which are rising medical costs, unequal benefits, and burdens among health insurance programs. One of the most important legacies of the U.S. occupation concerning Japanese healthcare issues is the unfinished work of reform that should have been completed when all options were on the table and open for debate a half-century ago. Today, in the twenty-first century, Japan as a nation is still struggling to finish this difficult task.

Notes

1 Sato Junichi and Kuroda Koichiro, eds, *Iryo shinwa no shakaigaku* [*Sociology of medical myth*] Kyoto: Sekai Shisosha, 1998, pp. 113, 115; Noguchi Yukio, *1940 nen taisei* [*The 1940 system*] Tokyo: Toyo Keizai Shimposha, 1995, chapter 3, pp. 9, 138.
2 Noguchi, *nen 1940 taisei*, pp. 140.
3 Sho Kashin, *Nihongata fukushi kokka no keisei to "jugonen senso"*[*Japanese style welfare state and the "15-year war"*], Kyoto: Minerva Shobo, 1998, i, iii, p. 15.
4 Ohkochi Kazuo, *Senji shakai seisakuron* [*Wartime social policies*], Tokyo: Jichosha, 1940, p. 4.
5 Tamai Kingo and Ohmori Maki, eds, *Shakai seisaku wo manabu hito no tameni* [*For those who study social policies*], Kyoto: Sekai Shisosha, 2000, p. 126.
6 Yutaka Fujino, *Koseisho no tanjo* [*Birth of the health and welfare ministry*], Kyoto: Kamogawa Shuppan, 2003, p. 64.

7 Ikegami Naoki and John Campbell, *Nihon no iryo* [*Healthcare in Japan*], Tokyo: Chuo Koronsha, 1996, p. 107.
8 "Zadankai" ["A Roundtable discussion"], *Ikai shuho*, 21 September 1940; Nakashizuka Michi, *Iryo hoken no gyosei to seiji* [*Administration and politics of health insurance*], Tokyo: Yoshikawa Kobunkan, 1998, p. 290.
9 "Jinko seisaku kakuritsu Yoko" Article 4, the cabinet decision, 22 January 1941 Online. Available HTTP: <http://www.ndl.go.jp/horei_jp/kakugi/txt/txt00302.htm> (accessed 6 July 2006).
10 Zenkoku Kokumin kenko hoken Dantai Chuokai, ed., *Kokumin kenko hoken 20nen shi* [*Twenty-year history of national health insurance*], Tokyo: Zenkoku Kokumin kenko hoken Dantai Chuokai, 1958, pp. 7, 9.
11 Kasahara Hidehiko, *Nihon no iryo gyosei* [*Japan's healthcare politics*], Tokyo: Keio Gijuku Daigaku Shuppankai, 1999, p. 102; Soeda Yoshiya *et al.*, *Koseisho shi no kenkyu* [*A study of history of the Ministry of Health and Welfare*], Tsukuba: Tsukuba University, 1993, p. 45.
12 Nomura Taku, *Senjika iryo seisaku noto* [*Health policy notes during the war*], Tokyo: Iryo Tosho Shuppansha, 1978, pp. 7–18.
13 Ibid., pp. 72–4.
14 Koseisho Gojunenshi Henshu Iinkai, *Koseisho gojunenshi* [*Fifty-year history of the Japanese Ministry of Health and Welfare*], Tokyo: Chuo Hoki Shuppann, 1988, pp. 435–6.
15 Nomura, *Senjika iryo seisaku noto*, p. 75.
16 Satoh and Kuroda, eds, *Iryo shinwa*, p. 115.
17 Nomura Taku, *Iryo to kokumin seikatsu* [*Healthcare and national life*], Tokyo: Aoki Shoten, 1981, pp. 85–6, 89, 91–6, 98–9, 101–2.
18 Nakashizuka, *Iryo hoken*, p. 338; Kosaka Fumiko, "Senso to kosei" ["War and welfare"], *Iwanami koza nihon tsushi*, vol. 19 Modern Era, No. 4, Tokyo: Iwanami Shoten, p. 336; Koseisho Hokenkyoku Kokumin kenko hoken ka, ed., *Kokumin kenkyo hoken gojunen Shi* [*Fifty-year history of the National Health Insurance*], Tokyo: Gyosei, 1989), pp. 11–12.
19 Nakashizuka Michi, "Iryo hoken seisaku no tenkai katei" ["Development process of health insurance policies"], *Nenpo kindai nihon kenkyu*, 15, 1993, 6; Saguchi Takashi, *Kokumin kenko hoken* [*National Health Insurance*], Tokyo: Koseikan, 1995, pp. 26–7.
20 Nakashizuka, *Iryo hoken*, p. 305.
21 Kasahara, *Iryo gyosei*, p. 93; Yoshihara Kenji and Wada Masaru, *Nihon iryo hoken seidoshi* [*History of Japanese health insurance system*], Tokyo: Toyo Keizai Shinposha, 1999, p. 103.
22 Matsuzaki Yasuko, "Sengo kaikakuki ni okeru shakai hosho koso no keisei katei" ["Formation process of social security vision during the postwar reform period"], *Shukutoku daigaku kenkyu kiyo*, vol. 27, 1993, pp. 1–23; Sugaya Akira, *Nihon iryo seisaku shi* [*History of Japanese healthcare policies*], Tokyo: Nihon Hyoronsha, 1977, p. 230; Yoshihara and Yoshida, *Nihon iryo*, p. 107; Koseisho 50nen Shi Henshu Iinkai, ed., *Koseisho 50nen shi-shiryohen* [*Fifty-year history of the Ministry of Health and Welfare: documents*], Tokyo: Chuo Hoki Shuppan, 1988, pp. 869–75.
23 Nakashizuka, *Iryo hoken*, p. 338.
24 Sir William Beveridge, *Social insurance and allied services: report*, London: H.M. Stationery Office, 1942.
25 Satoh and Kuroda, eds, *Iryo shinwa*, p. 105. Tokyo Daigaku Shakai Kagaku Kenkyujo, ed., *Fukushi kokka* [*Welfare state 1*], vol. 1 *Fukushi kokka no keisei* [*Formation of welfare state*], Tokyo: Tokyo Daigaku Shuppankai, 1984, pp. 3–4.
26 Tamai Kingo, *Bohin no sozo* [*Creation of poverty prevention*], Kyoto: Keibunsha, 1992, p. 288.

27 Takemae Eiji and Nakamura Takafusa, eds, *GHQ Nihon senryo shi* [*GHQ history of Japanese occupation*], vol. 23 *Shakai fukushi* [*Social welfare*], Tokyo: Nihon Tosho Center, 1996, p. 33.

28 G.C. Allen, *Japan's economic recovery*, London: Oxford University Press, 1958, pp. 28, 33; Catherine Edwards, "U.S. policy towards Japan, 1945–1951," Ph.D. dissertation, UCLA, 1977, p. 163; William Guttman, "Miracles of power," vol. 1, D.Phil. dissertation, University of Oxford, 1989, p. 72; GS Memo for the Chief, 24 April 1946, Hussey papers, University of Michigan in John Dower collection, personal collection of Professor John Dower at Massachusetts Institute of Technology.

29 Satoh and Kuroda, eds, *Iryo shinwa*, p. 112.

30 Takemae and Nakamura, *GHQ nihon Senryo Shi*, vol. 23, p. 10.

31 Kawakami Takeshi, *Gendai Nihon iryoshi* [*History of modern Japanese healthcare*], Tokyo: Keiso Shobo, 1973, p. 507.

32 Brigadier General Crawford F. Sams, "Medical care aspects of public health and welfare in Japan," PHW 01115, GHQ/SCAP Records, Public Health and Welfare Section, National Diet Library, Tokyo, Japan.

33 Zenkoku Kokumin kenko hoken Dantai Chuokai, ed., *20nen shi*, p. 109.

34 SCAPIN775 (27 February 1946); Sugiyama Akiko, *Senryoki no iryo kaikaku* [*Healthcare reform during the occupation*], Tokyo: Keiso Shobo, 1995, p. 95.

35 Takemae Eiji and Nakamura Takafusa, eds, *GHQ nihon senryo shi* [*GHQ history of Japanese occupation*], vol. 24 *Shakai hosho* [*Social security*], Tokyo: Nihon Tosho Center, 1996, p. 4.

36 Koyama Michio, *Gendai iryo hoshoron* [*Modern medical security*], Tokyo: Shakai Hoken Shinposha, 1969, p. 15.

37 Shakai Hosho Seido Shingikai, ed., *Shakai hosho no tenkai to shorai* [*Development and future of social security*], Tokyo: Hoken, 2000, p. 95.

38 Tokyo Daigaku Shakai Kagaku Kenkyujo, ed., *Fukushi kokka no keisei* p. 3; Satoh and Kuroda, eds, *Iryo shinwa*, p. 106.

39 Nakashizuka, *Iryo hoken*, p. 288.

40 Tamai, *Bohin no sozo*, pp. 300–2; Matsuzaki, "Sengo kaikakuki," pp. 13–14; Shakai Hosho Kenkyujo, ed., *Nihon shakai hosho shiryo I* [*Japanese social security documents I*], Tokyo: Shiseido, 1981, pp. 158–61.

41 Crawford F. Sams, Memorandum to Chief of Staff, 22 August 1947, PHW 162, GHQ/SCAP Records, Public Health and Welfare Section, National Diet Library, Tokyo, Japan.

42 C.F. Sams, "Nihon ni okeru koshu eisei" ["Public health in Japan"], *Koshu eiseigaku zasshi*, vol. 3, no. 5, 1948, pp. 264–5.

43 Zenkoku Kokumin kenko hoken Dantai Chuokai, ed., *20nen shi*, p. 109; Shakai Hosho Kenkyujo, ed., *Nihon shakai hosho shiryo* I, pp. 163–4.

44 Koseisho Gojunenshi Henshu Iinkai, *Koseisho gojunenshi*, p. 527.

45 Koseisho Hokenkyoku, *Iryo hoken hanseiki no kiroku* [*Documents of a half-century health insurance*], Tokyo: Shakai Hoken Hoki Kenkyukai, 1974, p. 118.

46 Zenkoku Kokumin kenko hoken Dantai Chuokai, ed., *20nen shi*, pp. 286–7; Saguchi, *Kokumin kenko hoken*, p. 82.

47 Nakashizuka Michi, "Iryo hoken seisaku no tenkai katei" ["Process of development of health insurance policies"], *Nempo kindai nihon kenkyu*, vol. 15, *Sengo nihon no shakai keizai seisaku*, December 1993, p. 9.

48 Zenkoku Kokumin kenko hoken Dantai Chuokai, ed., *20nen shi*, pp. 109, 297–303; Shakai Hosho Kenkyujo, ed., *Shiryo I*, pp. 163, 830, 832.

49 Shakai Hosho Kenkyujo, ed., *Shiryo I*, pp. 164–7.

50 The Constitution of Japan, available HTTP: <http://list.room.ne.jp/~lawtext/1946C-English.html> (accessed 6 July 2006).

51 Kondo Bunji, "Shakai hosho seide eno kankoku to kenko hoken"

["Recommendations for a social security system and health insurance"], *Kenko hoken*, vol. 3, no. 3, March 1949, p. 18.

52 Ohkochi Kazuo, "Shakai hosho to sono konkyo" ["Social security and its reasons"], *Byoin*, vol. 2, no. 1, January 1950, p. 5.

53 PH&W to ESS, "Check sheet," 15 December 1947, GHQ/SCAP Records, Public Health and Welfare Section, National Diet Library, Tokyo, Japan.

54 Shakai Hoken Seido Chosakai, "Sengo shakai hosho hattatsuki ni okeru shakai hoken seido chosakai ni tsuiteno kiroku" ["Documents about the social insurance system investigation committee during the development of postwar social security system"], *Shakai hoken jiho*, vol. 34, enlarged edition, p. 137; Shakai Hosho Kenkyujo, ed., *Sengo no shakai hosho* [Postwar social security], Tokyo: Shiseido, 1968, p. 22; Ohuchi Hyoe, ed., *Sengo ni okeru shakai hosho no tenkai* [*Development of social security in the postwar era*], Tokyo: Shiseido, 1961, pp. 23–5; Koyama Michio, *Sengo iryo hosho no shogen* [*Testimonies of postwar medical security*], Tokyo: Sogo Rodo Kenkyujo, 1985, p. 47.

55 Koyama, ed., *Shogen*, p. 56.

56 Koyama, *Gendai iryo hoshoron*, p. 114.

57 Shakai Hosho Kenkyujo, ed., *Shiryo I*, pp. 24–97; Koyama, ed., *no shogen*, p. 56; Sugaya, *Nihon iryo seisaku Shi*, p. 247.

58 Sugiyama, *Iryo kaikaku*, p. 197.

59 Nishioka Yukiyasu, "Gendai nihon iryo hensei no tokushitsu" ["Characteristics of modern Japanese healthcare organization"], *Shakai kagaku nenpo*, vol. 1, 1966, p. 261.

60 Shakai Hoken Seido Chosakai, "Sengo shakai hosho," p. 69.

61 Kawakami Takeshi and Kosaka Fumiko, *Sengo iryoshi josetsu* [*Introduction to postwar healthcare history*], Tokyo: Keiso Shobo, 1992, pp. 32–3.

62 "Report of the Mission of the American Medical Association," 7 December 1948, PHW 5055, GHQ/SCAP Records, Public Health and Welfare Section, National Diet Library, Tokyo, Japan.

63 Tatara Toshio, *Senryoki no fukushi kaikaku* [*Welfare reform during the occupation*], Tokyo: Tsutsui Shobo, 1997, p. 68; Shakai Hosho Kenkyujo, ed., *Shiryo I*, pp. 98–105; Murakami Kimiko, *Sengo shotoku hosho seido no kensho* [*Examination of postwar income security system*], Tokyo: Keiso Shobo, 2000, pp. 82–3.

64 Murakami, *Sengo shotoku*, p. 93; "Report of the Mission of the American Medical Association," December 1948, PHW 5055, GHQ/SCAP Records, Public Health and Welfare Section, National Diet Library, Tokyo, Japan.

65 As for the critical importance of the Dodge Line for the U.S. occupation of Japan, see Yoneyuki Sugita, *Pitfall or panacea: the irony of US power in occupied Japan 1945–1952*, New York: Routledge, 2003, chapter 3.

66 Kitaba Tsutomu, *Sengo shakai hosho no keiseib* [*Formation of postwar social security*], Tokyo: Chuo Hoki Shuppan, 2000, p. 44; Yokoyama Kazuhiko and Tada Hidenori, eds, *Nihon shakai hosho no rekishi* [*History of Japanese social security*], Tokyo: Gakubunsha, 1998, pp. 128–9.

67 Hayashi Shunichi, *Nihon shihon shugi ni okeru kokumi iryo no shomondai* [*Problems of national healthcare in Japanese capitalism*], Tokyo: Iryo Tosho Shuppansha, 1984, p. 62.

68 Kitaba, *Sengo shakai hosho no keisei*, pp. 45–6.

69 Ohkurasho Zaiseishishitsu, ed., *Watanabe Takeshi nikki* [*Watanabe Takeshi diary*], Tokyo: Toyo Keizai Shinposha, 1983, p. 314.

70 Howard Schonberger, *Senryo 1945–1952* [*Aftermath of war*], Tokyo: Jiji Tsushinsha, 1994, p. 264.

71 Yoshihara and Yoshida, *Nihon iryo*, p. 126.

72 Nakashizuka, *Iryo hoken*, p. 308.

73 Takemae and Nakamura, eds, *GHQ Nihon senryoshi*, vol. 24, p. 45.

74 Shakai Hosho Kenkyujo, ed., *Shiryo I*, pp. 171–87.
75 Crawford F. Sams to T. Kurokawa, Minister of Welfare, "Comments on the preliminary report of the Advisory Council on Social Security," 5 October 1950, GHQ/SCAP Records, Public Health and Welfare Section, National Diet Library, Tokyo, Japan.
76 Murakami, *Sengo shotoku*, p. 94.
77 Ibid., pp. 187–205.
78 Kondo Bunji, *Shakai hosho eno kankoku* [*Recommendation of social security*], Tokyo: Shakai Hoken Hoki Kenkyukai, 1950; Kudo Tsuneo, "Nihon no shakai hosho pulan" ["Japanese social security plan"], *Keizaigaku ronsan*, vol. 35, no. 56, February 1995, pp. 310–11; Sakamoto Shigeo, *Shakai hosho no rippo seisaku* [*Social security legislation policy*], Tokyo: Senshu Daigaku Shuppankyoku, 2001, p. 15; "Iryo hoken no sanjunen" ["Thirty years of health insurance"], *Shakai hoken junpo*, no. 1500, 1 April 1985, p. 16.
79 Shakai Hosho Seido Shingikai Jimukyoku, ed., *Shakai hosho seido shingikai 10nen no ayumi* [*10-year development of the advisory council on social security*], Tokyo: Shakai Hoken Hoki Kenkyukai, 1961, p. 207.
80 Shakai Hoken Seido Chosakai, "Shakai hoken seido chosakai ni tsuiteno kiroku," p. 70.
81 Nakashizuka, *Iryo hoken*, p. 312.
82 Ibid., p. 3.
83 Iida Tsuneo, *Gendai Nihon keizaishi jokan* [*Modern Japanese economic history*], vol. 1, Tokyo: Chikuma Shobo, 1976, p. 257; Hatano Sumio, "'Saigunbi' wo meguru seijirikigaku" ["The politics of Japanese rearmament"], *Journal of modern Japanese studies*, no. 11, 1989, pp. 181–6; Rekishigaku Kenkyukai, ed., *Nihon dojidaishi* [*Japanese contemporary history*], vol. 2, Tokyo: Aoki Shoten, 1990, p. 180; Ohtake Hideo, *Sengo Nihon boei mondai shiryoshu* [*Documents on postwar defense problems*], vol. 2, Tokyo: Sanichi Shobo, 1992, p. 82.
84 As for the U.S.–Japan alliance and economic growth in the 1950s, see Aaron Forsberg, *America and the Japanese miracle*, Chapel Hill, NC: University of North Carolina Press, 2000.
85 Tokita Tadahiko, *Nihon no iryo keizai* [*Japanese health economics*], Tokyo: Toyo Keizai Shinposha, 1995, p. 151.
86 Masumi Junnosuke, *Gendai Nihon no seiji taisei* [*Modern Japanese political system*], Tokyo: Iwanami Shoten, 1969, p. 76.
87 Nishioka, "Gendai nihon iryo," pp. 261–2.
88 Sugaya Akira, *Nihon iryo seidoshi* [*History of Japanese healthcare*], Tokyo: Hara Shobo, 1976, pp. 429–30; Hayashi, *Nihon shihon shugi*, p. 79.
89 Nishioka, "Gendai nihon iryo," p. 259; Nishioka Yukiyasu, *Gendai Nihon iryo seisakuron* [*Modern Japanese healthcare policies*], Tokyo: Rodo Junposha, 1985, p. 110; Hayashi, *Nihon shihon shugi*, pp. 78–9.
90 Shakai Hosho Seido Shingikai Jimukyoku, ed., *10nen no ayumi*, p. 237.
91 Shakai Hosho Kenkyujo, ed., *Sengo no shakai hosho*, p. 27.
92 Yokoyama and Tada, eds, *Nihon shakai hosho*, p. 133; Ohuchi, ed., *Sengo*, pp. 103–4.
93 Koseisho, *Shichinin iinkai no hokoku* [*Report by the Seven-Member Committee*], Tokyo: Koseisho, October 1955.
94 Kuroki Toshikatsu, *Nihon shakai hosho* [*Japanese social security*], Tokyo: Kobundo, 1959, p. 222; Yoshihara and Yoshida, *Nihon iryo*, p. 163.
95 Adachi Masaki, ed., *Fukushi kokka no rekishi to tenbo* [*History and outlook of welfare nation*], Kyoto: Horitsu Bunkasha, 1988, p. 100.
96 Shakai Hosho Seido Shingikai, *Iryo hosho seido ni kansuru kankoku to kakkai daihyo no hihan* [*Recommendation on a medical security system and criticisms from representatives from all quarters*], Tokyo: Shakai Hoken Shimposha, 1956.

97 Shakai Hosho Kenkyujo, ed., *Shiryo* I, pp. 621–2.
98 Ibid., p. 620.
99 Ibid., pp. 619–21.
100 Zenkoku Kokumin kenko hoken Dantai Chuokai, ed., *20nen shi*, p. 495.
101 Saguchi, *Kokumin kenko hoken*, p. 95.
102 Zenkoku Kokumin kenko hoken Dantai Chuokai, ed., *20nen shi*, p. 499.
103 Shakai Hosho Koza Hemsji Iinkai, ed., *Keizai hendo to shakai hosho* [*Economic fluctuation and social security*], Tokyo: Sogo Rodo Kenkyujo, 1981, p. 40.
104 Ohuchi, ed., *Sengo*, pp. 187–9.

7 Resident aliens

Forging the political status of Koreans in occupied Japan

Mark E. Caprio

Introduction

Declarations made before and immediately following the cessation of the Pacific War pledged the United States mission of the occupation of Japan, after disarming the erstwhile enemy of its military capacity and purging those responsible for the war, to be the introduction of democracy to its domestic politics. The same Potsdam Declaration that demanded Japan's "unconditional surrender" appended the notion that through occupation the democratic ideals of "[f]reedom of speech, of religion and of thought, as well as respect for the fundamental human rights shall be established." Article 14 of the 1946 postwar Constitution that the occupation forces imposed upon the Japanese people adopted the spirit of these ideals in its declaration that "[a]ll the people are equal under the law, and there shall be no discrimination in political, economic or social relations because of race, creed, sex, social status or family origin."[1]

One can debate the extent to which the occupation authorities were successful in introducing, in the words of W. Macmahon Ball, this "alien gift"[2] to the Japanese islands. It would be hard to dispute the fact, however, that Japanese democracy has demonstrated strength among its contemporaries in the post-World War II period. An important blemish in this record, though, remains in the state's treatment of its minorities. These peoples not only were denied political consideration as "Japanese" but also faced severe discrimination and at times non-recognition during the postwar period.[3] In particular, the plight of Japan's Korean population, due primarily to its size, its organization, and historical complications, has demanded (and attracted) a large amount of attention.

Complications between the Japanese and Korean peoples, of course, originated long before the Occupation forces arrived on Japan's shores; thus they are not to be considered a direct result of this seven-year period. Animosity between the two Northeast Asian neighbors manifested into images of superiority that predate Japan's Meiji period (1868–1912). Nor did one side monopolize these images: both sides continue to maintain claims of superiority in their politics, their culture, and their society.

Occupation authorities, well aware of these confrontational attitudes, however, directed a policy that resembled (and even exceeded) the segregation policies practiced by the Japanese over their thirty-five year period of colonial occupation. Koreans residing in Japan would be strongly encouraged to return to their "homeland"; if they chose to stay they would be subject to Japanese legal codes while remaining ineligible to participate in its society as Japanese citizens. Contrary to the optimistic ideals expressed in its rhetoric, occupation policy excluded them from participation in the Japanese democratic experiment.

Wartime images of the Koreans and United States preparation for occupation

United States documents from the occupation period often revealed the conviction that the majority of the Koreans living in Japan at this time had been brought to the islands by force to perform war-related labor. Thus, reports argue, it was reasonable to expect that the majority of this people wished to be repatriated. In fact many Japan-based Koreans had migrated to Japan before the outbreak of war.[4] Even during the war years (1937–1945), when Korean labor recruitment and conscription became policy, Japan brought a few more than 724,000 Koreans to the archipelago. This represents roughly 35 percent of the 2.1 million Korean residents who welcomed the allied occupation forces in 1945.[5] In addition to wartime forced labor, a large number of Koreans, drawn by relatively favorable wages and working conditions, migrated on their own to the Japanese islands, so much so that in 1942 the Japanese found it necessary to refuse entry to 5000 potential Korean immigrants.[6]

Up through the end of the war, the Korean resident population in Japan faced discrimination in a number of areas. Forced to maintain their family register (*koseki*) in Korea, the people were never expected to completely assimilate as Japanese even though they were taxed as such. They were, however, allowed suffrage rights in accordance with Japanese law. At a more informal level Korean labor provided Japanese industry with a cheaper pool of labor.[7] Those recruited during the early 1940s primarily replaced Japanese laborers conscripted into the military during the Pacific War. Korean residents, as a whole, never gained the trust of the local police, who protested many of the measures (such as making them Japanize their names) implemented to facilitate this population's assimilation as Japanese; preserving the Koreans' alien presence eased that institution's task of maintaining a vigilant eye on this potentially troublesome people.[8]

United States images of the Korean people had historically mirrored the prejudicial attitudes held by the Japanese. By the end of the nineteenth century the United States Government, under the presidency of Theodore Roosevelt, had all but written off the Koreans' ability to govern themselves.[9] It was the first foreign state to recognize Japan's annexation of the peninsula in 1910 and it seldom criticized Japanese colonial activities in Korea.[10] To this day many Koreans still contend that the failure of the United States (and other Western states) to take action against the Japanese intrusion represented a breach in the promises these states had made in the treaties they signed with the Korean government in the 1880s.[11]

This negative attitude prevailed as the United States prepared to occupy the Korean peninsula following the war's end. The wording in the Cairo Communiqué, compiled by the United States, China, and Great Britain in December 1943 in Cairo where they gathered to determine the postwar geopolitical world structure, reinforced these images, particularly in their decision to defer Korean independence for an unstated duration of time. Korean sovereignty would follow allied occupation "in due time." The United States justified this delay by repeating an argument frequently used by the Japanese to justify their occupation of the peninsula: the Korean people's inability to govern themselves.[12]

When the occupation of the Korean peninsula began in September 1945, the United States government directed the occupation forces to keep the Japanese (including the governor-general) and their Korean supporters at their posts until Koreans could be trained to replace them. Evidence suggests that Japanese influence prevailed even after Korean protests forced the United States to rescind this order and have the unwanted members of the former colonial bureaucracy replaced. Commanding General John Hodge admitted, for example, that he kept an ear directed toward the Japanese more often than toward the Korean.[13] One letter written by a Korean but intercepted by the occupying forces complained that Korean political parties found it necessary to find Japanese girls for officers of the American Military Government. It further complained that the military government still relied on Japanese, rather than Koreans, as interpreters.[14]

Documents written during the time that the United States was preparing for the occupation of Japan reveal a fairly sophisticated understanding of the diversity among the archipelago's Korean residents. Indeed, there was mention that members of this people, as liberated victims of Japanese oppression, could play a positive role in the everyday operations of the occupation. These same documents, however, reveal the aspiration that all non-Japanese would eventually be returned to their country, even while acknowledging that achieving this goal would be difficult, if not impossible.[15] Preparation to repatriate non-Japanese began soon after the Cairo meeting. Then the United States began gathering information on the Korean people by reading materials published by the Japanese and by conducting interviews with available Koreans. Those interrogated included Koreans living in the United States and Korean soldiers who had been captured by United States military forces. The interviews particularly focused on the inter ethnic relations shared by Japanese and Koreans, as well as Korean behavior following liberation – would they retaliate against their colonial occupiers? The negative portrayals of the Japanese that surfaced from these interviews only confirmed United States views that the Koreans and Japanese could not live together as neighbors either on the peninsula or the archipelago. Thus, Koreans in Japan and Japanese in Korea would have to be quickly repatriated.

The Office of Strategic Services authored in late June 1945 one of the first position papers to address occupational policy toward minorities. "Aliens in Japan" estimated that there were over two million Koreans, 40,000 Formosan Chinese, and 40,000 persons of other nationalities presently residing throughout the Japanese islands. The fact that almost 95 percent of all Japan-based foreigners were Korean tilted the attention of the report's compilers in the direction of this people.[16]

"Aliens in Japan" depicted the Koreans as a people of low social and economic position, a people that had failed to assimilate into Japanese society. They lived apart from, and rarely intermarried with, the dominant social group. The authors of the report emphasized the Korean people's transitory existence in Japan: they did not go to Japan with the idea of settling there; they sent back a rather large percentage of their earnings to family members in Korea. Japanese policies, as well, had curtailed any desire they might have had to make Japan their permanent home.[17] The report envisioned the image that the Japanese held toward the Koreans as follows:

> The Koreans, with few exceptions, are a distinct minority group, with a low social position. They are looked down upon by the Japanese and were the scapegoats on at least one occasion when natural disaster struck Japan. The Japanese attitude towards Koreans arises, in part, from the characteristics of the Koreans. Those who go to Japan are, in the main, very poor, uneducated, and unskilled, even by low Korean standards. Their language, culture, and manner of life are quite different from the Japanese, and the Koreans have attempted to maintain their old way of life, separate and distinct from the Japanese community. Koreans do not possess the Japanese fever for hard work, and to the energetic Japanese Koreans appear to be slow moving and lazy. The brevity of their stay in Japan makes them seem shiftless and lazy. The thrifty and austere Japanese also are appalled by the Korean fondness for food, elaborate ceremonies, impractical clothing, and gaudy decorations. It is also said that Koreans are not as conscious of cleanliness as the Japanese and that the Koreans live under miserable conditions in Japan because they know nothing better in Korea. On the other side, it should be borne in mind that Koreans remit or save a high percentage of their earnings and that Japanese prejudice and restrictions seriously limit housing possibilities.[18]

The tone of these images, although similar to that held by the Japanese, offered justification for Korean peninsula occupation and separate Japanese–Korean treatment in the archipelago occupation. "Aliens in Japan" concluded with a postwar "course of action." It estimated that about two million foreigners would be "in need of liberation, protection, or segregation from the Japanese." A more immediate problem, though, would be to take action against those aliens who constituted "a menace to Allied military operations." Such people, it advised, should be incarcerated. On the other hand, those who had endured a longer residence in Japan could be used to assist in the operations of the occupation forces. After screening for war criminals it advised that all foreigners who opted for repatriation be permitted passage to their homeland and that all those who wished to remain in Japan be granted liberty to stay. U.S. occupation policy would later adopt the stance against forcing non-Japanese repatriation.

All aliens were not, however, to be accorded equal treatment. "Aliens in Japan" recommended that for administrative purposes the Japan-based alien population be categorized into the following groups: Allied Prisoners of War (POWs), members of the Diplomatic Corps, imprisoned Allied citizens, and remaining foreigners. These categories, which were revised once the occupation operations commenced their duties, determined not only repatriation priority but also food rations (amount and kind) and legal status (whether a person was to be accorded extraterritoriality privileges).

Asian aliens were particularly open to suspicion. "Asiatics," the report noted, "may be either friendly or enemy; even those who became citizens might be either pro- or con-Allied; others might have collaborated with the Japanese." Every case, the report advised, must be investigated individually before their status was to be finalized.[19]

The report was rather generous in its recommendations for treatment of those foreigners who chose to remain in Japan rather than be repatriated. It concluded that in many cases the situation in such people's homeland might necessitate their continued residence in Japan. Discrimination against such people, it cautioned, must be eliminated at all costs. Indeed, the authors advised that this alien population be given priority of job opportunities over the Japanese. Specifically mentioned here was the case of the White Russians who would probably be the alien people with the least desire to return to their homeland.[20]

Late June 1945, a mere month and a half before the war's end, was still too early to anticipate the geopolitical structure of postwar East Asia. In particular the situation of the peoples of Japan's Northeast Asian colonies, the Taiwanese and Koreans, would be most affected by the postwar developments, namely the defeat of Nationalist Chinese to the Communists and the division of the Korean peninsula at the 38th parallel. The plight of the Korean people was particularly confusing due to their large numbers in

Japan and the political division of their country. To the contrary, the plight of the Taiwanese population in Japan was settled with relatively ease, thanks to the Nationalist Chinese' siding with the Allied forces. Both the Korean and the Taiwanese caused the occupation and Japanese police headaches by their illegal economic and political activities.

Occupation policy and Korean behavior

Within two months of Japan's surrender the State, War, and Navy Departments issued to the Supreme Commander for the Allied Powers (SCAP) one of the most important directives governing its occupation policy in Japan. In this document, titled "Basic Initial Post-Surrender Directive to Supreme Commander for the Allied Powers for the Occupation and Control of Japan," we find ambiguities surrounding the general status of the Korean population, as well as the most direct statement regarding their specific status vis-à-vis the Japanese. The directive read in part as follows:

> You will treat Formosan-Chinese and Koreans as liberated peoples in so far as military security permits. They are not included in the term "Japanese" as used in this directive but they have been Japanese subjects and may be treated by you, in case of necessity, as enemy nationals. They may be repatriated, if they so desire, under such regulations as you may establish. However, priority will be given to the repatriation of nationals of the United Nations.[21]

Ambiguity rested in the lack of a decisive statement regarding the Korean and Taiwanese as people to be liberated or incarcerated – they were not "Japanese" but they could be treated as such (i.e. as enemy). Among the problems in coming to a conclusion on this issue was the fact that a rather high number of these colonized peoples had participated directly in Japan's war efforts as soldiers. Indeed, as many as forty-four Koreans and Taiwanese would later be sentenced to death, and over 270 imprisoned as war criminals.[22]

That Japan's minority residents would not be considered as "Japanese" following the war was not a significant change from their pre-war and wartime status as subjects of the Japanese Empire – the Japanese government and people would have agreed with this classification. On the other hand, if not "Japanese," then of what political category were these people to be considered? Many had resided in Japan for the majority of their lives; others knew of no other "homeland." Indeed, until the establishment of the Nationalist Chinese government in Taiwan and the Republic of Korea government in the southern half of the Korean peninsula, no legitimate government existed to welcome these people upon their return to their ancestral land.

Nationalist China's early recognition as a member of the United Nations, and as one of the five Security Council members, greatly simplified the status of Japan's Taiwanese–Chinese population. Regardless of their opinion on the matter, they would be considered the responsibility of the Chinese government and thus entitled to all of the benefits that UN membership provided nationals of member states. As early as October 1945 the Chinese government ordered all Japan-based Chinese to register with this government to recover their Chinese nationality. It also established a mission in Japan for this purpose. Recognition as Chinese not only allowed them food rations as Allied nationals, but also exempted them from paying capital taxes to the Japanese government.[23]

The complications of the Korean resident in Japan intensified as those of the Taiwanese resident waned. The United States never considered the overseas Korean Provisional Government as its wartime ally or as a postwar legitimate representative of the Korean people. This non-recognition prevented the Korean population from attaining the status of Allied nationals following the war. Moreover, the division of the peninsula into U.S. and Soviet zones blocked this people from attaining United Nations status even after 1948, when legitimate governments were established in the north and the south. (The veto rights of members of the United Nations Security Council – which included the United States and the Soviet Union – allowed the two superpowers to block entry of each other's Korean client state.) It was only after this time that the occupation forces recognized the Korean government's right to establish a representative office in Japan to care for this people's needs. This office, however, represented the interests of but a minority of the Korean population in Japan. Previously, from 1946, SCAP entrusted the Japanese with the task of registering this population under the terms of the Alien Registration Act, promulgated that year.

The division of the Korean peninsula particularly complicated the status of Korean residents in Japan who were sympathetic to leftist ideology. Richard B. Finn, who served in the Diplomatic Section of SCAP and compiled a major "staff study" on Koreans in Japan, wrote that by 1948 at least half of the Korean population favored Japan's leftist elements.[24] Indeed, occupation documents demonstrate that United States administrators explained as "leftist" or "Communist" any Korean activity that they felt interfered with the occupation's administrative policies.[25] These generalizations were probably not far off the mark; the Japanese Communist Party was one of the few politically organized groups that lent the Korean people's plight a sympathetic ear. Korean leftists organized soon after the war's end; a meeting held on 15 October 1945 that gathered together 5000 delegates organized the *Chaeil Chosónjin Ryónmeng* (Japan-based Koreans Association, or *Choryón* for short).[26] The December 1945 demand issued by Kim Ty-yon [Kim Taeyon] – that Koreans be allowed to form a "People's Republic" in Japan – further strained Korean relations with occupation authorities. By September 1949 the SCAP's patience had run aground: it ordered the Japanese government to disband the organization.[27]

Communist activity on the Korean peninsula, as well, inflamed fears on the Japanese archipelago of the increased threat to the Japanese posed by Korean participation in Japan-based leftist activity. Japanese occupiers of the peninsula began reporting communist activity in Korea even before the United States occupation forces arrived. Soon after arriving, commanding officer John Hodge noted in his "Conditions on Korea" that the "situation in the South Korea (*sic*) makes extremely fertile ground for the establishment of Communism." From the autumn of 1946 the southern half of the peninsula was overrun by what the United States military interpreted as uprisings directed by leaders in P'yóngyang and Moscow.[28] Occupation authorities viewed the reverse flow of "repatriated" Koreans who illegally returned to Japan as the North, and by extension the Far East, Communist network, endeavoring to plant its agents on Japanese soil.[29]

Another thorn in occupation officials' sides (but in their minds not necessarily divorced from communist intentions) was Japan-based Taiwanese and Korean participation in black market activities that began to spread soon after Japan's defeat. One 1946 report estimated that there were some 20,000 Taiwanese engaging in the black market. This "unruly element," which included Koreans as well, was so feared that "there is one black market section in Tokyo in which Japanese police are afraid to enter unaccompanied by [U.S.] military police." When arrested, the two peoples faced different consequences: Taiwanese members were tried as foreigners by a commission that included Chinese and United States personnel; Koreans, on the other hand, were tried as Japanese in Japanese courts, as they qualified neither as Allied nationals nor United Nations citizens.[30]

With this record and reputation, both the United States occupation authorities and Japanese government officials united in the opinion that the best place for the former colonized aliens, and particularly those from Korea, was back in their homeland. The large numbers of people involved limited occupation policy to encouraging – rather than forcing – their repatriation. The comparatively difficult situation that the Korean peninsula faced caused planners to focus their attention more directly on their situation than on that of the Taiwanese.

SCAP policy initially glossed over its attitude to minorities, especially that regarding the treatment of Japan's Korean population. This reflected its attitude that the people's inevitable return to their homelands would solve all potential minority problems. The Japanese population would then revert to the homogeneous state it had enjoyed during the "isolation policy [it] held for [the] centuries" leading up to the time when Japan opened its borders to the Western world, in 1854.

SCAP directed the Japanese government to bear the financial responsibility for repatriation. Japan also was to ensure that these people received safe passage to their homes. As predicted, the majority of Japan-based aliens did return to their homeland. Yet, it would have been difficult for SCAP to foresee that as many as 600,000 Koreans would opt to remain in Japan. In addition to those who chose to stay, a large number of repatriated Koreans successfully, but illegally, returned to the Japanese islands after failing to re-establish themselves in Korean society.[31]

One of the biggest barriers that Koreans wishing to repatriate faced was the material limitation that SCAP officials placed on the amount of baggage and money with which they could return. Most damaging was the 1000 yen limitation on monetary possessions, an amount that officials calculated to be insufficient for one person to "exist for more than a few days, and . . . extremely inadequate to enable him to begin life anew."[32] All materials in excess of these limitations were impounded by occupation authorities until further notice. In January 1946, SCAP revised this policy to allow the Korean people to bring with them financial documents such as postal savings and bank passbooks, with the idea that their financial estate could be transferred to them at a later date. However, as Changsoo Lee points out, this revision was insignificant, as financial transactions between the two countries remained suspended from the end of the war.[33]

The United States authorities considered Koreans who chose to remain in Japan as people who intended to "retain" their "Japanese nationality." This placed them in a category separate from other foreign residents in Japan, which rendered them ineligible for benefits to which other alien groups were entitled. It also suggested the idea that the United States regarded the position of this "liberated people" as unchanged from that which they faced while under Japanese colonial rule. To add insult to injury, this status subjected the Korean residents to jurisdiction in the Japanese court system and required them to pay taxes that were, in part, used for war retributions. The U.S. justification for maintaining this status was rather practical: the sheer numbers of these people made any status change financially impractical.[34]

SCAP officials faced a dilemma: whereas they preferred that Japan-based Koreans return to their homeland, they insisted that these people be given a choice over where they wished to live. Occupation policy refused (as Japanese officials no doubt wished) to force Koreans to repatriate. In May 1948 the Diplomatic Section submitted a "staff study" that re-evaluated the situation of the Korean residents in Japan with the intention of advising a long-term policy designed to encourage repatriation. This report initiated a rather lively debate regarding the occupation's policy regarding the status and treatment of Koreans in Japan.[35]

The "staff study" borrowed aspects of the wartime "Aliens in Japan" view of Koreans in encouraging their repatriation. The Koreans presented a number of problems to both the occupation and Japanese authorities. They were intent on establishing political autonomy in Japan. They also participated in communist activities and thus helped strengthen ties that

linked communism on the Asian continent with that in Japan. Economically, the study continued, Koreans were infamous for their illegal black
market transitions that existed "beyond the control or tax authority of the
Japanese Government." Finally, socially the people represented a group
that did not readily assimilate with the Japanese "both because of the long-
standing prejudice of the latter and because of [their] uneducated and
generally underprivileged character." It was "undeniable," the report
offered, "that the Japanese would be only too happy to see all Koreans
leave Japan."[36]

Japanese aspirations for Korean repatriation, the study continued, were
not out of line with U.S. interests. Both felt it best that "as many Koreans
in Japan as possible return to Korea." The "staff study" supported this idea
(but contradicted its pejorative image of Japan-based Koreans) by adding
that their repatriation could contribute to Korean society "in manpower as
well as in skilled training and financial means acquired in Japan." Their
presence in Japan was "for the Japanese an almost complete liability"
because they drew heavily from the Japanese economy and contributed
little in taxes.

The compilers of the study, however, emphasized the need to continue
SCAP's fundamental policy: encouraging, rather than forcing, repatriation. Requiring Koreans *en masse* to return to their homeland would cause
major problems for the Korean peninsula. It would also create ill feelings
on the part of the Korean people toward the United States, to say nothing
of the major financial and social adjustments it would require in both
countries.[37]

Next, the study offered several recommendations toward implementing
a policy to attain its desired goals. One of its most welcome suggestions
was to raise the limits of financial property with which the Koreans could
repatriate to 100,000 yen. This adjustment would allow all but the wealthi-
est Koreans to return to Korea with their financial estates intact. It further
advised that the United States protect all assets in access of this limit by
depositing them in the owner's name for safekeeping. Also, occupation
policy should relax the rules governing the transfer of currency and property between Korea and Japan. The study also determined that weight
restrictions set on material property were within reason and not in need of
adjustment.[38]

The study further advanced that occupation policy must also reassess
the position of Koreans who opted to remain in Japan. It centered this discussion first, on whether these foreign residents should be accorded
United Nation member status, and second, on the position they should
occupy in Japanese society. Its compilers warned that Koreans would
demand (as they had in the past) United Nations privileges. However,
since Soviet opposition offered the recently formed Republic of Korea
little hope of gaining membership in this organization, their demands had
little chance of gaining acceptance. The Korean people, the study further

warned, would no doubt interpret this as discriminatory, being that Japan's Taiwanese residents had been granted this exalted status. The primary difference, it explained, was that the Republic of China held UN membership and Korea did not.

In lieu of United Nations member status, the "staff study" offered several options regarding the categorization of Japan-based Koreans. If, for example, SCAP were to allow the soon-to-be established Korean government permission to designate an official representative for residence in Japan, Korean residents could register and establish their Korean nationality (but not a status of foreign national) as a first step toward repatriation. It would be ill advised, the study cautioned, for the Korean government to offer blanket Korean nationality to this population. This would only increase the "threat of exaggerated claims by Koreans in Japan."[39]

The study did acknowledge that even reform in repatriation procedures would not convince all Japan-based Koreans to return to their country. Those who refused to register as Koreans, it advised, would retain the status of "Japanese nationality [as determined by] Japanese law," and thus remain subject to Japanese legal codes and the court system. The only exceptions would be for those Koreans who had been granted entry into Japan as foreign nationals, a select group chosen by the Korean government for their technological or scholastic potentials.

An important consideration that the study noted was that Koreans requesting repatriation were limited to returning to the southern half of the peninsula (the present-day Republic of Korea (ROK)). This limitation alone dissuaded a large number of Koreans from returning because of their ties with communism and other leftist ideologies.[40] To date, the study noted, the occupation forces had managed to return but 351 Koreans to their homes in northern Korea; even with policy reform the study's authors did not anticipate doing much better. Recommending that U.S. officials inform the ROK government "of the records and activities of all Korean communists who returned to Korea so that necessary measures can be taken" surely was not a policy that enhanced the chances of the plan attaining its stated goal: "to rid Japan of as many Korean communists as possible and prevent their re-entry to Japan."[41]

The "staff study" received compliments for its efforts – it was the most comprehensive review of the problem to date. It was criticized for its particulars, specifically regarding a number of its recommendations. The suggestion of increasing the financial amount that repatriated Koreans could take with them was readily endorsed by both the United States and Japanese authorities. On the other hand, many found the idea of Korean registration to be troublesome. Would this action not hinder occupation – and by extension Japanese – efforts to encourage these people to leave? Even if they were to register, but chose to remain in Japan, how would their status and treatment differ from that of Koreans who chose not to register?

William J. Sebald, the United States Political Advisor to SCAP, offered his comments on the report on February 1949. Reiterating the ultimate goal of this inquiry – "reducing the size of this difficult minority group" – he argued that "making them all Korean" would trigger the opposite effect: it would remove their incentive for returning to Korea. Not only would this deprive Korea of the "industrial and commercial skill it so eagerly desires," it would also "aggravate ... the worst source of friction" between Koreans and Japanese, the tendency of Japan-based Koreans to assert the privilege of non-Japanese status. As an "ultimate solution," Sebald recommended that the United States leave the matter for the Japanese and Korean governments to settle after both states had established sovereignty.[42]

A second issue emphasized in Sebald's critique of the study concerned the Korean government's registration of Japan-based Koreans. The United States, he stressed, must take measures, including the use of international law, to prevent this government body from altering the status of these people *en masse*, without taking into consideration their appropriateness of such action. The effect of a *carte blanche* registration of all Japan-based Koreans as "Korean nationals," even for those who did not state an intention of returning to Korea, he admitted, would mean little in legal terms, as the ROK was not a member of the United Nations. It would, however, give these residents an "undeniable psychological validity in the face of the present weak law enforcement in Japan and the ineffectual position of the country's disarmed police."[43] Sebald fortified his arguments by listing the crimes in which the Korean residents had been engaged since the end of the war. They blatantly disregarded Japanese police and legal authority by their participation in the black market and other illegal activities.

Sebald's privileged position allowed him close and frequent contact with the top SCAP brass, including General MacArthur himself. In August 1949 he summarized the Supreme Commander's views in a letter to the United States Secretary of State, writing that MacArthur

> had been quite positive in his decision to take no action at the present time looking to a clarification of the status of Koreans in Japan along the lines of the Mission's recommendations. He feels that registration of Koreans at this juncture would only confuse an already complicated situation and possibly raise more problems with respect to the Koreans here than it would solve.[44]

Alleviation of the plight of the Korean population in Japan appeared to stall from this point. The United States encouraged the Korean and Japanese governments to negotiate settlement in their relations even before the occupation officially closed its doors in 1952. However, the two sides failed to sign a treaty to solidify normal relations until over a decade later, in

1965, when they concluded agreements regarding normalization and the status of Japan-based Koreans.[45]

Complications in Korean repatriation and establishing Japanese residence

The debate over the status of Japan-based Koreans emphasized the United States' opinions as to why it felt the people should be encouraged to return, alluded to the Japanese' desire for them to return, and avoided any direct reference to the Korean government's position on the issue. It also offered little explanation regarding the economic and social situation on the Korean peninsula that discouraged their repatriation. A comprehensive understanding of this people's plight requires consideration of these factors.

The occupation's decision to take a hands-off position on this issue was no doubt strengthened by the diametrically opposed opinions held by the Japanese and Korean governments, both of which contributed to the debate on the Japan-based Koreans issue. In effect, both bodies expressed the idea that they did not want these people under their jurisdiction for similar reasons: the Japan-based Koreans' hybrid cultural characteristics soiled Korean and Japanese images of the homogeneous society that they sought to promote on the peninsula and on the archipelago. The Japanese and American administrations described these people as economic liabilities: they contributed little to the tax coffers, and the administrations feared the political sway they might wield if they were treated as citizens of the archipelago.

This issue entered a February 1949 discussion held between Richard B. Finn and Wajima Eiji, Director of the Control Bureau of the Japanese Foreign Office. Wajima emphasized that his government supported the position of absolute separation between the two peoples. Koreans in Japan, he explained, should be treated as "non-Japanese in all future legislation," and laws and regulations now in force should be amended "in such a way as to give [Koreans] the status of non-Japanese in every aspect of the administrative field." Here the Japanese official articulated a difference in the thinking modes between his government and the occupation authority. The U.S. view, thinking short-term, held it best that Koreans be included as Japanese nationals so as not to have to accord them the expensive foreign national status. The Japanese considered this problem as a long-term issue – the status of Japan-based Koreans after the occupation forces had packed up and gone home.

Wajima explained the Japanese government's reasoning behind its segregation thinking by rejuvenating a colonial idea – the Korean people as inferior to the Japanese. He boasted that "nearly all Koreans in Japan are extremely eager to acquire Japanese nationality," so much so that they were willing to pay up to two million yen to become adopted as Japanese.

The Japanese official then cited empirical research "proving" that the Koreans were an inferior race, one with "mental and social capacities" that "were of a primitive nature." Their "inferiority," he continued, "to a great extent motivates Japanese uncertainty and hostility in regard to the Koreans."[46]

The newly inaugurated South Korean government's position on this issue arrived in April 1949. To argue the need for their consideration as "Allied Nationals," it emphasized the suffering that these people had endured:

> ... regardless of their current domicile, the nationals of the Republic of Korea should be accorded treatment as Allied Nationals. This is especially so in regard to the Korean residents in Japan, in view of the unfavorable conditions under which they originally migrated to Japan, their prolonged suffering under the Japanese as an oppressed minority group, and the peculiar situation in which they are at the present.

The cover letter composed by the Korean diplomatic mission in Japan, under which the Korean government's submission was sent, emphasized that "the Republic of Korea has not requested any general repatriation of Koreans from Japan," an issue that should be settled as a provision of a peace treaty to be signed by South Korea and Japan.[47]

In these two documents we see Japanese and Korean official positions reaching the same general conclusion from different perspectives: the greater majority of Koreans residing in Japan should maintain a separate status, and be handled differently, from that of their Japanese neighbors. Both sides equally wanted nothing to do with this people – the Japanese government wanted them deported and the Korean government preferred that they remain in Japan. At the same time, the two sides independently agreed that this was an issue was to be resolved not by the American forces, but by the Japanese and Koreans when they were ready to sign a treaty to reconcile their differences.

Clearly, by expressing their preference that these culturally different people occupy separate spaces on both Korean and Japanese soil, the two sides united in their fears of the ideological baggage, as well as the potential trouble, they carried with them. Neither the South Korean nor the Japanese government wished to risk strengthening the leftist elements that disturbed their present conservative political dispositions. The South Korean media emphasized this in terms of the cultural factor – they lacked sufficient "Korean-ness." This point appeared in an April 1949 article titled "Cheil Chosŏn munhwa undong" [The cultural movement of Japan-based Korea]. Although not stating it directly, this Korean-language article suggested that Japan-based Koreans needed to strengthen their understanding of their ethnic heritage before they sought repatriation.[48] Another editorial that appeared in the *P'yŏnghwa ilbo* in early 1950 complemented this opinion by describing the Japan-based Korean problem as one that could not be solved until these people completed education on nation-building spirit.[49]

Finally, the discussion regarding repatriation of the Japan-based Koreans failed to give adequate attention to the situation that prevented Koreans from returning to their homeland in the first place. While acknowledging the limitations the authorities had placed on the amount of money with which they could return as problematic, as well as the ideological problems associated with a large number of Koreans in Japan, the discussion neglected to consider the problem of resettlement in a place that, essentially, was foreign for many. Not only did this complication prevent many from attempting to return, it also forced many of the repatriated to seek a means, and most often an illegal one, to return to Japan.

Adjusting the limitations on the amount of money with which Japan-based Koreans could return only solved the immediate problem – enabling them to repatriate with their financial estates. It did not address the long-term problems such as housing and employment. One letter intercepted by the military government in Korea explained as follows: "The conditions in Korea for repatriates is indeed deplorable, we have no means of livelihood, for we have no business, no homes, no food and our money was gone in a week."[50] For the majority of Koreans who chose to relocate to Japan, their migration had severed their ties with the Korean peninsula and forced them to opt for a difficult existence among a people who wished they would leave. Worst still was the position of their offspring born in Japan, who had little or no knowledge of their ancestral homeland and even fewer ties to its linguistic and cultural heritage. The people who had remained in Korea held little sympathy for those who had fled their country to seek their fortune elsewhere, be it in Manchuria or Japan.

Conclusion: The "ultimate solution" and the status of Japan-based Koreans

SCAP officials concluded in 1949 that determination of the status of the Korean population in Japan was a problem best left to the Japanese and South Korean governments once they sat down to negotiate a treaty to normalize their diplomatic relations. The two countries finally reached this milestone in 1965. At this time the two states also signed an "Agreement on Legal Status and Treatment of South Korean Residents in Japan," a document that in geographic terms included the vast majority of this population, but in ideological terms excluded close to half of them.[51]

The "Agreement" focused on defining the qualifications for permanent residency status for Koreans residing in Japan, based on the timing and continuity of their residency in Japan. In general, what was required of the individual was his or her arrival date preceding the 15 August 1945 surrender of Japan to the Allied forces. In addition, the individual had to demonstrate a sustained residence on the islands – those who had returned to Korea for any length of time were deemed ineligible.[52] Consideration was also given to the offspring of those who qualified for this status.

Much more problematic for the majority of this population was the stipulation that they had to register as Republic of Korea nationals in order to qualify. This virtually disqualified more than half of the 600,000 Korean residents in Japan who claimed membership in the Ch'ongryón [The General Federation of Korean Residents], the pro-North Korean group of Koreans in Japan.[53] The reward offered to those who submitted applications for permanent residence allowed for Japan's "appropriate consideration" in matters concerning "the education, livelihood protection and national health insurance coverage." The Japanese government would appropriate this favorable consideration, as well, to the financial affairs of those wishing to waive their rights to continued residence in Japan by repatriating to the Republic of Korea.[54] Omitted from this "Agreement" was consideration of those who opted not to register for permanent residence status.

The terms of the "Agreement" satisfied few of the Koreans living in Japan at the time of its signing. Even the pro-South Korean Mindan group protested the terms as presented in a draft within a week of its signing. On 17 June, over 10,000 of its members gathered at the Hibiya Public Hall to demand terms of greater equality with the Japanese regarding education and employment conditions. By contrast, the Ch'ongryón's protests, centered on the very negotiations themselves, which, upon success, solidified a two-Korea policy in Japanese diplomacy. Their status in Japan, which has remained precarious since this time, has been most directly affected by the highs and (mostly) lows of Japan–DPRK relations to date, with even the right to application for nationalization closed to them and their children because of their ideological disposition.[55]

The legacy of the United States occupation in terms of the plight of Japan's Korean residents is in its refusal to address the issue, rather than in any legislation that it introduced to include this minority in Japan's experiment in democracy. SCAP based its decision to refrain from actively engaging in this issue on its perception of the historical relationship of the two peoples, one that was tainted perhaps by images that the United States, as well, held of the Korean people from as early as the beginning of the twentieth century. It made it in the knowledge that the Japanese government desired to segregate these people from its democratic institutions following its release from occupation control. This policy no doubt was further influenced by the governments of South Korea and Japan, who believed the people's inclusion as state nationals to be a black mark on the postwar national identities they sought to forge.

The plight of the Japan-based Koreans began to improve from the late

1980s and early 1990s when the Japanese government removed one of the more controversial measures of the Alien Registration Act: finger-printing. Proposals in the Japanese Diet to reintroduce this practice in some form have carefully excluded non-Japanese with "special perman-ent residency" (*tokubetsu eijû ken*) status (which includes the Japan-based Korean and Chinese populations) from this requirement. This period has also seen a rise in the number of Japan-based Koreans naturalizing (*kikokuka*) and assimilating as Japanese, particularly after regulations for name changes were eased. At the same time the population continues to feel a backlash from swings in Seoul and P'yóngyang's relations with Tokyo. News that the DPRK had indeed kidnapped Japanese citizens pro-voked retaliatory hate activities against Korean schools – both the stu-dents (attacks) and the institutions (bomb threats). Thus, despite progress in treatment, the political status of Japan-based Koreans remains complex, much the same as it always has, ever since Koreans began to cross over in great numbers following the 1910 Japanese annexation of the Korean peninsula.

Notes

1 The Potsdam Declaration and the Japanese Constitution quoted from W. Macmahon Ball, *Japan: enemy or ally?*, New York: The John Day Company, 1949, p. 149.
2 Ibid., p. 150.
3 I draw attention here to then Prime Minister Nakasone Yasuhiro's 1986 comment regarding the United States' economic problems stemming from its minority peoples, a problem that the homogeneous Japanese people need not concern itself with, and the more recent "sankokujin" (third-country people) statement made by Tokyo governor Ishihara Shintarô.
4 Michael Weiner divides his study of this history into three phases of migration, 1910–1925, 1925–1938, and wartime migration. This last stage he divides into company-directed recruitment (1939–1941), government-assisted recruitment (1942–1944), and forced draft (1944–1945). While a distinction can be made in principle between "voluntary" and "forced" labor procurement, Weiner adds that "there were numerous instances where recruiting agencies made no attempt to distinguish voluntary recruitment from involuntary conscription," even between 1939 and 1944. See his *Race and migration in imperial Japan*, London: Routledge, 1994, pp. 194–5.
5 Korean mobilization was initiated by two pieces of legislation, both enacted in 1939: the National Labor Mobilization Act and the National Conscription Law. Throughout the six-year history of Korean labor recruitment and conscription, the Japanese were only once (in 1943) able to reach the quotas they had set (see the chart in ibid., p. 193). Heavy demand for such labor on the Korean peninsula, as well as in Manchuria, no doubt limited the pool of workers from which the Japanese could draw.
6 The Korean population in Japan more than doubled during this period. See ibid., p. 197.
7 A 1924 survey found Japanese-Korean wages differing by 5 to 50 percent, depending on the profession. See Higuchi Yûichi, *Nihon no chôsen-kankokujin* [*Japanese north Koreans–south Koreans*], Tokyo: Shinkôsha, 2002, p. 93.

8 Michael Weiner, *The origins of the Korean community in Japan, 1910–1923*, Manchester: Manchester University Press, 1989, p. 53.

9 United States images of the Japanese and Korean people have been well documented. U.S. president Theodore Roosevelt, for example, expressed as early as 1900 his belief in the Japanese right to control Korea, likening Japan's interests in the Sea of Japan (or, to the Koreans, the East Sea) to those of the United States in the Caribbean, Japan's relations with Korea to the United States' relations with Cuba. See Howard K. Beale, *Theodore Roosevelt and the rise of American world power*, Baltimore: Johns Hopkins Press, 1969, pp. 266–7. In 1904, American Minister to Korea, Horace Allen, articulated this point as follows: The Korean people "cannot govern themselves. They must have an overlord as they have had for all time. When it was not China, it was Russia or Japan. Let Japan have Korea outright." (See ibid., p. 319.) I outline the history of this image in my "Japanese and American Images of Koreans: a tale of two occupations," in Yoneyuki Sugita, Richard Jensen, and Jon Davidann, eds, *Trans-Pacific relations: America, Europe and Asia in the twentieth century*, Westport, CT: Praeger, 2003.

10 The one exception was following the 1919 March First Movement, a demonstration for Korean independence during which the Japanese killed hundreds of participants. The United States *Congressional Record* reveals a lengthy discussion on the Japanese slaughter of Korean Christians at this time. U.S. Congress, Senate, "Treaty of Peace with Germany," the 66th Congress, First session, *Congressional Record* 58, 9 October 1919: 6611–26.

11 One of the earlier challenges to U.S. policy at the time of Korean annexation was set before the U.S. Congress by the Georgian senator Thomas E. Watson, who questioned whether it was appropriate for Root to be honored with a valor medal by the National Arts Club after his having been the "principal author of the misfortunes of Korea, which misfortunes led to the persecution by Japan of the churches of Christ in that country." U.S. Congress, Senate, "Valor Medal for Root – National Arts Club will Honor Head of Mission to Russia," 67th Congress, second session, *Congressional Record* 62, 21 March 1920: 4182–6. For a more recent argument see John Edward Wilz, "Did the United States betray Korea in 1905?," *Pacific historical review*, 1985, pp. 245–6 and Yi Minsuk, "Miguk ùi tae Chosòn ch'inil chòngch'aek ùi ch'ulhyòn: ch'òngil chònchaenggi ùl chungsim uro"["The appearance of the pro-Japanese policy of the United States towards Korea during the Sino-Japanese War"], *Sachòng*, 40–1, June 1992, pp. 79–110.

12 Up to this time there were even some who recommended allowing Japan to maintain its presence in Korea even after the war, one example being Hugh Byas, *Government by assassination*, New York: Alfred A. Knopf, 1942, pp. 359–60.

13 Hodge's most infamous blunder was his labeling the Koreans as "the same breed of cats as the Japanese," an idea that he reportedly obtained from a Japanese general. See Mark Gayn, *Japan diary*, Rutland, VT: Charles E. Tuttle, Co, 1981, p. 359.

14 USAFIK G-2 Periodic Reports, 14 December 1945. One major reason for the American reliance on the Japanese was the simple fact that the United States had invested far more efforts in preparing for the occupation of Japan than for that of the Korean peninsula. Many of the members of the forces that arrived in Korea had been trained in Japanese, as we see in Warren Tsuneishi's account in a letter he sent to Don Keene on 12 September 1945. See Otis Cary, ed., *From a ruined empire: letters – Japan, China, Korea 1945–46*, Tokyo: Kodansha International, 1984, pp. 26–34.

15 One of the gravest misunderstandings of policy makers was the assumption that Japan-based Koreans had been considered "Japanese nationals" up to the

end of the war. For this reason many entertained the possibility that these people would eventually be able to choose acceptance of Japanese "citizenship" or maintenance of Japanese "nationality" as future options.

16　Office of Strategic Services, "Aliens in Japan," 29 June 1945. Included in "Occupation of Japan" United States Planning Documents, 1942–1945, Volume III of set located in the Japanese National Library, Kensei shiryô shitsu.

17　Ibid., pp. 5–13 and 15–16. The report did acknowledge the subtle, more recent, tendencies for Koreans to seek permanent settlement by noting a small rise in their intermarriage with Japanese, as well as in the number of Koreans having been born in Japan, ibid., p. 16.

18　Ibid., p. 14.

19　Ibid., p. 35.

20　Ibid., pp. 36–8.

21　"Basic Initial Post-Surrender Directive to Supreme Commander for the Allied Powers for the Occupation and Control of Japan," Division of Special Records, Foreign Office, Japanese Government. On-line version was available. HTTP: <http://www.ndl.go.jp/constitution/shiryo/01/036/036tx.html> (accessed on 11 July 2006).

22　Atsumi Aiko reports that there were 23 Koreans and 21 Taiwanese among the 984 individuals who were executed for war crimes. And of the 3,419 people sentenced to life or limited imprisonment, 125 were Korean and 147 were Taiwanese. See Atsumi Aiko, "Korean 'Imperial Soldiers': Remembering Colonialism and Crimes against Allied POWs," in T. Fujitani, Geofrey White, and Lisa Yoneyama, *Perilous memories: the Asia-Pacific war(s)*, Durham, NC: Duke University Press, 2001, p. 211.

23　Foreign Office Japanese Government, "Japanese Nationals in Detached Territories and the Peoples of those Territories Residing in Japan," in *Records of the United States Department of State relating to the internal affairs of Japan, 1945–49*, Reel 6, February 1948, pp. 9–10, Japan National Diet, Kensei Shitsu.

24　Richard B. Finn, *Winners in peace: MacArthur, Yoshida, and postwar Japan*, Berkeley: University of California Press, 1992, p. 238.

25　See, for example, documents concerning the 1948 Kobe–Osaka Riots following the School Education Law that closed many Korean schools, as contained in *Records of the United States Department of State relating to the internal affairs of Japan*. General William F. Dean, Military Governor of Korea, interpreted these riots as a communist effort to disrupt the electoral process in southern Korea. He wrote that the "Communist-inspired Koreans in Japan can only lose by such suicidal defiance of law as illustrated in the industrial areas of Kobe and Osaka . . . Election day is just four days from now . . . The activities of some Koreans in Japan are nothing but attempts to influence their native land's first democratic elections." See "General Dean's Answer to Written Press Questions of 6 May 1948," in *Records of the United States Department of State*, Reel 3.

26　See Changsoo Lee, "The Period of Repatriation, 1945–49," in Changsoo Lee and George De Vos, *Koreans in Japan: ethnic conflict and accommodation*, Berkeley: University of California Press, 1981, p. 62.

27　1949 was a busy year for administrative efforts to curb the communist threat. On 27 June, 2000 prisoners of war were repatriated from the Soviet Union, many of whom returned "waving red flags and singing communist songs." Also, July 1949 saw the largest number of railroad sabotage incidents during this period. Richard B. Finn writes of the "added hopes and fears that the communist revolution might not be far off." Richard B. Finn, *Winners in peace*, p. 229.

28　Bruce Cumings, *The origins of the Korean war: liberation and the emergence of separ-*

ate regimes, 1945–1947, Princeton: Princeton University Press, 1981, pp. 197, 351. Cumings concludes that other factors, including unemployment and poor rice distribution, caused the disturbances rather than communist revolutionary ambitions. See ibid., 378–9.

29 A 1948 "Staff Study" on Koreans in Japan noted, "Koreans moving between Korea and Japan serve as the link between Japanese communists and those of the continent of Asia – Korean, Chinese, and Russian." See "Staff Study Concerning Koreans in Japan," 16 August 1948, in *Records of the United States Department of State*, Reel 3.

30 "Subject of Nationality and Treatment of Formosans," in *Records of the United States Department of State*, Reel 1. Richard L.-G. Deverall, Chief of Labor Education in SCAP, writes that the Japanese government estimated that 3.5 million people engaged in black market activity. It repeatedly informed the occupation that all Koreans in Japan were a "bunch of black-marketeers." They failed to add, he continues, that "behind the black marketeering Koreans were sly Japanese politicians, purgees, and racketeers who found the Korean post-war status of 'Friendly ally' useful ... in alluding Japanese police detection or arrest." See his *Red star over Japan*, Calcutta: Temple Press, 1952, p. 256.

31 G-2 Reports from Korea recorded daily attempts by Koreans to smuggle their way back into Japan at a cost of between 1000 to 3000 yen. Between 24 September and 1 October 1947, for example, it reported intercepting six boats carrying 139 Koreans. These boats also carried supplies. On 5 November 1947, for example, the twenty-ton *Keishin Maru* which the Japanese police intercepted en route to Futagami, carried a cargo of twenty-one bushels of clothing, five cans of wheat gluten, ten gallons of alcohol, toilet articles and a crew of nine Koreans. On 14 November 1947 the reports included information on smuggling from northern Korea that attempted to bring into Japan "1030 bags of sulfur and a large quantity of communist propaganda literature." The boat on its return trip carried materials required by people residing on the Korean peninsula, as well.

32 This was reported in a memo titled "Critical Refugee Situation" and sent to the Governor General, Headquarters, USAFIX in Seoul by the Commanding General of the 40th Division on 26 December 1945. See *Gillette Papers*, vol. 1, Seoul: Hanlin University, Asian Culture Research Center, 1996, pp. 370–2.

33 Changsoo Lee, "The Period of Repatriation," p. 59.

34 The "Staff Study" cited above estimated that offering the Korean population these special privileges would require 80,287 additional tons of food annually, at a cost of over 12 million dollars.

35 This initial study appears to have been directed by Richard B. Finn. It is unfortunate that the occupation official did not devote more attention to this matter in his book *Winners in peace*, which devoted less than two pages to the issue. This account is consistent with other first-hand accounts of the occupation that also offer little consideration to Koreans or minorities. See also William J. Sebald with Russell Brines, *With MacArthur in Japan: a personal history of the occupation*, New York: W.W. Norton & Company Inc., 1965 and Beate Sirota Gordon, *The only woman in the room*, Tokyo: Kodansha International, 1997. Richard L.-G. Deverall's *Red Star over Japan* is more generous than the other accounts in this regard.

36 "Staff Study Concerning Koreans in Japan," pp. 2–3.

37 Ibid., pp. 3–4.

38 Ibid., pp. 4–5.

39 Ibid., pp. 8–9.

40 It must be noted that as the majority of Japan-based Koreans originally came from towns in the southern half of the peninsula their reluctance to return was not necessarily based on their physical ties to the North. See Sonia Ryang, *North*

Koreans in Japan: language, ideology, and identity, Boulder: Westview Press, 1997, p. 3.

41 Solutions are listed in "Staff Study Concerning Koreans in Japan," pp. 7–9. The newly installed Rhee administration in South Korea was particularly harsh toward Koreans returning from Japan.

42 William J. Sebald, "Status of Koreans in Japan," interoffice memo dated 18 February 1949 from the United States Political Advisor for Japan. Located in *Records of the United States Department of State relating to the internal affairs of Japan,* Reel 15.

43 Ibid., p. 4

44 William J. Sebald to Secretary of State, 15 August 1949, contained in ibid. He also entertained briefly the idea of enlisting the Japanese government's cooperation in accepting its Korean residents as Japanese citizens. This possibility, he argued, was not feasible for a number of reasons. First, the Japanese government was unlikely to endorse such a proposal. Primarily, it would argue that the loyalty of those Koreans permitted Japanese citizenship would be divided between their ethnic and adopted homelands, with more affinity bestowed upon the former. Sebald also expressed concern that this change would strengthen the leftist elements in Japan by swelling their numbers with enfranchised Koreans of radical persuasion.

45 The anti-Japanese sentiments of President Syngman Rhee are often cited as the reason behind this delay. The Korean official did express his desire to negotiate settlement with the Japanese on a number of occasions, and his belief that the communist threat was greater than past disagreements with his country's former colonial overlords. The *Nippon Times* reported on 17 February 1950 the following from a speech Rhee made during his visit to Tokyo at this time: ". . . one of the questions in my mind is whether there is any possibility of improving the relations between Korea and Japan. I shall be glad to discuss this with Gen. MacArthur as well as some high officials of the Japanese government . . . Instead of quarreling over the unhappy past if the Japanese realize their danger as we do [I am] willing to co-exchange views with some of the Japanese government officials who have views similar to mine." The newspaper headlined this story as "Rhee calls on Japanese to join anti-red battle."

46 Richard B. Finn, "Memorandum of Conversation: Koreans in Japan," 3 February 1949, in *Records of the United States Department of State relating to the internal affairs of Japan,* Reel 15.

47 Letter and enclosure from the Korean diplomatic mission in Japan to the Supreme Commander for the Allied Powers, Tokyo dated 7 April 1949, contained in *Records of the United States Department of State relating to the internal affairs of Japan,* Reel 15.

48 "Cheil Chosón munhwa undong" ["The Cultural movement of Japan-based Korea"], *Cheil Chosón munhwa nyón kan,* April 1949, pp. 50–61.

49 "Chaeil kyop'o munje" ["The Japan-based Korean resident problem"], *Pyónghwa ilbo,* 4 January 1950. This editorial in particular noted the leftist ideology of this group as problematic.

50 HQ, USAFIK G-2 Periodic Reports, 7 September 1946.

51 Terms of this "Agreement" are taken from the "unofficial translation of the gist of the agreement" carried in "Accord on status of S. Koreans here," *Japan Times,* 23 June 1965.

52 Changsoon Lee documents two cases of Koreans ineligible for permanent residence status because of their inability to prove their continued residency due to their complicated circumstances. Mr. P., for example, had changed his name on several occasions following his escape from a coalmine in Niigata and thus was not able to provide a residence record bearing his real name. See

Changsoon Lee, "The legal Status of Koreans," in Changsoon Lee and George De Vos, *Koreans in Japan*, p. 148.

53 Determining the exact number of Koreans that this provision affected is problematic because a sizable number of this group was registered with both the pro-South Mindan and the pro-North Ch'ongryón. Sonia Ryang, herself a "stateless person" for decades, who finally was granted a United States green card once she established herself as a scholar at Johns Hopkins University, estimates that around 220,000 Koreans were affected by this ruling. See Sonia Ryang's introduction to her edited volume, *Koreans in Japan: voices from the margin*, London: Routledge, 2000, p. 5. The 18 June 1965 issue of the *Japan Times* stated that over half of the 600,000 Japan-based Koreans belonged to the Ch'ongryón.

54 The Japanese government had permitted repatriation to North Korea for a short period from January 1959. This action, which returned over 88,000 Koreans (and some Japanese spouses) to North Korea, lasted through 1967. Initially, Japan's granting this permission infuriated the South Korean government and stalled normalization negotiations. For discussion on this history see Sonia Ryang, "The North Korean homeland of Koreans in Japan," pp. 35–9.

55 Much of the discrimination against the Korean population has been directed at this group, in particular at the schools in which their children study.

8 Occupation policy and postwar Sino-Japanese relations

Severing economic ties

Sayuri Guthrie-Shimizu

Introduction

Nominally a multi-national enterprise implemented through collective decision-making mechanisms (the Far Eastern Commission and the Allied Council in Tokyo), the Allied occupation of Japan was for all practical purposes a project in nation rebuilding executed single-handedly by the United States. Because of the overriding U.S. dominance in the post-surrender occupation, Japan was spared the misfortune of prolonged national partitioning and extended occupation that befell jointly-occupied areas such as Korea and Germany. On the other hand, the reframing of the Japanese state and social reforms undertaken during the postwar occupation were almost completely shaped by America's national priorities.

The rift between the United States and the Soviet Union that came into bold relief by 1947 in the Eastern Mediterranean and central Europe ushered in a protracted global confrontation that would soon bear the brand of the Cold War. The effects of this superpower stand-off soon began to reverberate into America's occupation policy towards Japan. As the hostility spun out of the Cold War proliferated in scope and magnified in intensity elsewhere in the world, the central tenet of American policy enforced in occupied Japan began to shift from reform revolving around demilitarization and democratization to industrial recovery and the stabilization of the domestic political order.

In October 1949, the civil war in China ended with the Nationalist government's flight to the island of Taiwan and the proclamation of the People's Republic of China with Beijing as its capital. This conclusion to a violent and turbulent chapter in China's modern history marked the defeat of Washington's scenario for postwar East Asia, predicated upon the consolidation of a pro-Western unified government in the Chinese mainland serving as the keystone of a stable regional order. As the United States recalibrated its regional strategy for Asia, Japan was inescapably required to formulate its China policy within the bounds of the reconstituted U.S. strategic imperatives during and even after the end of the occupation. The outbreak of the Korean War in June 1950 determined that the range of actions Japan might be allowed to take during the war's duration would be narrowed further.[1]

Despite this powerful external constraint, however, many Japanese sought to define their nation's place in postwar East Asia in ways autonomous of strategic imperatives imposed by the American occupation overlord. These Japanese took as a given the integration of the world economy, a process that had become patently inexorable in the interwar period, and would now be fueled by the United States' paramount economic power and military might. At the same time, these pan-Asianist visionaries presupposed that Japan would continue to play a key role in an emerging regional order and sought to minimize the area's economic reliance on the United States to secure its leadership. In other words, they envisioned East Asia's post-World War II economic integration in ways that would obviate over-dependency on the United States, the world's uncontested economic powerhouse that had emerged unscathed from the recent war.

Since the type of forced regionalism instigated by Japanese militarists in the 1930s and wartime was no longer tenable in the postwar world, a number of Japanese came to view economic regionalism as their nation's "orthodox" diplomatic objective, albeit refashioned for the new era. It appeared to them at the close of the 1940s that the time was ripe for its fulfillment. As historian Inoue Toshikazu has aptly noted, Japan's vision for Asia following the liquidation of its colonial empire not only reflected a sea change in the nation's ideological orientation occasioned by this cataclysmic moment in national history. The structural evolution of international relations since the early decades of the 20th century also framed the context within which the postwar Japanese hopes and aspirations regarding Asia were shaped and articulated.[2]

Those Japanese who tackled the problem of repairing the nation's tattered relations with China similarly had to factor in these legacies of the preceding half-century in their postwar planning. Now stripped of overseas possessions in the Korean peninsula and Taiwan, could the Japanese economy be viable without trading with the Chinese continent, another important pre-war destination for its manufactured goods and a key source of industrial raw materials and foodstuffs? Was it not imperative to maintain commercial relations with the Chinese mainland, particularly its northwest provinces, for the sake of Japan's postwar reconstruction and long-term economic rehabilitation, regardless of the outcome of the Chinese civil war and directions America's Far Eastern policy might take in the gathering clouds of the Cold War? It would probably be impossible to recoup the Japanese investments in China, but could these lost assets be converted into a foothold through which Japan might interject itself into China's anticipated postwar economic development? These questions, with their postwar implications, came to the fore just as policy makers, traders, and other private sector individuals recalibrated their plans regarding China. In addressing these questions, the Japanese customarily legitimated their positions on the basis of "affinity" with China deriving from the two nations' historical and cultural ties and geographical proximity. This chapter will examine the economic aspects of Japan's grasp for the Chinese mainland in the early postwar period to illuminate one way that the defeated nation sought but failed to free itself from the binding dictates of America's Far Eastern policy under the occupation and subtly coercive directives from Washington after restoring independence. This sideshow in the reconfiguration of East Asia will help highlight the power-laden realities of the postwar U.S.–Japan partnership in which Japan's commercial ties with the colossal yet untapped intra-regional market came to be all but severed. It will also weave a tale of how Japanese visions for regional solidarity, lined by stable economic networks, were forced to lie dormant for nearly two decades under the combined weight of America's Cold War fiats and multilateral trade sanctions that the United States enforced against the Asian communist state.[3]

Japanese nationals and the Chinese civil war

In considering early postwar Japanese efforts to re-establish commercial networks with the Chinese continent, one is inevitably struck by the powerful grip of a national myth steeped in ambivalence and nostalgia towards the Asian "neighbor." Amid the military and political uncertainties over the war that resumed between the Nationalist and Communist forces on the Chinese continent, Japan's emotional investments in the lost colonial frontier and belief in the inevitability of Sino-Japanese unity created a variety of political plots and military maneuvers as by-products. One of the earliest examples of such ill-conceived activities by Japanese nationals overtaken by the myth of China–Japan brotherhood was an unauthorized military campaign carried out by now-defunct Japanese imperial army officers and troops in China's Shanxi province. Waged jointly with troops under the command of provincial chief Yan Xishan, this military action against the advancing People's Liberation Army could be best characterized as a runaway act of ragtag Japanese officers and soldiers trying desperately to leave a mark on the unfolding civil war in China. It did not receive sanction from the Nationalist government's central leadership, the U.S. military personnel stationed in China, nor the Japanese government. The unauthorized campaign came to an ignominious end with the battle of Taiyuan in the spring of 1949.[4]

The saga of the so-called "White Group" was another example of the doomed Japanese efforts at perpetuating Sino-Japanese brotherhood. After Jiang Jieshi's retreat to Taiwan, the so-called "White Group" organized around former commander of the China Expeditionary Forces Okamura Yasuji secretly sailed from Japan via Hong Kong to the island bastion of the beleaguered Nationalist government. These Japanese "volunteers" participated in the military training of the Chinese Nationalist Army as adjunct instructors at the Yuan Shan Training Institute located north of Taibei. The presence of the "Japanese military advisory group" in Taiwan was not sanctioned by the Allied occupation authorities in Tokyo or the Japanese government. But the group's activities in the country under martial law continued through much of the early Cold War period. Despite SCAP's efforts to stamp out unlawful maritime travels by members of the White Group between Kyushu and Taiwan, and the White Group's frequent clashes with the American military personnel in Taibei, the clandestine stream of retired Japanese army officers to Taiwan could not be cut off for a long time. It was not until 1969 that the last band of the White Group reported its mission completed and returned to Japan.[5]

While these military operations and political maneuvers were being carried out in defiance of SCAP's directives and the Japanese government's cease and desist orders, Japanese civilians inspired by a similarly persistent sense of affinity with China engaged in more benign activities that received at least tacit government approval. After their nation's defeat by the Allies, a great number of Japanese technicians and engineers disregarded the government's official repatriation program and continued to practice their professional skills in China. With varying degrees of voluntariness, they performed services that helped keep the Chinese economy running amid the chaos of the civil war.[6] According to a study by Daqing Yang, these Japanese technical experts and engineers remained mostly in Manchuria and areas around Shanghai. They supervised technical training at Nationalist-controlled manufacturing plants, shared managerial know-how at business offices, and trained experts at educational and medical facilities confiscated by the local Chinese authorities at the time of Japans surrender. The Foreign Ministry's leadership viewed favorably these civilian activities, although performed in defiance of their official repatriation directives. Prime Minister Shigemitsu Mamoru, for instance, believed that such civilian contributions might lay the foundation for future Sino-Japanese economic cooperation. The Chinese Nationalist authorities also welcomed the lingering presence of these Japanese civilians in areas under their control. Mired in the protracted war with the Communist forces, Jiang Jieshi and his aides had to ensure that the operation of manufacturing plants, mines, and railroads continued in Tianjin, Beijing, several key cities in Manchuria and the lower Yangzi River. Due to the shortage of trained local personnel, the Nationalists found it imperative to retain the service of Japanese nationals to handle day-to-day operations. In the long term, such technical training was expected to segue to economic development of a unified China under Nationalist leadership.[7]

In the early phase of the civil war, some elements within the Nationalist government resisted Jiang's attempt to retain Japanese services at industrial plants and technical facilities. The most vocal opposition to the this informal postwar Sino-Japanese economic partnership, however, came from the U.S. military personnel stationed in China. Concerned that the Japanese civilian activities were in fact a government-coordinated ruse to retain a foothold in China, General Albert Wedmeyer, commander of the U.S. military advisory mission, requested in October 1945 that the repatriation of Japanese nationals from mainland China be completed by the summer of 1946. He also questioned the Nationalist government's desire to permit Japanese engineers to remain in areas under its control. In early 1946, however, the Nationalist government concluded that the 1000 Japanese engineers who had been permitted to stay in Taiwan after Japanese surrender were not enough to maintain necessary production levels and that 5000 more trained experts were needed. As a result, 7000 Japanese engineers and their dependents, numbering approximately 28,000, were permitted to remain in Taiwan on the basis of Jiang's agreement with the United States.

The Nationalist leadership applied the same retention policy to Japanese engineers and experts in areas in the Chinese continent under its control. When the initial postwar repatriation program expired in June 1946, the Nationalist authorities informed Washington that they would continue to permit Japanese engineers to work in continental China, excluding Manchuria. The U.S. government agreed to this, and over 10,000 Japanese engineers and experts remained in mainland China beyond the summer of 1946. A majority of the retained Japanese, however, ended up handing over their professional responsibilities to local Chinese counterparts within 18 months and returned to Japan. One reason for this relatively swift changeover was that the Nationalist government, fearful that the Communists might get hold of the Japanese nationals' expertise, began to encourage and expedite their repatriation as its standing in the on-going civil war quickly deteriorated. By early 1948, when the People's Liberation Army advanced further into central and southern China, the number of Japanese engineers remaining in the Nationalist-controlled area had dwindled to an estimated 1300. From this point on, the trans-oceanic network of human resources and the infrastructure of informal Sino-Japanese technological partnership tapered off.[8]

American policy regarding the resumption of Sino-Japanese trade

In contrast to the ideological anti-communism that was beginning to ossify U.S. domestic politics and diplomacy towards Europe, the Truman administration's China policy remained relatively flexible for a brief time after the civil war there ended in Communist victory. In a similar vein, the administration maintained surprisingly pragmatic attitudes towards Japan's relationship with the Communist state entrenching itself in the near-by continent, at least in the realm of commercial transactions. From Tokyo, SCAP instituted a policy that allowed Japanese barter trade with exporters and importers operating out of mainland China, so long as the transactions were limited to non-strategic materials and civilian goods. This flexibility was necessitated by the fact that SCAP understood Japan's need for supplies of foodstuffs and essential industrial raw materials available from China in the absence of alternative sources. In compliance with East–West trade warfare policy then being formulated in Washington, however, SCAP carefully checked the content of commercial transactions made between Japanese nationals and Chinese traders and conducted via Tientsin, Tianjin, and Hong Kong to prevent strategic items from being passed into Communist hands.[9]

Japan's foreign commerce, placed under the SCAP's command at the inception of the Allied occupation, returned to civilian hands in December 1949 for exports and January 1950 for imports. Even before the resumption of normal trade, Japanese traders who had conducted business with the Chinese before the outbreak of war attempted to contact the Chinese revolutionary authorities who gained ascendancy in the civil war. These efforts received a boost when these trading houses, mostly small, family-operated, and concentrated in Western Japan, succeeded in early 1949 in opening a channel of communication with a local trade representative office that the Communist central leadership had recently opened in Tientsin. The structure of the Chinese revolutionary regime's foreign trade regulation was gradually taking shape at the time. As they expanded areas under their control, the communist authorities instituted new foreign trade regulations. North China first came under their commercial jurisdiction, followed by Eastern China, and finally Southern China. In the sequence of administrative expansion, the Communist regime opened local branches of its foreign trade agency in Tientsin (Huabei district), Shanghai (Huazhong district), and Guangzhou (Huanan district). After ensconcing itself in the capital city of Beijing, the Communist government proclaimed foreign exchange and trade control ordinances to integrate locally-administered commercial activities into its centralized governing structure. Due to a dearth of foreign exchange currency, the regime was forced to conduct foreign trade by barter for the time being. In early 1950, a Tokyo trading firm finalized a contract with the Tientsin overseas trade office to import 90,000 tons of salt. It was the People's Republic of China's first export to Japan under Allied occupation.[10]

While these private-sector overtures began to produce trickles of trade with the Chinese mainland, the result remained just that: trickles. By the time the Chinese civil war ended, mainland China's share in Japan's total foreign trade had shrunk to a small fraction of the pre-war ratio of 35 percent. In 1950, Japan's trade with mainland China, including diversion trade via Hong Kong using the British merchant marine, amounted to approximately $95 million, a meager 6 percent of Japan's total foreign trade that year. The bulk of Japan's estimated $45 million exports to the Chinese mainland were textile and steel products. Japan's imports from the Chinese continent, about $50 million in estimated value, were coking coal, iron ore, salt, soybeans, and miscellaneous foodstuffs. Japanese expectations for resuming trade with New China were expansive, but the reality surrounding the trade was grim at best. Both Japan and China lacked means of international financial settlements, as well as adequate maritime transport capabilities.[11]

International circumstances conspired to keep the trade unspectacular. As has been noted earlier, the United States government retained a pragmatic approach to Sino-Japanese trade even after the Communist takeover of the Chinese mainland. In March 1950, the State Department decided to permit barter trade in non-strategic materials between occupied Japan and mainland China, and the Japanese government officials and private-sector traders lost no time in submitting to the SCAP lists of items they wished to ship to the People's Republic of China (PRC). The outbreak of the military conflict on the Korean peninsula that summer, however, repainted the entire picture. Once the Beijing regime sent in volunteer troops and came into direct clash with United Nations forces, what remained of the U.S. flexibility disappeared. At that point, the PRC was catapulted to the top of the Truman administration's list of mortal enemies and it became one of the key targets of the multilateral embargo system then being institutionalized under U.S. leadership.[12]

In response to the PRC's military intervention, the Truman administration launched unilateral economic sanctions against the added battlefield foe on the basis of U.S. domestic legislation. It also requested that America's Western allies and nations under its occupation, such as Japan, tow the line. As a first step towards coordinated multilateral sanctions, the Truman administration engineered the adoption of a resolution by the United Nations General Assembly in January 1951 that condemned the PRC as a military aggressor. In May, it also succeeded in passing a UN resolution that banned the export of strategic materials, arms, and munitions to the PRC and North Korea. For about a year thereafter, the Truman administration sought to consolidate the multilateral structure aimed at putting economic squeezes on the PRC. The series of diplomatic efforts along these lines culminated in the creation of the China Committee, a multilateral embargo organization that targeted the Soviet Union and Eastern Europe. In the summer of 1952, the China Committee was launched as a sub-organ of the Consultative Group (CG) headquartered in Paris. This new organization enforced trade embargo programs directed at China and North Korea that were much more sweeping and rigorous than those imposed on Western trade with the Soviet Union and Eastern Europe.[13]

In addition to these efforts in the multilateral arena, the U.S. government proceeded to restrict commercial transactions in non-strategic materials, permitted prior to the Korean War's outbreak, between Japan and the continental China. The SCAP possessed two administrative authorities to achieve this objective. One was direct regulation of occupied Japan's external trade through the government issuance of export licenses to private-sector traders and manufacturers. The other, more indirect in enforcement, was to have the Japanese government limit foreign exchange allocations to be used for the purpose of trading with China. Between the fall of 1950 and the early months of 1951, the SCAP progressively tightened the control of commercial transactions between Japan, ports in China's northeast, North Korea, Hong Kong, and Macao in these domestic administrative avenues. The list of embargoed goods that the Japanese government administered thus came to be even more extensive and rigorous than those compiled in pursuance of the UN embargo resolution and agreement among members of the Consultative Group. By the time the San Francisco Peace Conference was convened in September 1951, the Japanese government was required by SCAP to embargo all exportable goods to the PRC except textiles and other innocuous consumer goods, and a handful of agricultural and marine products. In more specific terms, the anti-PRC embargo program the Japanese government administered at the tail end of the Allied occupation covered approximately 400 items over and above the Consultative Group's common list, the severity and scope of which ranked just below that of the U.S., Canada, South Korea, and Taiwan.[14]

Japanese government policy and private sector activities regarding trade with the PRC

In implementing the new imperative of curbing commercial transactions between Japan and the Chinese continent, the SCAP encountered a number of difficulties, tangible and otherwise. Among the most formidable obstacles for the United States to conquer was the sense of affinity widely shared by the Japanese populace towards the Chinese continent and a pan-Asian identity sustained by a persistent collective nostalgia. As the Chinese Civil War moved towards a decisive Communist victory in late 1948, the exodus of Japanese nationals repatriating from central and southern China accelerated. Even then, the Japanese government and public expressed surprisingly little ideological aversion to the revolutionary government now angling to dominate the Chinese mainland. Prime Minister Yoshida Shigeru represented such non-doctrinaire, or opportunistic, Japanese attitudes towards the prospects of a communist-controlled China. As a trade partner, Yoshida famously declared, he did not care if China was "red or green." He professed to a faith in the inevitability of Japan–PRC economic coupling, arguing that the island nation and the Chinese mainland were "naturally complementary markets." He did not shy away from projecting that Sino-Japanese trade would lead to Communist-controlled China's economic dependency on Japan and induce estrangement between the Asian communist state and the Soviet Union, in overall benefit to the Western capitalist world.[15]

As epitomized by the avowedly anti-communist prime minister's views, the Japanese pining for the Chinese continental market transcended ideological differences. This universal desire pervaded the government bureaucracy charged with foreign trade as well. When the Chinese Communist Party leadership promulgated its foreign trade ordinances, the Economic Stabilization Board (ESB) eagerly obtained their texts to assess the prospects of continental trade after an anticipated Communist takeover of the Chinese mainland. A thoroughgoing study of the announced legal requirements led the ESB to make optimistic forecasts that the Chinese would continue to provide markets for Japan's light manufacturing goods such as textiles and textile machines, and would remain key sources of foodstuffs, fuels, and industrial raw materials regardless of the central authority's ideological coloration. The ESB's analysts delightedly emphasized that the Chinese trade did not require dollar settlements, a heavy burden on cash-depleted Japan, or long-distance maritime shipping.[16]

The enthusiasm for trading with China under the Chinese Communist Party's administrative regime was not only openly expressed by Liberal Party members and other conservatives aligned with Yoshida, but shared also by opposition members of the typically fractious national legislature. In May 1949, Diet members interested in commerce with the Chinese continent formed the Dietmen's League for the Promotion of Sino-Japanese trade. This bipartisan parliamentary caucus encompassed conservatives, middle-of-the-roaders and progressive legislatures agreeing to join hands to restore and expand Sino-Japanese trade while setting aside the thorny and sure-to-be-divisive issue of diplomatic relations. With its original membership roster listing side by side the names of Liberals and members of the Socialist and Communist parties, this ideologically motley group was held together solely by the aspiration of re-establishing stable trade relations with mainland China. The League's first high-profile action came with the sponsoring and adoption of an upper-house resolution in early 1950, urging the Yoshida cabinet to take "all measures possible by setting aside political and ideological differences" towards the resumption of direct trade with mainland China. The resolution was designed partially to send a welcoming signal to the PRC proclaimed in Beijing a few months before.[17]

Japanese traders with pre-war connections to the Chinese continent learned, to their great delight, that the newly established foreign trade office in Tientsin was seeking to clarify barter trade procedures with prospective business partners. This reciprocal show of interest spurred several private sector groups to form non-governmental functional equivalents to the Dietmen's League in the spring of 1949. One of the most politically influential of these groups was the Sino-Japanese Trade Promotion Association (SJTPA). Ideologically, this was a left-leaning organization whose members included progressive intellectuals, members of labor unions, Chinese nationals residing in Japan, and members of the Socialist and Communist Parties. Yet the group also included politically conservative small and medium-sized traders who had been engaged in Chinese trade before the war. In keeping with its leftist political orientation, the prospectus put together by the group's founding members stated that Sino-Japanese trade was not only key to achieving Japan's economic self-support but should also help Japan reform its industrial structure. Trade with New China would help foster "peaceful" industry in Japan and build a democratic national economy. Japan would also contribute to its postwar economic development by providing China with capital goods and Western science and technology.

The establishment of the left-leaning organization generated similar initiatives from the conservative end of the political spectrum. The Sino-Japanese Trade Association was one such spin-off. Launched by leading businessmen and industrial leaders, the organization made clear from its inception its intention to keep progressive elements and leftist ideologues at arm's length. Yet, as seen from its charter, this group in fact shared several common thematic elements with those declared in the founding prospectus of its leftist rival organization. Befitting its conservative political bent, the SJTA's founding document made no mention of Japan's transfer to a peaceful and democratic national economy, but it articulated a belief that Japan's postwar economic rehabilitation and New China's aspirations could stand together. Now unified by a centralized government, China's economy would evolve from a collage of pre-modern fragmented agricultural communities into a consolidated national market. As the sole industrialized power in Asia, the SJTA contended, Japan was uniquely positioned to provide capital and consumer goods that would be needed by its communist neighbor in the course of economic development. Compatibility between the economic agendas of the two independent Asian nations thus became Japan's new orthodoxy by the end of the Allied occupation.

American policy and Sino-Japanese trade

As the year 1951 dawned, diplomatic maneuvers revolving around a Japanese peace treaty picked up speed. Once an end to the Allied occupation of Japan loomed as a realistic prospect, the State Department and SCAP faced the new task of containing Japan's dealing with the PRC within the bounds of America's Far Eastern strategy. In political and diplomatic realms, that meant ensuring that the PRC would not be permitted to participate in World War II peace-making for Asia and that the Japanese government would accept that international arrangement. In the economic arena, it entailed obtaining Japanese consent to continue the existing controls on trade with the PRC, even though they went above and beyond what was expected of most other Western allies. As for the first objective, John Foster Dulles, the State Department's counsel in charge of the Japanese peace treaty, crafted an agreement with Great Britain that prevented both Beijing and Taibei from occupying a seat at the peace table. Dulles supplemented this baseline strategy with the so-called Yoshida Letter, a bilateral pledge exacted from the Japanese prime minister to negotiate a separate peace treaty with the Chinese Nationalists.[18] Historians have long puzzled over the true intent Yoshida invested in this letter.[19] Regardless of what Yoshida sought to achieve with his subtly prevaricating promise, the Japanese government establishing governmental relations with the Republic of China in April 1952 prevented it, as fully intended by Dulles, from adopting a "two Chinas policy" in the short run.

To achieve the other goal – securing Japan's pledge to maintain the draconian embargo standards of its commercial transactions with the PRC – the Truman administration opted to use a combination of less coercive methods. Based on the bipartisan clamors heard from the chambers of the Diet and public opinion, the United States was keenly aware of the possibility, or surety, that the Japanese government, once released from SCAP's administrative dictates, would seek greater leeway in trading with the PRC. Yet the State Department was initially reluctant to pressure the Japanese to retain the existing administrative regimen regarding PRC trade controls. At a time when Japan's public opinion was polarized over the question of "total" versus "partial" peace, Yoshida and his cabinet were already vulnerable to charges of being obsequious to U.S. demands. The department's Japan experts believed that Washington's overbearing behavior in economic matters would compound the problem and preferred to secure Japanese compliance indirectly. Hoisting the banner of the United Nations mandate was a good start, for gaining UN membership was one of Japan's top post-independence national priorities. SCAP thus engineered Yoshida's public statement that pledged his government to honor the UN embargo resolution against the PRC after Japan had regained its sovereignty.[20]

The Truman administration knew full well, though, that tethering Yoshida to the UN embargo resolution was hardly enough to stamp out Japan's PRC trade fever. In 1951, market forces appeared to be working decidedly against the United States in this regard. Goods reaching Japanese ports from the Chinese mainland were much cheaper than American equivalents that had to be hauled across the Pacific. The Commerce Department estimated, for example, the cost of coking coal shipments to Japan from China to be about $15,000 per ton, about half that required for U.S. shipments. Chinese sources also held a distinct advantage in terms of maritime shipping. In 1951, Japan's ocean transport capabilities were about half of what they had been in the 1930s. U.S. policy makers realized that the draw of purchasing Chinese goods out of the port of Tienjin remained so long as the British merchant marine levied higher freight rates on Japanese traders.[21]

Further complicating the matter for the U.S. government was the mode of PRC–Japan trade settlement: barter. Suffering from a serious dearth of dollars, Japan found the PRC, another cash-strapped economy, to be one of precious few trading partners from whom it could purchase needed foodstuffs and industrial raw materials without tapping into its meager dollar holdings. Prior to the San Francisco Peace Conference, legal experts within the U.S. government concluded that the Federal Assets Control Act (FACA), the legal instrument the Truman administration deployed to make the U.S. dollar unavailable to Beijing as a tender in foreign trade settlements, was impotent in stopping the PRC's trade with Japan. To counter Washington's use of this financial tool in economic warfare against the PRC, the Chinese Communist Party (CCP) leadership designated the pound sterling and the Swiss franc as its means of international settlement. As a result, even if Japan and the PRC were to establish an open account to avoid cash settlements, U.S. dollars would not be used as its nominal settlement medium. This rendered the FSCA powerless to curtail their transactions.[22]

The U.S. government encountered similarly unexpected difficulty in its efforts to halt diversion trade via Hong Kong, an avenue of commerce with the Chinese continent that the Japanese bureaucracy used to thwart U.S. financial intervention. In the 1951 Anglo-Japanese Payments Agreement, the Japanese Finance Ministry agreed to use the pound sterling for trade settlement with Hong Kong. Three years earlier, occupied Japan had signed a provisional payments agreement with Great Britain that included the so-called "dollar clause." According to this provision, if Japan accumulated pound sterling trade surplus beyond a certain level, it could make up to two annual requests to the British treasury that the surplus be converted to U.S. dollars. The British government, citing the serious worldwide dollar gap and the decline of Britain's economic standing after World War II, claimed that this obligation was unduly burdensome. When the Anglo-Japanese payments agreement was renegotiated, the Japanese government agreed to eliminate the dollar clause from the revised accord, reverting Hong Kong's status from the dollar-denominated open account area to the sterling settlement area. While these new currency arrangements reflected the attempted consolidation of the sterling area in Asia by the British treasury, the motives for Japanese acquiescence were complex, or so the State Department suspected. There was an ever-present risk that the British government would deny the Japanese use of the pound sterling as a tender of settlement in Sino-Japanese trade if Tokyo refused to relinquish the dollar clause. More importantly, United States officials surmised that, by designating Hong Kong as the sterling area, Japan hoped to preclude U.S. intervention in its diversion trade that it carried out through Great Britain's Far Eastern entrepot.[23]

The Japanese ingenuity was matched by an equally persistent U.S. effort to find other ways to choke off Sino-Japanese diversion trade. The Bank of Japan obtaining a $40 million import loan from the U.S. Export–Import Bank provided one important opportunity. In the spring of 1951, this bank provided the loan to finance the Japanese government's purchase of surplus raw cotton from the U.S. With the receipt of U.S. public funds, Japan became bound by the provisions of the U.S. Battle Act, which required recipients of U.S. foreign aid to abide by its export control policies against the Communist bloc. This requirement curtailed diversion trade with the Chinese mainland as it obligated the Japanese government to guarantee that items on the U.S. Battle List would not be re-exported to the PRC via Hong Kong. It also required export license controls and end-use checks, after exported goods left Japanese ports, be used to monitor against infringements. Two months before the San Francisco Peace Conference, the United States transferred these administrative functions from SCAP to the Ministry of International Trade and Industry (MITI).[24]

The way the newly created Ministry handled this mandate revealed that Japanese officialdom was hardly a monolithic entity. Prior to the administrative handover, SCAP and the State Department had predicted that the Foreign Ministry's mainline faction would faithfully execute Yoshida's declared intent to comply with the UN embargo to win confidence among members of the Western community. For the same reason, the United States expected Yoshida and the Foreign Ministry to maintain Japan's PRC embargo beyond multilateral levels even after the end of the occupation. Conversely, the U.S. suspected that MITI and the Economic Stabilization Board might adopt lax standards in trade regulation to promote trade with the PRC, or simply to please domestic interest groups. Policy makers in the Truman administration began to realize that post-independence Japan must be firmly locked into a system of clearly defined international obligations regarding Chinese trade to eliminate both these uncertainties and room for excessive discretion.[25]

U.S.–Japan diplomacy over multilateral trade controls

During the period between the signing and ratification of the San Francisco Peace Treaty, trade officials locked horns out of the spotlight of high-level diplomacy over the shape of Japan's future embargo program. In April 1952, the Commerce and State Departments dispatched a team of specialists to Tokyo to discuss with the Japanese administration its post-occupation policies for trade regulation. This experts' conference broke down over how to interpret Japan's domestic enabling legislation to control foreign trade, the Foreign Exchange and Trade Control Law, and Cabinet Order 378 issued in December 1949 containing a list of goods that required MITI's export licensing. The Ministry regarded this list simply as an enumeration of goods requiring export licensing, rather than an embargo list. This interpretation gave MITI discretion to approve the export of any item on the list regardless of its final destination, including the PRC. Furthermore, the U.S. delegation was astounded to learn that MITI planned to release from licensing requirement not only relatively non-controversial items such as paper, wooden products, and dyestuffs, but also transportation and communication equipment, construction materials, and machines tools. These items the U.S. government regarded as strategic or of dual utility.[26]

MITI's head, Takahashi Ryutaro, also caused a stir in the Diet, where trade with the PRC emerged as a focus of the most rancorous domestic political debate confronting Yoshida and his cabinet. At the first post-independence legislative session, the Dietmen's League engineered the adoption of a resolution urging the government to place Japan's China trade controls on a par with other Western nations. Here, members of the Yoshida cabinet exhibited a confounding disarray of official governmental positions regarding what constituted appropriate "multilateral levels." Foreign Minister Okazaki stated before a committee of legislators that the U.S. Battle Act and the UN embargo resolution made it impossible for the Japanese government to relax the current level of trade controls; appropriate "multilateral levels" could only be achieved after Western countries raised their trade restrictions to the Japanese level. At the same questioning session, however, Takahashi openly demurred, arguing that Japan's controls should be lowered to the CG level if multilateral parity was to be achieved. The U.S. embassy in Tokyo was also informed that MITI at a working level had decided to license the export of contested items to the PRC as counter exports in their barter trade.[27]

These developments in Tokyo led trade officials in the State and Commerce Departments to conclude that it was imperative to make the Japanese government accept the principle of prior consultation with the U.S. before any export items could be decontrolled. The United States became even more convinced of this necessity after a piece of disquieting news arrived from Moscow. In April 1952, the Communist camp convened the Moscow International Economic Conference, with delegations from forty-nine nations in attendance. Reflecting a subtle change in the CCP's attitudes towards Japan after gaining independence, Nan Han-chen, the president of the Chinese People's Bank and a co-convener of the Moscow conference, extended an invitation to Japan's "progressive elements." In an open letter, Nan foregrounded the theme of Sino-Japanese affinity and solidarity among Asian peoples. Both China and Japan shared a stake in fostering Asia's intra-regional trade and cultural exchange and in raising their standard of living. From the podium of the Communist-sponsored economic conference, Nan urged the Japanese people to free themselves from the shackles of the U.S.-instigated trade embargo obsequiously worn by "Yoshida and his clique," to take an important first step towards build-ing a lasting peace in Asia.[28]

At the request of the U.S. embassy, the Foreign Ministry withheld pass-ports from Japanese nationals seeking to attend the Moscow Conference. Despite this obstruction, three opposition legislators, Kora Tomi, Miyakoshi Kisuke, and Hoashi Kei, traveled to Moscow via several Euro-pean cities and took part in the gathering. This "exploit" received major coverage in the Japanese media and cheers from prominent political figures, including members of Yoshida's Liberal Party. In Moscow, the three national legislators met with the PRC's second-ranking foreign trade officer, Rei Len-min, and followed him to Beijing after the conference. Resulting from this unauthorized visit was a "private-sector" trade agree-ment signed by the three opposition legislators and Nan, who acted as chairman of the China's International Trade Promotion Committee. This agreement provided for barter trade in the amount of 300,000 pounds one way, with goods divided into three mutually exchangeable categories. Category 1, accounting for 40 percent of trade, included goods of prin-cipal interest to Japan (iron ore, coal, soy beans) and strategic goods banned from export to the PRC by the U.S. Battle Act. Beijing clearly intended to extract these latter items from Japan as counter-exports in barter trade.[29]

Despite the public exuberance, the agreement amounted in inter-national law to nothing more than a written intention to conduct barter trade. In practical terms, whether it would lead to any sizable growth in trade was suspect, for the absence of a formal payments agreement between the two governments made open account settlements impossible. Furthermore, the absence of sizable foreign exchange reserves held by either nation precluded any cash settlements in the foreseeable future. Both the Japanese government and the U.S. embassy in Tokyo understood all this, but they fretted over the agreement's symbolic value. These politi-cians, after all, had succeeded in defying the travel ban and reached out to the rival Communist regime a mere two months after the Japanese govern-ment had established formal relations with the Chinese Nationalists. Because of the Japanese signatories' status as Diet members, there was no way to avoid the aura of official sanction being attached to the trade accord in public perception. Yoshida and the Foreign Ministry could not dismiss those who hailed their action as "reds" or dangerous radicals, since they included a prominent Liberal Party member (and future prime minister), Ishibashi Tanzan. In addition, Hoashi's trip to Moscow and Beijing had been partially financed by traders and small business owners in the Kansai area, a constituency of the ruling party.[30]

Following the agreement's signature, the U.S. embassy continued to enlist the assistance of the Foreign Ministry in blocking Kansai area traders and manufacturers from traveling to Hong Kong to negotiate busi-ness transactions involving the mainland. Another key player, MITI, was not so cooperative. Despite the embassy's repeated complaints, MITI offi-cials repeatedly leaked to the press stories of American opposition to Japan's relaxation of its embargo against the PRC. The Ministry also incurred the embassy's displeasure by working with the left-leaning SJTPA to draft administrative ordinances concerning barter trade with the PRC. MITI's assertion of expansive administrative leeway and Diet members' high-profile maneuverings made it imperative for Washington to make the Japanese government assume clearly delineated international obligations embedded in a multilateral embargo system. Initially, the State Depart-ment considered the option of using Japanese membership in COCOM to gain its cooperation. The idea of COCOM membership appealed to the Japanese government as well. The Yoshida wing of the Liberal Party and pro-U.S. officials within the Foreign Ministry tended to see COCOM mem-bership as a visible embodiment of Japan's long-awaited return to the international community. Officials in MITI and the Economic Stabiliza-tion Agency, on the other hand, envisioned COCOM membership as a means to help Japan reduce its China trade controls to Western European levels.[31]

The question of Japan's possible accession to COCOM was subsumed into on-going discussions within the Truman administration over the mul-tilateral trade embargo system's future in the Far East. The Defense and Commerce departments maintained that a separate mechanism for con-trolling Western trade with Asian Communist states must be developed to enforce effective sanctions for the duration of the Korean War. Defense also believed that Japan was a geographical misfit in COCOM, an organi-zation that at the time was slated for integration into the North Atlantic Treaty Organization (NATO). In the end, the Truman administration reached consensus along the lines proposed by the Commerce and Defense departments.[32] The Japanese Foreign Ministry initially resisted the U.S. plan to establish a separate embargo mechanism for the Far East. By mid-June 1952, it had agreed to cooperate under the condition that the new group would be a sub-organ of the CG, equal in status to COCOM and based in Paris. The Japanese concession came shortly after Takahashi had openly contradicted Okazaki before the Diet. The Foreign Ministry's top echelon wished to expedite the process by clarifying Japan's inter-national obligations with regard to trade with the PRC.[33]

In late July, five countries with stakes in trade with the PRC (the U.S., Great Britain, France, Canada, and Japan) gathered in Washington to discuss a multilateral embargo regime that specifically targeted Asian Communist states. Great Britain spearheaded the support of Japan's acces-sion to COCOM as an equal member, or alternatively the formation of a separate Far Eastern embargo organization. London's motive was hardly altruistic: it wanted to deflect Japan's future economic thrusts towards China's northeast, away from southern China and Southeast Asia where its own economic interests were concentrated. France and Canada's support of Britain's proposal for Japan's admittance into the multilateral embargo regime on an equal footing in effect isolated the U.S. The five-power consensus delivered, at the end of the Washington conference, a new embargo organ dedicated to the Far East as a sub-organ of the CG, parallel in rank to COCOM that policed Western trade with the Soviet Union and Eastern Europe. Japan gained admittance to the CG and was inaugurated as a charter member of the China Committee, the new Far Eastern embargo group formerly launched in September 1952.[34]

The U.S. delegation at this conference had to pressure Japan bilaterally to retain restrictions of trade with the PRC above and beyond those of the China Committee's other charter members. The task fell on Under-Secretary of State Harold Linder, who requested Minister Ryuji Takeuchi of the Japanese embassy, Japan's chief negotiator at the conference, to agree to stricter trade controls with China as a bilateral arrangement. Formally titled "the U.S.–Japan Bilateral Understanding Regarding Trade Controls against Communist China," the document signed by Linder and Takeuchi on 5 September bound Japan to retain all embargo items listed in COCOM, under COCOM's quantitative control and supervision, and in the U.S. Battle Act. In addition, in the event that Japan sought to ship dual utility items to the PRC as counter-exports in barter trade negotiated by private-sector traders and manufacturers, the agreement stipulated that all transactions must be strictly regulated through MITI's export licensing. Should MITI wish to release goods from a licensing requirement, the agreement stipulated that the ministry consult with the United States regarding this change. The agreement left no ambiguities or room for maneuver as to what the Japanese government was now obligated to do so as to play its role in economically strangling the Communist regime that the United States considered to be Asia's paramount military threat.[35]

Conclusion

The bilateral understanding on China trade controls into which the Yoshida government grudgingly entered just months after Japan regained national sovereignty would have far-reaching and long-lasting implications for Japan's post-occupation trade control system. As the government agency charged with regulating Japan's commercial relations with the PRC, MITI was given the daunting administrative responsibility of enforcing an embargo on all exportable items deemed strategic by a multilateral organization (the China Committee) and the U.S. government. In addition, consultation with the United States before exporting dual utility items became part of post-occupation Japan's routine administrative procedures governing its foreign trade. Despite these layers of embargo and monitoring in the forms of bilateral understanding and multilateral agreements, imposed by the U.S. government (and particularly the military) continued to be haunted by suspicions that MITI would try to chisel a damaging hole in the multilateral anti-PRC embargo system by abusing its discretionary powers in export licensing. This U.S. suspicion would remain unallayed throughout the duration of the Korean War and even beyond. The series of U.S.–Japan pre-consultations held during the Cold War over Japan's gradual decontrol of goods exportable to the PRC were invariably contentious and often acrimonious.

The Japanese economy, in the transition from postwar reconstruction to peacetime sustained growth, would draw its sustenance primarily from trade with the Western world in the absence of a stable commercial relationship with the Chinese mainland or a spectacular growth of intra-Asian trade. After Yoshida's exit from office, Japan's trade with the PRC would see a slight increase during the premierships of Hatoyama and Ishibashi, but Sino-Japanese trade remained insignificant. After the Nagasaki flag incident of May 1958, commercial relations between Japan and the PRC were all but severed. During Japan's high-speed growth period that began with the dawning of the 1960s, Japan's foreign trade became overwhelmingly reliant on economic relations with the Western capitalist world, particularly the United States. Like diplomatic relations with the PRC, cultivation of intra-regional trade with the Chinese mainland through peaceful means, a smoldering Japanese dream from the pre-war years, would remain an unattainable vision until the U.S. government effected a major reorientation of its Far Eastern policy by seeking ties with the PRC from the early 1970s.

Notes

1 For general surveys of postwar Sino-Japanese relations, see Tanaka Akihiko, *Nitchu kankei 1945–1990* [*Japan–China relations, 1945–1990*], Tokyo: Tokyo Daigaku shuppankai, 1991; Soeya Yoshihide, *Nippon gaiko to chugoku 1945–1972* [*Japanese diplomacy and China, 1945–1972*], Tokyo: Keio Tsushin, 1995; Chen, Zhao-bin *Sengo Nippon no Chugoku seisaku* [*Postwar Japan's China policy*], Tokyo: Tokyo Daigaku shuppankai, 2000.
2 Inoue Toshikazu, *Nippon gaikoshi kogi* [*Japan's diplomatic history lecture*], Tokyo: Iwanami Shoten, 2003, pp. 118–20.
3 Ibid., p. 120.
4 Jono Hiroshi, *Sansei dokuritsu senki* [*Records of war of independence for Shanxi*], Tokyo: Sekkasha, 1967; Kono Michiko "Nippon rikugun no taienyouzan kosaku" ["The Japanese Army's Taiyuan Operation"], in Eto Shinkichi Sensei Koki Kinen Ronbunshu Henshu Iinkai, ed., *20 seiki Ajia no kokusai kankei* [Twentieth century Asian international relations], vol. 2, Tokyo: Harashobo, 1995, pp. 105–33; Yuasa Shigehiro, "'Kyoryoku de toitsu' ka 'jakutai de bunretsu' ka: dainiji taisen senchu sengo ni okeru Nichibei ryokoku no Chugokukan no hikaku kosatsu" ["'Strong and united' or 'weak and divided'? A comparative study of Japanese views of China: wartime vs. postwar"], *Tokyo joshidaigaku kiyo*, vol. 48, no. 1, pp. 40–4.
5 For activities by members of the White Army, see Nakamura Yuetsu, *Paidan-Taiwangun wo tsukutta Nippon shokotachi* [*The White Army–Taiwan military formed by Japanese officers*], Tokyo: Fuyo Shobo, 1995. For information on former Japanese imperial army officers and soldiers who participated with the campaigns by

218   S. Guthrie-Shimizu

the Chinese Communist army, see Furukawa Mantaro, *Itetsuku daichi no uta-jinmin kaihogun Nipponjin heishitachi* [*The song of the frozen land: Japanese soldiers in the people's liberation army*], Tokyo: Sanseido, 1984.

6 Donald G. Gillin and Charles Etter, "Staying on: Japanese soldiers and civilians in China, 1945–1949," *Journal of Asian studies*, vol. 42, no. 3, 1983, pp. 497–518.

7 Daqing Yang, "Resurrecting the empire? Japanese technicians in postwar China, 1945–1959," Harold Fuess (ed.), *The Japanese empire in East Asia and its postwar legacy*, Monographien aus dem Deutschen Institut fur Japanstudien der PHILIPP Franz von Siebold Stiftung, Band 22, 1998, pp. 185–205.

8 According to Daqing Yang, a sizable number of Japanese technicians and experts remained on the Chinese mainland even after the 1949 Communist takeover. Some Japanese contributed to medical services for the Chinese People's Liberation Army during the Korean War. Ibid., p. 200.

9 MSC 41, 28 February 1949, "United States policy regarding trade with China," *Harry S. Truman Papers*, President's Secretary Files, box 205, Harry S. Truman Library, Independence, Missouri; NSC 48/2, "The position of the United States with respect to Asia," 30 December 1949, *Foreign relations of the United States (FRUS)*, 1949, 7:1215–20; *Ajia keizai shiryo*, no. 44, pp. 2–3.

10 Furukawa Mantaro, *Nitchu sengo keizaishi* [*Japan–China postwar economic history*], Tokyo: Hara Shobo, 1981, pp. 20–30; *Ajia keizai shiryo*, no. 46, pp. 1–19.

11 "Chukyo to shochiiki ni taisuru boeki kanri-Showa nijunananen shigatsumade" ["Trade control towards the People's Republic of China and its surrounding areas: until July, 1952"], 15 July 1952, "Tai kyosanken tosei kankei ikken," Ministry of Foreign Affairs Record, E '4.1.0.6.1, Foreign Ministry Archives, Tokyo Japan (hereafter cited as MOFA Trade Control Files); *Ajia keizai shiryo*, no. 47, pp. 15–25, no. 48, pp. 22–34; *Ajia keizai junpo*, no. 51, pp. 7–8, no. 62, p. 51, no. 63, pp. 4–10; "Trade between Japan and China and adjacent Communist areas," 16 May 1951, Department of State Decimal Files (DC), 493.94/5-1651, National Archives (NA), College Park, Maryland.

12 Sayuri Shimizu, *Creating people of plenty: the United States and Japan's economic alternatives, 1950–1960*, Kent: Kent State University Press, 2001, pp. 49–50; *Ajia keizai junpo*, no. 74, pp. 29–30, no. 76, pp. 1–8.

13 Kato Yoko, *Amerika no sekai senryaku to kokomu* [*America's global strategy and COCOM*], Tokyo: Yushindo, 1992, pp. 110–11.

14 "Chukyo to shochiiki ni taisuru boeki kanri-Showa Nijunananen shigatsu made," 15 July 1952, MOFA Files; *Ajia keizai junpo*, no. 83, pp. 1–4.

15 Nancy Tucker, "American policy toward Sino-Japanese trade in the postwar years," *Diplomatic history* 8, Summer 1984, p. 193.

16 Kato, *Amerika no sekai senryaku*, pp. 10–11.

17 Nitchu boeki sokushin giin renmei, ed., *Nitchu kankei shiryoshu* [*Materials on Japan–China relations*], Tokyo: Nitchu boeki sokushin giin renmei, 1967, pp. 21–2.

18 Furukawa, *Itetsuku daichi no uta-jinmin kaihogun*, pp. 20–5; Nitchu kokkokaifuku sokushin giin renmei, ed., *Nitchu kankei shiryoshu*, Tokyo: Nitchu kokko kaifuku sokushin giin renmei, 1972, pp. 1–3; Hirano Yoshitaro, "Nitchu boeki undo no hajimari," in *Ajia keizai junpo*, pp. 526–27.

19 For historians' interpretations on the true intent of the Yoshida Letter, see Chin, *Sengo nippon no chugoku seisaku*, pp. 1–3 and En Kokukin, "Gaiatsu riyo gaiko toshiteno 'Yoshida shokan'" ["The 'Yoshida letter' as a case of the diplomacy of outside pressure"], in *Hitotsubashi ronso*, vol. 107, no. 1, 1992.

20 "Trade between Japan and China," Hemmendinger to Dulles, 15 January 1952, DF, 493.9441/1-1552; "Chukyo to shochiiki ni taisuru boeki kanri," "Shireibu oboegaki-yushutsu kanriboekirei kaisei ni kansuruken" ["The memo of the

General Headquarters regarding the export control law"], 28 May 1951, MOFA Files.

21 Allison to Hemmendinger, 20 December 1951, DF, 493.949/12-2051, *Ajia keizai Junpo*, no. 77, p. 28, no. 78, pp. 19–20, no. 80, pp. 17–18.
22 Allison to Hemmendinger, 20 December 1951; *Ajia keizai junpo*, no. 93, pp. 1–11.
23 Diehl to Barnett, 2 November 1951, DF, 493.9431/11-251; McClurkin to Allison, 20 December 1951, DF, 493.949/12-2051, *Daquoban*, 27 August 1950; *Ajia keizai junpo*, no. 87, p. 20.
24 "Shireibu oboegaki," 15 March 1952, MOFA Files; Warning to Hemmendinger, 26 January 1952, DF, 493.949/1-2652.
25 McClurkin to Allison, 15 February 1952, DF, 493.94/2-552; telegram from Araki to Asakai, 28 July 1952, MOFA Files.
26 Ibid.
27 *Asahi Shinbun*, 24 and 29 May 1952; Murphy to Acheson, 30 May 1952, DF, 493.949/5-3052; *Ajia keizai junpo*, no. 125, pp. 1–9.
28 Furukawa, *Itetsuku daichi no uta-jinmin kaihogun*, pp. 36–44; Nan Han-chen letter, 14 February 1952, *Nitchu kankei shiryoshu*, 1967, pp. 134–5; Hoashi Kei, *Soren chugoku ryoko* [*A trip through China and the Soviet Union*], Tokyo: Mainichi Shinbunsha, 1985, pp. 4–57; Kora Tomi, *Hisen wo ikiru* [*Life of pacifism*], Tokyo: Domesu Shuppan, 1983, pp. 140–6; *Ajia keizai junpo*, no. 132, 1–4; no. 134, pp. 24–5.
29 Murphy to Acheson, 31 May 1952, DF, 493.949/5-3142; Hoashi Kei and Wakimura Yoshitaro, "Chukyo boeki ha kanoka" ["Is Red China trade possible?"], in *Sekai*, no. 81, pp. 133–5; *Ajia keizai junpo*, no. 143, 1–25, no. 151, pp. 1–9.
30 Nan Han-chen to Nitchu boeki sokushinkai [Nan Han-chen and the Japan–China trade promotion association], 27 December 1951, *Nitchu kankei shiryo*, 1967, pp. 133–5.
31 Kerr to Department of State, 3 June 1952, DF, 493.9431/6-352, 8 August 1952, DF, 493.9431/8-852.
32 Acheson to the embassy in Paris, 11 April 1952, DF, 400-949/6-1752; Murphy to Acheson, 28 May 1952, DF, 400.949/5-2852; Allison to Acheson, 31 May 1952, DF, 499.949/5-3142.
33 "Chukyo to Shochiikini Taisuru Boeki Kanri," telegram from Araki to Okazaki, 24 June 1952, 27 June 1952, MOFA Files.
34 Young to Johnson, 2 August 1952, DF, 499.949/8-452; "Understanding between Japan and the United States concerning the control of exports to Communist China," DF, 493.009/9-552; telegram from Araki to Okazaki, 1 August 1952, telegram from Okazaki to Araki, 2 August 1952, MOFA Files; *Ajia keizai junpo*, no. 153, pp. 1–8.
35 Circular telegram, 19 September 1952, DF, 400.949/9-1952.

9   A secondary affair

United States economic foreign policy and Japan, 1945–1968

Michael A. Barnhart

The history of United States economic foreign policy has been distinguished by scholarly neglect for most of the twentieth century. With the exception of a brief flurry of interest in tariffs, stimulated in the 1930s by the experience of the Great Depression and a newfound belief in the need for freer trade, diplomatic historians have overwhelmingly concentrated their efforts on the study of political, strategic, and even social, intellectual, and cultural aspects of America's relations with the world.

This concentration seems curious. Since at least the Bretton Woods Conference of 1944, and arguably a good deal earlier, the primary goal of U.S. diplomacy has been the creation and maintenance of an order that is overwhelmingly economic in definition and character. Contrary to much of the documentary classification and escapades surrounding military of intelligence issues, the record of U.S. economic foreign policy is as open as it is copious.

Even so, it is simple enough to deduce the chief causes of this neglect. Economic foreign policy rarely came to the attention of top policymakers as such. It virtually never mattered to the American military or intelligence communities. There were no economic "crises" during the period under consideration in this paper – if by "crisis" we mean an interval in which its subject consumed nearly all the time of top policy makers. Even those outside this period, whether the London Economic Conference of 1933 or the demise of the very short-lived Bretton Woods system in 1971 and 1973, have little of the excitement attending the dramas of Cuba or Berlin. Last, but hardly least, tracking the record of American foreign economic policy requires excursions in the main unfamiliar to historians of foreign policy and usually unexplored by economic historians. In part, this is because foreign economic policy was not easily compartmentalized within the White House and the State and Defense departments. During this era (or any other), economic policy was the result of protracted negotiation not only with foreign governments but also between the Executive and Congress, and diplomatic historians have shown nearly as great an allergy to treating of Congress as they have in considering economic issues. In part, economic policy is ignored because it was made, at times crucially, by agencies entirely outside the government, such as the American banking community. While the flow of trade was and always will remain a vital component of foreign economic affairs, the bottom line, both figuratively and literally, was the flow of capital. An examination of that flow, barely begun in this study, is as imperative to understanding U.S.–Japan relations during this era as it is difficult.

The study of U.S. economic foreign policy with Japan has suffered not only from this general inattention, but also from two themes – perhaps better described as obsessions – influencing those who do practice in this area and era. The first was the search for origins of America's Vietnam War. Some accounts, such as William S. Borden's *The Pacific Alliance*,[1] were seized upon in claims that Washington's quest to ensure Japan's swift economic recovery through access to cheap raw materials led to an initial interest in Southeast Asia and thus America's eventual tragedy there. The second theme has been the chronic trade difficulties afflicting U.S.–Japanese relations since the 1970s and the suspicion that clever, even insidious, Japanese diplomats cunningly took advantage of American economic naïveté and Washington's desire to stop the Kremlin no matter what the cost in order to execute "an economic Pearl Harbor" or, as former Senator Paul Tsongas claimed, win the Cold War.[2]

But if the past is taken on its own merits, rather than upon these two current concerns, a quite different pattern emerges in American economic foreign policy and Japan. That policy was shaped primarily by struggles between the American Executive and Congress, neither one of which saw Japan as at all central to its concerns in those struggles. And that policy was shaped secondarily by struggles among agencies, some within the executive branch (such as the Department of State *versus* the Department of Agriculture), and some not (the American Export-Import Bank against the putatively non-American World Bank, for example), which likewise hardly saw Japan as central in their disputes. Greatly unlike American economic policy toward Europe, which was well debated in Washington on its own merits, which had a dedicated cadre of senior American "Atlanticist" policy makers who often succeeded in connecting it to key issues in the Cold War, and which enjoyed the support of well-connected (and well-traveled) Europeans, there really was no American economic policy *toward* Japan during these years. Instead, American economic policy considered Japan as an important but distinctly secondary affair to the greater issues of Europe and Congress. Japan, one might say, pursued its own policies to take advantage of that relative inattention.

Inattention may not have been an option for Washington during the years of the occupation, but American economic policy in Japan during those years nevertheless was chiefly colored by the clash between the Executive and Congress. By early 1947 senior State Department officials such as Dean Acheson and Paul Nitze had concluded that Japan was an economic wreck that had to be rehabilitated rapidly to enable Tokyo to become a reliable partner in the emerging Cold War. It was simple enough to compel U.S. occupation partners in the Far Eastern Commission to sharply limit Japan's reparations obligations, but Japan needed positive funding as well. Stuffing the U.S. army's occupation budget was one alternative copiously pursued. Extending the occupation itself ensured that this alternative remained open for as long as possible. But Congress proved reluctant to extend actual recovery funding unless it was tied to domestic interests, such as a $150 million credit line offered to the Japanese authorities to purchase American raw cotton.[3]

Given Congress's reluctance to provide either direct relief aid or, more important for the long run, capital for industrial reconstruction and development, Americans in Japan were compelled to resort to drastic methods. The Dodge Line (named after American banker Joseph Dodge) instituted austerity for already hard-pressed Japanese consumers not only to control inflation but also to liquidate a Japanese domestic market and thus force Japan to export. Dodge retired the Japanese government's debt using American Government and Relief in Occupied Areas (GARIOA) counterpart funds and encouraged investment in coal, shipbuilding and electric power industries.[4] He also overrode prior American economic studies in pegging the exchange rate at 360 yen to the dollar – an artificially high ratio that facilitated Japanese exports.[5]

Those exports grew, but to the sterling area, not Southeast Asia or the United States, and Japan's dollar shortage actually worsened through 1949 and 1950. By April 1950 Japanese Finance Minister Ikeda Hayato was on his way to Washington to request fundamental revisions in the Dodge Line, not the least being the abandonment of austerity. There, representatives from the State and Treasury departments railed against continued British opposition to sterling–dollar convertibility but did nothing about it. A proposal for a "yen fund," allowing Japan to buy American goods in yen, which the United States would then loan or grant to Southeast Asian nations, received little encouragement (and even less optimism) until the American military began casting about for ways to increase assistance to that area.[6]

The immediate savior was the outbreak of war in Korea and large American military procurement spending in Japan, a good deal of it under the terms of the Mutual Defense Assistance Act of 1949. But this salvation was short lived. Japan regained sovereignty in early 1952 just as this spending began to drop and Japan's dollar shortage difficulties (in fact general capital shortages) resurfaced. State Department efforts that year to enter into long-term procurement arrangements encountered stiff resistance in Congress as Japan's overall trade deficit ballooned toward $750 million.

The new Eisenhower administration demonstrated few signs to suggest improvement. Although Secretary of State John Foster Dulles had first-hand experience with Japanese leaders, he was not inclined to press for a showdown with Congress over aid to Japan, or for that matter an overall set of American foreign economic policies beneficial to Tokyo. Nor was the president. Eisenhower quickly abandoned efforts to secure a long-term renewal of executive authority under the Reciprocal Trade Agreements Act in exchange for a one-year extension, and that at the price of his agreeing not to enter into tariff negotiations for the interim.[7]

The timing of these arrangements could hardly have been worse for Japan, which had just initialed a Treaty of Commerce and Navigation with the United States in April 1953.[8] This was not a bilateral affair, as both Tokyo and Washington were eager to have Japan gain accession into the General Agreement on Tariffs and Trade (GATT). But accession required tariff criteria that could best be met by negotiation – a possibility that Eisenhower had negotiated away during the critical year in which such talks would have been most important. The resulting finesse – temporary GATT membership for Japan – hardly pleased Tokyo, especially since 1953 saw a record trade deficit.[9]

Nevertheless, American economic foreign policy provided substantial aid to Japan during this crucial period, if not always intentionally. Japan had joined the World Bank (technically, the International Bank for Reconstruction and Development) in August 1952. The resulting Bank mission to Japan drew up a dismal forecast for Japan's economic prospects. Yet this was good news in a sense. The Bank had defined its mission as aiding development and Japan appeared as a prime candidate. The Bank's staff, moreover, felt most comfortable issuing loans for the specific development of industrial infrastructure, especially in transportation and energy generation. The Bank's loan terms did not require trade liberalization, and were quite generous in permitting domestic procurement.[10] Needless to say, Japan was a perfect fit and one of the World Bank's heaviest borrowers between 1952 and 1966.

Even so, the Bank might not have lent so quickly but for a key dispute in 1952–1953 with the U.S. government's Export-Import Bank. The Export-Import Bank had agreed to extend two loans worth $40 million to finance Japan's purchase of generating equipment for steam power plants from Westinghouse and General Electric. Eugene Black, president of the World Bank, strongly felt that these purchases infringed upon the central loan mission of his institution. He bitterly complained to the Departments of State and Treasury and threatened to withhold all loans to Japan if the deal went through. Black won this fight and the World Bank took over these loans. But Japan was the chief victor as both the Export-Import Bank and the World Bank copiously supplied it capital far into the 1960s.[11]

These infusions of capital would aid Japan's creation of its successful industries of that decade and later, but they did little to address its pressing trade issues, going into 1954. Fortune again smiled as the communists overran French positions at Dien Bien Phu that spring, allowing Eisenhower to accuse Congress of weakening a critical American ally in Asia at a critical moment. That, and the political wiles of Speaker Sam Rayburn, secured renewal of the Reciprocal Trade Agreements Act and enabled Eisenhower to extend substantial American tariff concessions to other nations in exchange for their agreement to support Japan's full membership in GATT.[12] Congress also obliged Japan with generous treatment under Public Law 480, a scheme to promote the "sale" of American agricultural products.[13]

It would exaggerate to say that these resolutions of 1954 were primarily responsible for Japan's economic takeoff, but 1955 and 1956 were very good years for its foreign trade. Clarence Randall, Eisenhower's free trade advocate, had been retained as Chairman of the Committee on Foreign Economic Policy and visited Tokyo in late 1956.

Randall marveled at Japan's trade surplus and lauded Japanese efforts. But he remained cautious. Too much of Japan's foreign exchange earnings (about 20 percent) was still due to U.S. defense expenditures in Japan.[14] Japan was still capital poor and could not compete internationally in heavy industries such as steel or chemicals. Prospects for an integrated Asian market to benefit Japan were dim. Fortunately, bilateral American–Japanese trade was flourishing, with Japan the largest purchaser of important American products such as cotton and grains.[15]

In fact, to some American textile companies and political leaders in the American South, Japan was purchasing all too much cotton. As early as the summer of 1955 their demands for a textile import quota had reached Eisenhower, who was surprised to learn that the United States had guaranteed Japan a minimum floor of textile imports as part of the GATT concessionary negotiations.[16] Dulles fended off complaints from Japanese leaders[17] but was able to defeat a 1956 congressional attempt to impose import quotas on Japanese textiles only by securing Tokyo's agreement to voluntary export restraints through 1957.[18] By the end of that year, Japanese textile imports had declined significantly and the issue disappeared, for a time.

Tokyo complained about these arrangements, noting that Japan again had lapsed into a trade deficit, especially with the United States. Kishi Nobusuke, a rising political star, pointed out that renewed austerity steps were emboldening the Japanese left, especially the teachers' union. Foreign Minister Fujiyama Aiichiro argued that many of the exporters hurt by American (or Japanese voluntary) trade restrictions were small, vulnerable, and lured by the prospect of trade with communist China. They appealed for a suspension of American anti-trust provisions over Japanese export arrangements to American markets and for the creation of a special East Asian development bank.[19]

Washington was unsympathetic for a variety of reasons. Deeply concerned about the rising Soviet economic threat,[20] the Eisenhower administration had resolved to press much harder for general arrangements toward Western economic integration rather than the bilateral suggestions of Kishi and Fujiyama. Randall, C. Douglas Dillon, Henry Owen, and George Ball were powerful proponents of enlarging the Organization for European Economic Cooperation (OEEC) into a much broader entity that would include the United States, Canada, and Japan.[21]

As well, economic foreign policy makers worried about America's lapse into a trade deficit.[22] In 1958 and 1959 these worries were not great. Practically everyone, including the most senior experts at the International Monetary Fund (IMF), believed the situation only temporary and even desirable as a way to end the dollar shortage difficulties that had plagued the early 1950s.[23] There was some sentiment for pressuring Europe to ease the United States' burden by providing more support for the North Atlantic Treaty Organization (NATO) and lowering tariffs and other barriers to American agricultural goods.[24] But while U.S. ambassador to Japan Douglas MacArthur II did protest Japanese trade "discrimination and restrictionism," there was little effort made to compel adjustments in American–Japanese trade and investment patterns.[25]

Little effort was made due to a number of considerations. Foremost was a desire to avoid increasing tensions during the crucial renegotiation of the Japanese–American Security Treaty and, to a lesser degree, the final settlement of occupation-era GARIOA fund repayments. The Americans also recognized that Japan did not enjoy a colossal trade surplus with the United States.[26] Japanese leaders were correct when they argued that Japan was just emerging from a highly volatile trading environment and, despite a strong record of growth since 1955, remained highly dependent upon low global trade barriers, especially with the United States. Contrary to growing suspicions of the Europeans, Washington harbored no fears of the emergence of a Japanese economic bloc. By early 1958 Secretary of the Treasury Robert Anderson was thoroughly alarmed by America's balance of payments position, but his recommendations – calling upon allies to eliminate import quotas and reduce tariffs on American goods as well as shoulder part of the mutual defense burden – targeted Europe, not Japan.[27] Indeed, while Washington resolved to actively discourage further World Bank loans to Italy and France, and was determined to reduce or eliminate military aid to Italy and the Low Countries (and press West Germany for greater support of U.S. forces there),[28] Japan escaped these pressures altogether.[29]

This is not to say that concerns over the Security Treaty muted all complaints. Nor were American policy makers oblivious to the possibility of future frictions in the new decade. Prime Minister Kishi's visit to Washington in January 1960 was preceded by protests over declining American military assistance and P.L. 480 aid to Japan, coupled with reminders that Japan's need for foreign trade could well motivate increased dealings with Red China. The Americans were willing to accept such dealings, but rather pointedly reminded Kishi that the Chinese could turn fickle, as they had two years earlier in abruptly severing a number of trade agreements. Privately, Dillon and J. Graham Parsons[30] were indeed concerned about Japan's heavy dependence upon the American export market. Correctly noting that, for the foreseeable future, Japan could not count on expanding exports to the less developed countries, the only opening appeared to be Western Europe. Unfortunately, trends in what would become the European Economic Community (EEC), as well as continued strong British opposition to Japanese imports, pointed in the opposite direction. Japanese protectionism, especially barriers to capital investment, provided both Europeans and Americans ample grounds for resistance.[31]

Still, there was no prospect of serious American pressure on Japan after John F. Kennedy's victory in the 1960 presidential contest. Kennedy had openly criticized "Republican protectionism" during his campaign. He advocated sharply lower barriers to international trade as one way to grow out of the recession of 1960 and the surest guarantee to win the economic struggle against the communist bloc. Indeed, Kennedy had openly embraced the Keynesian philosophies of the Democratic Advisory Council during his run for the presidency.[32] Before the end of his first year in office, Kennedy was calling for the Reciprocal Trade Agreements Act to be replaced (its latest renewal due to expire in June 1962) to permit sweeping reductions in American trade restrictions as a way to induce similar liberalization elsewhere.[33] Besides, Kennedy had received positively glowing reports on Japan's assistance as an economic ally. Japan was America's second largest export market and took large amounts of surplus agricultural goods. Tokyo's reparations agreements with various East and Southeast Asian nations were aiding their economic development just as the Cold War focused attention upon these regions. While the pace of Japan's import liberalization left something to be desired, it was a move in the right direction. And Prime Minister Ikeda had moved swiftly to settle the GARIOA issue, providing payments to the United States of nearly $500 million.[34]

Kennedy's Trade Expansion Act was roundly attacked by Republicans in Congress, especially Senator Prescott Bush of Connecticut. Bush argued that lower trade barriers might indeed encourage more international trade, but to the further detriment of the American balance-of-payments deficit thanks to Japan. The Europeans imposed quotas upon Japanese imports because Japan had lower labor costs. Why shouldn't the United States have quotas against the EEC for the same reason?[35] By October 1962, however, Kennedy had his law at the cheap price of continued voluntary export restriction in textiles embodied in a "long-term arrangement" (LTA) covering these goods,[36] and an agreement that a Special Trade Representative (STR) would oversee economic negotiations instead of the State Department.[37]

Kennedy thinkers (such as Dillon, Owen, and Ball) believed that the chief cause of American payments deficits was home grown, not Tokyo. A substantial amount of capital was flowing out of the United States through private investment overseas,[38] government expenditures (primarily to support American forces abroad and foreign aid), and tourism. Curbing tourism would be unpopular. Reducing foreign aid was out of the question under the New Frontier. But Kennedy was quite willing to pressure Europe, especially West Germany, to increase support for American forces there.

There would be no similar pressure on Japan, however, for a number of compelling reasons. There were not large numbers of American ground forces in Japan to begin with. The major installations were on Okinawa, which operated under American sovereignty and thus a dollar economy. But at base, Kennedy was not willing to press Japan because he was not sure of its economic strength or political resilience. After all, Japan itself had often lapsed into trade deficits. It constantly had run a large negative balance with the United States. If the American market were shut off, or if undue strain were otherwise placed on the Japanese economy, it might easily turn to trade with China or even the Soviet Union. Senior advisor Walt Rostow and U.S. ambassador to Japan, Edwin Reischauer, stressed that the roots of democracy in Japan were shallow[39] and the stem itself a foreign transplant of recent vintage. There was no viable moderate-left political force to buffer the communist extreme, and the security treaty riots of 1960 had demonstrated how much turmoil lay just under the surface of Japanese politics.

Instead, Kennedy sought to appeal to Japan by offering economic attractions. He proposed the creation of a New Pacific Community to rival the Common Market. He sharply increased American payments for the Okinawa base facilities and granted All Nippon Airways, a Japanese carrier, daily landing rights at Naha.[40] He agreed to establish the U.S.–Japan Committee on Trade and Economic Affairs, a mechanism for regular consultation among business and government leaders from both countries and strongly opposed by the American lumber and textile industries.[41] He issued an Executive Order allowing exceptions to the "Buy American" Act for American government procurement overseas. When howls of congressional opposition led to a bill to observe 7 December as "Infamy Day," Kennedy personally took charge of the successful effort to kill it.[42]

Even so, American–Japanese relations were not altogether smooth during the second half of Kennedy's presidency. The joint committee was well received in Tokyo, but the new community was not. It was too obviously a Cold War device to forestall overtures for trade with communist nations[43] and a way to reduce Japan's role in the newly-forming Organization for Economic Cooperation and Development (OECD, the successor to the OEEC) even further.[44] Textile and a range of other issues provided chronic irritation and a warning from George Ball that Japan was being pressed too hard in response to American domestic interests, a consideration that encouraged a presidential goodwill trip to Japan in February 1962.[45]

The opening salvos of the Kennedy Round also highlighted Japanese–American differences. Washington pushed for linear tariff reductions rather than item-by-item ones. The approach was not popular in Europe, which already had lower rates than the U.S., nor was it favored by Japan. This meant no European–Japanese alliance, however. Indeed, Ikeda had been irritated by the Trade Expansion Act's passage. To him, it seemed (and in fact it was) geared almost entirely to U.S.–European trade issues, promised to lower U.S. trade barriers to European exports, and at the price of continued "voluntary" restraints on Japanese exports in the American market. Nor had the Americans done anything to have the Common Market lower obstacles to Japanese exports to Europe in conjunction with Ikeda's trip there in the autumn of 1962. These complaints produced a quick trip by the first Special Trade Representative, Christian Herter, to Tokyo in April 1963 with promises to press the EEC to end quotas on Japanese imports if Japan dropped its objections to the linear approach. Ikeda agreed.[46]

As importantly, other American financial initiatives bid fair to injure Japan's prosperity significantly, none more than the Interest Equalization Tax, which Kennedy proposed in June 1963. The Interest Equalization Tax was the result of Kennedy's increasing frustration at his inability to reverse the flow of dollars from the United States. Reducing American foreign aid or military spending overseas were not attractive options, nor was a general increase in the domestic discount rate. Drawing on American tranches with the IMF to counterbalance the outflow was rejected out of hand, as was a reversion to protectionism to achieve similar results.[47] Compelling other nations to buy additional U.S. Treasury securities or to convert their existing holdings into long-term obligations struck Treasury Secretary Douglas Dillon as the equivalent of debt rescheduling, befitting Brazil or Argentina but not the United States.[48] Kennedy and Dillon thought much of the problem was due to private American capital going to Europe to get behind the tariff walls that the new European Economic Community seemed certain to raise. They were reluctant to directly discourage this flow. Instead, they struck upon restricting foreign access to American capital markets through a tax on foreign borrowings.

Simply put, the equalization tax raised the effective cost of borrowing capital in American markets by one percent in order to discourage the, as Ball put it, "marginal borrowing" of dollars by Europeans.[49] There was a good deal of such borrowing, however, by the Japanese (and American banks operating in Japan) under arrangements that made Japan's capital markets especially vulnerable to restrictions on access to American ones.[50] Japan's reaction was a swift dispatch of Foreign Minister Ôhira Masayoshi, who predicted that Japan would find borrowing difficult and experience a substantial capital shortage. Had the United States even bothered to study this possibility?[51] Could Japan be granted an exemption from the tax, as Canada would be? American replies were not encouraging.[52] Nor were American protests concerning Japanese changes to foreign investment laws that appeared to make such investment more difficult than ever.[53] These new troubles led Kennedy to decide in October 1963 to visit Japan in early 1964, a trip that Secretary of State Dean Rusk made in the slain president's stead.

Under Lyndon Johnson, Japan at last would win its exemption from the interest equalization tax,[54] but at a price. In return, Tokyo promised that it would hold its balance of American dollars rather than convert them into gold.[55] This was hardly a policy exception. It was a continuation of American attempts to impose de facto controls on the use and flow of international capital, which still overwhelmingly meant the dollar and the pound.[56] Canada, which already had enjoyed the exemption, was compelled to accept an actual cap on the dollar reserves it could hold. The Johnson administration enjoyed less success in forcing Europe, especially the always nettlesome French,[57] to agree to similar terms and resorted in February 1965 to calls for voluntary restraints on transfer of American capital abroad.[58]

The "dollar overhang," already serious when Johnson became president, grew worse during his administration despite these measures.[59] One straightforward solution would have been to drive the United States' trade balance into greater surplus by increasing exports or reducing imports.[60] But the latter option was unappealing. Johnson was strongly committed to the idea of free trade and uncomfortable with trade restrictions, especially on a Japan that had cooperated in the capital control affair and that still needed to "export or die." So Washington would grant a liberalized export quota for textiles to Japan and Hong Kong[61] in 1965–1966. When Warren Christopher led a delegation of American wool-makers to Japan in June 1965 to secure a voluntary export restriction in those goods, he declined to press the issue after a Japanese rebuff.[62] Most famously, Johnson committed his administration to making the "Kennedy Round" of trade reduction negotiations under the GATT a success.

It was a sincere but awkward commitment, made so by a congressionally-imposed deadline on presidential negotiating authority. The Americans remained chiefly concerned with Europe, especially European barriers to American agricultural exports. The Europeans simply stonewalled until the deadline approached in the spring of 1967. Rather than accept failed negotiations, the United States agreed to take agriculture off the table.[63] The resulting agreement was hardly a mere symbolic victory for "free trade," however. Tariffs on industrial goods were greatly reduced, with Washington giving concessions on imports valued at $8.5 billion and gaining reductions on exports worth $8.1 billion.[64]

For most of the Johnson administration, though, U.S.–Japan economic relations were not overly fractious. In part, there was little concern because few Americans could conceive of a robust Japanese economy. During hearings on the Trade Expansion Act, Director Nelson A. Stitt of the U.S.–Japan Trade Council had assured Congress that Japan simply lacked the capacity to increase its exports to the United States by much.[65] A presidential strongarm tactic in mid-1965 to force Japan to liberalize its investment practices backfired badly as many American companies protested the possible loss of their markets in Japan if Tokyo retaliated. Besides, if worst came to worst, Tokyo had a good record of agreeing to voluntary export restraints and appeared far more accommodating to American imports than the EEC, which in 1967 proceeded to adopt a Value Added Tax (VAT) that clearly discouraged imports of all kinds.[66]

In addition, there were persuasive political reasons for avoiding friction with Japan. Japan was a quiet supporter of the American war effort in Vietnam.[67] The return of Okinawa had to be confronted therefore at a moment when U.S. military facilities there appeared more valuable than ever. Where there were powerful domestic interests to balance these reasons, as with textiles, American officials could be prodded into action. But the story of the end of the 1960s was not terribly different from that of the early 1950s: "diplomatic" considerations outweighed parochial, "economic" ones. The sea change would come only after concerns about the Cold War were eclipsed by rising anxiety in Washington that there was another struggle afoot and America was losing it.

Even so, American and Japanese negotiators at the Kennedy Round talks in Geneva found an increasing number of nettlesome trade issues arising. None became openly fractious, as would happen in the Nixon years. But by the end of the Kennedy Round there was a more tangible feeling in Washington of exasperation over Japan's continued excuses for special treatment even as Tokyo insisted that it was part of the industrial West.

Typical were the Japanese explanations at the early 1964 meetings of the U.S.–Japan Committee on Trade and Economic Affairs. Finance Minister Tanaka Kakuei complained of the hardships of joining the OECD (which Japan had strongly sought) and adhering to Article Eight of the IMF (ceasing foreign exchange restriction) while Japan's per capita income and productivity remained under one-fifth of the American. MITI chief Fukuda Hajime predicted that these liberalization steps would unleash a flood of imports into Japan, ruining Japan's many small businesses. And new, therefore technologically advanced industries, also enjoyed a flood of imports from the United States. Novel processes developed in the United States for making synthetic fibers had led a dozen Japanese firms to apply for permission to acquire the technology and receive American investment to start production. To approve them all would result in reckless expansion of capacity. Instead of understanding Japan's difficulties, the United States insisted that Japan expand its Voluntary Export Restraints (most annoyingly to cover woolens), and imposed the Interest Equalization Tax, possibly a cotton equalization fee, and considered new "anti-dumping" measures even as it was eliminating military assistance.[68]

In that year, at any rate, the Americans were a good deal more understanding of Japan's difficulties than they would become. Reischauer, Bundy, and Ball noted a variety of Japanese grievances. These ranged from an American denial of air routes to JAL, fisheries disputes, and the ever-present woolens issue, to American pressures on Japan to liberalize trade and investment rules as a price for full entry into the IMF, OECD, and participation in GATT's Kennedy Round negotiations as an industrial nation just as the ever-obstinate Congress was pressing for protectionist measures (crabbing in the Bering Sea, for example) and firmer implementation of U.S. anti-dumping provisions. The timing was especially unfortunate, since new prime minister Sato was a firm and public supporter of American policies and had a right to expect, as Reischauer put it, "demonstrable benefits as quid pro quo on economic front."[69]

Yet by 1967 American attitudes toward Japan had soured considerably. One factor was the result of the Kennedy Round itself. Contemporary studies admitted that while American–EEC concessions were roughly equivalent, Japan (and Britain and Canada) had gotten more than they had given. Japanese protection over items such as color film, computers and calculators, and pharmaceuticals (automobiles and air conditioners were also priority items) irritated American negotiators. By mid-1966 these economic diplomats were rejecting out of hand Japanese complaints about "Buy American" legislation.[70] In this light, Tokyo's balking over the food-aid issue appeared distinctly unhelpful,[71] and last-round Japanese withdrawals of tariff concessions prompted similar American pullbacks, to Washington's disappointment.[72]

Congress was vocally dissatisfied with the results of the Kennedy Round and, by implication, the Trade Expansion Act. One particularly sore point involved a complicated deal in chemical tariffs which entailed the elimination of existing legislation.[73] Congress felt that Special Trade Representative William Roth's team had presumed too much and refused to enact the repeal. In February, the American steel industry had charged that its Japanese competitors were dumping products on the U.S. market as a result of excess Japanese capacity.[74] For the first time, industry representatives were joined by the steelworkers' union. American textile interests pushed for an international accord covering wool, similar to the Long-Term Arrangement already negotiated for cotton, a push targeted at Japan and supported by British manufacturers.[75] Although Johnson vowed to veto any import quota bill (many were before Congress), he did resort increasingly to "voluntary" export restraints. As ominously, Congress refused to renew any trade bill in 1967, and close questioning of STR William Roth by Wilbur Mills in March 1968 led to a damning litany of complaints about a closed Japanese market to American goods and investment.[76] Mills' Ways and Means Committee held marathon hearings on trade issues in June and July of 1968 that focused attention, and a good portion of the upcoming presidential campaign, on America's declining competitiveness in international trade.[77]

Unhappily for Japan, these concerns coincided with renewed and redoubled American worries over increasingly large and chronic balance of payments deficits. By 1967 there was open talk, in fact, of a crisis. The surrender of sterling in November led to massive European purchases of gold and a resulting assault on the dollar in 1968. Japan was increasingly singled out as the ally doing least to "burden-share," especially in terms of obligingly purchasing American military hardware. American eyes increasingly glared at a growing bilateral trade imbalance in Tokyo's favor, and a Japan that was, at least among OECD member states, uniquely closed to American investment. Treasury memoranda in early 1967 singled out Japan's bilateral surplus with the United States. Worse, Japan's deficit with the rest of Asia, Latin America, and especially the Middle East ruled out the possibility of a "Dollar Bloc" as some senators and David Rockefeller had suggested.[78] An American proposal that Japan invest in long-term securities (a solution Dillon, just a few years earlier, had scoffed at) met a cool reception in Tokyo. The Pentagon saw increased Japanese purchases of U.S. military equipment as a solution to the need to boost Japanese readiness while reducing its trade and payments imbalances. Rusk, however, thought prospects "dismal" given Tokyo's refusal to increase its defense budget overall and its resistance to buying outside Japan. At the same time, the U.S. Treasury was projecting future surges in Japanese payments surpluses with the United States that would overwhelm any such purchases even if they could be arranged. All this while Japan balked at an even minimal commitment of funds to the Kennedy Round's food aid program.[79]

There is a measure of irony in this sea of change. The story of U.S. economic policy and Japan from 1945 to 1968 is essentially a story of the United States setting the economic agenda of the West and ensuring that Europe and Japan subscribed to that agenda. Primary American concerns during these years were directed toward Europe, and rightly so. Washington saw Japan as economically unsteady, as many Japanese did themselves. The dominant conservative coalition in Japan during these years, especially after the formation of the Liberal Democratic Party shortly after the occupation's end, pushed hard and, for the most part, successfully in securing swift Japanese membership as a full partner in the postwar economic order, from membership in the GATT to the OECD. The most vital, if not entirely intended, result was open access to the American market on a scale impossible to imagine before the Second World War.[80]

The United States indeed was accommodating in opening its market to Japanese goods, but it is difficult to see how else it might have acted under the circumstances, especially given European resistance to accepting

Japanese products and the sheer impossibility of Japan relying heavily upon Southeast Asia – a region wracked by war and poverty throughout this period. Equally undesirable was for Japan to reopen trade with the communist states, at least on a large scale.[81] U.S. financial foreign policy, likewise, was determined in Washington and dominated by concerns over dollar shortages (for about a decade after the war) and dollar surpluses (a decade after that) in Europe.

Throughout the 1960s the United States could have accepted higher domestic interest rates instead of the dodge of the interest equalization tax and the compulsory restraints on transfer of funds abroad that took effect in early 1968 (around the time of Johnson's decision to finally rein in the escalation of the war in Vietnam). But it did not. Washington could have accepted a "Mansfield solution" and reduced its military and hence financial burden in Europe, but the Executive Branch never took this option seriously and never thought, at least during the 1950s and 1960s, that the American burden in Japan was especially great anyway. Perhaps Washington might have pressured the World Bank to restrict its capital development loans to Japan. Congress might have been less generous in its unmeaning provision of substantial aid such as the P.L. 480 program. But it is difficult to imagine scenarios where such pressure or parsimony were likely. It is just as difficult to see a foreign conspiracy, certainly not one made in Japan, as the root of American economic difficulties by the end of the 1960s.

In retrospect, it seems curious that Japanese–American friction would emerge so powerfully and centrally and survive so well in the years that followed. Whether this result arose from the elimination of the factors that contributed to the relative harmony discussed here or from the rise of a different constellation of American and Japanese priorities has been primarily the focus of the previous chapters. But the signs in this period point heavily toward the growing American concern over a weakening balance of payments position, and a growing suspicion that Japan was doing a great deal more to harm than to help that position after decades, in Washington's view, of American assistance and even charity. That Tokyo felt rushed into equality – trade and financial liberalization – barely a decade after the occupation ended mattered to all too few people in Washington, for all too brief a time, and for all too clear a reason: from 1952 to 1968 American policy makers viewed their economic relationship with Japan as a secondary affair. It would not remain so much longer.

Notes

1 William S. Borden, *The Pacific alliance: United States foreign economic policy and Japanese trade recovery, 1947–1955*, Madison: University of Wisconsin Press, 1984. Reviews of Borden's book stressed this connection more heavily than he did.

A recent example chronicling the interests of senior State Department officials in Southeast Asia for Japan's sake is Ronald McGlothen, *Controlling the waves*, New York: Norton, 1993, pp. 43–52, 75–6, and especially chapter 6.

2 For "economic Pearl Harbor," see *The Wall Street Journal*, 16 May 1989, A9.

3 Borden, *Pacific alliance*, p. 75. Japan quickly became a leading export market for American agricultural products. The cotton itself was turned into textiles and exported, chiefly to British imperial areas, where it earned a considerable balance of sterling. SCAP negotiated a foreign exchange payments agreement with the sterling area in May 1948, but at the price of agreeing to Britain's insistence that the sterling not be convertible into dollar balances.

4 Borden, *Pacific alliance*, pp. 89–93.

5 Even so, the ¥360=$1 rate elicited a good deal of Japanese protest. Robert C. Angel, *explaining economic policy failure: Japan in the 1969–71 international monetary crisis*, New York: Columbia University Press, 1991, p. 37. See also Theodore Cohen, *Remaking Japan: the American occupation as new deal*, New York: Free Press, 1987.

6 Borden, *Pacific alliance*, pp. 136–7.

7 Aaron Forsberg, "Eisenhower and Japanese economic recovery: the politics of integration with the Western trading bloc, 1952–1955," *The Journal of American-East Asian relations*, 5, Spring 1996, pp. 57–76. Eisenhower also established a special commission under Clarence Randall to make trade policy recommendations, naming congressional protectionists Milliken, Simpson, and Reed to it.

8 The treaty permitted continued restrictions on American capital investment in Japan for purposes of gaining voting control of Japanese companies. One effect was to markedly restrict all forms of direct foreign investment in Japan. This effect, however, hardly meant that Japan was denied capital funding from abroad. See below.

9 This deficit contributed to Japan's first drawing from the IMF of $110 million in 1953. Robert V. Roosa, *The United States and Japan in the international monetary system, 1946–1985*, New York: Group of Thirty, 1986, p. 2.

10 Edward S. Mason and Robert E. Asher, *The World Bank since Bretton Woods*, Washington, D.C.: The Brookings Institution, 1973, pp. 276–7. Angel points out that throughout the 1950s Japan went through cycles of boom, which created shortages of exchange reserves, compelling tight money policies which led to recessions, which, in turn, replenished the exchange reserves. Angel, *Explaining economic policy failure*, chapter 2.

11 Mason and Asher, *The World Bank*, pp. 500–1. From October 1953 to July 1966, the World Bank would lend $857 million to Japan. From March 1956 to November 1969, the Export-Import Bank lent $886 million. Remarkably, the Bank permitted Japan to use some of the loans for yen (internal) costs. Warren S. Hunsberger, *Japan and the United States in world trade*, New York: Harper & Row, 1964, p. 73. Black's threat had substance, in part because the World Bank had initially declined loans to Japan on grounds of inadequate creditworthiness. Substantially pressure from the American government, which had unique access to loan applications, overrode the Bank's opposition. Catherine Gwin, *U.S. relations with the World Bank, 1945–92*, Washington, D.C.: The Brookings Institution, 1994, p. 71.

12 Forsberg, "Eisenhower and Japanese economic recovery," pp. 69–74.

13 Borden, *Pacific alliance*, pp. 182–5. Of the initial $400 million earmarked for P.L. 480 in Fiscal Year 1955, over one-third went to Japan. Department of State, *Foreign Relations of the United States [FRUS], 1955–1957*, v. 9, Washington, D.C.: U.S.G.P.O., 1987, pp. 286–9. Not all P.L. 480 provisions were giveaways. Some incurred repayment obligations on soft loans that became much "harder" for the Americans in the late 1960s.

14 In fact, American assistance, including procurement orders, was responsible for funding 20 percent of Japan's imports of goods and services from 1945 through 1962. Hunsberger, *Japan and the United States*, New York: Harper & Row, 1964, p. 35.

15 *FRUS, 1955–57*, v. 9, pp. 29–43. Randall's views were closely incorporated into NCS 5516/1, see *FRUS, 1955–57*, v. 23, pt. 1, pp. 52–62. There was a squeeze in the grain trade during these years. Britain's earlier refusal to permit sterling–dollar convertibility, continued under GATT exception clauses, had channeled Japanese grain imports toward the sterling area. The United States had to consider renewing its membership in the International Wheat Agreement in 1956. Washington blocked GATT endorsement of the agreement but Commerce and Treasury lined up against State and Agriculture in an unsuccessful attempt to end U.S. adherence to the agreement's terms. Congress was the arbiter, as it supported adherence so long as domestic agricultural policies [and P.L. 480] were not interfered with. See Burton I. Kaufman, *Trade and aid: Eisenhower's foreign economic policy, 1953–1961*, Baltimore: The Johns Hopkins University Press, 1982, chapter 5.

16 *FRUS, 1955–57*, v. 9, pp. 144–50.

17 Shigemitsu, Kono, and Kishi, who visited Washington in late August 1955. *FRUS, 1955–57*, v. 23, pt. 2, pp. 111–16.

18 *FRUS, 1955–7*, v. 23, pt. 1, pp. 183–7. Randall's committee agreed that American GATT concessions had helped lead to a "flood" of Japanese textile imports, but dismissed claims of injury to the American industry and argued, with dubious political sense, that if Japanese mills could buy American raw cotton at cheaper prices than American mills, then U.S. domestic price support programs ought to be revised. *FRUS, 1955–57*, v. 9, pp. 179–82. These arguments led the following Kennedy administration to consider an "export tax" as an equivalent, see below.

19 *FRUS, 1955–57*, v. 23, pt. 1, pp. 479–83, 488–504.

20 That is, that the Soviet bloc would overtake the West in the production of many key industrial products. Steel gap, anyone?

21 Pascaline Winand, *Eisenhower, Kennedy, and the United States of Europe*, New York: St. Martin's Press, 1993, pp. 128–9. A related initiative was British membership in the Common Market. Washington recognized, however, that full Japanese membership in the OEEC or whatever replaced it would complicate efforts to resolve outstanding problems with Europe. *FRUS, 1958–60*, v. 4, pp. 58–62.

22 *FRUS, 1958–60*, v. 4, pp. 82–6. The first warnings about a deteriorating American position appear to have come in April 1955, when Treasury Secretary George Humphrey warned of shrinking gold stocks. A year later, he briefed the Cabinet formally about the deterioration, warning of declining American competitiveness due to high labor costs and large American military expenditures. See John W. Sloan, *Eisenhower and the management of prosperity*, Lawrence: University of Kansas Press, 1991, pp. 129–30.

23 Margaret G. deVries, *The international monetary fund, 1966–1971; Volume I: Narrative*, Washington, D.C.: International Monetary Fund, 1976, p. 485.

24 Winand, *Eisenhower, Kennedy, and the United States of Europe*, p. 135.

25 *FRUS, 1958–60*, v. 18, pp. 206–12, 214–21, 226–9.

26 In fact, Japan had run large trade deficits in 1956 and 1957, compelling an IMF drawing by the spring of 1957. A second deficit in 1961 compelled negotiations for a stand-by arrangement with the IMF that year. Harold James, *International monetary cooperation since Bretton Woods*, Washington, D.C.: International Monetary Fund and New York: Oxford University Press, 1996, pp. 116–17.

27 Sloan, *Eisenhower and the management of prosperity*, p. 130.

28 *FRUS, 1958–60*, v. 4, pp. 134–9, 142–7.

29 There were complaints about the inordinately high telephone rates Japan charged U.S. forces in Japan. *FRUS 1958–60*, v. 18, pp. 268–73.
30 Parsons was Assistant Secretary of State for Far Eastern Affairs.
31 National Security Archive Record Number (henceforth NSA) 77111; 77110; 77115; 77112. German Chancellor Adenauer, meeting with Eisenhower before a trip to Japan, was more concerned than the President about Japanese trade with China and sought a German–Japanese–American communiqué that would somehow bind Tokyo. Dillon pointed out that there was a draft communiqué that applied to NATO, but Japan hardly could be included. When Adenauer suggested that a wider term be found to include NATO and Japan, Dillon noted the opposition of Europe and Britain to any such connections, given possible trade complications. NSA 77107. The Americans saw bigger trouble ahead in Japan's burgeoning labor force and substantial capital expansion, which would entail sharply increased exports. To where? Japan hoped eventually to cultivate South and Southeast Asia, but lacked the capital to develop those areas, hence Tokyo's desire for Western capital assistance there. NSA 77115.
32 Sloan, *Eisenhower and the management of prosperity*, p. 66.
33 Winand, *Eisenhower, Kennedy, and the United States of Europe*, chapter 7.
34 NSA 76495, 76504, 79424. To be precise, the GARIOA settlement was for $490 million over fifteen years at 2.5 percent with the proceeds to be used for aid programs. By 1967–1968, Washington would press for an acceleration of these payments. Cleverly, Ikeda had arranged for the payments to come out of the Japan Development Bank (not general revenues), which had been capitalized originally with GARIOA counterpart funds. NSA 79441; *FRUS, 1961–3*, v. 22, pp. 682–5, 726–7.
35 Winand, *Eisenhower, Kennedy, and the United States of Europe*, p. 181.
36 The LTA was irksome to Tokyo inasmuch as it froze Japanese textile exports to the United States while doing little to curb increased American purchases of such goods from Honk Kong and elsewhere. It especially bothered Nobuhiko Ushiba, the Foreign Ministry's textile expert. Ushiba would go on to be Japan's key representative in the GATT "Kennedy Round" negotiations. NSA 76042.
37 Robert A. Pastor, *Congress and the politics of U.S. foreign economic policy, 1929–1976*, Berkeley: University of California Press, 1980, p. 109. As well, Congress, chiefly Wilbur Mills, secured direct representation in the U.S. delegation to the ensuing Kennedy Round of trade negotiations. Steve Dryden, *Trade warriors: USTR and the American crusade for free trade*, New York: Oxford University Press, 1995, p. 52.
38 A brief account with statistics can be found in Pastor, *Congress and politics*, p. 205. U.S. foreign direct investment grew from $19.3 billion in 1955 to $32.7 billion in 1960.
39 The "shallow roots" terminology rapidly entered official country and regional briefing papers on Japan that also stressed the country's strong "neutralist sentiments." NSA 79307. In addition, there were a number of technical reasons why Japan was spared American pressure at the start of the Kennedy years. Japan was not a member of the OEEC or OECD until 1964. The OECD's Working Party 3 (WP-3) has been formed in April 1961 to oversee multilateral efforts to adjust international balance of payments imbalances. Nor was Japan a charter member of the "Gold Pool," established in December 1958 for similar reasons, in part because Japanese gold reserves were nugatory. Roosa, *The United States and Japan in the international monetary system*, p. 9.
40 From $6 million annually to $150 million. Kennedy also reiterated Dulles' earlier confirmation of Japan's "residual sovereignty" over the Ryukyus.
41 The joint committee, which indeed would play a major role in U.S.–Japanese

relations for the rest of the decade, was modeled after a similar U.S.–Canadian body. An important catalyst was a Japanese diplomat active in American and Canadian economic affairs in the 1950's: Kiyoaki Kikuchi. Interview with Kiyoaki Kikuchi, 15 March 1997, San Diego, California.

42 Timothy P. Maga, *Hands across the sea: U.S.–Japan relations, 1961–1981,* Athens: Ohio University Press, 1997, p. 35.

43 This was a primary reason why Australia was included as well. The Australians had a similar (and more public) reaction.

44 In fact, Kennedy initially had been reluctant to push for Japanese membership in OECD in the face of British opposition and his belief that the organization ought to be a "tool" of the "Atlantic Community." He shared concerns that the OECD's Trade Committee might come to replace the GATT as the chief venue for resolving economic disputes. NSA 76488; *FRUS, 1961–3,* v. 22, pp. 693–6. Full membership finally came in July 1963 with Prime Minister Ikeda acknowledging American help in November. Ibid., pp. 805–6.

45 Kennedy had considered an "equalization fee" on exports of raw cotton to bring its price abroad in line with the American (subsidized) equivalent. Tokyo immediately protested such a step as an indirect tariff hike, which of course it would have been. NSA 75111; 76482. The Agency for International Development blocked Japanese firms from bidding on fertilizer procurement contracts for South Korea and the Defense Department had stopped oil purchases from a Japanese supplier. See Ball to Rusk, 9 February 1962. *FRUS, 1961–3,* v. 9, pp. 517–19. Consideration of adding woolens to textile export arrangements was another irritant. Kennedy had made a pledge to American wool manufacturers under a mistaken impression, provoking loud if private protests from Ball and the Japanese. Ibid., pp. 532–6, 555–7, 570–2, 572–6, 580, 585–8, 619–20. Kennedy did hike American tariffs on wool carpets in March 1962, but mollified Tokyo somewhat by refusing a Tariff Commission recommendation to do the same for mosaic tiles and baseball gloves. John W. Evans, *The Kennedy round in American trade policy: the twilight of the GATT?,* Cambridge: Harvard University Press, 1971, pp. 168–70. Japanese requests for civil air rights into New York and beyond (to Europe) were vetoed. *FRUS, 1961–3,* v. 22, p. 677. American automobile manufacturers complained of their inability to export directly to Japan and to invest in Japanese automotive companies, prompting Commerce Department discussions with MITI Minister Fukuda, who explained that Japanese roads were "narrow and congested." *FRUS, 1961–3,* v. 22, 754–7.

46 Thomas B. Curtis and John R. Vastive, Jr., *The Kennedy round and the future of American trade,* New York: Preager, 1971, chapter 2; Dryden, p. 67; NSA 76008. Ikeda had also been unhappy with U.S. anti-dumping legislation, which negated American tariff concessions in steel. Evans, p. 226. Rusk favored Japanese membership in OECD and hoped that increased Japanese exports would result. As he noted in February to Gilpatric, "The principal limiting factor to steadily expanding United States civilian exports to Japan will continue to be Japan's ability to earn the foreign exchange necessary to pay for them." NSA 75917.

47 *FRUS, 1961–63,* v. 9, pp. 15–18, 25–6, 49–50, 51–62. Of interest is a blunt memorandum from John Kenneth Galbraith to Kennedy in August 1963 arguing that the Kennedy Round's lowering of tariffs would only worsen the balance of payments deficit. Galbraith advocated tariff surcharges on EEC manufactured goods and accepting the trade war that would ensue. Ibid., pp. 78–86.

48 *FRUS, 1961–63,* v. 9, pp. 160–4. Dillon was overruled. The Treasury floated "Roosa bonds," expressly designed to be held by foreign central banks. James, *International monetary cooperation since Bretton Woods,* pp. 152–62. By 1967–1968, American pressure for conversion into longer-term securities (Roosa bonds

were one- and two-year instruments) was persistent and Japan was applauded for bending to it. Indeed, in August 1967 Japan even announced (to the OECD's Working Party 3 charged with monitoring global capital movements) specific reserve targets. James, *International monetary cooperation since Bretton Woods*, pp. 192–7.

49   *FRUS, 1961–63*, v. 22, p. 779.

50   There were a number of reasons for this vulnerability. The Bank of Japan held a comparatively very small amount of gold and foreign currency reserves versus Japan's current account payments. As well, it was common for Japanese banks, and American banks in Japan using Japanese nationals, to borrow dollars and deposit them and then borrow yen from the banks which would receive kickbacks and, in 1963, attractive interest rates. But the borrowers typically used these funds for long-term capital investment projects while the deposits were overwhelmingly short term. Leon Hollerman, *Japan's dependence on the world economy: the approach toward economic liberalization*, Princeton: Princeton University Press, 1967, pp. 110–13. Hollerman notes the large *keiretsu* combinations at this time were investing extremely heavily in plant and equipment to expand production capacity massively. Hollerman, *Japan's dependence on the world economy*, pp. 61–2. Much of this expansion was driven by competition for domestic market share, to be sure, but it nevertheless led to the export boom so noticeable by 1967–1968 in the United States. It is possible to speculate that some of this investment was also driven by fears that, after the investment liberalization promised for 1964 and Japan's full membership in the GATT and OECD in April that year, capital might be available only with the strings of equity stakes by foreigners, especially in the automotive and consumer electronics sectors.

51   In fact, Ball himself had raised the problem the tax would create for Japan and Canada. Dillon was sympathetic, as was Roger Hilsman, to whom Ohira had been particularly blunt. *FRUS, 1961–63*, v. 9, pp. 51–62; NSA 76462.

52   It appears that, at least in part, American reluctance to extend exceptions to Japan arose from German complaints of unequal treatment. *FRUS, 1961–3*, v. 9, pp. 180–1, 181–4.

53   Ibid., pp. 799–800. It was not lost on the Japanese that the Interest Equalization Tax did not apply to direct investment overseas by American corporations.

54   The tax went into effect in September 1964 but was applied retroactively to all transactions made after 18 July 1963. The exemption, for new securities issued or guaranteed by the Japanese Government up to $100 million, was granted in February 1965. The tax was to have expired at the end of 1965 but was extended for two years. Hollerman, *Japan's dependence on the world economy*, p. 122n. But the initial and prolonged Japanese complaints over the tax put off even the normally sympathetic Reischauer as they dragged on. In November 1963 he noted that the tax had not affected Japan's ability to raise foreign capital or its overall economic performance, and it was regrettable that Japan delayed trade liberalization measures in the meantime. NSA 75949. One reason why the tax may have had minimal effect is that American bankers wishing to loan to Japan simply adjusted the period of the loans by a month or two to avoid the tax's jurisdiction (conversation with Ed Miller, SHAFR in 1997).

55   Fred L. Block, *The origins of international economic disorder*, Berkeley: University of California Press, 1977, p. 184.

56   A central facet of American foreign economic policy during the Johnson years was a protracted and ultimately unsuccessful defense of the pound to prevent its devaluation, which finally occurred in November 1967. The reasons were not hard to see. From 1964 to 1967 Britain's Labour government ran an expan-

sionary domestic policy, recorded high balance-of-payments deficits, experienced a large "overhang" abroad of the pound, yet still maintained a global military presence. The parallels to America were obvious and disturbing.

57 In January 1965 the French government announced that henceforth it would convert all new accruals of dollars into gold. Diane Kunz, *Butter and guns*, New York: Free Press, 1997, p. 164.

58 The American capital controls were partially successful, prompting international fears of a capital liquidity crisis in the mid-1960s and the origins of Special Drawing Rights (SDRs) at the International Monetary Fund.

59 The Interest Equalization Tax, at least as it applied to Japan, failed to reduce the American balance of payments deficit to any degree. In fact, American direct investment in Japan, which was not subject to the tax, fell the first year after its implementation while lending from American banks, on terms usually of 34 or 35 months to avoid the tax, more than doubled during the same period. Hollerman, *Japan's dependence on the world economy*, p. 142.

60 Another option was to retrench the American military commitment to NATO, as proposed by Senator Mike Mansfield on several occasions. It received renewed attention in 1967 when West German Chancellor Erhard asked to be excused from a German obligation to make purchases of American goods worth $1 billion to offset American military expenditures in Germany. Kunz, *Butter and guns*, pp. 164–70.

61 Hong Kong textile exporters had been quick to take advantage of the restraints imposed upon their Japanese competitors, which had prompted Japanese complaints as early as 1961 and thence Hong Kong's inclusion in the export arrangements. *FRUS, 1961–63*, v. 9, pp. 479–84; *FRUS, 1961–3*, v. 22, pp. 687–9.

62 Alfred E. Eckes, Jr., *Opening America's market: U.S. foreign trade policy since 1776*, Chapel Hill: University of North Carolina Press, 1995, p. 183.

63 The one sop towards (American) agricultural interests, and American desires that the Kennedy Round negotiations appear to do something for the "developing countries" was an agreement among the industrial powers to contribute food aid. Ironically, this agreement led to considerable friction with Japan, which, as a large importer of agricultural goods, argued that its food aid would have to come directly from its foreign exchange reserves in the form of purchases from abroad, as it had no domestic surplus to offer. After an initial stand marked by considerable friction with Tokyo, Washington ultimately conceded this point as well and secured an exception permitting Japan to contribute non-food goods. Curtis and Vastine, *The Kennedy round and the future of American trade*, pp. 55–8.

64 Eckes, *Opening America's market*, pp. 199–200.

65 Ibid., pp. 186–7.

66 Pastor, *Congress and the politics of U.S. foreign economic policy*, pp. 115–20. Japan and Europe would agree to a VER covering steel in January 1969. The textile situation was more complicated.

67 The question of American aid and direct military procurements requires more investigation.

68 NSA 73313, 76687, 79301, 79303. Military aid to Japan was to end after 1964 although existing commitments (such as co-production of the F-104) would linger. As an aside, the U.S. Department of Defense doggedly pursued ways to dump equipment on Japan in exchange for Japanese aid to Vietnam, such as a proposed barter of two Nike-Hercules battalions at a "bargain" for $27 million or more of aid. The Pentagon was willing to have the aid go elsewhere in Southeast Asia since it could then reduce its MAP amount to the recipient and redirect it to Saigon. NSA 76698.

69 NSA 79716, 79666, 79705. Bundy suggested several such quids: an increase in

the cotton textile quota for Japan for 1965 and a larger role for Tokyo in administering the Ryukyus. As it was, by the end of 1965 Japan had received a $100m per year exemption on the Interest Equalization Tax and won its case on air route extension. NSA 79693.

70 As Martin Hirabayashi, who headed the U.S.–Japan bilateral negotiations during the Kennedy Round, observed, "Even with present U.S. offshore procurement practices, which were instigated as a result of our deteriorating balance of payment position, Japanese firms have done extremely well and are again obtaining increased orders because of the exigencies of the Vietnam emergency." NSA GATT E114.

71 Japanese intransigence over food aid had nearly wrecked the entire agreement as other food importers, such as Scandinavia, had threatened withdrawal. Evans, *The Kennedy round in American trade policy*, pp. 270–1. Japan's position, explained by Ushiba, was that food aid should be part of the International Wheat Agreement and, thus, include the USSR. This was not exactly what American Cold Warriors had in mind. NSA GATT E150.

72 Dryden, *Trade warriors*, pp. 107, 110. The United States reduced duties on Japanese imports worth $1.44 billion in exchange for concessions on $667 million. A more detailed breakdown of the concessions can be found in Ernest H. Preeg, *Traders and diplomats*, Washington, D.C.: Brookings, 1970, p. 214. Japan offered substantial tariff reductions in steel and textiles, precisely those areas where its competitive prowess was greatest.

73 Passed in 1922 creating the American Selling Price (ASP) basis for duties. Japan was implicated in the chemicals agreement as well. Abolition of the byzantine ASP system would have given Japanese rubber-soled footwear and canned clams (!) substantial tariff benefits, but Tokyo refused to offer any concessions in return. Evans, *The Kennedy round in American trade policy*, p. 272.

74 There was a measure of truth to these charges. Japan's steel making production had increased from 34.7 million metric tons in 1963 to 52.6 million in 1966 and exports from 7.9 million to 14.1 million in the same period. This increase, however, was only a part of a global surge in steel production and production capacity, a good deal of it fueled by official American (and World Bank) development programs. House Ways and Means chairman Wilbur Mills took up steel's cause and, with Assistant Secretary of State for Economic Affairs Anthony Solomon, secured voluntary export restraints to run from 1968 to 1971. The immediate result, given a boom in steel demand in 1968–1969, was a substantial price hike by American steel makers. Curtis and Vastine, *The Kennedy round and the future of American trade*, pp. 144–53.

75 Although American woolen manufacturers led the way in voicing concerns over increased Japanese sales in the United States, Dean Rusk saw a way to avoid charges of protectionism by opening consultations in March 1964 with the British, suggesting that an international marketing agreement might restore some sales Britain had lost in America due to Japanese competition. The British government was opposed to such an arrangement. While Rusk, George Ball, and U. Alexis Johnson were hopeful that Italy and Japan would agree (incorrectly: Japan was well aware of U.S.–EEC discussions and opposed any deal on wool), London's opposition forestalled progress. Ball and STR Christian Herter, moreover, were reluctant to press the issue, arguing that the American woolen industry was not badly injured and, in any event its injury came more from the increasing popularity of synthetic fibers among consumers. Despite Johnson's promises to Congress, in brief, wool was not an issue worth friction with Japan or the EEC. Johnson did not agree. He took up wool during his meeting with Sato in early 1965 and sent Warren Christopher to Japan, accompanied by American textile industry "observers" to stiffen State

Department resolve. The result was a series of blunt exchanges with Japanese counterparts, who reminded the Americans that their real enemies were the North Vietnamese. *FRUS, 1964–68*, v. 9: pp. 568–75, 582–4, 609–11; Vinod K. Aggarwal, *Liberal protectionism: the international politics of organized textile trade*, Berkeley: University of California Press, 1985, pp. 95–8.

76 Dryden, *Trade warriors*, chapter 6.
77 Evans, *The Kennedy round in American trade policy*, pp. 301–3.
78 The idea had been for members of such a bloc to have agreed never to convert their dollars into gold. Japan might well have agreed to such a stipulation itself (though Treasury thought Tokyo would demand some trade concessions in return), but the point would be moot if those dollars were simply shipped to nations that would convert them. NSA 77237.
79 Hollerman, *Japan's dependence on the world economy*, p. 273; NSA 65935, 27498, 74715. The bilateral surplus in Japan's favor was forecast, in September 1967, to grow from $2 billion in 1968 to $5.2 billion by 1972.
80 A good discussion of Japanese efforts to enter the American-sponsored economic order can be found in Aaron Forsberg, *America and the Japanese miracle: the cold war context of Japan's postwar economic revival, 1950–1960*, Chapel Hill: University of North Carolina Press, 2000. A fascinating analysis of pre-war economic warfare and, in its final chapter, postwar planning for accommodation with Japan is Edward S. Miller, *Bankrupting the enemy: the U.S. financial siege of Japan before Pearl Harbor*, Annapolis: U.S. Naval Institute Press (forthcoming).
81 The Southeast Asian situation was beginning to change by the end of the 1960s, however, as Japanese trade with Hong Kong, Taiwan, Singapore, and the Philippines increased. Trade Bulletin Corporation, *1971 foreign trade white paper of Japan*, Tokyo: Trade Bulletin Corporation, 1971, Book One, pp. 4–5. As for trade with Communist states, there was relatively little concern to minor trading with the Soviet Union or Communist China raised at any of the Joint Economic Committee meetings for example, although the United States was actively interested in ending Japanese purchases of Cuban sugar.

Index

For Product Safety Concerns and Information please contact our EU
representative GPSR@taylorandfrancis.com
Taylor & Francis Verlag GmbH, Kaufingerstraße 24, 80331 München, Germany

www.ingramcontent.com/pod-product-compliance
Lightning Source LLC
Chambersburg PA
CBHW050417280326
41932CB00013BA/1893